ISLA

PETTER NESSER

Islamist Terrorism in Europe

A History

OXFORD
UNIVERSITY PRESS

Oxford University Press is a department of the
University of Oxford. It furthers the University's objective
of excellence in research, scholarship, and education
by publishing worldwide.

Oxford   New York

Auckland   Cape Town   Dar es Salaam   Hong Kong   Karachi
Kuala Lumpur   Madrid   Melbourne   Mexico City   Nairobi
New Delhi   Shanghai   Taipei   Toronto

With offices in

Argentina   Austria   Brazil   Chile   Czech Republic   France   Greece
Guatemala   Hungary   Italy   Japan   Poland   Portugal   Singapore
South Korea   Switzerland   Thailand   Turkey   Ukraine   Vietnam

Oxford is a registered trade mark of Oxford University Press
in the UK and certain other countries.

Published in the United States of America by
Oxford University Press
198 Madison Avenue, New York, NY 10016

Library of Congress Cataloging-in-Publication Data is available
Petter Nesser.
Islamist Terrorism in Europe: A History.
ISBN: 9780190909123

Printed in India on acid-free paper

CONTENTS

ACKNOWLEDGEMENTS

I owe a debt of gratitude to many people for helping bring this book to fruition. First and foremost I thank my colleague, mentor and good friend Brynjar Lia. He introduced me to jihadism studies to begin with and advised me to explore Islamist terrorism in Europe long before the phenomenon was considered a major security challenge in the public eye. Brynjar supervised my doctoral thesis on which this book is based, and I have benefitted enormously from his vast knowledge of the Middle East, Islamism and terrorism. He is my role model academically and in so many ways beyond that.

My doctoral thesis was completed while working for the Norwegian Defence Research Establishment (FFI), and its terrorism research project (TERRA). I thank my employer, the FFI, for facilitating the PhD thesis and the book project and for valuing academic publishing. This is not something to be taken for granted in the think tank realm, and I am grateful and proud to be at such an enlightened institution.

I thank former heads of the FFI Analysis Department Ragnvald Solstrand and Jan Erik Torp, as well as the current head of the Analysis Department Espen Skjelland and manager of the terrorism research project Espen Berg-Knutsen, for backing me. I thank the rest of the crew at the security policy division for their support and for providing an inspiring and friendly research environment.

I further thank my colleague and friend Thomas Hegghammer for invaluable help in transforming the thesis into a book. It has truly been a privilege to be able to tap into his extensive experience in authorship and jihadism studies.

I thank former colleagues Hanna Rogan and Tine Gade for annotated translations of French and Spanish sources and Jane Chanaa for copyediting my doctoral thesis.

ACKNOWLEDGEMENTS

My colleague Anne Stenersen deserves a special thank you. Anne and I co-authored an article on the modus operandi of jihadism in Europe, which forms the basis for Chapter Two of this book.

A number of people have contributed, directly and indirectly, to making this book happen. Many are scholars in Middle East studies or terrorism research from around the world, with whom I have cooperated on various occasions and regard as colleagues and friends. These scholars have generously shared sources with me and offered advice on the facts presented, as well as methodological issues. I have also been in contact with several expert journalists in the field, who kindly shared sources and insights with me in relation to the events which the book covers.

In alphabetical order I highlight Cheryl Benard, Laila Bokhari, Peter Bergen, Tore Bjørgo, Jeffrey Checkel, Lindsay Clutterbuck, Martha Crenshaw, Hans Davidsen, Rohan Gunaratna, Ellen Haugestad, Bruce Hoffman, Stéphane Lacroix, William McCants, Roel Meijer, Yassin Musharbash, Sean O'Neill, Peter Neumann, Tore Nyhamar, Rafaello Pantucci, Rudolph Peters, Tom Quiggin, Magnus Ranstorp, Fernando Reinares, Anders Romarheim, Martin Rudner, Ronald Sandee, Alex Schmid, Morten Skjoldager, Guido Steinberg, Michael Taarnby, Truls Tønnessen, Dominique Thomas, Joas Wagemakers and Lawrence Wright.

I would also like to thank security officials who shared knowledge with me on the condition of anonymity. They deserve praise for the hard work they do to keep us safe.

I thank my editor Michael Dwyer for supporting me and believing in the book. I am also truly grateful to the book's peer reviewers for setting the bar so high, something that improved the end result tenfold. Further I would like to thank my copyeditor Tim Page for his brilliant work towards the end of the project. He captured the style I was aiming for, and his careful attention to details uncovered some embarrassing errors at the last minute.

Last I thank my beloved family for always being there for me.

Flaws and inaccuracies that slipped through the thorough reviews are my responsibility alone.

CONVENTIONS

Transliteration

This study uses the transliterations most commonly found in the sources when addressing Arabic names. This makes it easier for readers to search online for additional sources. When addressing Arabic words and expressions that do not frequently appear in Western sources, I use a simplified transliteration omitting the letter 'ع' (*ayn*), the letter 'ء' (*hamza*), and the letter and female de-nominator 'ة' (*tamarbuta*) leaving the belonging vocals. The letter 'ي' (i.e. a long i) is transliterated 'iyy' in the middle of a word, and simply "i" at the end of words. Long vowels and double letter 'ّ' (*shadda*) are omitted leaving only the attached vocal. The letter 'غ' (*ghayn*) is transliterated 'gh', the letter 'خ' (*kha*) is transliterated 'kh'. The letter 'ظ' (*dha*) is transliterated 'z', and the letter 'ط' (*tha*) 'th'. French transliterations from Arabic have become standard when addressing North African names. When French transliterations of names or expressions have appeared in the sources I have used this standard.

Names and biographies

This study contains much biographical material. All biographies have been retrieved from media sources and judicial papers. For research ethical reasons, information about people who have not been prosecuted is kept to a minimum, especially in connection with pending investigations and trials. This does not apply to well-known members of al-Qaida and likeminded groups, who have evaded prosecution and continue to be active. When people operate under aliases, as clandestine terrorists often do, I use the most common one when addressing them. I do not name family members of suspects and convicts unless they have been prosecuted. Because age is generally considered a significant factor in relation to political violence, I indicate the age of people addressed in the case studies. I use age at the approximate time of a crime as standard reference.

Endnotes

Most sources are available online, apart from books, judicial papers and interviews. I also have copies of all Internet sources referenced on file. Because of space limitations I have kept references to a minimum, and as simple and short as possible. This means that access dates and URLs have been omitted in the published version. Exceptions from this rule have been made for certain primary sources and blog posts referenced. Some of the interviewees for the book have been anonymized.

ABBREVIATIONS

AQI	Al-Qaida in Iraq
AQAP	Al-Qaida in the Arabian Peninsula
QAP	Al-Qaida on the Arabian Peninsula (pre-2009)
AQIM	Al-Qaida in the Islamic Maghreb
Tawhid	Al-Tawhid wa'l-Jihad
AI	Ansar al-Islam
GIA	Armed Islamic Group
GSPC	Salafi Group for Call and Combat
MIA	Armed Islamic Movement
PET	Danish Police Security Service
EIJ	Egyptian Islamic Jihad
EDL	English Defence League
FATA	Federally Administered Tribal Areas
HuA	Harakat-ul-Ansar
HUJI	Harkat-ul-Jihad al-Islami
HuM	Harakat-ul-Mujahidin
IEDs	Improvised Explosive Devices
ISI	Inter-Services Intelligence Directorate
IG	Egyptian Islamic Group
IJU	Islamic Jihad Union
LIDD	Islamic League for Preaching and Jihad
IMK	Islamic Movement of Kurdistan
IMU	Islamic Movement of Uzbekistan
AIS	Islamic Salvation Army
FIS	Islamic Salvation Front
ISIS/IS	Islamic State

ABBREVIATIONS

JAN	Jabhat al-Nusra
JeM	Jaysh-e-Mohammed
LeT	Laskhar-e-Taiba
FAI	Lebanese Fatah al-Islam
LIFG	Libyan Islamic Fighting Group
MAK	Maktab al-Khidamat
MICG	Moroccan Islamic Combatant Group
NWFP	North West Frontier Province
FLN	Pan-Arab National Liberation Front
TNSM	Tehrik Nifaz Shariat Muhammadi
TTP	Tehrik Taliban Pakistan
TIFG	Tunisian Islamic Fighting Group
ETIM	East Turkestan Islamic Movement

PROLOGUE

Islamist Terrorism in Europe presents the historical background for today's jihadi terrorist threat to Europe, which is dominated by the "Islamic State" (IS). The book traces the chain of events, from the early 1990s until the present day, which led jihadism to become the main terrorist threat in the region.

As I was writing the conclusion for the first edition in January 2015, al-Qaida terrorists raided the offices of the *Charlie Hebdo* magazine in Paris, killing staff and a policeman who arrived at the scene. When the book was first released in November 2015, IS terrorists massacred concertgoers at the Bataclan concert hall in the same city, in the deadliest attacks by militant Islamists in Europe since the 2004 Madrid bombings. This paperback edition comes at a time when jihadi attack activity has reached unprecedented levels in the region. As I argue in the epilogue, there has been an "IS-effect" on European jihadism.

The main features of this "IS-effect" are threefold. First, European jihadi networks have grown rapidly in scope and strength since the outbreak of the Arab Spring and particularly since the war in Syria in 2011. Second, there has been a steep rise in the number of terrorist plots. Third, more plots than ever go under the radar of security services and result in deadly attacks.

The high number of plots and executed attacks across Europe has spurred heated debates on the causes of the threat, and how best to deal with them.

In these debates, IS's terrorism in Europe tends to be portrayed as a new phenomenon and different from that of al-Qaida. It is often alleged that IS pursues different objectives, attracts different people, and recruits differently from al-Qaida. A typical argument is that al-Qaida's strategic goal was to push European States to cut ties with the US, whereas IS merely seeks to cause chaos in the region through acts of random violence.

Another widespread notion is that European IS terrorists are not as religiously motivated as those belonging to al-Qaida, and are instead driven by personal grievances and failings. Another common misperception is that most IS terrorists in Europe are "lone wolves", who act on their own without interacting with organized networks. "Lone wolves" are in fact very rare in European jihadism. I find it problematic that sweeping generalizations are being drawn from insufficient data related to recent attacks.

If one instead looks at the historical evolution of European jihadism over time, and draws a comparison between al-Qaida and IS, one will find they are surprisingly similar. The differences between the groups are nearly negligible in Europe. The "IS-effect" in Europe is mainly one of scope; the core dynamics of the threat have not changed.

Many terrorists operating for IS in Europe until recently belonged to al-Qaida-networks. IS, by and large, wants to achieve the same goals as al-Qaida by attacking European countries. The two organizations recruit in the same way and use transnational networks to do so, and they attract the same kinds of people. Recruits come from various backgrounds and join networks for different reasons, but once they are inside, they become indoctrinated with an extremist form of Islam, and act accordingly.

When debating what causes the escalating threat, many have pointed to flawed integration and social discontent among Muslims in the countries being targeted. Others have argued that the increased threat is a direct consequence of increased immigration.

In reality, such factors have limited impact on the emergence of jihadi terrorist cells in Europe, on variation in the threat level, and on which countries become targeted. This has been the case both historically and presently.

The jihadi terrorist threat in Europe is a transnational phenomenon, and to obtain a nuanced and realistic understanding of how terrorist cells emerge, we need to pay attention to the threat's historical roots, and the interplay between "homegrown" extremists inside Europe and jihadi groups in conflict zones. The central element in this interplay is a particular kind of terrorist I refer to as an "entrepreneur"—someone who builds and guides terrorist cells. These terrorists play a crucial role in making the threat more streamlined, more ideological, and more shaped by events outside of Europe than many are aware of.

This book will not settle any of the highly politicized debates on jihadi terrorism in Europe. It is my hope, however, that the detailed empirical approach and the analytical tools presented can inform the debates surrounding this subject, and bring about a clearer understanding of the threat's roots and drivers.

European jihadism is a complex phenomenon. After more than ten years of research on the topic I have become aware of how problematic it is to make generalizations. I am convinced that we need to move beyond the search for one-factor explanations (for example ideology vs socio-economic factors), and rather to disaggregate the problem into smaller components and look at the interplay between them, with a view to breaking the cycles that bring about terrorist violence. I concretize how this might be done throughout the book and in the epilogue. Meanwhile, although this book is rather dystopian in its conclusions, I hope that the reader will find it rewarding to engage with the various case studies presented, and reflect on how they resonate with ongoing debates, be it in the public sphere or in academia.

January 2018

INTRODUCTION

This book recounts the history of jihadi terrorism in Europe from the Air France hijack in 1994 to the raid on the offices of *Charlie Hebdo* in 2015. It examines a range of terrorist plots throughout the region over a twenty-year period in which individual terrorist cells launched, or sought to launch, a number of deadly attacks. The book aims to explain why these terrorist plots happened when they did and where they did, and to shed light on what goes on inside European jihadi networks more generally. It seeks to demonstrate how jihadi terrorism in Europe emerged through an intricate interplay between foreign and European factors, between top-down and bottom-up processes of radicalization, and between social and ideological motivations. The book questions the tendency to view transnational jihadism either as a strategic threat or a social movement and discards the notion that explanations for jihadism in Europe can be reduced to a single or just a few factors.

While the book stresses the complexity involved in the emergence of terrorist cells, it also emphasizes the interaction between the cells and the transnational networks emanating from the 1980s Afghan jihad. It highlights how this interaction is facilitated by certain types of terrorist who are referred to as "entrepreneurs" because they build cells and provide them with a rationale and purpose. Entrepreneurs are often the leaders of terrorist cells, but they can also be radical preachers or fulfill other functions in extremist networks surrounding operational cells. The entrepreneurs come from diverse backgrounds, but are generally committed, charismatic activists with a talent for manipulating people. They tend to be veterans in the field of jihad who have spent time in conflict zones. In Europe, jihadi entrepreneurs bring together frustrated "misfits" and "drifters," introduce them to a sub-culture where they can find community and identity, and translate far-flung grievances into a militant

1

worldview and violent activism. In the context of terrorist cells, entrepreneurs provide a link between the cell and armed groups in conflict zones. Consequently, the jihadi threat to Europe is more organized than is commonly assumed. It is largely determined by the ability of al-Qaida or similar groups to groom entrepreneurs within Europe. The notion of entrepreneurs helps answer the question as to why terrorist cells commonly composed of youths who seem to be non-political and non-ideological commit terrorism in accordance with al-Qaida's ideas. The case studies presented here suggest that the militancy of a determined few count most in the emergence of jihadi terrorism in Europe.

The significance of ideological leader-types does not contradict the idea that social dynamics and grievances matter in radicalization, however. Social factors and ideology are indeed working together in shaping the jihadi threat to Europe. The book identifies overall changes in the terrorist threat and the actor landscape. In the 1990s, jihadi attacks in Europe were linked to the Algerian Civil War and the Armed Islamic Group (GIA). In the early 2000s, al-Qaida emerged with a global jihad offensive in European countries mainly aimed at Jewish and the American targets, but following the invasion of Iraq in 2003 jihadi attacks in Europe increasingly aimed to deter and avenge European contributions to the War on Terror after 9/11.

Europe came to play a central role in the mobilization of transnational jihadism and experienced high levels of jihadi terrorism simply because the region has hosted many militants involved in armed conflicts around the world. The region emerged as an ideological center and recruitment ground for al-Qaida and likeminded groups in the 1990s. Jihadis have organized support networks in European countries for numerous groups in multiple conflict zones such as Afghanistan, Pakistan, Bosnia, Algeria, Iraq, Somalia, Yemen and Syria. These networks have raised funds, spread propaganda, recruited fighters and given birth to terrorist cells. Thousands of Islamists living in Europe have traveled to conflict zones as foreign fighters, and no other region in the West is home to as many jihad veterans as Europe. This connection between Europe-based extremism and the conflict zones of the Muslim world plays a vital role in the emergence of terrorist cells in Europe today.

Jihadi terrorism in Europe is a paradox on many levels. First, Europe has never received a great deal of attention in jihadi ideology and Europeans are not the main enemy of al-Qaida. Secondly, Europe has been valuable for jihadis as a sanctuary from which they can support armed groups in Muslim countries. According to strategic logic, the region should thus feel safe from attacks. Finally, and as is discussed extensively in this book, jihadi ideology forbids Muslims who live in non-Muslim countries from harming those who provide protection. Although these inconsistencies make the terrorist threat in Europe all the more intriguing and challenging to understand, explanations are to be found in the interplay between local European extremists, armed groups abroad and jihad ideology.

Existing research

Despite the growing threat jihadi terrorism poses to European security, the academic literature on this topic is scarce. Only a handful of books have covered the phenomenon from a European perspective.[1] These have mainly concentrated on patterns in homegrown radicalization, focusing on a limited number of cases primarily in the period after 9/11. In contrast to the current book, which is actor-focused, previous studies have offered a more policy-oriented approach. The existing body of academic literature on jihadism in Europe has tended to focus on extremism in the wider sense of the term, as well as stressing societal European explanations such as immigration policies and failed integration.

While failed integration is clearly a factor in individual radicalization, it does not explain why, when and where jihadis attacks occur in Europe. This study aims to identify how factors such as failed integration interplay with many other factors, such as extremist group dynamics and the strategies of foreign terrorist groups, in shaping the terrorist threat inside Europe. Although very few books explore jihadism in Europe from a regional perspective, there are a growing number of articles and reports dealing with different dimensions of the regional terrorist threat, such as recruitment and modus operandi.[2] These studies, including my own work, provide lessons for the analyses presented here and are cited where relevant. There is also a growing body of empirical literature focusing on specific countries, which provides valuable in-depth knowledge of local networks and plots, and is used as sources in this study.[3]

Two competing explanations have dominated the debate on the jihadi threat to the West: Bruce Hoffman's "leader-led jihad" perspective and Marc Sageman's "leaderless jihad" perspective. Although there is a growing consensus as to the need for new and more fine-grained models, Sageman and Hoffman's opposing theories are useful starting points for this study. Hoffman's "top-down" model portrays the threat to the West as al-Qaida-led

3

to a large extent, and surmises that attacks in Western countries happen according to al-Qaida's strategic aims.[4] Attacks in Europe are designed to create fissures among counter-terrorism allies and to deter European countries from interfering in conflicts in which al-Qaida has interests. Here, organizations and ideology are the main driving forces behind attacks. Organizations recruit, indoctrinate and train people, providing them with terrorist tasks.

Sageman's "bottom-up" model portrays the threat to the West as initiated by an Internet-based social movement composed of second-generation immigrants and converts, and formed inside Western countries.[5] This movement is inspired by al-Qaida but is largely detached from its networks and the armed struggles of Muslim countries. Radical youths join jihad mostly for social reasons, such as knowing someone on the inside, and they also hold social grievances. The main reasons they turn to violence are not ideology or strategy. They become attracted to militancy because they are frustrated with their lives and feel discriminated against, and hence they become involved in jihadism as a way to rebel against their parents and society, and to gain identity, respect, recognition and the moral high ground. According to the "the bottom-up" model, people join jihad out of ulterior motives, not ideology, and organizations are merely a backdrop and enabler for terrorist violence.

Leader-led jihad might explain certain aspects of high-profile incidents in Europe. There is little doubt that al-Qaida was involved in the plans to bomb the Christmas market in Strasbourg in 2000 and in the plots against US embassies and military installations in France, Belgium and Italy in 2001–2. Al-Qaida was also involved in several plots to use poisons as weapons in the UK and France before 2003, the bombings of the London Underground in 2005 and a plot to bomb transatlantic airliners taking off from Heathrow in 2006, as well as in several plans to strike individuals and institutions involved in the publication of cartoons of the Prophet Muhammad after 2005. However, although al-Qaida recruited, trained and provided direction to people involved in these terrorist acts, the exact nature and level of the organization's control, and the extent to which the plots reflected al-Qaida's strategy, were not clear. Additionally, there were aspects of these and other plots, such as the ways in which the terrorists joined jihadism, which were more consistent with a leaderless jihad. There were few traces of al-Qaida in the 2004 murder of the filmmaker Theo van Gogh by a Dutch Moroccan in Amsterdam, for example. There was also little to suggest any al-Qaida involvement in the plots of the Danish terrorist cells uncovered in 2005 and 2006 (the Glostrup and Vollsmose cells), and several plots by single-actor terrorists after 2008 (e.g.

the shooting of American soldiers at Frankfurt airport by the Kosovar Arid Uka in 2011). Social grievances, social networks and social media were key elements in leading these groups and individuals to turn to violence.

Although the leader-led vs leaderless perspectives capture dimensions of most plots in Europe, they also lead to reductionism and confirmation bias. The threat to the West is either organization-driven, top-down and foreign, or social-movement driven, bottom-up and local (homegrown). In reality, such dichotomies rarely capture the whole picture. Second, cultivating one of the perspectives may lead to an overemphasis on aspects of terrorism cases confirming the chosen model. Leaderless jihad may go too far in interpreting the involvement of young criminals as a sign that ideology does not play an important role. The leader-led model, conversely, may go too far in interpreting al-Qaida's involvement as a sign of strategic sophistication. The ever-changing nature of transnational jihadism is bound to render parsimonious models swiftly outdated. The fast-paced shifts in relations among jihadi movements in today's Middle East are a case in point, as new actors emerge which could represent new approaches to jihad in the West.

In other words, the leader-led/leaderless distinction is not necessarily the most useful approach. The perspectives apply to different stages in the processes leading to terrorism, Sageman's mainly to how individuals join networks, and Hoffman's to how terrorist cells are used strategically—the former too early and the latter too late to capture fully what goes on inside cells. To arrive at a nuanced understanding it is necessary to establish a more complete picture of the cells' internal dynamics, and how the behavior of cells is affected by the context as well as individual members.

Terminology

This book examines jihadi terrorist cells and plots in Europe. "Terrorist plot" refers to planned, prepared and executed attacks. Although "terrorist" is a contested concept, there is no reason to problematize it here. The essence of terrorism is the use of violent attacks to spread fear with the intention of sending a political message.[6] With this in mind, there is little ambiguity concerning the cases addressed in this book, which mostly involve plans to conduct bombings or shootings against non-combatants inside peaceful European societies. "Terrorist cell" refers to a secretive group composed of two or more people who cooperate in efforts to stage terrorist attacks. However, many of the terrorist plots addressed in this book were undertaken by individuals who will be referred to as "single-actor terrorists." A further distinction is made between "solo-terrorists," who attack by themselves but have links to and receive support and direction from networks, and "lone wolves" who operate completely on their own and only draw inspiration from organized terrorists. Further, "cell" refers primarily to perpetrators and "plot" mainly to their actions. The term "jihadi" refers to individuals, groups, networks and ideologies emanating from the Arab-based foreign fighter movement of the 1980s Afghan jihad.[7] The "Afghan-Arab movement" emerged as a particular strand of militant Islamism. It led to the internationalization of post-colonial Islamist insurgencies against Arab regimes and gave rise to the idea of global jihad, and the tactic of targeting the United States and Israel to achieve the strategic aim of defeating Arab dictatorships.

Ideologically, al-Qaida and likeminded movements are referred to as "Salafi-jihadis." Simply put, this means they combine revolutionary Islam originating from Egypt with fundamentalist Islam as practiced in Saudi Arabia (Salafism or Wahhabism).[8] The salafi dimension has implications for jihadi terrorism in Europe in that acts of jihadi violence must find justification and precedent in the traditions, or hadith, of the Prophet Muhammad. For example, a verdict by a recognized Salafi scholar on the individual duty of Muslims to kill people who insult the Prophet contributed to a higher proportion of attacks against people and institutions accused of doing so. It should be emphasized that the dependence of jihadis (Salafi) on religious justification by no means contradicts strategic thinking. On the contrary, the movement has a strong tradition of producing strategic texts and evaluating the fruitfulness of its means of struggle.[9] In jihadi thought, religious tenets and strategy go hand-in-hand as the militants consider it a religious duty to mimic the warfare strategies and tactics pursued by the first Muslims.

I further distinguish between "extremists," who support violence but do not generally take part themselves, and "militants" who engage in violence. "Militant" is used as a synonym for "jihadi." Although lines are blurred between non-violent and violent extremism, movements in Europe such as Hizb ut-Tahrir and al-Muhajiroun are generally dubbed "extremist," whereas al-Qaida and likeminded actors are referred to as "jihadis" and "militants." The process through which people become extremists is referred to as "radicalization." I will return to the process of radicalization when discussing various components of terrorist cells and the different pathways involved in joining a cell. Another word that needs further explanation is "homegrown." In terrorism research, "homegrown" usually denotes the idea that terrorists have been born and bred in in the West and hold Western citizenship. This book uses the term in the same way, but adds an extra layer when discussing terrorist plots. A terrorist plot is considered "homegrown" if it emerges without interaction (online or face-to-face) with militants internationally (i.e. interaction with militants abroad did not relate to the plotting of attacks).

When referring to armed Islamist groups in Muslim countries I sometimes address them as "mujahidin" (holy warriors). "Jihadi" and "mujahid" hold the same meaning, but the former usually denotes militants operating transnationally, whereas the latter is used to refer to locally focused actors. The Afghan Taliban's fighters are "mujahidin" according to this definition. "Al-Qaida" refers to the organization Osama bin Laden established in Peshawar in the late 1980s. Al-Qaida "branches" are groups in Muslim countries which have taken the al-Qaida name, such as al-Qaida in the Arabian Peninsula (AQAP), or al-Qaida in the Islamic Maghreb (AQIM), or have vowed allegiance to the organization's leader, such as al-Shabaab in Somalia. Al-Qaida affiliates are groups that have a close relationship to al-Qaida without necessarily having vowed allegiance to the leader. The Uzbek Islamic Jihad Union (IJU) might serve as an example here. The branches and affiliates will also be described as "regional" because they operate across state borders.[10] "Europe" refers to Western Europe, and excludes Russia and the former Eastern Bloc countries. I refer to jihadi activities in other parts of the West, such as the United States, Canada and Australia, solely for context.

What this book is not about

This book provides a detailed picture of the way in which terrorist cells emerge and why, but it lacks counterfactuals and control groups. It clearly focuses on those few who become terrorists and not the vast majority of European Muslims who oppose terrorism. While the book details the backgrounds of many terrorists to illustrate their pathway to militancy, socio-economic metrics are not a focus as such. Previous research on the socio-economics of jihadis has yet to detect systematic differences between them and non-jihadis. Terrorism research has also found that people from all backgrounds can become terrorists under certain circumstances.[11] The case studies presented here support the pluralism of social background, but they also suggest that certain terrorists, with certain social characteristics and personalities, are crucial for the formation of terrorist cells.

This book pays much attention to foreign fighters (understood as Muslims living in the West who travel to conflict zones in Muslim countries and interact with militants). However, it does not study foreign fighting as such, but rather its impact on the threat in Europe.[12] The Arab Spring and the Syrian uprising re-actualized the relationship between foreign fighting and international terrorism. Research based on historical data suggests that relatively few foreign fighters (one out of nine, at most) become involved in international terrorism.[13] However, those few that do become involved tend to be more capable and dangerous than those without experience. Europe is geographically close to areas in the Middle East and North Africa where jihadis fight local governments and foreign occupiers. Armed conflicts in Muslim countries have contributed to terrorism in Europe in the past and will do so in the future. European fighters in Syria today are obtaining contacts and experiences that will make some of them a threat to European security. However, the jihadi threat in Europe also involves terrorists who have become radicalized by local extremists, or whose radicalization took place online, with limited or no connections to conflict zones.

Questions

This book addresses several questions: What are the main components involved in the emergence of jihadi cells in Europe? Who are the terrorists? Why and how do they radicalize? Why and how do they join forces and form cells? How do terrorists radicalize together in the context of the cells? What is the relationship between terrorist cells and local extremist networks? What is the relationship between cells and jihadis abroad? What are the internal structures, hierarchies and roles within cells, and how do they affect the cells' behavior? What contextual factors influence a cell's decision to strike at a certain point of time and location? By observing plots across time and space this study identifies common components in the emergence of cells and plots and how these components relate to one another.

Components of terrorist plots

Jihadi terrorist plots in Europe usually involve interaction between a cell and extremist networks in the attack country, as well as international networks. This pattern has been consistent over time: it applies equally to GIA's terrorism in France in the 1990s, the al-Qaida-linked London attacks in 2005 and the attacks on the offices of *Charlie Hebdo* in 2015. The terrorists almost always interact with radical preachers or other kinds of extremist leaders. The interaction with preachers usually predates attacks, but there are also rare examples of terrorists contacting preachers in connection with attacks. The Madrid bombers' attempts to call preachers and ask for permission to blow themselves up while surrounded in Leganés is a case in point.[14]

Meeting places are another vital component of jihadi terrorist cell formation in Europe. The terrorists examined here often met in radical mosques, although they also met in prisons, educational institutions and NGOs. Single-actor terrorists also sought out meeting places for extremists during their radicalization. Members of the German Sauerland cell (2007) were radicalized in the context of a radical mosque and a university study circle before connecting with mujahidin in Waziristan. The Hofstadgroup in the Netherlands (2004) gathered in an Internet café/phone center and in the apartment of the lead member who assassinated Theo van Gogh. Mehdi Nemmouche, who attacked the Jewish Museum in Brussels in 2014, was radicalized by Islamist extremists in prison before joining the Syrian jihad on release. Over time, online platforms have supplemented radical mosques and other venues as meeting places and a way to access radical preachers. The attack by Arid Uka on US soldiers at Frankfurt Airport in 2011 exemplifies how terrorists in rare instances interacted with extremists solely on social media. Research has highlighted the role of physical meeting places in jihadi networks, and the extent to which virtual platforms might fully replace face-to-face interaction has been a subject of debate.[15] The continued flow of European extremists to conflict zones despite the high risks involved and all possibilities to pursue jihadism online suggest that real-life activism is still of great importance to jihadis, however.

Motivation, which is derived from many sources, is a crucial ingredient in any terrorist attack. Jihadi terrorism in Europe is linked to local, regional and international events which jihadis present as a war on Islam. The invasions of Afghanistan and Iraq were followed by an increase in the number of terrorist plots. The arrests of radical preachers and other Islamists seem to have affected the level of terrorist plotting, as has the publication of cartoons of the Prophet Muhammad in European media. The motivating effect of such events finds a considerable amount of anecdotal support in the case studies presented throughout this book, and the next chapter will suggest a connection between plots in Europe and events in Palestine. Several high-profile attacks on Jewish targets, such as the Mohammed Merah attacks in Southern France, followed Israeli operations and the killing of civilians in Gaza. The motivating effect of events such as invasions, cartoons and Palestine finds support in most research on militant Islamism, albeit emphasized to varying degrees. However, vast numbers of Muslims (and non-Muslims) are outraged by Israeli actions in Palestine, and only a tiny fraction of extremists resort to violence. This demonstrates that political grievances only partially explain extremism and terrorism. For such grievances to translate into terrorism they need to resonate with the personal backgrounds and experiences of individuals, and to be given direction through interaction with militants and their ideology.

The terrorist plots researched in this book involved all kinds of people. They included multiple nationalities, first- and second-generation immigrants, as well as converts. Most were young men, with some exceptions, such as the almost fifty-year-old David Coleman Headley who planned to bomb the offices of the Danish newspaper *Jyllands-Posten* in 2010. Several plots, for example those attributed to the Hofstadgroup (2004), have also involved women in support functions, and there has been one single-actor attack by a woman (the attempt by British Bengali Roshonara Choudhry to kill the British MP Stephen Timms). Some of the terrorists were poor and generally troubled people, such as the unemployed drug addict Shadi Abdullah who was involved in plans to attack Jews in Germany in 2002. Others were well-functioning and relatively well-off individuals, such as Mohammed Siddique Khan who led the cell that staged suicide attacks in London in 2005. Rather unexpectedly, some of the terrorists were highly educated, such as the Tunisian Sarhane Ben Abdelmajid Fakhet (head of the cell behind the attacks in Madrid in 2004) who was about to finish a doctorate in economics when he turned to jihadism. However, the vast majority lacked higher education. It was not uncommon for jihadis in Europe to have criminal records (including petty crime, fraud, trafficking, armed robbery and various acts of violence). The foot soldiers in the Madrid bombings, for example, were recruited from a criminal network. On the other hand, there were also law-abiding citizens involved in terrorist attacks with no known criminal record. The best example of this is the plot involving medical doctors who attempted to bomb Glasgow Airport and nightclubs in London in 2007. This diversity in their social profile finds support in existing research on the sociology of Islamists in Europe and al-Qaida's global networks.[16]

If the backgrounds of jihadis in Europe varied, then so too did their personalities. Some have been described as strong, charismatic and manipulative, others as weak, impressionable and easily manipulated. Some of the terrorists were opinionated, fiercely political and ideologically informed. Some were quiet and withdrawn, while others were outgoing and action-oriented. Some were calm and controlled, whereas others had a temper, displaying rage and violent tendencies. Some were kind, polite and emphatic, whereas others were rude, or threatening. For example, as I will explore in detail below, there was a world of difference between the articulate and calculating schoolteacher who led the London bombers and the reckless delinquent Mohammed Merah who massacred Jewish school children in Southern France.

Although backgrounds and personalities differed and the terrorists joined cells in various ways, there were recurring patterns. Most were affiliated with non-violent extremism before turning violent. The Woolwich killer Michael Adebolajo's mixing with Anjem Choudary's network in the years before the attack is an example here. Research on radicalization highlights the ability of extremists to inflict "moral shocks" on followers, which causes them to engage in soul-searching and makes them question their established worldviews. Searching for answers, they may experience "cognitive opening," leading them to buy into extremist conspiracy theories.[17] In the context of Islamism, extremists expose recruits to propaganda showing atrocities against Muslims, as well as spectacular jihadi attacks, such as 9/11. The shock then leads them to search for answers in ideology and to a religious awakening and radicalization based upon jihadi interpretations of Islam. Personal crises and tragedies also tilted individuals towards extremism in many instances. The death of the mother of the terrorist who murdered Theo van Gogh is one of numerous examples of how people started to radicalize when affected by personal misfortune.

However, radicalization could also be triggered, or amplified, by other, less intuitive factors. For example, in some instances radicalization involved conversion, or rediscovering, childhood faith. Studies have indicated that converts radicalize faster and more intensively than people who have grown up with Islam.[18] Converts may have to prove themselves more than native Muslims, although such mechanisms have yet to be substantiated by rigorous research. For those who rediscovered faith, many were not pious in the past. They did not pray regularly or attend mosques. They smoked, drank alcohol, kept girlfriends outside marriage or pursued other habits frowned upon in Islam. Rediscovering faith seems to have involved a counter-reaction in many instances whereby jihadis seek to cleanse themselves of past sins.

A pattern which finds support in radicalization research is that most jihadi terrorists in Europe were recruited via friends and relatives.[19] The story of how the leader of a terrorist cell in Germany in 2002, Mohammed Abu Dhess, recruited his childhood friend from Jordan is one of the many examples discussed in this book. Shared backgrounds and identity and interpersonal trust may create a hospitable atmosphere for radicalization under given circumstances.

Finally, travels to conflict zones have also facilitated radicalization. The majority of plots in Europe involved at least one cell member who had spent time with armed groups abroad, and these individuals tended to be more extreme upon returning home. Research has yet to theorize the effect of foreign fighting on radicalization, and proponents of leaderless jihad argue it is not a necessary component of the process. However, several studies have documented a relationship between foreign fighting and international terrorism, and this book will show how foreign fighting is a common feature of jihadi socialization, and how foreign fighters tend to end up as entrepreneurs of terrorist cells.

None of the components addressed can explain why, when and where terrorist cells emerge. Many Muslims in Europe interact with extremists locally and internationally, offline or online, without resorting to terrorism. Many seek out radical preachers without committing terrorist acts. Scores of Muslims despair over the situation in Palestine without resorting to terrorism. Similarly, most people experience personal tragedies and many convert or rediscover faith without radicalizing. Spending time with relatives and people who have a shared background also has no radicalizing effect on its own. And though many Muslims have gone to conflict zones, only a minority dabbles in international terrorism.

Types of jihadi terrorists in Europe

In order to explain terrorist cell formation, it is necessary to examine how the various components addressed work together in the context of plots. For this purpose I introduce a typology of jihadi terrorists in Europe. The typology is based upon what the terrorists said and did before, during and sometimes after their involvement in terrorism, and how others depicted them. It focuses on the core members of cells involved in plotting attacks and distinguishes between "the entrepreneur," "the protégé," "the misfit" and "the drifter." Each type radicalizes and joins cells differently and plays different roles; they fulfill different functions and influence the behavior of cells in different ways. This typology is a new way to approach data in studies of terrorist cell formation. It provides a tool to assess the relative importance of factors leading to jihadi terrorist plots in Europe.[20]

The entrepreneurs and their protégés are far more important than others in the emergence of terrorist plots. These individuals pursue ideological–political motives and run errands for militant groups in conflict zones. They proactively seek out organized extremist and militant networks in Europe and abroad, and allow themselves to become recruits in terrorist projects. In turn they recruit, socialize and manipulate others to join them. The misfits and drifters are the numerical majority. However, they become militants in a more passive way and for a host of reasons other than politics and ideology. Their radicalization pathways are characterized more by personal problems, deprivation and a lack of options, identity crises, loyalty to friends and relatives, adventure and youthful rebellion. They become terrorists by way of coincidence because they encounter and befriend "entrepreneurs," or because they are related to such individuals in one way or another. Although they may take the initiative to interact with extremists on some level, they are usually approached and lured into terrorist networks and tend to be at the receiving end of the radicalization process.

The categorizations used here are by no means exhaustive. Some of the terrorists defy categorization, and in other cases it is impossible to find sufficient information about them. Sometimes the overall composure of the cell does not fit the pattern, as for example when certain cells are dominated by "misfits." Throughout the period examined in this book, terrorist plots increasingly involved a single-actor terrorist who resembled one or a combination of the four prototypes.

The entrepreneur

Entrepreneurs are crucial for a terrorist cell to form and take action. They are religious–political activists who have a strong sense of justice. They seek out radical mosques, preachers and propaganda, and listen to and draw inspiration from militant ideologues. Entrepreneurs proactively connect with extremist networks, militant groups and training camps in conflict zones. As a result, they can nearly always be characterized as foreign fighters. In the context of a terrorist cell, they recruit, socialize and train the other cell members. They stage activities that promote group cohesion, take on a leading role in political and ideological discussions and refer group members to acknowledged jihadi preachers and ideologues for further guidance. They are in charge of the cell's operational activities and its external relations with jihadi organizations, networks and operational and ideological mentors—both in Europe and internationally. They are usually (but not always) senior to and more experienced and educated than their accomplices, and sometimes they are family men. They are passionate about social and political causes, and demand respect from their surroundings. They do not appear to resort to violence primarily for their own sake, but for something they consider a greater good and a religious duty. They aspire to do right by those they identify with, framed as the community of true believers, or the Muslim Nation.

Although hard to measure, the entrepreneurs examined here seem to have had a genuine concern for the suffering of Muslims in all conflicts addressed by jihadi movements. They are rarely involved in party politics, but may dedicate themselves to Islamic NGOs and take part in the activities of broader Islamist extremist movements. They tend to have high aspirations, and sometimes have failed to achieve their own personal ambitions. Entrepreneurs embrace jihadi thought gradually through an intellectual process, through activism and idealism, and call for social and political justice. They tend to be well read and well traveled, and sometimes they contribute to the jihadi field with their own ideas through propaganda, preaching or by producing ideological material. Frustrated by politics and the poor prospects of having much influence through non-violent means, entrepreneurs seek alternative ways to make a difference, and become attracted to the action-oriented approach of the jihadis.

They ultimately take on a terrorist project for al-Qaida or likeminded groups in Europe. Entrepreneurs do not represent formal authority associated with hierarchical organizations or charismatic leadership associated with movements. Their authority seems to be based primarily on being more knowledgeable in political and religious matters than their peers; they are better connected and skilled in matters related to jihadi activities, and they generally possess charismatic qualities and a talent for influencing and manipulating others. The Algerian Djamel Beghal, who ran a terrorist network for al-Qaida in Europe in 2001 (examined in Chapter Four), is the archetypical entrepreneur. Even from behind bars he was able to radicalize perpetrators of subsequent terrorist plots in Europe. The leader of the London bombers, Mohammed Siddique Khan (discussed in Chapter Six), is another example.

The protégé

Although similar to entrepreneurs, protégés are always junior and inferior. This character serves the function of being second-in-command. Protégés and entrepreneurs have a special bond resulting from a longtime friendship and shared background. Protégés are trusted with important tasks and are privy to the details of a plot, as well the cell's connection to organized networks. The two characters may go on trips together, or attend training camps abroad without involving other members of the cell. Like entrepreneurs, protégés show signs of being devout idealists with a strong personality and sense of justice. Protégés admire and idealize entrepreneurs. They embrace militant ideology and become part of a terrorist cell project via a combination of loyalty to entrepreneurs and intellectually justified activism (social, religious and political).

The dominant driving force in protégés' radicalization (parallel to that of entrepreneurs) are political grievances related to the persecution of, and the injustices suffered by, Muslims. Protégés tend to be intelligent, well educated and well mannered, excelling in their professional, academic and social lives. As a result of their skills and education, they provide the cell with resources or expertise (e.g. bomb-making skills, IT-skills or the provision of finance). They are usually young with limited life experience, and are impressionable and quite easily manipulated by senior figures they respect and look up to (such as entrepreneurs, or other mentors, including militant preachers).

The presence of a protégé type in cells speaks to the relative sophistication of the entrepreneur and the ideology they convey to the other members. It illustrates how jihadi thought may appeal to highly intelligent, socially skilled and sometimes economically well-off people, social segments that, according to rational arguments, would have a lot to lose by engaging in terrorist activity. The interplay between Djamel Beghal and his accomplice Kamel Daoudi, discussed in Chapter Four, perfectly illustrates the entrepreneur–protégé dynamics, as does the interplay between Mohammed Siddique Khan and his second-in-command, Shehzad Tanweer, explored in Chapter Six. Indicative of the commitment of entrepreneurs and their protégés, there are hardly any examples of such characters having regrets or turning informants in if they get arrested, as has been the case with the next two categories I will address: the misfit and the drifter. On the contrary, in trials and rare press interviews, captured terrorists who have played the part of an entrepreneur or protégé rarely show signs of remorse and remain consistent in their belief that they pursued a legitimate course of action.

The misfit

Jihadi terrorist cells in Europe often involve a category I refer to as misfits. Personal misfortune plays a much bigger role in the radicalization of misfits than it does for the other categories of cell members. Misfits are individuals who do not perform well socially and tend to have a troubled background as well as a criminal record. They appear to be far less ideologically informed and committed than entrepreneurs and protégés. Misfits also tend to possess weaker and more hesitant personalities, and display more personal vulnerabilities than the other categories (to the extent it is possible to generalize from the available data). Misfits become part of a militant religious circle primarily as a means to cope with personal problems, or out of loyalty to friends and kin, or some combination of the two.

In some instances their motivation for connecting with religious militants involves a form of personal salvation or desire to cleanse themselves of past sins. Misfits are often recruited in prison or via criminal networks. They tend to lack proper education, but may be streetwise and physically fit. Indeed, several of the misfits discussed in this book have been involved in sports, and some have even been highly talented athletes. Misfits are typically approached by an entrepreneur or a protégé with whom they share a common background. They may offer to help get the misfit back on the straight and narrow, returning them to the right path by encouraging them to join their militant religious terrorist project. Misfits do not enjoy much influence within the cell, and serious disagreements sometimes occur between misfits and other cell members, including entrepreneurs.

Misfits often display violent tendencies and may have had criminal convictions before becoming involved with extremism and militancy. Because they tend to be physically fit, have violent tendencies and are familiar with criminal practices, misfits qualify for practical tasks at the operational level. They may be put in charge of acquiring weapons, for example, or placing bombs on to a target. The failed Tunisian footballer Nizar Trabelsi in Beghal's network and the London bomber Hasib Hussain joined terrorism according to the misfit trajectory. As opposed to the overall consistency and persistence of the political–religious convictions associated with entrepreneurs and protégés, the misfit may voice regrets, or turn an informant in when captured. Misfits typically justify their actions by referring to social grievances including underemployment, drug abuse or of having been exposed to racism and other injustices. Owing to their individualized justifications, and their secondary role in terrorist cell formation and behavior compared to entrepreneurial figures, the misfits' motivations should rarely be seen as reflecting the terrorist cell as a whole.

The drifter

The final category of jihadi terrorist cell members in Europe, drifters, may actually represent the majority of the individuals who become involved in terrorist plotting. Moreover, their inclusion in a terrorist cell is consistent with the dominant theories on radicalization, which emphasize the importance of social connections and group processes in radicalization and recruitment for terrorist networks. Yet it might be argued that drifters play a somewhat insignificant role in determining the emergence of cells and plots. Drifters may possess a similar overall background to entrepreneurs, protégés and misfits. But they differ from the other ideal-types mainly by having less specific reasons for becoming involved with extremism. Drifters tend to lack a strong agenda. Their motives for interacting with extremists are primarily related to fulfilling social commitments and obtaining social rewards. Only in exceptional circumstances do they appear to have been strongly politicized or ideological before connecting with militant friends and acquaintances, and they have rarely experienced serious social troubles. It can be argued that they become a member of a terrorist cell primarily by being in the wrong place at the wrong time, or being socially connected to the wrong people (entrepreneurs and protégés).

Drifters could have gone in an entirely different direction if they had connected with different people. It is thus mainly the obligations that lie in friendship, common background and shared experiences which determine where they end up more than the personal grievances associated with the misfits, and the political grievances and ideas associated with entrepreneurs and protégés. Drifters are rarely entrusted with the most important tasks in a cell, possibly because of their volatile characteristics and relative lack of devotion, and they are rarely privy to the precise details of an impending terrorist operation. However, they represent manpower, and fulfill important support functions in a cell. While it may be unclear exactly what causes drifters to radicalize, there are indications that youthful rebellion, a search for identity and adventure, or the lack of viable options are more pronounced driving forces than in the case of entrepreneurs, protégés and misfits. An affiliate of Beghal's terrorist network, Johan Bonte, who was the brother of Beghal's wife, is an example of this category. It was a family connection that put him in contact with an entrepreneur and he appears to have had a subordinate role in the plot.

The typology singles out three main pathways to becoming a terrorist, each involving different driving forces. Entrepreneurs and protégés are driven mainly by political grievances, ideology and activism. Misfits are driven mainly by personal grievances, whereas drifters tend to end up in cells because they have a social tie to someone on the inside. Social networks facilitate the inclusion of all categories, but are most significant in the inclusion of misfits and drifters, relatively speaking. Entrepreneurs and protégés play a more important role in hatching a terrorist plot than the other categories. They are the ones who build cells, connect them to a broader network, provide them with an ideological rationale and set attack plans in motion. This deconstruction of a terrorist cell is a useful analytical tool. It creates a differentiated picture of what motivates people to form a cell, how cell members relate to each other and the outside world, and how leader-led and leaderless aspects converge inside cells. It also indicates that we should be careful about making theoretical assumptions based on what characterizes the majority of jihadi activists when explaining the formation of terrorist cells. The typology also has certain implications for the prevention of jihadi terrorism in Europe, and these will be addressed in the final chapter of this book.

Together, entrepreneurs, protégés, misfits and drifters have appeared in terrorist plots featuring different configurations of the components involved in terrorist cell formation throughout the period examined in the book. Some cells were top-down, others bottom-up. Some were initiated from abroad and some locally. Some cells emerged from mosques, others online. Some were motivated mostly by the war in Iraq, others by cartoons. The only consistent feature is that no cells have formed in the absence of entrepreneurs.

Method and sources

The method of this book is the case study. I examine multiple case studies of terrorist cells emerging in Europe under changing contextual circumstances in the period between 1994 and 2015. I explore all of the components involved in terrorist cell formation and how they interplay with each other. As indicators of what caused plots to emerge I look at the perpetrators' backgrounds and network connections, the statements attributed to them, and their actions, including the modus operandi of the attack plans. As the available information about terrorist plots is by definition incomplete, I combine different indicators, check the consistency between them and interpret them jointly. I carefully assess the immediate and broader context of plots in the country where attacks were going to happen, regionally in Europe, and internationally. Some aspects of the plots, such as the backgrounds of terrorists and their ties to local extremists, are well documented, whereas other aspects, such as foreign travel, can be murky, require interpretation and involve a substantial margin of error.

While I rely a great deal on surveying how people become terrorists and on interpreting what they have said, I also look at their modus operandi. Because terrorists communicate through violence, the weapons and tactics they employ and the targets they select are highly revealing as to the reason why certain plots emerged. The modus operandi will therefore be addressed in a separate chapter (Chapter Two) as well as in the individual case studies. Knowing that al-Qaida prefers certain bombs, tactics and targets, for example, could tie one given cell to al-Qaida and global jihad, although other indicators must be taken into consideration. Other groups besides al-Qaida have operated in Europe, and terrorists' motives involve a personal dimension which affects terrorist cell formation and behavior.

In analyzing the case studies presented here, the book also pays careful attention to the context of plots. Terrorists pursue multiple agendas and what they say about their motives cannot always be taken at face value. It is therefore necessary to assess events and developments occurring in Europe and internationally which may have influenced a cell, whether its members refer to them or not. The cases were selected from a comprehensive open source chronology of jihadi terrorist incidents in Europe since 1994, which can be accessed via the book's electronic appendix (www.hurstpublishers.com/book/islamist-terrorism-in-europe). This was chosen as the starting point because 1994 was the year of the first clear example of a jihadi terrorist plot, when members of the al-Qaida-linked GIA hijacked an Air France jet in Algeria with the aim of crashing it in Paris in a suicide mission.

The book is based on media sources, expert interviews, judicial papers and jihadi primary source material. It also collates insights from existing studies. Media sources have a reputation for sensationalism and inaccuracies. However, the media is still a vitally important tool in terrorism research. Media rarely misses out on significant events and several journalists are de facto terrorism experts, with access to primary sources within law enforcement and even terrorists. Although media sources are by definition secondary sources, they also contain primary source material such as statements, witness accounts or published memoirs, judicial documents and leaked intelligence documents. As well as media sources, I have also collected judicial papers, which can generally be viewed as reliable sources. Finally, I have consulted academics and security officials in countries where plots occurred, as they often possess unique local insights. All sources involve margins of error and potential bias. Journalists may ignore facts to pursue a certain angle, for example, and security officials may want to exaggerate a threat, while academics may possess theoretical bias, and judicial sources may miss out on the international aspects of plots. I have consequently gauged each source critically, and have triangulated them where possible.

Furthermore, as information on terrorist incidents is rarely complete, I have categorized such incidents according to the extent to which they fulfilled the following criteria: (1) known jihadi perpetrator(s); (2) identified target; and (3) solid evidence (bomb-materials, suicide notes). Well-documented incidents were categorized as "category 1" cases (C1), whereas less-documented incidents were defined as "category 2" (C2) and "category 3" cases (C3). In most cases, the level of documentation corresponds to the seriousness of terrorist plots (major, lethal attacks generate large numbers of sources). However, there have been many examples of plots that initially seemed insignificant and later turned out to be serious when additional information emerged. My categorization system seeks to provide a nuanced sense of the threat, and at the same time to ensure that all serious plots are registered.

The time factor is crucial when assessing terrorist plots. An attack may look very different when time passes and new information comes to light. For example, it took nearly six years to establish the fact that the 2004 Madrid bombings were not the sole work of homegrown terrorists but were instead connected to al-Qaida via a Moroccan handler named Amer Azizi. My case studies focus on well-documented C1 plots, which I assessed as being typical of the threat situation in different time intervals and illustrated continuities and discontinuities in terrorist cell formation. However, I also include C2 incidents when discussing the scope of the threat and trends in modus operandi. Occasionally I also address C3 incidents, which involved significant aspects despite being too poorly documented to conduct in-depth analysis. Selecting well-documented and typical plots in such a way requires prior knowledge about the universe of the available cases. In quantitative research such selection is prohibited, but in qualitative work it might be considered a strength.[21]

Outline

The book is divided into nine chapters. Chapter One investigates how jihadi networks have evolved in Europe since their emergence in the early 1990s and traces their origins to the "Afghan-Arab" foreign fighter movement of the 1980s Afghan jihad. It also situates jihadis in the broader Islamist landscape. The chapter provides the necessary context for the case studies presented in subsequent chapters. It addresses individuals, groups, networks, radical mosques and training camps which have played a part in the emergence of jihadi terrorism in Europe. It shows how Islamist extremists in Europe were interwoven with transnational jihadi networks and how the former provided crucial support for the latter in terms of propaganda, money, weapons and recruits. The chapter provides a background for explaining why many terrorist cells in Europe grew out of support networks for foreign jihadis.

Chapter Two provides an overview of trends in the scope and modus operandi of jihadi terrorism in Europe since 1994 and offers a tentative discussion of why they change. It maps variation in the occurrence and geographical distribution of plots throughout the period examined in the book. It provides an overview of trends in weapon types, attack types and target types which will be employed as indicators of terrorists' group affiliations and motives throughout the book. It further addresses the ratio of group-based versus single-actor terrorism, and the extent to which foreign fighters were involved in plots, which has varied throughout the book's timeline for different reasons. The chapter concludes by commenting briefly on the way jihadi terrorism in Europe is financed because this relates to the formation of terrorist cells.

Chapter Three examines the GIA's terrorist campaign in France in the mid-1990s. This was a cornerstone historical case because it was the first example of jihadi terrorism in Europe, and an early example of jihadis internationalizing their (mainly) national struggles. Moreover, the GIA campaign involved networks and individuals that continue to shape the jihadi threat in Europe and have surfaced in terrorism investigations up until the present day.

Chapter Four examines several terrorist plots in the period from 2000 to 2004 which had dual ties to al-Qaida in Afghanistan and terrorist groups in the Middle East and North Africa. The cells were pursuing attacks on US and Jewish targets in Europe and demonstrated how al-Qaida aimed to include Europe as one front in the global jihad. The cases also exemplified how ties to groups in Muslim countries influenced the terrorists' motives and actions.

Chapter Five analyzes the circumstances of the Madrid attacks (M-11) and the murder of Theo van Gogh in the Netherlands in 2004 and looks at the occupation and invasion of Iraq as a motivation for jihadi terrorism in Europe in 2003–5. This chapter also problematizes the notion of "homegrown" terrorism in relation to these cases.

Chapter Six explores three Pakistani-based terrorist cells in the UK between 2004 and 2006. These cells represented a new pattern, as people from Pakistani origins had rarely been involved in plots in Europe until then. The cases also demonstrate how al-Qaida, which was regrouping in the Af-Pak region after the invasion and occupation of Afghanistan, managed to exploit extremists in the UK for continued global jihad in Europe, and how changes in the relationship between Islamists and the state in Pakistan and radicalization over Iraq contributed to this development.

Chapter Seven examines five terrorist cells in 2005–7 which signify a pattern where jihadi terrorism in Europe was becoming increasingly diversified and involved more nationalities, combining people who were born and bred in the region and immigrants. These cases also demonstrate how al-Qaida's regional branches began taking an interest in Europe, and how the motivational landscape was widening. In addition to invasions and counter-terrorism, insults against Islam in Europe gained in significance as motives in this period. These cases also illustrate that while jihadi plots had largely been confined to continental Europe and the UK, now the threat was also expanding north, affecting Scandinavia.

Chapter Eight outlines a number of plots in Europe in the period 2008–10, a period in which al-Qaida's central organization was under pressure, whereas its regional branches and affiliates were on the rise. The period was also characterized by the proliferation of jihadism in social media, and, as the chapter argues, all of these factors contributed to the rise of single-actor terrorism as a preferred tactic of European jihadis. By 2008, the publication and re-publication of cartoons of the Prophet Muhammad had also become a major theme in al-Qaida propaganda seeking to encourage attacks by individuals in the West, something which added to the threat of solo-terrorism in Europe.

Chapter Nine examines jihadi terrorism in wake of the Arab Spring and death of bin Laden. It details a situation where the threat to Europe was becoming increasingly heterogeneous, combining trends from the past with new features. The rise of the Islamic State (IS) in Syria and Iraq has complicated the picture further in creating a volatile and unpredictable threat situation from 2014 onwards. Chapter Nine also concludes the study by addressing the shock attacks on the offices of *Charlie Hebdo* and the hostage-taking at a Jewish supermarket in Paris, January 2015. By viewing these attacks from a historical perspective, the chapter ties together knots from different phases of jihadism in Europe including GIA's terrorism in the 1990s, the threat from al-Qaida throughout the 2000s and the emerging threat from IS.

1

FROM AFGHANISTAN TO EUROPE

This chapter takes stock of the emergence of jihadism in Europe and traces the origin of the phenomenon to the "Afghan-Arab" foreign fighter movement. It looks at how jihadis in Europe came to reflect the Afghan-Arabs' transformation from a loose alliance of Arab groups fighting Arab dictatorships into a transnational project targeting the West. The chapter emphasizes how jihadis in Europe thrived on charismatic leaders, much like the mother-movement in Afghanistan. Radical preachers and entrepreneurs were crucial in building the support networks for international jihad in Europe that gradually emerged as a terrorist threat.

The history of jihadi terrorism in Europe is largely one of how interaction between local networks and militants in conflict zones produced attack cells. I describe how jihadi networks in Europe became centered on the UK, but also stretched across the region, and how jihadis in different countries fulfilled different functions vis-à-vis armed groups internationally. The chapter sheds light on how jihadis in Europe exploited the freedoms of democracies while creating a subculture around radical mosques and social media activism. I will also discuss what gave radical preachers their authority and the methods they used to recruit, and how these self-appointed pundits harnessed the mythology of jihad and focused on war crimes against Muslims while shaping the identity and enemy perceptions of youths. With the aim of inducing moral shocks in subjects, they focused partly on atrocities in Muslim countries and partly on injustices against Muslims in the West. By linking these issues, they were able to frame them as evidence of a conspiracy between corrupt Muslim leaders and the West against oppressed, authentic Muslims.

When reaching out to second-generation immigrants and converts, preacher-recruiters made their message available to a Western audience. This included preaching in English and exploiting the universal language of imagery to stir emotions. The chapter also addresses the sociocultural aspects of recruitment. The jihadi subculture in Europe offered community and activities for youths, such as religious seminars, public rallies and paramilitary training. Like other social movements, it also offered an identity through distinct symbolism (logos and flags), appearance (beards, *jalabiyyas* and headscarves), rituals (prayer) and jihad hymns (*nasheed*). For some immigrant youths caught between cultures with limited opportunities in the job market, jihadism was the ultimate form of youth rebellion and a way to achieve status. While the chapter addresses general processes of recruitment and radicalization throughout Europe, it also focuses on the most vigorous and influential network in the UK, which was the center of gravity and the mother ship for extremists in other countries.

I explore the background and activities of three UK-based preachers, Abu Qatada, Abu Hamza and Omar Bakri Mohammed, who facilitated the rise of jihadism in Europe in the 1990s and have remained figureheads ever since. They also played an important role in shaping the ideology and praxis of the European jihadis. They cooperated with and assisted extremists in other European countries in setting up networks modeled on the UK's. Via their personal experiences and international contacts, they ensured that jihadis in Europe became interwoven with a transnational movement. Although these preachers have been arrested or have left Europe, they have continued to influence followers in Europe from behind bars and through their henchmen such as Anjem Choudary.

The chapter begins with an account of the rise of the Afghan-Arab movement and al-Qaida as it relates to jihadism in Europe. This is followed by an examination of Europe's place in jihadi thought and what the ideology says about fighting in non-Muslim lands. The chapter concludes by exploring the dynamics involved in the emergence and spread of jihadi networks in Europe, as well as the interplay between leaders, their recruits and the ideology.

Afghan-Arabs

The 1979 Soviet invasion of Afghanistan was part of a perfect storm for the emergence of transnational militant Sunni Islam in the period that followed.[1] The invasion coincided with the Shia revolution in Iran, which not only demonstrated the political power of Islam but also heightened tensions and enmity along the Sunni–Shia divide. Many Sunnis felt they were facing an existential struggle. Sunni Arab regimes had suffered humiliating defeats in wars against Israel in 1948, 1967 and 1973, leading to the occupation of Palestine and US–Israeli dominance in the Middle East. Islamist movements across the Arab world accused their rulers of treachery for forging alliances with Western powers and introducing Westernized political systems.

Coinciding with the invasion of Afghanistan and the Iranian revolution, the Arab world saw several revolts in Egypt, Saudi Arabia, Algeria and Syria. In Egypt, the groups Egyptian Islamic Jihad (EIJ) and Islamic Group (IG) attempted to overthrow the regimes of Anwar al-Sadat and Hosni Mubarak.[2] In Saudi Arabia, followers of the charismatic Islamist Juhayman al-Utaybi besieged the Grand Mosque in Mecca with the intention of igniting an Islamic revolution.[3] In Algeria, the Armed Islamic Movement (MIA) attacked the state.[4] And in Syria, the Muslim Brotherhood besieged the city of Hama with the aim of toppling Hafez al-Assad.[5] However, all of these campaigns were harshly suppressed, causing a spiral of violence. At the geopolitical level, the Soviet invasion of Afghanistan was seen as a threat to US and Saudi Arabian interests in the region. With Pakistan's assistance, the Americans and the Saudis channeled billions of dollars to the Afghan mujahidin. Thousands of Muslims worldwide volunteered to support the Afghans, mostly with humanitarian aid, but some also joined the armed struggle.[6]

Much like the foreign fighters of today, Muslims traveled to the Afghan warzone for various reasons: some out of religious fervor, while others were seeking adventure and companionship or simply chasing the myth surrounding the jihad.[7] Muslim governments, NGOs and private donors facilitated the recruitment of volunteers. Islamist movements, such as the Muslim Brotherhood, sent money, doctors and engineers to provide shelter and medical services for Afghan refugees (al-Qaida's Ayman al-Zawahiri was one of the doctors).

These were the circumstances under which a small number of Arab foreign fighters (primarily Algerians, Egyptians and Saudis) joined the armed conflict. They were recruited by the Palestinian Abdullah Azzam who was seen as the "godfather" of the foreign fighters in Afghanistan until his death in mysterious circumstances in 1989.[8] Azzam was born in Jenin in 1941 and lived as a fugitive in Jordan after the 1967 war. He obtained a doctorate in Islamic jurisprudence from al-Azhar, Cairo, in 1973. After being expelled from Jordan because of his fierce pro-Palestinian activism he settled as an imam in Jeddah, Saudi Arabia. In 1981 Azzam obtained a post as a lecturer at the International

Islamic University in Islamabad, Pakistan. He became absorbed into the Afghan cause, and established ties to Afghan warlords. Azzam preached that it was an individual duty for all Muslims to join jihad. He traversed the world raising funds and recruiting together with the spiritual guide of the Egyptian IG, Omar Abdel-Rahman. However, it was in Saudi Arabia that Azzam recruited his most valuable asset, the Islamist son of a Saudi-Yemeni building entrepreneur and billionaire, Osama bin Laden, who emerged as a main financer for the Arab mujahidin and the founder of al-Qaida.

At the end of 1984, the two men established al-Qaida's forerunner, Maktab al-Khidamat (MAK), for the purpose of fundraising and recruitment, as well as propaganda such as the *al-Jihad* magazine which reported from the battlefield. Because of Azzam's ties to Afghan warlords, the first Arab fighters joined Afghan mujahidin factions. They later became organized under MAK before many of them joined bin Laden's spin-off group, al-Qaida.[9] Many of the Arab recruits were military novices, but some of them were also experienced fighters. Among the Algerians, for example, some had fought in the Algerian War of Liberation, while some had taken up arms against the regime during the 1970s and some had served in the army. Likewise, Egyptian Islamists who were involved in coup attempts in the 1970s and 1980s had been in the military. Algerians and Egyptians therefore acted as trainers among the Arabs in Afghanistan, and several of them would later become involved in insurgencies such as the Algerian Civil War and international terrorism for al-Qaida and affiliated groups.[10]

The relationship between the Afghan mujahidin and the foreign fighters was ridden by power struggles as well as ideological and cultural frictions. This led the foreign fighters to isolate themselves. In 1984–5 Azzam established the Guesthouse of Abu Uthman in Peshawar and the Sada training camp on the Afghan border for Arabs only.[11] Bin Laden subsequently established two other camps solely for Arabs, al-Arin and al-Masada. In 1986 he went on to establish a special front, independent from Azzam and MAK, named al-Ansar, in Jaji, Paktia. Al-Ansar comprised fighters from Saudi Arabia, Egypt and Algeria. During Ramadan in 1987, al-Ansar fighters led by bin Laden successfully defeated Soviet Special Forces in what became known as "the battle of Jaji."[12] This victory boosted the Arabs' morale and contributed to the myth of the Afghan jihad: that a small band of committed believers could defeat superpowers. The fact bin Laden personally oversaw the battle contributed to the myth surrounding his persona: the pious billionaire son ready to sacrifice his wealth and life for God. The Jaji victory set the stage for the formation of the organization that most profoundly came to shape the terrorist threat in Europe—al-Qaida.

Al-Qaida

Al-Qaida was founded in Peshawar, Pakistan, after the battle of Jaji and before the Soviet withdrawal, in 1988.[13] It was set up as an Arab paramilitary organization designed to carry the banner of jihad after Afghanistan, with the aim of overthrowing Arab dictators, freeing Muslims from foreign occupation, liberating Palestine and ultimately re-establishing the Caliphate.[14] In the 1990s bin Laden and Ayman al-Zawahiri developed the strategy of a "global jihad" with the intention of deterring Western powers from interfering in Muslim affairs. While the evolution of al-Qaida cannot be treated in-depth here, I highlight issues of particular relevance to jihadi terrorism in Europe: the organization's section for external operations; its training camps and alliance politics; and its role in fomenting the idea and praxis of global jihad among Islamists that were primarily focused on national struggles.

Bin Laden set up a hierarchical organization with a central leadership, an advisory council and committees overseeing different functions and activities such as military, religious and financial affairs, as well as media and propaganda.[15] With regard to international terrorism, al-Qaida organized a special section for external (out of Afghanistan) operations in the latter half of the 1990s.[16] This section is shrouded in secrecy, but different sources suggest it was headed first by the former Egyptian Army soldier Mohammed Atef (Abu Hafs al-Masri) until his death in 2001. From then on it was overseen by the chief planner of 9/11, the Pakistani Khalid Sheikh Mohammed, until his arrest in 2003. It is believed that the section was headed by the Egyptian Hamza Rabiyyah al-Masri between 2003 and 2005 until he was killed by a drone. He was in turn replaced by another Egyptian, Abu Ubaydah al-Masri, who oversaw international operations until he died from a disease in 2007. The sources are vague concerning who was in charge of al-Qaida's out-of-Af-Pak attacks after 2007, but it is believed that a third Egyptian, Abu Jihad al-Masri, oversaw such operations for a while in 2008 before he too was killed by a drone strike in the very same year. In 2009, information from terrorist investigations in Europe and the United States indicated that the section was led by one Abu Saleh al-Somali (a Somalian). He was also killed by a drone strike at the end of that year, and several sources have since speculated that an al-Qaida veteran known as Saif al-Adel, who fled to Iran after the 2001 invasion of Afghanistan, subsequently took charge. If this is true, he has been the longest serving supervisor of external operations in al-Qaida's history.

It is believed that al-Adel has been held in some sort of house arrest in Iran together with other al-Qaida members, including bin Laden's son, Saad. The rationale for the Iranian authorities to keep high-ranking al-Qaida members in semi-captivity is unclear. It has been suggested that Iran has sought to avoid al-Qaida attacks in the country, while at the same time it has sought to keep the door open to future cooperation with the organization in the event of a large-scale confrontation with the United States and Israel.[17] In any event, there are indications that al-Qaida figures in Iran have enjoyed relative freedom to engage in international terrorism. According to some sources, al-Adel was central in moving al-Qaida towards a strategy of small, frequent attacks instead of spectaculars like 9/11.

Apart from the section's leaders, terrorism investigations have identified multiple individuals involved in facilitating attack cells operating in European countries on behalf of al-Qaida. In 2001–2, for example, the Palestinian Abu Zubaydah and the Algerian Abu Doha helped set up several al-Qaida-linked cells in Europe, although, as I will discuss in Chapter Four, the former's role is disputed. Furthermore, there are strong indications that the Moroccan Amer Azizi played a role in organizing the cell that bombed Madrid in 2004.[18] In subsequent years, a Libyan known as Abu Faraj al-Libi, an Iraqi known as Abd al-Hadi al-Iraqi, the British-Pakistani Rashid Rauf and a US-Saudi citizen Adnan Shukrijumah are also thought to have acted as facilitators of several high-profile plots in Europe and the United States.

What is known about al-Qaida's external operations is part of the puzzle when assessing the emergence of plots in Europe. Part of the same puzzle is the organization's training camps. Contacts between European jihadis and al-Qaida are usually traced to these camps, mostly in Af-Pak, but also elsewhere. Training camps were at the crux of al-Qaida's alliance-building and recruitment from the outset.[19] Imagery from al-Qaida's training camps, showing black-clad trainees in military exercises and jumping through rings of fire, have gained cult-status and is being mimicked by groups such as Jabhat al-Nusra and ISIS/IS in the Middle East today.

Camps and alliances

Within the training camps, al-Qaida traded resources (training, money, brand name) for support, cooperation and protection. Shortly after its foundation, the organization set up a training camp named al-Faruq in Khost, which was later moved to Kandahar.[20] This was the organization's main facility until 2001, and it offered basic military training and courses in ideology. Most of the recruits in al-Qaida's formative period were Arabs, but over time more and more nationalities attended the camp, including Europeans. Recruits were handpicked from al-Faruq for advanced training at Khalden and the Derunta camp in Jalalabad, which offered specialized courses in bomb-making. At Derunta, al-Qaida also supervised experiments with chemical and biological agents and conducted research into nuclear capabilities.[21] Neither Khalden nor Derunta were al-Qaida camps as such, but the supervisors of the camps (mostly Egyptians, Algerians and Libyans) cooperated with the organization and exchanged recruits.[22] Until 2001 al-Faruq, Khalden and Derunta were attended by a number people who became involved in terrorist plots in Europe. In the late 1990s al-Qaida also helped set up a training camp in Herat on the Afghan–Iranian border supervised by the Jordanian Abu Musab al-Zarqawi, who later emerged as the leader of al-Qaida in Iraq (AQI).

When al-Qaida's camps were demolished in 2001, bin Laden's organization relocated to the Af-Pak border region. From Pakistan, the group continued to train terrorists for international attacks, but no longer in fixed locations. Training now happened inside abandoned buildings, or in mobile training units moving around in remote areas of the Northern Pakistani badlands.[23] The Afghan jihad created strong bonds between the foreign fighters, but after the war most saw no place for themselves in Afghanistan and wanted to return home to fight their own regimes. Some of the Arabs who were prevented from returning by their national security services stayed behind in Afghanistan and maintained training camps.[24] Others found their way to Europe where they supported militant Islamists in Muslim countries.

Bin Laden returned to Saudi Arabia where he offered to use al-Qaida against the emerging threat from Saddam Hussein. The monarchy declined the offer and instead welcomed US forces into the country. This infuriated bin Laden to the extent that he criticized the kingdom, had his citizenship revoked and went into exile in Sudan.[25] In Sudan he was accompanied by loyal supporters, such as al-Zawahiri's faction of the EIJ. From Sudan al-Qaida continued to cooperate with Arab jihadis, while also reaching out to non-Arab groups. Al-Qaida sent fighters to battle American forces in Somalia and the Serbs in Bosnia. Bin Laden helped fund al-Qaida-style training camps in places such as the Philippines, Bangladesh, Tajikistan, Eritrea, Burma, and Malaysia.[26] In the Arab world, bin Laden helped fund the GIA in Algeria and extended support to the radical faction of the Egyptian IG. Bin Laden and al-Zawahiri also cooperated with the Libyan Islamic Fighting Group (LIFG), which declared jihad against the Libyan regime in 1995, and established ties to the Moroccan Islamic Combatant Group (MICG), which later became involved in the Madrid bombings.

While networking in the Muslim world, bin Laden also looked to Europe, which was becoming a sanctuary and support base for Islamists of all sorts in the early 1990s. He set up a propaganda front in London under the leadership of the Saudi Khalid al-Fawwas, and logistics cells in Madrid, Milan, Hamburg and other European cities that were part of a growing jihadi support network in the region.[27]

Upon returning to Afghanistan in 1996, bin Laden forged a strategic alliance with the Taliban, a movement which was emerging in Pakistan.[28] He reopened the training camps, which once again became a popular destination for militant Muslims. From the camps, al-Qaida maintained alliances with old partners and built new ones, while setting up the section for external operations and dispersing terrorist cells internationally. After declaring jihad against America in 1996 and "Jews and Crusaders" in 1998, the network began pursuing global jihad by bombing US embassies in Kenya and Tanzania, blowing up a US warship on the coast of Yemen in 2000 and launching the world's deadliest terrorist attacks on 9/11.

These attacks were controversial among jihadis, and the US-led invasion put an end to the longtime sanctuary in Afghanistan. From its new sanctuary in the Northern Pakistani tribal region, the Federally Administered Tribal Areas (FATA) and the North West Frontier Province (NWFP) after 2001, al-Qaida continued to cooperate with various Afghan Taliban factions while forging strategic alliances and cooperating with several Pakistani jihad groups, such as Harakat-ul-Ansar/Harakat-ul-Mujahidin (HuM), Jaysh-e-Mohammed (JeM), Laskhar-e-Taiba (LeT), the Pakistani Taliban, Tehrik Taliban Pakistan (TTP), the Haqqani Network and Harkat-ul-Jihad al-Islami (HUJI).[29] The organization also forged ties with several militant outfits from Pakistan's neighboring countries that started operating out of the lawless Af-Pak border region, such as Islamic Movement of Uzbekistan (IMU) and its splinter-group, the Islamic Jihad Union (JIU), as well as the Uighur East Turkestan Islamic Movement (ETIM) from Xinjiang in western China.

Al-Qaida's relations with Arab groups changed throughout the 2000s. Some groups stayed loyal to al-Qaida, whereas others sought autonomy or challenged its position. There were also examples of groups distancing themselves from al-Qaida for a period before returning to the fold. For example, as mentioned earlier, in 1999 a group of Jordanians under the leadership of al-Zarqawi set up an organization and a training camp named al-Tawhid wa'l-Jihad (Tawhid) in Herat, Afghanistan, with support from al-Qaida.[30] This group operated in a relatively autonomous way in the early 2000s, initiating terrorist plots against Jewish interests in the Middle East and Europe, before focusing on the jihad in Iraq after the invasion. Tawhid also organized international recruitment for the Iraqi jihad, including in Europe, in cooperation with several North African jihadi groups and the Iraqi-Kurdish Ansar al-Islam movement.

From 2004 onwards al-Zarqawi's group came to function as al-Qaida's official branch in Iraq, taking the name "al-Qaida in the Land of the Two Rivers," more commonly known as al-Qaida in Iraq (AQI). The group sought autonomy after a fierce conflict between al-Zarqawi and al-Qaida's central leadership. Following al-Zarqawi's death in 2006, the group started operating under the name Islamic State of Iraq (ISI), before severing all ties and challenging al-Qaida's position under the names Islamic State of Iraq and Sham (ISIS) in 2013 and Islamic State (IS) in 2014. Around 2000, Tunisian jihadis established a militant group called the Tunisian Islamic Fighting Group (TIFG), which established ties to al-Qaida and became part of its network in Europe. As for the Algerian jihadis, the GIA severed its ties to al-Qaida in the mid-1990s, but bin Laden supported the spin-off group named the Salafi Group for Call and Combat (GSPC), which came to pursue an on-and-off relationship with al-Qaida. In 2003, GSPC announced its support for global jihad and the parties grew closer, partly because they interacted in Europe. In 2007 GSPC vowed loyalty to bin Laden and took the name al-Qaida in the Islamic Maghreb (AQIM). In the time leading up to the Iraq war, between 2001 and 2003, al-Qaida also nurtured ties to the Kurdish group Ansar al-Islam (AI), which grew out of the Islamic Movement of Kurdistan (IMK) formed by veterans of the Afghan jihad.[31] AI emerged as a key player in the Iraqi war theater following the invasion and cooperated with other jihadis (including al-Zarqawi's Tawhid) in an effort to bring European recruits to Iraq, via Syria.[32]

While their exact roles were unclear in many instances, all of the jihadi groups and networks mentioned here surfaced in terrorism investigations in Europe. What is beyond doubt is that interactions between networks in Europe and al-Qaida's affiliates in Af-Pak and other conflict zones are one of the main reasons why the region has faced an increasing terrorist threat from jihadism.

Europe in jihadi thought

Before detailing why and how jihadi networks emerged in Europe, it should be emphasized that Europe had not been a major topic in jihadi thought and jihadis had to overcome ideological obstacles to justify attacks in the region. Al-Qaida and likeminded movements are referred to as "Salafi-jihadi."[33] This means they combine revolutionary Islam, associated with the Egyptian thinker Sayyid Qutb, with fundamentalist, purist Islam as practiced in Saudi Arabia (Salafism or Wahhabism). The jihadis have reworked elements from the writings of Qutb and Salafi scholars, the most important of which is the Syrian medieval scholar Ibn Taymiyyah, into a deployable narrative for the armed struggles of today. Qutb called upon Muslims to excommunicate (announce *takfir* on) rulers violating Islamic law, whereas Taymiyyah wrote extensively on the duty to wage jihad against foreign occupiers of Muslim lands (in his time the Mongols, and in modern times Russia and the US–Israeli "crusader" alliance). Taymiyyah also issued a fatwa on the duty to kill people who insult the Prophet Muhammad, which influenced many jihadi terrorists in Europe.

Salafi-jihadism has emerged as a genre within militant Islamist ideology, best represented by the webpage "Minbar al-Tawhid wa'l-Jihad," hosted by the Jordanian ideologue Abu Mohammed al-Maqdisi. This website contains the writings and speeches of a community of pundits propagating jihad in some form.[34] Most of this material calls for jihad against Arab rulers and occupiers of Muslim countries and there is little dealing with jihad in the West. To the best of my knowledge there is no major text focusing on jihad in Europe. In order to obtain a sense of the militants' stance on terrorism in Europe it is therefore necessary to interpret discourses scattered across texts, statements, threats and propaganda, while also paying attention to how jihadis have justified attacks in Europe.

There is a general idea among jihadis that they are to reoccupy European territories held by Muslims at the height of the Islamic expansion, such as areas in southern Spain, referred to as al-Andalus. Calls for reoccupying al-Andalus are common in Islamist propaganda. When the non-jihadi Hizb-ut-Tahrir calls for re-establishing the Caliphate, al-Andalus is part of their vision.[35] Al-Qaida has called for the re-occupation of al-Andalus in several statements, but seemingly for symbolic reasons and usually when addressing followers in the Maghreb region adjacent to Spain.[36] Jihadis in Maghreb do refer to al-Andalus in propaganda and threats, and al-Qaida's Algerian branch AQIM even named its media-wing al-Andalus.[37] At the same time, as discussed in Chapter Three, AQIM and other groups in North Africa are more focused on combating their regimes at home than international terrorism, and nearly all their operations happened at the national and regional level rather than in the West.

Europe was a side-topic in al-Qaida's broader vision of global jihad until the mid-2000s.[38] When the organization's leaders addressed Europe in statements before 2001, they usually rebuked France and the UK for interfering in Muslim affairs and causing the loss of Palestine during their colonial past. Al-Qaida issued warnings that Europeans should not support or take part in America's policies in the Middle East, but rarely threatened to attack Europeans themselves. When several European countries participated in the invasion of Afghanistan they received threats from al-Qaida, but only in general terms.

This changed when several European countries participated in the invasion of Iraq. From then on, al-Qaida began to issue direct threats against Europeans (see Chapter Five). However, discourses among jihadis indicate that many felt uneasy about attacks in Europe. There were ideological and pragmatic reasons for this. For most Islamists, Europe was an ideal place from which to support movements in Muslim countries. European democracies functioned as sanctuaries where activists could disseminate propaganda, raise funds and recruit new members. As they were also protected by the right to free speech, militants could go much further in their propaganda than in any authoritarian regime via radical mosques, un-censored Internet and even the mainstream media. This, combined with the fact that the ideology of al-Qaida and like-minded movements forbids them from doing anything that undermines jihad, may have restrained terrorism in Europe.[39]

Moreover, according to a Salafi-jihadi ideological principle known as the "covenant of security" (*aqd aman*), which is acknowledged by most jihadis, Muslims who enjoy the protection of a non-Muslim state through citizenship or other rights are forbidden to put the state and its citizens in harm's way.[40] However, according to ideologues, such a covenant ceases to be valid if the state in question engages in warfare against Muslims and/or arrests Muslims and/or insults the Prophet Muhammad and Islam. As I will show in the next chapter, there were spikes in terrorist plots in Europe in connection with the invasions of Afghanistan and Iraq, arrests of Islamists and the publication of Muhammad cartoons. Whether or not such variation can be attributed to ideology or other factors is debatable, but the covenant of security exemplifies how jihadis in Europe may ideologically justify attacks in Europe under given circumstances. I surmise that jihadi interpretations of the covenant of security have affected the threat level in Europe, and will offer evidence to that effect after taking a closer look at the emergence and mobilization of jihadi networks in the region.

Jihadis enter Europe

Al-Qaida and its affiliates began to set up networks for fundraising, weapons smuggling, propaganda and recruitment in Europe in the early 1990s. The networks became centered on veteran activists and radical preachers and involved both nationally focused jihadis and militants with an internationalist outlook. The support networks came to span most European countries, but the jihadi community in London and the UK has always been the largest, most active and influential.

The influx of jihadis into Europe was partly a calculated strategy by armed groups in need of a rear base when fighting regimes in Middle East. However, it was also a necessity because many jihadis faced persecution in their home countries and experienced difficulties finding safe haven elsewhere. Jihadis came to constitute a somewhat insulated part of a growing Islamist scene in Europe composed of a wide spectrum of activists who had been forced to take refuge in the region as asylum seekers, workers, students or illegal immigrants. Most of these Islamists followed common immigration patterns.[41] They typically entered countries which once had Muslim colonies, such as the UK, France, or otherwise had close bilateral relations with Muslim countries, such as Germany—Asians and Middle Easterners settled in the UK, North Africans in France and Turks in Germany.

Many political Islamists in the UK, for example, were of Pakistani and Bengali origin. Islamist refugees in Europe were often associated with international movements such as the Muslim Brotherhood and Hizb ut-Tahrir. During the 1980s, Islamist youth organizations began to proliferate in UK universities, providing services and activities for Muslim students.[42] Europe's Islamist scene also included non-political Salafis (quietist Madkhalis or Wahhabis), mystical Sufis, and Tablighis dedicated to worship, missionary and social work. From Europe, political Islamists supported their counterparts in places such as Egypt, Syria, Jordan and Pakistan. In Europe they enjoyed protection (political asylum), political freedoms (freedom of speech and assembly), economic opportunities (employment) and social safety (legal rights and welfare systems). While focusing mainly on their home countries, Islamists also initiated activism to improve the situation for Muslims in Europe. Moreover, they began to protest against European foreign policies, such as support for Israel and Arab regimes, and domestic events and policies seen as discriminating against or being insulting to Muslims: the publication of Salman Rushdie's *Satanic Verses* (1988) and the ban on headscarves in France, for example.[43]

The relationship between jihadis and political Islamists (politicos) in Europe was characterized by mutual resentment, with the two competing against each other for new recruits.[44] The jihadis mocked the politicos for pursuing democracy and neglecting Islamic law and jihad. By lambasting political groups, jihadis strengthened their own identity and were able to present themselves as the radical alternative. Some jihadis also began practicing moral policing (*hisba*) against fellow Muslims for not adhering to Islam, or as a means to control fundraising channels and places of worship.[45] Jihadis also came to exploit non-violent movements such as Tabligh for recruitment purposes, with a number of Tablighis ultimately being recruited to terrorist cells in Europe.

Commandos behind enemy lines

The memoirs of Abu Musab al-Suri, a founding member of al-Qaida and strategic thinker for the global jihad movement, provide a unique account of why jihadis settled in Europe. A former Syrian Muslim Brother, al-Suri participated in the Afghan jihad and spent several years in Spain and the UK as a propagandist for al-Qaida and the GIA. At times he also acted as a liaison between al-Qaida and the Taliban inside Afghanistan, and between al-Qaida in Afghanistan and its international networks.

Al-Suri spent years as a military trainer in Afghanistan. He authored the doctrine of "decentralized jihad," considered the blueprint of how al-Qaida operated in the late 2000s—pursuing small-scale attacks and solo terrorism.[46] In his memoirs focusing on his time in London as part of a GIA media cell, he presented Britain, France and the rest of Europe as a window of opportunity and a crucial strategic factor which would be "beneficial to us to push the jihadi current forward in a new phase after the Afghanistan-period," and which would be "almost like a mission by special commandos operating behind the enemy lines," providing "rear logistical services" to national Islamist struggles.[47] According to al-Suri, the jihadis in Europe were playing a strategic "game," and he emphasized its "political–security–media" as opposed to the "military" dimension.[48]

Al-Suri's strong personal ties to Algerian militants are probably the reason why he emphasized the insurgency in Algeria as the primary mobilizing cause for the post-Afghanistan "jihadi current."[49] According to al-Suri, "from the beginning of 1994 the hopes of all jihadis were linked to the Algerian cause and that it would be the second step for the Afghan-Arabs towards the Arab world after the Afghanistan period."[50] However, it should be noted that even if Algeria was the main rallying point in the 1990s, jihadis in Europe also supported several other armed struggles in the Middle East, East Africa, Asia and the Caucasus at that time (e.g. Islamists fighting US forces in Somalia, terrorism campaigns against the Egyptian, Libyan and Jordanian regimes; and the wars in Bosnia and Chechnya).

By "rear logistical services" al-Suri was referring to fundraising, weapons smuggling, propaganda and recruitment. Several terrorist cells analyzed in this book have taken part in such activities before plotting attacks. Jihadis in Europe have raised funds through a combination of legal and illicit business activities, collections from mosques, NGOs and criminal networks. Money was channeled from European to Muslim countries via bank transactions, airmail, couriers, NGOs and the informal hawala money transfer system. In addition to raising funds for their counterparts abroad, jihadis in Europe have also generated funds to maintain the support networks as such, covering living expenses, meeting places, travel, propaganda activities and weapons procurement.[51] Weapons and ammunition were obtained on the black market and then smuggled to the Middle East and North Africa in cars and boats. In his memoirs, a Moroccan who infiltrated European jihadi networks on behalf of the security services in the mid-1990s claimed that the weapons smuggling activities were confined to the Schengen countries due to their limited border controls.[52]

While functioning as a rear base for national struggles in the Muslim world, Europe also became a recruitment ground for the transnational jihad movement. Radical preachers who acted as authority figures and teachers of ideology played a vital role in the recruitment. They operated out of radical mosques where they gave religious sermons and exposed recruits to propaganda detailing injustices against Muslims and the virtues of the mujahidin. Europe's jihadis began to employ the Internet for propaganda in the early 1990s, a phenomenon that accelerated with the arrest of radical preachers and the closure of radical mosques following 9/11.

"Londonistan"

London was at the heart of the jihadi sub-culture in Europe. From the British capital a critical mass of radical preachers who had spent time in Af-Pak, Bosnia and other conflict zones acted as leaders and recruiters within a growing jihadi scene. These veteran militants also acted as religious guides for foreign armed groups. French security officials invented the name "Londonistan" in part because of the many jihadis in London, and partly because the city became a transit station for recruits heading for training camps in Afghanistan.[53] "Londonistan" became slang for the tendency of the British authorities to turn a blind eye to extremism and to offer sanctuary to terrorists. London also emerged as a main venue for ideological debate among jihadis. Al-Suri claimed that his stay in London in the early 1990s placed him at the "center of events," and, when Italian police investigated an AQI recruitment network in 2003, agents tapped a phone call in which a key suspect characterized London as the "nerve center."[54] Jihadis from all over Europe gravitated toward London to attend sermons by (in)famous radical preachers, and make necessary contacts and arrangements for joining camps and groups overseas.

Why did London become the hub? It has been suggested that British immigration and security policies, such as lax immigration controls, naive multiculturalism and a security apparatus focusing on the Irish Republican Army (IRA) rather than Islamist extremism were to blame.[55] However, UK laws and immigration policies did not differ a great deal from other European countries, and the UK security services did not ignore the Islamists but instead pursued a strategy of mitigating threats. It is more likely that the centrality of the UK was caused by a chain of unfortunate coincidences which led to certain jihadis who enjoyed a particularly high status and authority ending up in the country. These high-profile activists were in turn followed by loyal supporters, creating the critical mass needed to spark further recruitment. In his account of the jihadi heyday in Europe, al-Suri characterized London in the 1990s as "the new 'Peshawar' of the Islamic awakening, especially for the jihadis."[56] He emphasized two factors which made London suitable for mobilization: the opportunities for media outreach through Arabic newspapers and the UK's imperial history, which tied Britain to the Islamic world and contributed to a density of Islamist movements and pundits.

However, while the significance of London cannot be overstated, jihadi networks also emerged all over Britain and the rest of Europe. In the UK, jihadis took root in Luton, Manchester, Birmingham, Leicester and other cities. In Italy a cultural center and mosque in Milan (Viale Jenner) emerged as a jihadi hub during the 1990s.[57] There, a leader within the Egyptian IG, Anwar Shaban, organized the recruitment of foreign fighters to the Bosnian jihad. The mosque continued to be a meeting place for jihadis until the early 2000s, together with other radical mosques in Rome, Cremona and other Italian cities. Similarly, in Spain a core jihadi network formed around the Syrian Afghanistan veteran Abu Dahdah and radical mosques in Madrid during the 1990s, but jihadis were also active in other Spanish cities, such as Barcelona and Valencia.[58]

In Germany, the al-Quds Mosque in Hamburg was the main hub before 9/11. The Syrian Afghanistan veteran and al-Qaida affiliate Mamoun Darkanzali came to act as imam at the mosque, and it was also the venue which sheltered the 9/11 suicide pilots when they prepared in Germany.[59] Jihadi networks emerged in multiple German cities such as Frankfurt, Munich, Düsseldorf, Krefeld and Neu-Ulm in Bavaria. In the 1990s Belgium saw the rise of fervent jihadi networks linked to the GIA, the MICG and al-Qaida. Belgian jihadis operated out of several cities, including the capital Brussels, Antwerp and the city of Maaseik bordering the Netherlands.[60] Jihadi support networks emerged in the Netherlands in the 1990s, and in the early 2000s a notorious Dutch-based terrorist network formed under the influence of a Syrian extremist named Radwan al-Issa in The Hague and Amsterdam.[61] In Denmark, the Copenhagen-based Moroccan Said Mansour acted as a jihadi propagandist in the 1990s, and in the mid-2000s a militant network formed around a radical Palestinian preacher named Abu Ahmed.[62] The Danish network was not confined to Copenhagen but also included other cities such as Aarhus. Throughout the 2000s organized jihadi activism also blossomed in neighboring Sweden and Norway, a development which intensified with the outbreak of the Syrian Civil War.[63] The jihadi networks that spread throughout Europe usually had a connection to the core network in the UK as well as armed groups in Muslim countries. As will become evident, the same pattern characterized operational terrorist cells from the 1990s until 2015.

All over Europe jihadis organized themselves in similar ways, pursued similar activities and maintained similar transnational connections. Under the guidance of radical preachers, they infiltrated and sometimes took over mosques, or gathered in various community centers, private homes and commercial facilities. From such places and online they initiated cooperation with counterparts locally, regionally and internationally. The role of radical preachers as network entrepreneurs cannot be overstated as jihadi movements have always thrived on charismatic leadership. Recruits are expected to vow allegiance (*baiyya*) to leaders and follow their guidelines. Leader–follower dynamics pervade the jihadi phenomenon from the macro-, movement-level to the micro-level of operative cells.

Preachers

Three radical preachers personify "Londonistan" and were crucial to the rise and growth of jihadism in Europe: Jordanian-Palestinian Abu Qatada, the Egyptian Abu Hamza and the Syrian Omar Bakri Mohammed (Omar Bakri). They have remained symbols and ideologues for European jihadis despite their repeated periods of imprisonment and the fact they no longer live in Europe. The trio ran radical mosques, activist groups and propaganda outlets. They networked with militants in Europe, and internationally, and they produced ideological essays, books and audio-visual lectures and propaganda.

The preachers differed in their ideological focus and the causes they rallied. They consequently catered to different audiences. While competing for recruits and resources, they also shared goals and cooperated. Their different visions and approaches complemented each other in resonating with different jihadi trends and types of activist. Qatada was the chief ideologue for the first Arab jihad veterans coming to Europe. While many of these veterans had ties to al-Qaida, they focused primarily on jihad in their home countries. Hamza and Bakri emerged as ideologues and recruiters of a new generation of jihadis in Europe. This generation was comprised of immigrants and converts who embraced ideas of global jihad against the West to a greater extent. I will spend some space on the preachers' personal backgrounds as they illustrate the role of authority figures in building networks and the shift in European jihadism from being focused on Muslim countries to embracing global jihad. As my case studies will show, they also radicalized and inspired numerous people plotting terrorist attacks in Europe.

Qatada hails from Bethlehem and his family was forced into exile in Jordan during the Arab–Israeli wars.[64] As a youth he joined Tabligh and obtained a BA in Islamic jurisprudence from the University of Amman in 1984. He became a Salafi during the course of his military service and started to mix with militant Islamists before joining anti-regime activism in Jordan. After experiencing troubles with the authorities, Qatada traveled to Peshawar where he completed his MA in Islamic jurisprudence and acted as a religious teacher among the Arab foreign fighters.[65] In 1993 he applied for asylum in the UK for himself and his family, and started to preach at the Four Feathers Youth

Club in London. While living under UK protection on UK welfare, he rallied support for Islamists in Algeria, Chechnya, Bosnia and the Middle East before a growing number of Afghan-Arabs who were finding their way to London. He also entertained relations with al-Qaida in Afghanistan and its cells in Spain, Germany and other countries.

Together with al-Suri, he edited the propaganda magazine of the Algerian GIA, *al-Ansar*, and helped to edit the magazine of the LIFG, *al-Fajr*, and EIJ's magazine, *al-Mujahidun*. These magazines reported from jihad zones and disseminated messages from armed groups and ideologues. Qatada functioned as an ideologue for the GIA by writing essays and legal opinions in support of the group's atrocities. However, in mid-1996 the GIA murdered some emissaries from the LIFG who went to Algeria to offer their support in the war on the regime. This incident caused a major row among international jihadis, and Qatada was forced to denounce the group.[66] In the latter half of the 1990s he focused his activism on the jihad in Chechnya until he was arrested in 2001. Although Qatada remained imprisoned in the UK until he was deported to Jordan in July 2013, he was able to smuggle messages to his followers via prison networks and visitors, which were then published online.

After investigators recovered videos of Qatada's sermons from apartments used by the 9/11 suicide pilots in Hamburg, he became known as al-Qaida's "spiritual ambassador" to Europe. This image was exacerbated by his celebration of the 9/11-pilots as martyrs, and an essay he wrote providing religious justification for the attacks. However, while publicly endorsing al-Qaida, a jihadi insider claimed that Qatada opposed 9/11, and that he saw operations in the West as counterproductive. This is consistent with the preacher's ideological focus. Qatada's writings confirm that he is primarily a religious puritan concerned with jihad in the Middle East. He lambasts the "deviant" political Islamists who dabble in democracy and the "polytheist" sufis and other sects who worship gods other than Allah. Yet for Qatada the most important enemies are the "apostate" Arab dictators, and especially the Hashemite of Jordan. With regard to Islam's external enemies, he is mostly concerned with the long-term goal of abolishing Israel and reconquering Palestine.

Qatada's significance lies in his role as an identity builder. Because of his contacts in Peshawar and his command of theology, he was exactly the kind of figure Europe's first jihadis needed to gather around and position themselves vis-à-vis competing Islamist trends. He did not play a direct role in the advent of jihadi terrorism in Europe, however. While Qatada is known to have radicalized people plotting attacks in Europe he was ambivalent about global jihad. As I will discuss later, a similar ambivalence characterized terrorist cells in Europe composed of Arab jihadis who looked up to Qatada as a religious authority. For them, attacks in Europe were primarily a means to achieve something in Muslim countries. The new generation of jihadis in Europe saw things differently. Activists of the new generation included European citizens who were less invested in Middle East conflicts than the Afghan-Arabs and who were far more receptive to al-Qaida's call for jihad against the West.

Qatada's pupil, Abu Hamza al-Masri (the Egyptian), became a popular preacher among the new generation and he unequivocally supported al-Qaida.[67] In the 1990s, Hamza preached to a congregation primarily made up of North African extremists, but over time he attracted a multinational crowd including second-generation immigrants of Middle Eastern backgrounds and converts. Hamza was born in Alexandria and arrived in London as an engineering student in 1979. He married a British woman and obtained a residence permit in 1982. He was not pious at the time, and even worked as a nightclub bouncer for a while. He turned to religion after his divorce, and when on hajj he encountered Abdullah Azzam who introduced him to the concept of jihad.

In 1991 Hamza moved to Afghanistan where he became a bomb-maker at the Derunta camp. After losing his hands and an eye in an explosives accident he returned to the UK where he studied under Qatada and established himself as an independent preacher. In 1994 he formed the North African-based Supporters of Shariah organization. This group supported jihad in Algeria, Bosnia, Yemen and Chechnya. It ran a website and staged rallies and sent recruits to jihadi training camps abroad. In 1995 Hamza joined the Bosnian jihad, which elevated his status and extended his international contacts. When he returned to Britain in 1997 Hamza became the leader of Friday prayers at the Finsbury Park Mosque, which became a magnet for young extremists. From Finsbury Park he continued to support the GIA long after the group had become an outcast for its extremism.

However, when the GIA went completely off the rails by declaring war on the Algerian people and fellow Islamists (LIFG envoys), Hamza was also forced to end his support and took a special interest in the Islamic Army of Aden-Abyan of Yemen instead. In the late 1990s, members of the Supporters of Shariah organization (including Hamza's son) became involved in terrorist bombings against Christians in Aden and kidnappings of Western tourists in Abyan.[68] At one point Hamza was also involved in an attempt to set up a jihadi training camp in Bly, Oregon, for which he was prosecuted in the

United States. He was arrested in 2004 and charged with soliciting murder and supporting terrorism, and remained incarcerated until 2012 when he was extradited to the United States where he was tried and found guilty of additional terrorism charges.[69] Despite the fact that he has been out of circulation since 2004, Hamza has remained an inspiration for a number of terrorists pursuing global jihad in Europe.

The Syrian preacher Omar Bakri eventually became even more influential among young European jihadis than Hamza.[70] One of Bakri's most significant achievements was his role in radicalizing many Pakistanis who became involved in international terrorism, and he has also served as an ideologue and facilitator for European foreign fighters traveling to Syria after the Arab Spring. Although he is often dismissed as a loudmouth or clown, Bakri was the first "Londonistan"-preacher to set up a jihadi organization in Europe. Moreover, he has been attributed with higher levels of education than Qatada and Hamza, and according to his author biography, he completed a doctoral thesis.[71]

Born in Syria in 1958, Bakri enrolled in Islamic boarding schools from the age of five. He obtained a BA in Islamic jurisprudence from the University of Damascus at the age of seventeen and completed his MA in the same subject at the Imaam Uzaie University in Lebanon. He was persecuted by the Syrian secret police as a member of the Syrian Muslim Brotherhood, and in 1979 he moved to Saudi Arabia, where he claims to have finalized a PhD on the Caliphate system in Islam.[72] In Saudi Arabia Bakri set up a local branch of the international radical Islamist organization, Hizb ut-Tahrir. This organization, which was founded in Jerusalem in the 1950s, works for the establishment of a global Caliphate. While pursuing an extremist discourse and supporting jihad, Hizb ut-Tahrir generally works through non-violent political means. The organization's central leadership opposed the formation of a Saudi branch and shut it down. Bakri then formed his own organization, al-Muhajiroun (The Emigrants), in Jeddah in 1983, which was more extreme.

In 1985 the Saudi authorities expelled Bakri because he was perceived to be a security threat. Bakri then planned to head for Pakistan, which he considered the ideal place for an Islamic revolution. He ended up in the UK because he had a multiple entry visa from an earlier visit, and continued movement-building there. Interestingly, he first set up a new branch of Hizb ut-Tahrir, which had some 400 members by 1990. Hizb ut-Tahrir was more radical than other Islamist trends in the UK during the 1980s, and appealed to educated people, many of whom were Pakistanis. By working through a semi-militant movement, Bakri was able to attract a relatively broad following which he could later build upon. In 1996 Bakri broke with Hizb ut-Tahrir and re-activated al-Muhajiroun. By 2000 the group had some 160 members, around 700 affiliates and 7,000 sympathizers worldwide. The organization also created sub-divisions in more than thirty UK cities and international branches in Lebanon, Ireland, Pakistan and the United States. Like Hizb ut-Tahrir, al-Muhajiroun became popular among British-Pakistanis.

Al-Muhajiroun gained notoriety through its aggressive media profile by lambasting Western culture and glorifying 9/11.

Furthermore, its uncompromising, reckless style seemed to attract disillusioned moderate Islamists in search of alternative forms of activism. Bakri built an impressive recruitment apparatus focused on the Kashmiri jihad from his headquarters in Edmonton, near Tottenham. He staged public rallies and conferences in the UK that were attended by extremists from all over Europe.[73] He boasted about having sent hundreds of recruits to training camps in Pakistan, but maintained that his followers represented no threat to the UK because they were bound by the aforementioned covenant of security. However, in late 2004 Bakri decided to disband al-Muhajiroun when some of its members (and former members) were linked to a suicide bombing in Tel Aviv in 2003 and a plot to stage a truck bombing in London in 2004. The organization resurfaced shortly afterwards under a number of different labels such as al-Ghurabaa and the Saved Sect, and later Islam4UK.[74]

After the 7/7 bombings in London, which involved individuals associated with al-Muhajiroun and al-Qaida, the preacher fled Britain and settled in Tripoli, Lebanon. He was never allowed to return, but continued to guide acolytes in the UK and other countries via social media. In his absence, al-Muhajiroun's spin-off groups in the UK were led by people like the Jamaican Abu Izzadeen, the British-Pakistani Abu Uzair and Bakri's protégé, the lawyer Anjem Choudary, who also hailed from Pakistan.[75] Choudary emerged as Europe's main jihadi proselytizer in the absence of Bakri, although he acted on Bakri's behalf, and not as an independent ideologue. In January 2005, six months before the 7/7 attacks, Bakri issued a statement via the chat website PalTalk in which he annulled the covenant of security between Muslims and Britain. The significance of this statement has not been appreciated fully. It was the first time a radical preacher with a substantive following in Europe had declared jihad against a European country. In subsequent years many terrorist plots in Europe involved young Europeans who had been influenced by Bakri and al-Muhajiroun.

Recruitment

Although other preachers in Europe, and elsewhere, influenced the jihadis based in Europe, the trio of Qatada, Hamza and Bakri played unique roles in building the networks. These preachers were in the right place at the right time and had what it took to cater to the needs of a European jihad movement in the making. Although they were based in the UK, they networked extensively with counterparts throughout Europe, either face-to-face when activists traveled to London to meet with them, via phone or online. They became the main figureheads of a transnational jihadi subculture spanning the whole of Europe. All three had received a religious education and had credible backgrounds in activism. Qatada and Hamza had spent time in conflict zones, whereas Bakri had experience in political activism and organizational work. All three were charismatic and interesting speakers and they also had a sense of populism, rallying the right causes at the right moment.

Qatada appealed strongly to the Afghan-Arabs because he had acted as a religious teacher in Peshawar, because he preached in classical Arabic and because he provided religious justification for excommunicating and fighting Arab dictators, which was their main concern. His role as an ideologue for the GIA at the height of its popularity also elevated his position on the international scene. Qatada wore Afghan-style clothes and surrounded himself with a close-knit band of elite jihadis (such as Abu Doha and Djamel Beghal, discussed in subsequent chapters), who traveled between Europe and Afghanistan functioning as gatekeepers for al-Qaida's training camps.[76] He gained a reputation as a genuine scholar because of his seriousness, command of theology and writing skills, and because he produced essays and books that became classics of the jihadi curriculum. Online videos show him to be a highly confident speaker, presenting his messages before the audience through one-way, top-down communication, leaving little room for dialogue.[77]

Hamza pursued a different style. The Egyptian had a rough appearance and combat experience, with the wounds to show for it. Sporting a hook where his hands used to be and a matching eye-patch, the pirate-like jihadi became a public spectacle who made an impression on recruits. Perhaps as a result of his time as a nightclub bouncer, he came across as streetwise and well versed in young people's language. In his online sermons he uses a direct style of preaching, aggressive in tone, but shifting to humor, irony and sarcasm, welcoming questions from the audience, but ridiculing critical voices.[78]

Hamza was known to emphasize face-to-face interaction with his followers.[79] He gave special lectures for trusted men behind closed doors, and just like Qatada he surrounded himself with close peers who helped recruit and coordinate his followers. When addressing recruits, Hamza stressed the duty of preparing for jihad and he organized rudimentary training camps in Wales and Scotland for his followers, even hiring former SAS soldiers as instructors on one occasion. He pursued extensive international networking and called upon some of his loyal men to cooperate with American extremists in setting up a training facility in Oregon. According to one informant who infiltrated Finsbury Park, after al-Qaida's announcement of global jihad in 1998, Hamza's main project was to support al-Qaida and the Taliban, and recruit for training camps in Afghanistan.[80] Until his arrest he functioned as a gatekeeper for the camps in such a way that a letter of introduction from him granted access. Hamza and his followers were also pioneers in employing the Internet in propaganda and recruitment. He distributed articles and books, in addition to video-taped speeches, via the Supporters of Shariah website and its electronic newsletter. The website also published other audio-visual content, such as videos of atrocities against Muslims in Bosnia and Chechnya, which functioned as radicalization triggers for many jihadi recruits in the 1990s.[81] As well as spreading propaganda online, Supporters of Shariah members sold books and cassettes at sermons and public rallies and via Islamic bookshops, with the sales providing a source of income for the group.

Whereas Hamza primarily recruited under-educated and unemployed North Africans, Bakri focused on university campuses where he targeted second-generation Pakistanis from the middle class. Moreover, while Qatada and Hamza gained credibility from their time in conflict zones, Bakri had to place a greater emphasis on his academic credentials and organizational skills. Bakri's sermons were more educational and interactive than those of Qatada and Hamza. Online videos show how he actively involves the audience in discussions by listening to and answering their questions in a respectful way. In the videos Bakri has a friendlier, more approachable appearance than the other preachers, and at times he even makes jokes.[82]

A similar style was adopted by his protégé Anjem Choudary, who rose to prominence when Bakri went to Lebanon. Bakri was known for his use of subtle techniques in recruitment, with new recruits being socialized via a step-by-step process within an organizational framework. Al-Muhajiroun introduced a cunning praxis of recruitment, which meant that members were trained in how to approach new recruits, engage them in discussions and provide them with information. They would then urge the new recruits to consider the pros and cons of al-Muhajiroun's program compared to that of competing Islamists. This recruitment strategy meant that recruits felt they were in control of the situation and were making their own choices, whereas in reality they were being indoctrinated.[83] Bakri's approach to recruitment was more open, dialogue-based and bottom-up than Qatada and Hamza's approach, something which may have had a special appeal to Europeanized Muslims. Al-Muhajiroun also organized meetings, conferences and camps offering religious education and physical training before sending recruits to camps in Pakistan.

Like Qatada and Hamza, Bakri surrounded himself with an entourage of junior leaders and recruiters, such as the former lawyer and co-founder of al-Muhajiroun, Choudary, who took over the day-to-day administration of Bakri's following after he relocated to Lebanon. From its centers in Tottenham, Luton and a number of other UK cities, Bakri and his acolytes focused their mobilization efforts around the Kashmiri jihad, while continuously lambasting Arab regimes and campaigning fiercely against "Western decadence," paying special attention to homosexuality. Al-Muhajiroun also operated several websites, one of which was administered by the organization's office in Lahore, Pakistan.

While the London preachers' differing backgrounds, ideological priorities and mobilization methods made it possible to attract different types of followers, the differences between each of the men also generated conflict. The followers of Hamza and Qatada, for example, criticized Bakri for his lack of combat experience, whereas Bakri's followers defended him by reference to his academic accomplishments. Hamza and Qatada's followers also accused Bakri of being a spy because he had never been arrested in Britain, whereas Bakri's followers suggested Qatada was a spy for talking to MI5.[84]

Some level of polarization among the preachers' audiences is likely to have had a positive effect on recruitment in that it led their followers to become increasingly passionate about the individual preachers. Variation in the social make-up of the preachers' congregations also allowed people from different backgrounds to connect with leaders accommodating their special grievances and needs. Moreover, despite the factionalism, there were porous boundaries between preachers' followings, and activists drifted back and forth "preacher-shopping"—sometimes activists would attend Bakri's lectures for education, for example, and shift to Hamza's for more passion and action.[85] On a number of occasions there were also joint rallies gathering people from Hamza, Bakri and Qatada's followings.

The preachers and their followers formed a sub-culture which was spreading throughout Europe.[86] This sub-culture was not solely about going to lectures, gathering money and training, but also involved a quest for identity and opposition to societies from which the young Islamists felt detached. Extremists in London and other European cities developed their own distinct style of clothing combining *jalabiyyas*, military fatigues, boots and headscarves. Pictures and videos of Hamza's lectures in the streets after the closure of Finsbury Park Mosque vividly illustrate this phenomenon.[87] Another socio-cultural praxis was the singing of jihad hymns (*nasheed*). This is a key element in jihadi propaganda videos, and it also serves as a bonding activity when jihadis gather together. *Nasheed* are sung in Arabic, which is another jihadi obsession. All Islamists strive to have command of God's language, and Arabic courses proliferate on jihadi websites. Lectures by radical preachers, such as Bakri, also set out to train recruits in Arabic and explain Arabic theological terms.

Moreover, many extremists from Europe attended language courses in Egypt, Syria and other places on their pathway to militancy. However, many of them struggled to gain fluency and instead mixed the religious terms with their mother tongue, creating a hybrid lingo characteristic of European jihadis. Many activists also dropped out of school and started bullying their parents and siblings for being impious and having adopted Western ways which violated Islamic law. This illustrates how the newfound interest in hardliner Islam often represented a rebellion, not just against society but also in generational terms. However, while radicalization involved social and cultural dimensions, all actions by Salafi-jihadis need to find Islamic justification through hadith and ideologues they recognize. This raises the question of how, and from whom, jihadi terrorists in Europe obtained permission to launch terrorist attacks.

Covenant of security

Radical preachers and recruiters in Europe openly and fiercely justified jihad in Muslim countries, but their stance on attacks in the West was more ambiguous. There were several reasons for this. First, in the wake of 9/11, voicing support for terrorism could land Islamists in jail and jeopardize important support networks. At the same time, it was ideologically controversial for jihadis to be living in the West in the first place, and there were ideological regulations on jihad in non-Muslim states. The main ideological obstacle was the covenant of security. This is an established principle in Islam, one not taken lightly by jihadis, even by al-Qaida. To remove this hindrance the terrorists had to consult thinkers in Europe and internationally.

The covenant of security finds precedent in hadith. According to Salafi-jihadi scholars, Muslims should live in Islamic countries governed by Islamic law in "dar al-Islam" (the abode of Islam) and generally avoid mixing with "kuffar" (unbelievers). The reason for this is to avoid being contaminated by un-Islamic influences. Muslims are only permitted to stay in "dar al-kufr" (the abode of unbelief) based on the example of the first Muslims' exile in Medina, and under a covenant of security (*aqd aman*). This principle states that Muslims can seek refuge among unbelievers when they are in a weak position during times of war, under a mutual agreement not to harm each other.

The purpose of the covenant was to allow Muslims to regain their strength in order to resume fighting as soon as possible. Based on the example of the first Muslims, the arrangement can last no longer than ten years and is cancelled as soon as believers regain their ability to fight. As well as a number of other conditions (discussed subsequently), the covenant is also automatically cancelled if the host state attacks Muslims or Muslim lands.[88] A further exception from the rule requiring Muslims to avoid mixing with non-Muslims is that it is permissible to pose as a non-Muslim and infiltrate a non-Muslim state to carry out operations behind enemy lines during times of war. This was cited as justification for the 9/11-pilots' visits to nightclubs, for example. Operations behind enemy lines have also been grounded in the hadith about one of the Prophet's men, Mohammed bin Maslama, who infiltrated the Jewish clan Banu Nadir to kill a poet, Ka'b Ibn al-Ashraf, who had insulted the Prophet Muhammad.[89] According to the hadith he asked the Prophet for permission to do so and received a positive answer. This hadith was also cited by bin Laden and others as justification for attacks on the offices of *Jyllands-Posten* and the Danish cartoonists.[90]

The ideologues in London had different views as to whether the covenant of security applied to jihadis living in the West. One (less well-known) London-based radical preacher hailing from Syria, Abu Basir al-Tartousi, strongly supported jihad in the Muslim world, but condemned attacks in the West such as 9/11 and the London bombings because the attackers were either protected citizens of Western states, or enjoyed the status of visitors as they had applied for visas.[91] Among the high-profile preachers, Bakri was a vocal proponent of covenants and during the 1990s and early 2000s he preached that a covenant was in place in Britain. Bakri maintained that Muslims with Western citizenship were forbidden from attacking their countries. However, he also argued they were allowed to attack other Western countries (as had been the case with the 9/11-pilots who traveled from Germany to the United States). He also preached that Muslim citizens of non-Muslim countries were allowed to attack their country if they, after an individual assessment, found the country to be at war with Muslims and were arresting Muslims on "a large scale."[92] Bakri renounced the covenant of security between Britain and British Muslims in January 2005, six months before the London bombings, because of the UK's involvement in the Iraq war and the rise in arrests of Islamists.[93]

Bakri's stance on covenants is interesting because it makes a strong case for the impact of ideology and preachers on the actions of European jihadis. Bakri held sway over al-Muhajiroun, and it is significant that members of his group were not involved in any plots to attack the UK before he annulled the covenant. Many members of the group had been involved in international attacks, in Kashmir, India and in Israel before the time of the annulment, but not in the UK. From 2005 onwards there were a number of plots in Britain by Bakri's acolytes (which also involved links to al-Qaida). Interestingly, there was one bomb plot uncovered in London in March 2004 by British-Pakistanis who had left Bakri's group in 2002 because he had placed restrictions on targeting Britain. They instead oriented themselves towards Hamza and al-Qaida in Af-Pak. After Bakri had left for Lebanon following the London bombings, two of his minions, Abu Izzadeen and Abu Uzair, expressed support for the atrocity while referring to the annulment of the covenant and bin Laden's ultimatum that Europeans would face attacks unless forces were pulled from Iraq.[94]

Qatada recognized the principle of covenants provided they lasted no longer than ten years.[95] However, he also said that non-Muslim countries were at war with Muslims "by default," and hence covenants had no practical relevance. Interestingly, a former personal assistant of Qatada's said that although he publicly supported 9/11, he had told him privately that he opposed the attacks, likely because they could undermine the national struggles that were Qatada's main concern.[96]

Hamza generally supported attacks in the West, but he too spoke of the covenant of security between Muslims and Britain, although this was probably a tactic to fend off unwanted attention from the security services. In an online video he referred to the idea of a security pact limiting attacks in the West with one word: "crap."[97] Another UK-based radical preacher, Abdullah al-Faisal, also lectured that the idea of a covenant of security was misguided and simply served as an excuse for not fighting.[98] He was cited as the main inspiration for the Jamaican member of the cell who launched the London bombings in 2005. He was imprisoned and deported to Jamaica on his release in 2007.

The discourse on covenants was not confined to Europe, and once al-Qaida understood that the principle could hamper recruitment, the organization led an effort to inform Muslims in the West that covenants were now invalid. This seems to have been prompted by criticisms from a former leader of EIJ and co-founder of al-Qaida, Sayyid Imam Sharif, who claimed that the organization's international terrorism violated covenants of security.[99] This led al-Zawahiri to publish a response, entitled *The Exoneration*, in which a whole chapter was dedicated to covenants and the reasons they no longer applied.[100] Al-Zawahiri argued that if security contracts ever governed the relationship between Muslims and non-Muslims in the West, they had been violated first by the invasions of Muslim countries, but more definitively by the publication of cartoons depicting the Prophet. He also emphasized how it was permissible for the 9/11-pilots to deceive the enemy by entering the United States as students and tourists because the Prophet's companions also entered into fake treaties with the aim of defeating their enemies.

With regard to formal security contracts, al-Zawahiri underscored their mutual nature and presented a series of examples of Western violations. These included the permission granted by the European allies of the United States for the CIA to arrest Muslims on their territories (i.e. extraordinary rendition), thereby demonstrating how ownership of a residence visa or other rights had failed to make Muslims safe. He also referred to the fact that Muslims in Western countries had been forced to pay taxes which financed warfare against Muslims, how Muslims in Western countries were prevented from offering their children proper Islamic education and from practicing their religion, and finally, how Western countries permitted insults against the Prophet. In its eagerness to reach out to Western recruits, al-Qaida proactively sought to prevent the constraining effects of covenants and, conversely, exploit the potential for radicalization that lie in exposing violations.

Ibn Taymiyyah's rulings on individual punishment for anyone insulting the Prophet Muhammad emerged as an important tool in achieving this goal. Quoting Ibn Taymiyyah's works, al-Zawahiri stressed how the Prophet distinguished between non-Muslims who "have merely broken a contract and those who in addition have offended the Muslims." The killing of the latter was "specifically commanded."[101] The meaning of this, al-Zawahiri explained, was that insults against Islam, the Quran and the Prophet are the gravest sins (even graver than war on Muslims) and they demanded the punishment of death. *The Exoneration* was part of a propaganda offensive by al-Qaida and its affiliates at a time when jihadis were facing pressure on several fronts in 2007–8. This campaign involved exploiting new social media, and placing more emphasis on interactivity, such as a question-and-answer session where al-Zawahiri would respond to questions from followers, critics and the press.[102]

However, the part of the jihadi social media offensive which came to have the greatest impact on the threat in Europe was the launching of AQAP's *Inspire* magazine and the online preaching by the group's ideologue, the American-Yemeni Anwar al-Awlaki.[103] This charismatic jihadi spoke in eloquent English directly to the new generation of jihadis in the West, and called upon them to support jihad in any way they could, anywhere, calling specifically for individual attacks on US targets in Western countries. Accompanied by the glossy *Inspire* magazine, cultivating a cross-over between popular youth culture and jihad mythology attracting militants of the new generation, al-Awlaki inspired multiple terrorist cells in Europe and also played a role as a handler in a few incidents addressed in Chapter Eight. While calling for jihad in the West, al-Awlaki also had to address the issue of the covenant of security and wrote an article in *Inspire* magazine no. 4 where he laid down arguments as to why covenants were invalid.

Al-Awlaki filled a void in European jihadism towards the late 2000s, when most radical preachers in Europe went in-and-out of prisons, and those who were not, such as Choudary, had to balance within the boundaries of law, keeping a low profile regarding jihad in the West. However, it is a popular misconception that al-Awlaki somehow replaced other ideologues for jihadis in the West. Although *Inspire* magazine and speeches by al-Awlaki were consumed by most terrorists operating in Europe after 2009, most of them had been radicalized by people like Bakri and other jihad entrepreneurs, and they drew inspiration from a number of ideologues, including the medieval scholar Ibn Taymiyyah, Qatada, Hamza, the Jordanian Abu Mohammed al-Maqdisi and Salafi-jihadi scholars from Saudi Arabia. This will become clearer later in the book when exploring the concrete terrorist cells and what caused them to emerge. Before moving on to the case studies I now present the overall trends of how jihadis have operated in Europe and some tentative explanations of their behavior.

2

SCOPE AND MODUS OPERANDI

There is a close connection between the "who," the "why" and the "how" of jihadi terrorism in Europe.[1] Terrorists communicate through violence, and factors such as timing and modus operandi provide clues as to why terrorist cells emerge when they do, where they do and the way in which they do. Terrorists need money for weapons and training in how to use them, something which also calls for discussing trends in how jihadi terrorist cells in Europe have been financed, and the extent to which the terrorists have traveled to conflict zones (foreign fighting).

This chapter provides an overview of how jihadi terrorists in Europe have operated. Based upon surveys combining qualitative and quantitative data, I look at the variation in the occurrence of plots over time and the changes in the context in which such plots take place. I also examine variation in weapons, tactics and target selection. I further provide tentative explanations as to why trends change and what it means for the emergence of cells.

Overall, the total number of plots in Europe has increased and seems to be increasing. At the same time, the level of plotting has fluctuated with events in Europe and internationally affecting jihadism, such as the invasion of Iraq and the publication of cartoons of the Prophet Muhammad. As for modus operandi, the targeting has grown increasingly discriminate over time. Through the 1990s and early 2000s jihadi terrorism in Europe was characterized by random mass casualty attacks on transportation, such as the Madrid bombings. From the late 2000s it became more common to target Jews, artists who had drawn Muhammad cartoons, or soldiers in uniform.

Attack types and weapon types have also diversified. In the 1990s and early 2000s, jihadis in Europe operated in groups and planned bombings with certain types of explosives. From the late 2000s, more terrorists worked alone, using a broader repertoire of weapons, including crude bombs, knives, axes and guns. Terrorist groups tend to become increasingly politicized and strategic over time, and trends toward discriminate attacks may have reflected the jihadis' need for legitimacy and support, whereas changes in tactics likely reflected an adaptation to counter-terrorism efforts. As for the financing of jihadi terrorism in Europe, a survey has identified a trend towards self-financed cells, something which is linked to the pattern of smaller and cheaper plots.[2] The last trend addressed in this chapter is the involvement of foreign fighters. I indicate that the vast majority of jihadi terrorist cells in Europe involved at least one individual with foreign fighter experience, and as will become clear in my case studies, they usually functioned as entrepreneurs.

Scope of plots

Besides spreading fear, terrorism is also about sending political messages. The timing of plots therefore indicates the factors which may have led cells to emerge. The year-by-year overview of the scope of jihadi terrorist plots in Europe in figure 1 shows considerable variation.[3]

The first spike in incidents occurred in 1995. It was caused by the GIA's bombing campaign in France. These were the first attacks by jihadis in Europe and were linked to the civil war in Algeria. The GIA's terrorism in France also coincided with the war in Bosnia. As will be discussed in the next chapter, the Bosnian jihad was a mobilizing cause for Islamists in Europe. Many traveled from Europe to Bosnia as foreign fighters and at least one of them, the GIA-linked convert Christophe Caze, became involved in terrorism in Europe (in France, 1996). In the period from 1996 to 2000 there were almost no concrete plots in the region. Then, from 2000 onwards, there was a gradual upswing and new peaks in 2003–4. The increase in plotting from the turn of millennium must be understood in the context of al-Qaida's global jihad, declared in 1998, which was followed by a number of attacks on US interests and culminated in 9/11. The unprecedented number of plots in 2003–4 took place amid the invasion of Iraq, which involved European countries, and emerged as the number one cause for jihadis worldwide.[4] The most lethal attacks in Europe so far, the Madrid bombings, also occurred in 2004. Moreover, 2004 saw the first attack in Europe justified by insults against Islam, the murder of

Theo van Gogh in Amsterdam. It should also be noted that the increase in plots in 2000–4 coincided with the second Palestinian Intifada (2000–5) and the Israeli counter-attacks which killed many civilians. Jihadis present the liberation of Jerusalem as an ultimate objective, and Palestine must always be considered when assessing triggers for jihadism.

After 2004 the number of plots stabilized at a lower level before reaching a new peak in 2010. The period 2004–10 was marked by a series of developments which help explain why the number of plots neither increased nor abated. In 2005 the Danish newspaper *Jyllands-Posten* published cartoons of the Prophet Muhammad, which angered Muslims and emerged as an important justification for terrorism. The republication of the cartoons by European media kept breathing new life into the crisis. The period 2005–7 also saw the al-Qaida-led bombings of the London underground (7/7), and other high-profile plots, such as plans to down transatlantic jets by al-Qaida (2006), an attempt to bomb German trains in 2006 by terrorists linked to AQI, a plot to bomb nightclubs in London and Glasgow International Airport in 2007 by terrorists linked to AQI, and several plots in Scandinavia (discussed in Chapter Seven).

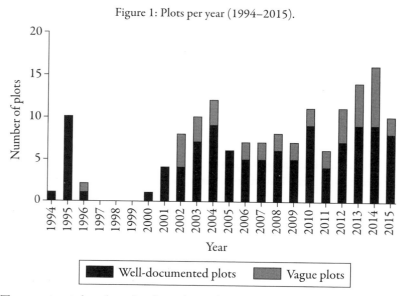

Figure 1: Plots per year (1994–2015).

The overview is based on the chronology of incidents presented in the electronic appendix, last updated on 1 July 2015 (N=151).

Around 2007, global jihadis shifted attention to Af-Pak for a while after being focused on Iraq for several years. The renewed interest in Af-Pak could in principle have enhanced al-Qaida's ability to attract recruits from Europe. However, at the same time, by 2007 al-Qaida in Af-Pak was losing many leaders to drones. Also, al-Qaida and allied Pakistani groups embarked on a terrorist campaign against the Pakistani state, which led to incursions by the Pakistani Army in the tribal areas. These factors made it harder for al-Qaida to pursue international attacks, at least in the short term. At the same time, in 2007–9 several of al-Qaida's branches and affiliates in Iraq, Yemen, Somalia and Algeria began to engage in international terrorism.

From around 2008 there was an increase in terrorist plots in Europe linked to al-Qaida's affiliates, especially AQAP. After the publication of Muhammad cartoons in Denmark in 2005 and more so after the establishment AQAP in 2009, global jihadis began to call for "decentralized jihad," with attacks being launched by independent supporters in the West. This new focus on decentralized jihad translated into plots by single terrorists in Europe. This development was accentuated by a watershed shift in jihadi propaganda around 2008, when jihadis turned to Twitter, Facebook, YouTube and other social media.[5] Several developments may be relevant for the peak in plotting during 2010. The launch of AQAP's *Inspire* magazine aimed at Muslims in the West was significant. The Israeli incursions in Gaza in 2009 should also be taken into account. Moreover, the political campaign to outlaw religious headscarves in France generated threats from al-Qaida in 2009.[6]

In 2011 the number of plots dropped, before reaching high levels again from 2012 onwards. The downturn in 2011 could be linked to the jihadis' disarray following the death of bin Laden and the Arab Spring, whereas the increase from 2012 on must be seen in relation to jihadi mobilization over Syria. This year-by-year overview shows that that the number of plots increases in connection with European interference in Muslim world conflicts, events in Europe considered insulting to Islam and terrorist campaigns by groups such as GIA and al-Qaida. It is also noteworthy that spikes in plotting tend to be followed by a downturn in the following year, something which could be ascribed to counter-terrorism measures. The fact that activity picks up again speaks to the sustainability of the threat and indicates that current counter-terrorism efforts are insufficient or counter-productive. Variation in the number of plots provides clues, but is one out of many indicators of what causes cells to occur. The terrorists' modus operandi provides additional input.

Modus Operandi

A survey of the modus operandi of jihadi terrorists in Europe in 1994–2013 found that al-Qaida and its branches had the strongest influence on threat patterns in Europe.[7] The study, which was based on 122 incidents, identified two main trends: increasingly selective targeting and diversification of weapons and tactics. The changes were seen most clearly in the data by comparing the situation before and after 2008.

The period around 2008 was characterized by developments in the field of transnational jihadism which were bound to influence the threat. Al-Qaida in Af-Pak had been weakened by drone strikes, while its regional affiliates started plotting international attacks. In this situation, a trend towards discriminate attacks may have reflected al-Qaida's need for legitimacy and support under pressure from the War on Terror and competition from other groups. By focusing on discriminate targets, the organization may have hoped to win sympathy and make up for the critique it faced following mass-casualty attacks which also killed Muslims, such as 9/11.[8] However, al-Qaida did not abandon mass-casualty terrorism. Rather, by widening the repertoire to include both indiscriminate and discriminate attacks, the organization sought to fulfill a dual need of upholding its reputation as the world's most dangerous terrorist organization on the one hand, and winning sympathy from broader audiences on the other. The trend towards diversity in weapons and tactics likely reflected tactical adaptations to Western security measures, but also the fact that new actors were now joining the global jihad. A full worthy analysis of modus operandi in 2014–15 was not available at the time of writing. Most incidents from 2014 onwards seem in line with trends outlined here though—including the plots linked to ISIS/IS.

Weapons

Overall, trends in the types of weapons used by jihadis in Europe indicated that terrorist groups in conflict zones held sway over European cells, mostly via interaction at training camps, but also online. Improvised Explosive Devices (IEDs) have been the preferred weapon. Nearly all plots before 2001, 78 percent of plots in 2001–7 and 65 percent of plots in 2008–13 involved IEDs. Home-Made Explosives (HMEs) have become more common since 2008, while military and commercial explosives (such as the dynamite used by the Madrid bombers) have become less common.

Patterns in the type of explosives used have been strongly influenced by groups outside the region. In the 1990s, cells supervised by the GIA used chlorate mixtures (a low explosive) in closed containers such as gas canisters and pressure cookers. From 2001, plots linked to al-Qaida involved peroxide-based mixtures (a high explosive). Beginning in 2004, several plots linked to groups in Af-Pak and Iraq involved cylinder bombs, while fertilizer has been employed by some al-Qaida cells and independent terrorists from 2004 onwards. From 2010 several plots linked to AQAP either involved the advanced explosive PETN in plots against aviation, or very crude devices made out of gunpowder from fireworks. New types of explosives have usually emerged in Europe as result of training or assistance from al-Qaida and like-minded groups in conflict zones, or via recipes spread by such groups online. Interestingly, bomb recipes already accessible online were rarely used before they had been promoted by a group.[9]

Over time, there has been an increase in plots involving knives and firearms. Knives and firearms occurred in one plot before 2001, 7.3 percent of plots in 2001–7 and in 33 percent of plots in 2008–13. Only one attack reached fruition using knives/firearms before 2008, compared to seven attacks in 2008–13. The increase in the use of handheld weapons was linked to discriminate targeting and an increase in assassinations, both of which will be addressed shortly.

There was a decline in the number of plots involving chemical, biological, radiological or nuclear (CBRN) materials over time. This could stem from the trend towards discriminate targeting, as well as reduced capabilities in the area of CBRN. CBRN materials occurred in no plots before 2001, six plots in 2001–7 and were absent from plots in 2008–13. Four out of six CBRN plots in 2001–7 involved poisonous chemicals or toxins. One plot involved a plan to create a "dirty bomb" from a radiological substance and one incident involved plans to attack the Borssele nuclear power plant by Dutch terrorists in 2004. The jihadis' interest in CBRN is linked to programs run by al-Qaida in Afghanistan before 2001 which aimed to develop a CBRN capability for global jihad. Nearly all of the limited number of incidents involving CBRN in Europe could be traced to this program, and the absence of such plots after 2001 suggests that the demolition of al-Qaida camps reduced this threat in the region.[10]

Tactics

Most terrorist plots by jihadis in Europe involved bombings. This was the case with almost 80 percent of plots before 2008 and 65 percent of plots in 2008–13. However, assassinations and armed assaults have become more common over time. There was only one assassination plot before 2001, whereas in

2001–7 this increased to 4.9 percent of plots with a further increase to 25 percent of plots in 2008–13. Most of the bombing plots were aimed at public sites and transportation. There were only eight plans to attack aviation, and only one, poorly documented plot to attack at sea (a ferry).

The means that were used, or were intended to be used, in the bomb plots varied from hand grenades to truck bombs. So far the jihadis' attempts to use truck bombs have been foiled, but such attacks have the potential to be very deadly. One example was a plan to bomb the canteen of a US military base in Belgium in 2001 and another was a plan to detonate truck bombs made out of fertilizer in Central London in 2004. The preference for bombs is hardly surprising as al-Qaida and affiliated jihad groups have used bombs successfully and possess expertize in this area. It is still somewhat surprising, however, that the proportion of plots involving bombs stayed at more than 60 percent in 2008–13 as the threat was becoming increasingly discriminate. Moreover, anecdotal evidence suggests that restrictions on buying chemicals for bombs led jihadis to turn to handguns. For example, the French-Algerian gunman Mohammed Merah told police negotiators he chose a shooting spree over bombing for exactly these reasons.[11]

Few hostage situations have been created by jihadis in Europe. In 1994–2013 there were only three plans to take hostages, and none of them ever came to fruition. However, all of these plots were potentially large scale and happened after the notorious 2008 attacks by jihadi terrorists in Mumbai, India, which involved mobile crews of gunmen attacking several sites in the city before taking hostages at the Oberoi Trident Hotel. Most of the European jihadis' plans involving hostage-taking have drawn inspiration from the attacks in India, to the extent they were described as "Mumbai-style" plots. An actual "Mumbai-style" attack occurred with the massacres at the offices of *Charlie Hebdo* and a Jewish super-market in Paris, January 2015. The increase in Mumbai-style plots in 2008–13 is another indicator of how the threat to Europe has been shaped by involvement or inspiration from foreign terrorist groups.[12]

Whereas Mumbai-style plots usually require manpower, the most significant change in the tactics of jihadis in Europe in 2008–13 was the rise in single-actor plots. Before 2008 only 12 percent of jihadi terrorist incidents involved a single-actor, whereas in 2008–13 the proportion had increased to 38 percent. However, groups of two or more terrorists remained the most common cell configuration, occurring in more than 60 percent of all plots, also in 2008–13. It is noteworthy that as much as 70 percent of the plots involving single actors went undetected and reached the execution stage in the period surveyed, while group-based plots were foiled in almost 80 percent of the cases.

Several factors contributed to the rise in single-actor terrorism and the pattern will be discussed thoroughly in Chapter Eight. In part, the jihadis were forced to rely on independent cells and individuals to uphold the threat to the West—given the pressure they were facing from drone strikes and counter-terrorism measures. Relying upon strategic thinking about decentralized jihad and theological texts justifying attacks to avenge insults against Islam, al-Qaida called upon supporters in the West to act alone. The call for individual jihad was spread through the propaganda machinery in social media and AQAP's *Inspire* magazine, which was tailored to a Western audience. The contagion of successful attacks, such as the shootings at Fort Hood in 2009, also contributed to the rise in solo-terrorism.

Targets

As terrorists communicate through violence, target selection is a central indicator of what motivates cells.[13] Over time, an increasing proportion of jihadi plots in Europe were discriminate and aimed at sub-national entities, communities and individuals rather than the public. The GIA's terrorism in France in the 1990s involved only a few incidents of a discriminate character, such as the attempt to bomb a Jewish children's school and the assassination of an imam. In 2001–7 around 20 percent of plots were discriminate, whereas al-Qaida's mass casualty modus operandi dominated the picture.

In 2008–13, as much as 55 percent of all plots were targeted discriminately and random attacks were decreasing. The majority of discriminate plots were aimed as institutions, artists and politicians perceived to be anti-Islam. Another category of plots targeted military objects, in particular military personnel in public areas. A third category of plots targeted Jews. In the first category were plots to attack the offices of *Jyllands-Posten* and individual artists who had drawn Muhammad cartoons, or other media figures perceived to be anti-Islam. The latter included the Swedish artist Lars Vilks and Danish author and Islam critic Lars Hedegaard. The targeting of individuals perceived as being anti-Islam contributed to a rise in assassination plots, which also involved other target categories.

The first assassination by jihadis in Europe was the GIA's killing of an imam in Paris who was associated with the competing Islamic Salvation Front (FIS) movement. The next incident occurred in 2004, when a Dutch-Moroccan jihadi (inspired by al-Qaida in Iraq) murdered and tried to decapitate the

Dutch filmmaker Theo van Gogh on the streets of Amsterdam for being anti-Islam. There was then a further rise in assassination attempts following the publication of cartoons of the Prophet Muhammad in Denmark and other European countries. Assassinations are an attack mode suitable for individuals, and the attack type was promoted massively in jihadi propaganda from the 2000s onwards. On a number of occasions, al-Qaida figures have encouraged followers to carry out assassinations, especially of those who insult the Prophet. As will be discussed in Chapter Eight, they evoked verdicts by Salafi scholars prescribing the death penalty for such acts.

The jihadi assassination plots in Europe have generally targeted individuals of little strategic value. The most high-ranking politician eyed as a target was the mayor of London, Boris Johnson. Overall, the assassination plots seem to have been driven by revenge and symbolism rather than strategy. This also applies to an increased number of plots targeting military personnel in Europe over time. Jihadi leaders have been calling for and threatening attacks on soldiers outside conflict zones and this has translated into several incidents, the most lethal one being the shooting spree at Fort Hood in 2009. The role model for the Fort Hood shooter, AQAP's ideologue Anwar al-Awlaki, talked about the permissibility of attacking Western soldiers in their home countries, and the idea was promoted in *Inspire* magazine.[14] In 2014, the spokesman for IS in Syria–Iraq also called for attacks on soldiers in the West.[15]

Attacking military personnel in public places emerged as a modus operandi among jihadis in Europe in 2011, with the Kosovar Arid Uka's attack against a shuttle bus carrying US soldiers at Frankfurt international airport in 2011, followed by Mohammed Merah's attacks in 2012 and stabbings of soldiers in the UK and France in 2013 (Chapters Eight and Nine). There was only one well-documented plot involving similar modus operandi before 2008, when a UK-based terrorist cell, inspired by AQI, planned to abduct and behead a British Muslim soldier who had served in Iraq, and videotape the ordeal, in January 2007. As for the targeting of Jews and Jewish interests, the struggle against Israel and its policies in Palestine has always been a core issue for jihadis and needs no further explanation.

Another development pointing to an increased focus on killing discriminately is that the number of plots against aviation and public transportation has declined over time. The GIA's attacks in France in the 1990s targeted aviation, transportation and public sites. Before 2008, there were nine well-documented plots against transportation and seven plots against aviation, whereas 2008–13 saw only three plots against aviation and three plots against buses, trains or metro systems. Yet the threat against crowded public areas has largely remained constant (fifteen well-documented incidents before 2008 and nine in 2008–13). The decline in the number of plots targeting aviation must be seen in light of increased security measures, but this does not apply to public transportation such as buses and trains. The continued threat against public areas can only be interpreted as a sign that random mass casualty terrorism will not be fully abandoned by jihadis in Europe.

Discriminate aspects of the threat in Europe are also expressed by the fact that some countries and nationalities face a higher threat than others. Because some nationalities rank higher as enemies for the jihadis, there is no one-to-one relationship between where plots occurred and what enemies the terrorists set out to harm. For example, although quite a few terrorist plots happened in Germany, most were aimed at Jewish, US or French targets rather than Germany as such. This could serve as one indicator that Germany was lower in the jihadis' enemy ranking than, for example, the UK, where almost every plot was aimed at British targets. Table 1 illustrates the discrepancy between countries where plots occur and the nationalities which have been targeted.

Table 1: Plot country versus target nationality (1994–2013).

Country	No. of plots	No. of plots where plot country was target	%
France	24	16	67 %
UK	23	19	83 %
Germany and Switzerland	12	3	25 %
Scandinavia	11	9	82 %
Italy	10	6	60 %

Data from Nesser and Stenersen, "The Modus Operandi of Jihadi Terrorists in Europe." The table includes eighty well-documented incidents where it was possible to identify targets (N=80).

At the same time, the fact that multiple plots occurred in Germany demonstrates that the country hosted extremists with both the will and capacity to resort to terrorism there. In addition to being a country in which jihadis plotted attacks, Germany has also been a staging ground for attacks in other countries, most famously 9/11, but also other cases such as a plot to bomb the Christmas market in Strasbourg (Chapter Four). The survey of the modus operandi of jihadis in Europe on which this chapter is based grouped

Scandinavian countries together and found that the UK and France have experienced the most plots over time, followed by Germany, the Scandinavian countries and Italy.[16] Plots in the UK mainly targeted the UK; plots in France were aimed at French, US, Jewish and Russian targets; whereas many plots in Italy and Germany targeted US or Jewish people and interests. The most striking development in the geographical distribution of plots was the increased threat in Scandinavia (Figure 2).

This development started in 2005, and unlike Germany, as many as 82 percent of the plots in Scandinavia were directed against Scandinavian targets. Nearly all of the plots were aimed at people and institutions involved in the publication of Muhammad cartoons, but there were also incidents not immediately linked to the cartoons affair, such as the case of the Stockholm bomber in 2010 and assassination plots against the Swedish artist Lars Vilks and the Danish Islam critic Lars Hedegaard.

Throughout 1994–2013 there was also a tendency towards fewer plots against US targets compared to European ones. In 2001–3, there was a clear tendency to target American interests in Europe. This was in tune with al-Qaida's vision of global jihad, which was aimed mainly at the United States

Figure 2: Geographical distribution of plots over time (1994–2013).

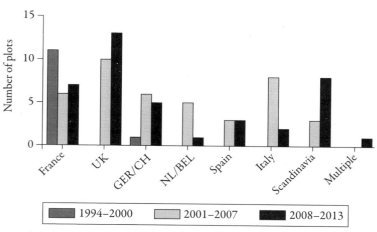

Figure is based on Nesser and Stenersen, "The Modus Operandi of Jihadi Terrorists in Europe". It includes ninety-three well-documented incidents (N=93). Scandinavian countries have been grouped together in the output, as have the Netherlands (NL) and Belgium (BEL), and Germany and Switzerland (CH).

rather than Europe. The pattern started to change in 2003–5, when jihadis increasingly targeted European interests. This was primarily a result of European involvement in the Iraq war. Over time more motives to harm Europeans emerged, such as the Muhammad cartoons and arrests of Islamists. Tellingly, as much as 15 percent of all plots in 2008–13 targeted *Jyllands-Posten* or the cartoonists, while only 10 percent of the plots in the same period targeted the United States. Overall, the increase in plots against European targets compared to American ones illustrates how al-Qaida's global jihad came to involve America's allies to a greater extent from the Iraq war onwards.

This development was mainly a reaction to Europe's contribution to the War on Terror. However, as will be discussed many times throughout the book, terrorist attacks in Europe also found justification in jihadi ideology. Before the Iraq war Islamist militants in Europe claimed to live in the region under a religiously defined security pact between them and their host states. According to this pact, they were forbidden to attack the countries as long as they felt secure and were allowed to practice Islam.

However, in the mid-2000s several ideologues annulled the pact on the grounds that European countries had participated in the wars in Afghanistan and Iraq, insulted the Prophet and persecuted Muslims. Symptomatically, many terrorists in Europe have since stressed wars, persecution and insults against Islam when justifying their actions. The Stockholm suicide bomber's reference to the Swedish contribution in Afghanistan and anti-Islam artwork by Lars Vilks was one out of numerous examples. In 2008–13 most plots in Europe targeted the UK (30 percent), followed by Scandinavia (20 percent) and France (13 percent). However, from 2013 there was an upsurge of incidents in France again, which will be addressed towards the end of the book.

A trend towards discriminate terrorism by jihadis in Europe is somewhat counterintuitive. Randomness is a hallmark of terrorism, given its aim of instilling fear in populations. Discriminate attacks are less suitable for frightening an overall population, but are easier to justify politically and religiously than random ones. Discriminate attacks speak to a larger segment of Muslims than the ultra-extreme that usually become attracted to jihadism, and could therefore represent an attempt to win support and recruit among a far-flung audience to be reached via social media. However, as indicated earlier, the trend towards discriminate targeting does not represent a major shift.

Al-Qaida has continued to plan mass atrocities in Europe, in addition to targeted plots. An article from AQAP's *Inspire* magazine in 2012 illustrates the duality. It called upon assassins to combine "selective hits" on "military personnel and political leaders," but also "for mass hits" to hurt the enemies' infrastructure and economy.[17] A recent report on the financing of jihadi terrorism in Europe, based upon analyses of forty cases, identifies a similar duality.[18] The study indicates that the terrorists have been moving away from large-scale terrorist plans reliant on transfers from foreign terrorists, to smaller plots by self-financed cells. However, the report also points to exceptions from the general rule such as the plans to bring down transatlantic jets by al-Qaida's branch in Yemen.

Money

The report found that in 90 percent of the cases the terrorists were involved in activities to generate money for the attacks themselves. Further, only 25 percent of the cells received money transfers from al-Qaida or similar groups (i.e. some involved both). Also, the proportion of cells receiving transfers from foreign groups declined over the time-span surveyed (1994–2013), whereas self-financing increased. The report highlighted how jihadi terrorist plots in Europe were generally low-cost, with 75 percent of cases estimated at less than 10,000 USD, whereas only three cases, the Madrid bombings, a plot to bomb a market place in Strasbourg and the terrorist network behind the string of attacks by the GIA in France in the 1990s (all attacks) were estimated to have cost more than 20,000 USD.

Moreover, the report painted a picture of how jihadis in Europe mostly funded their attacks through trivial means such as salaries and savings (73 percent), and criminal means such as the illegal trade in drugs or commodities and theft (38 percent). In line with trends in modus operandi, the study found that support from foreign groups usually applied to big cells pursuing ambitious attacks. The report also highlighted how the involvement of foreign fighters in cells increased the likelihood of external funding. This leads to the final point I address regarding overall patterns in jihadi terrorist cell formation in Europe: the foreign fighter factor.

Foreign fighters

Most jihadi plots in Europe involved people who had trained or fought in conflict zones. The GIA's cells in France in the 1990s involved people who had fought with mujahidin in Afghanistan and Algeria. Al-Qaida-linked cells in Europe in the 2000s involved people who were trained at the group's camps in Afghanistan, and throughout the 2000s cells involved people who had stayed in Af-Pak and other areas hosting mujahidin, such as Chechnya, Bosnia, Somalia and Yemen. As the War on Terror hardened after 9/11, it became more difficult for European Islamists to reach conflict zones undetected, though many still went.

Stenersen and Nesser's "Jihadism in Western Europe Dataset" indicates that more than 90 percent of cells before 2001 involved at least one foreign fighter, more than 70 percent in 2001–7 and more than 50 percent in 2008–13.[19] Numbers seem to have dropped, but there are many missing values, and numbers for the two last periods could be closer to 80 percent if cases where information was scarce involved foreign fighters. The large contingent of foreign fighters in Syria is expected to intensify the jihadi threat in Europe, and there have already been several incidents involving Syria veterans, as will be discussed in Chapter Nine.

The effect of foreign fighters on the emergence of terrorist cells in Europe is best captured through a qualitative study. The case studies in the forthcoming chapters will show how people with foreign fighter experience played central roles in cells. They functioned as entrepreneurs who built cells, led them and linked them to militant networks internationally. They were typically the point of contact when advice and instructions where channeled between foreign terrorist groups and cells in Europe. Foreign fighters were sometimes part of attack cells, whereas in other instances they functioned as handlers or advisors of cells, leaving the scene before attacks were set in motion. Exceptions from foreign fighter involvement were genuinely home-grown cells and lone wolves, but in some instances these had drawn inspiration from foreign fighters they knew or were aware of (e.g. people who acted as radical preachers or propagandists online).

There are also examples of solo-terrorists who initiated plots from the bottom-up by traveling abroad to interact with mujahidin, obtaining the necessary training, returning and carrying out attacks by themselves. The prime example of this pattern was Mohammed Merah. However, while most entrepreneurs had been foreign fighters, the same was not true the other way around. Many foreign fighters had different roles in cells and most foreign fighters did not resort to international terrorism. The book will now move from overall trends to the case study of networks and cells. I begin by turning the clock back to 1994–5 and the first examples of jihadi terrorism in Europe, when Algerian jihadis of the GIA launched a series of attacks in France.

3

THE ALGERIA FACTOR (1994–2000)

This chapter recounts the circumstances and aftermath of a GIA terrorist campaign in France in 1995. The campaign was the first example of jihadi terrorism in Europe and it involved networks and individuals that would continue to shape the terrorist threat in Europe in years to come. The campaign began in December 1994 when GIA fighters hijacked an airliner in Algeria with the aim of crashing it in Paris. It continued in the summer of 1995 with the murder of an imam and a series of bombings in the French capital and other cities, which left eight dead and injured some 200. Subsequent years saw several terrorist incidents in France and Belgium involving people linked to the GIA or its spin-off group GSPC. Both the 1995 attacks and subsequent incidents involved people who had spent time with armed groups in Algeria, Afghanistan or Bosnia. The GIA's terrorism in France (and Belgium) is usually understood as a side-effect of the Algerian Civil War.[1]

Based on a new reading of the sources I endorse the view that events in Algeria were the main driving forces behind GIA terrorism in Europe. However, my account stresses how the group's bombings in France were a starting point and blueprint for a new threat to Europe, which was increasingly global in word and deed. Like subsequent cases of jihadi terrorism in Europe, GIA cells involved both a national, Algerian dimension, a regional European dimension, and an international dimension. In order to interpret the GIA's actions in Europe, it should be noted that the group was set up with help from al-Qaida and was informed by the Afghan-Arabs' international understanding of jihad. At the same time, the GIA fought primarily against the regime and competing Islamists inside Algeria, and had to balance its international aspirations and need for outside support with achieving objectives in the national battlefield.

In exploring the reasons why GIA took its war to Europe, the following account highlights how the GIA's leader at the time of the attacks, Djamel Zitouni, was influenced by veterans of the Afghan jihad who had returned to Algeria. As for the dynamics of how GIA's European terrorist cells emerged, I highlight how they formed around entrepreneurs in France and other European countries who were linked to GIA's leaders in Algeria and jihadis in Afghanistan. These veteran activists acted upon orders from the GIA in Algeria and recruited from Algerian Afghanistan veterans and young extremists in Europe. The entrepreneurs also helped organize, fund and prepare the cells.

As discussed in the previous chapter, the war in Algeria was the number one cause for jihadi terrorism in Europe during the 1990s. Although many of the GIA's actions inside Algeria caused friction among jihadis internationally, the attacks in France were popular, and the people involved were eulogized as heroes or martyrs. Also, several people involved in the attacks would continue to take part in jihadism in Europe and have surfaced in terrorism investigations up until the present day. Before taking a closer look at how the campaign in France unfolded, I give some historical background to the GIA. It shows how the group has always been composed of national and international elements and how this was reflected in the terrorist network striking France.

GIA

In the early 1990s Algeria drifted into civil war between the regime (supported by France) and the Islamists (supported by international counterparts). The war lasted a decade and killed more than 100,000 people. It was triggered by the cancellation of Algeria's first democratic elections in which the FIS was poised to win, but there were also many underlying reasons, such as the national history of violent struggle and economic factors.[2] During the War of Liberation (1954–62) the Pan-Arab National Liberation Front (FLN) and the Islamists fought side-by-side sporting Islamic symbols. In the absence of a common enemy, ideological differences surfaced. Algeria was in a political and economic crisis, and the presidents of the FLN, Ahmad Ben Bellah (1962–5), Houari Boumédienne (1965–78) and Chadli Benjedid (1979–92), had failed to tackle the problems involved in state-building, including the need to satisfy the expectations of the population.

By the end of the 1980s the economy was in constant decline and abuses of power and corruption proliferated.[3] In order to deal with the economic crises and stay in power, the FLN cut ties with the Soviet Union and sought alliances with Western powers. Rapprochement with France and the United States was highly unpopular among the population and the Islamists in particular. In consequence, the elites of the FLN became increasingly distant from the common people and the Islamists. The Islamists soon became a political factor, promising community, safety and identity in the name of Islam, and the provision of social services ignored by the state.[4] In the 1970s the Islamist opposition grew increasingly militant.

In 1979 the Armed Islamic Movement (MIA) was formed under the leadership of a war hero from the Liberation War, Mustafa Bouyali. MIA was the first militant group in Algeria to target the state in the name of jihad. In 1982 the authorities cracked down on MIA and arrested some 200 members. Many of those who escaped joined the Afghan jihad as foreign fighters. MIA became the mother of subsequent jihadi trends in Algeria.[5] Two of the movement's leaders, Abd al-Qadir al-Shubuti and Mansuri al-Meliani, co-founded the GIA after being released from prison in 1989. In 1988 countrywide riots broke out against the regime because of the deteriorating economic situation. Panicking soldiers shot and killed demonstrators, creating a revolutionary atmosphere. President Benjedid tried to calm the situation by announcing his intention to hold free elections in the period between 1990 and 1992.

After the riots, Algeria's Islamists joined forces in the FIS. FIS aimed to Islamize Algeria via political activism and party politics. The movement was established in the al-Sunnah Mosque in Baab al-Waad, Algiers, in February 1989.[6] Two heroes of the Liberation War, the university professor, Abbas Madani, and the schoolteacher, Ali Belhadj, led FIS until they were arrested in June 1991. Belhadj was the leader of the radical faction of the party. While the organization initially met with skepticism from Algerian Salafis and jihadis opposed to democracy, FIS managed to mobilize moderate and radical groups and the majority of the people for elections. The party recruited mostly from Algerian variants of the Muslim Brotherhood, for example the "Algerianists" (jazara) headed by Mohammed Said and Abd al-Rasaq Rajam. FIS also recruited former members of MIA and Algerians who had fought as foreign fighters in Afghanistan and had returned home.

The movement was well organized, dividing Algeria into administrative zones, establishing countrywide offices as well as support groups in Europe.[7] Despite infighting and infiltration by the security services, in 1991 FIS won the municipal elections and started mobilizing for the general elections, which were held in 1992 and resulted in a landslide victory. On 11 January Benjedid dissolved the parliament and resigned. Subsequently, secularist army officers (widely believed to have been under pressure from France and the United States) cancelled the election results. The subsequent imprisonments of Madani and Belhadj added to the tensions and the stage was set for armed confrontation and the rise of the GIA.[8]

After the cancellation of the elections, Algeria's revolutionary Islamists took up arms within the framework of the GIA. The group was partly a product of Algerian guerrilla traditions and partly an off-shoot from the Afghan-Arab movement. It aimed to topple the regime, rid Algeria of Western dominance, and announce an Islamic state. The GIA grew increasingly extreme and internationally oriented over time. The group first targeted the regime. In 1993 it declared war on its political opponents in Algeria. In the fall of 1993 GIA declared war on foreigners in Algeria, and then began bombing French cities in 1995. And from 1995 onwards the GIA reached its highest level of extremism by initiating a war against other Islamists and the general population.

The GIA emerged as an association of Algerian militants between 1989 and October 1992. It was composed of three segments: veterans of MIA under the leadership of Abd al-Qadir al-Shubuti, returned foreign fighters from Afghanistan under the leadership of Qari Said and Mansuri al-Meliani, and violent Islamist youth gangs from Algiers's suburbs under the leadership of Mohammed Alal and Abd al-Haq Layada.[9] The Algerian al-Qaida member Qari Said is believed to have been the founder of the group. He returned to Algeria with a group of Afghanistan veterans in 1991, and had been given money by bin Laden to form an Algerian jihadi group.[10] Said first tried to recruit MIA veteran Abd al-Qadir al-Shubuti as leader for the returned foreign fighters to ensure legitimacy inside Algeria. This was necessary because many of the foreign fighters had been away for some time and were said to have become strangers to their own country. Shubuti rejected the offer and instead formed his own group, Movement for the Islamic State (MEI). Said then approached another MIA veteran released from jail in 1989, Mansuri al-Meliani, whom he convinced that the returned foreign fighters possessed the necessary resources and skills to challenge the regime.[11]

The different segments of the GIA fulfilled different functions. MIA veterans had experience in guerilla war inside Algeria, whereas the returned foreign fighters brought with them a web of connections outside Algeria, resources and new ideas of international jihad. The youth gangs had rudimentary ideological knowledge and lacked fighting experience, but many possessed the fervor of born-again-believers and knew their way around the Algerian suburbs.[12] Herein lies a parallel to how jihadi terrorist cells in Europe would come to combine foreign fighters and homegrown youth. At GIA's founding meeting, the foreign fighters were represented by Ahmad al-Wud. Al-Shubuti represented MEI. Abd al-Haq Layada and Ali Zouabri, brother of GIA's last emir, the infamous Antar Zouabri, represented the youth fighter group of Mohammed Alal.[13]

Like al-Qaida, the GIA was set up as a hierarchical organization, with a central leadership, an advisory council, an executive body, local branches throughout the country and international networks in North Africa, Europe and even the United States. The group ran training camps in the southern deserts and the mountains northeast of Algiers, which was its main base. The GIA also had access to guesthouses and camps in Pakistan and Afghanistan.[14] The group divided Algeria into nine zones, each headed by a local emir and controlled by a battalion (*katiba*) of fighters. The main battalions were the Green Battalion (Katibat al-Khadra), the Supporters' Battalion (Katibat al-Ansar), the Fixed Battalion (Katibat al-Ithabat), the Sunnah Battalion (Katibat al-Sunnah) and the Horror Battalion (Katibat al-Hawal).[15] The group was funded mainly through donations and crime. Support networks in Western countries were a significant source of income, in addition to criminal activities in Algeria, its neighboring countries and Europe, including bank robberies, trafficking and fraud.[16]

GIA support cells emerged in a number of European countries, such as France, Belgium, Spain, Sweden, Denmark and the UK. These cells were involved in fundraising, weapons smuggling, recruitment and propaganda, and they also sheltered jihadis on the run from law enforcement, or in transit between Algeria and Afghanistan. In order to raise funds, GIA supporters collected charity money or taxes from worshippers at mosques, traded drugs, forged and sold documents, and smuggled stolen cars, weapons and other goods. Weapons were usually purchased from former Eastern Bloc states and smuggled to Algeria via France, Spain and Morocco, or to Algerian camps in Afghanistan.

The GIA ran an organized system of recruitment in Europe, whereby recruiters would approach youths in mosques and Islamic charities, or in prisons, in an effort to persuade them to join jihad.[17] As part of the recruitment, the GIA distributed propaganda via three channels: Arabic newspapers in London, propaganda leaflets and on websites.[18] A core element in the propaganda was the media front supervised by Qatada, Abu Musab al-Suri, Hamza and others in London from 1993 to 1994, which was called "the family of the supporters" (Usrat al-Ansar). It distributed GIA's magazines *al-Ansar*, *al-Shahada* (the testament) and *al-Jama'a* (the group), as well as the magazines of the Libyan Islamic Fighting Group (LIFG), *al-Fajr* (the dawn) and EIJ's *al-Mujahidun*. One of the administrators was the Afghanistan veteran Rachid Ramda. Another Algerian involved in propaganda and recruitment was Ali Touchent. Ramda and Touchent were entrepreneurs in the network of cells that attacked France in 1995.

Emirs and radicalization

Like in Afghanistan and Europe, radicalization and internationalization of Algerian Islamism was driven by charismatic leaders and internal power struggles. Under the leadership of its first emir, Layada, who had fought with MIA against the regime, the GIA concentrated on targeting the police, army and other state institutions in Algeria. However, when Afghanistan veterans gained leading positions in the group from 1993 onwards it grew more violent and internationally oriented. After Layada was arrested in Morocco, where he was trying to set up regional weapons smuggling networks, leadership was transferred to Aish bin Amar, who was killed by security forces in August 1993. The next emir, the Afghanistan veteran Saif Allah Jafar al-Afghani, announced "he who fights us with the pen, we will fight with the sword," and urged his followers to attack intellectuals and journalists who criticized the GIA.[19] In October 1993 the GIA kidnapped three French diplomats working at the consulate in Algiers. The hostages were released in early November carrying a letter from al-Afghani warning that all foreigners who had not left the country by the end of the month would be killed.

This letter initiated the GIA's war on foreigners which ultimately led to the attacks in France.[20] Al-Afghani was killed in February 1994 and replaced by another Afghanistan veteran, Sherif Ghousmi, who continued the targeting of foreigners. He also orchestrated unification between the GIA and the radical FIS, such as the Algerianists. Although the unification was initially perceived as a strength, it eventually led to disagreements between GIA's internationalists and the nationally focused FIS militants. Infighting also made the group vulnerable to infiltration. The internal conflicts peaked over who should replace Ghousmi as emir when he was killed by security forces in 1994. The Algerianists' candidate was Ghousmi's deputy chief, Mahfuz Tajin.

However, several GIA leaders opposed Tajin's candidature because he was not considered a pious man, and because it was rumored he had sent fighters to train with the Shia Hizbullah movement in Lebanon.[21] These accusations prompted an investigation to be opened against him, during which the emir of the dreaded Green Battalion, Djamel Zitouni, stepped up and took Ghousmi's place through intimidation and force.

Born in Birkhadem, Algiers, in 1968, Zitouni was an unlikely leader for a group which had been overseen by experienced Islamists. He had little formal education and, unusually for a jihadi leader, he preferred to speak French and had only a poor mastery of Arabic. Zitouni worked as a slaughterer and chicken salesman, was married with no children, and first joined FIS and became deputy chief of the local FIS office.

He was arrested in connection with the upheavals in 1991 and thrown into a desert jail, where he met and befriended prominent Afghanistan veterans who would became part of the GIA, including the group's third and fourth emirs, al-Afghani and Ghousmi. Once he was out of jail Zitouni joined the GIA and earned a reputation as a fierce warrior. He was initially appointed emir of a local battalion in Birkhadem and later became emir for the GIA's most lethal armed force, the Green Battalion. The battalion was made up of about forty fighters handpicked by Zitouni for their fighting skills. It executed successful attacks on the security forces and was behind the kidnapping of French diplomats which initiated the war on foreigners in 1993. After seizing power by force, Zitouni proceeded to run the GIA with an iron fist. One of his first acts as leader was to declare that it was time to take the battle to France.[22]

The fact that Zitouni was recruited and socialized by people with foreign fighter experience, who saw the national Algerian struggle as part of something wider, may have affected his decision to strike the French at home. Overall, statements by the GIA and its followers in Europe suggest that the group drew most of its ideas from the Afghan-Arab movement.[23] In fact, no Algerian ever made the top tiers of jihad ideologues, and the London-based Abu Musab al-Suri, who maintained close relations with GIA's Afghan-Arab founders, argued that the group educated its recruits in the writings of Qutb, al-Zawahiri and himself, rather than referring them to Algerian thinkers.[24] This means that Zitouni, who headed the GIA when the group struck inside France, was exposed to the ideology of the Afghan-Arabs, something which was reflected in his statements up until the terrorist campaign in France. Zitouni emphasized the group's Salafi creed, blamed Western colonialism for the suffering of Muslims and called for an armed struggle against all enemies not only inside but also outside Algeria.[25]

The France attacks

A member of GIA's advisory council, Omar Sheiki, explained that there was internal discord within the GIA's leadership about the legitimacy and fruitfulness of attacking inside France, but Zitouni overrode the dissenters. According to Sheiki:

> The decision to attack the metro was taken by Zitouni personally. There was an agreement that we should send a letter to Chirac and invite him to Islam. Zitouni said to us that we had to attack France, but that we had to contact Chirac because he was of the people of the book, and so we invited him to Islam and Monotheism. But when he sent the letter Zitouni speeded up the matter and said he should attack France. Then the members of the advisory council said to him that Chirac had not answered the letter yet, so why do you want to involve us in war? The majority of the council was against involving us in a battle with France at such a level especially deep inside France. But Zitouni insisted and kept making the case that the council was only advisory and not binding. He said that "I can consult you and not respond, and I can also not consult you ... for I am emir and the highest judge."[26]

Together with the GIA's chief of external operations, Radwan Abu Basir, Zitouni then set the attack plans in motion. On 24 December 1994, four GIA fighters hijacked Air France Flight 8969 at Houari Boumedienne Airport. The plane was going to Paris and it is believed that Zitouni wanted the hijackers to down the aircraft over the city in a suicide mission.[27] The hijack operation was headed by the twenty-five-year-old Abdul Abdullah Yahia, the son of local employees at the French embassy in Algiers. The terrorists took control of the aircraft after disguising themselves as policemen. After tough negotiations with Algerian and French authorities, during which three hostages were killed, the aircraft was allowed to take off, and headed for French airspace. The negotiators managed to convince the terrorists that they lacked sufficient fuel to fly to Paris because the plane's motors had been running during the stand-off in Algiers. The flight was then diverted to Marseilles airport where it was stormed by French commandos. The counter-terrorism operation succeeded without further loss of life, except for the terrorists.

The GIA subsequently organized a series of attacks in France in the summer of 1995. On 11 July 1995, the terrorists murdered an imam and co-founder of FIS, eighty-five-year-old sheikh Abd al-Baqi Sahraoui and his bodyguard in a mosque on Rue Myrrah in Paris. This remains the only example of competing Islamists attacking each other in Europe. Sahraoui was shot twice in the head with a Winchester revolver. The imam and other FIS leaders in Europe had received threats from the GIA shortly before the incident. The murder weapon was later retrieved from a backpack of the French-Algerian Khaled Kelkal, who was the operational leader of the cell that staged most of the bombings in France.

Shortly after Sahraoui's killing, a number of homemade bombs were placed onboard, or near, public transportation in Paris, some of which exploded. The most lethal and potentially most lethal attacks were the time-bombs that exploded on board a subway train at the Saint-Michel station in Paris on 25 July 1995 (which killed eight people and injured eighty-six), a large bomb-device detected on a high-speed (TGV) railway track north of Lyon (which failed to detonate), and a car-bomb that exploded outside a Jewish school in Lyon on 7 September (the school hosted some 700 children). The bomb outside the school was set to explode when the pupils came out of the building, but because the school's clock ran slow the attack only caused injuries and material damage.

The attacks in France led to a Europe-wide manhunt for Algerian Islamists. Several members of the terrorist network avoided arrests and went underground in the UK and Belgium, while others escaped to Algeria, Afghanistan or Scandinavia.[28] During the fall of 1995, Belgian, Italian, German, Swiss and UK authorities arrested a number of terrorist suspects, as did other European security services. On 29 September French police rounded up Khaled Kelkal and his childhood friend and accomplice Karim Koussa outside Lyon. Kelkal was shot dead while Koussa was seriously wounded in a shootout. The attacks aimed to murder randomly selected French citizens en masse, and after the first wave of attacks in Paris there were also attempted attacks in Lille and Lyon.

Several of the terrorists had received training in the al-Qaida-associated Khalden training camp in Afghanistan. Others had trained in Algeria or France. The investigations indicated that the attackers received money and instructions from Algeria via the aforementioned Rachid Ramda in London, and a recruiter named Ali Touchent who moved between France, Belgium and the UK in the period leading up to the attacks.[29] All of the bomb devices were constructed in a similar way, and were built by the terrorists themselves guided by two instructors sent to France from Algeria by the GIA, as well as instruction videos. The explosives were made of sodium chlorate, sulfur, black powder and charcoal, with the bombs being placed inside butane gas containers or pressure cookers. The devices varied in size and weight, and some of them were packed with nails and bolts to produce shrapnel. All of the bombs were set off by timers, except for the TGV derailing attempt, which employed a mechanical detonating system.[30]

The terrorists took several counter-surveillance measures when preparing for the attacks. The network was organized into compartmentalized cells, and communications between them were kept at a minimum. They also set up multiple "safe-houses" (apartments) for preparatory activities, and the cell members bore aliases and communicated with each other in codes. The main attack cell headed by Kelkal also organized its own training camp in the woods outside Lyon. Apart from the Air France hijacking, none of the attacks were suicide missions. In general, suicide attacks were not yet a widespread tactic among Islamists in the 1990s.[31] However, although the GIA rarely equipped fighters with suicide belts, the group emphasized the virtues of martyrdom, and hailed its martyrs.[32]

Building cells

Overall, the targeting of the French public seemed designed to deter French interference in Algeria and to avenge arrests of GIA members in Europe. The targeting of a Jewish children's school reflected broader international efforts by Islamists to punish Israel for Palestine, but it also placed a strain on French–Israeli relations. The background and radicalization of the terrorists varied between leaders and foot soldiers. The leaders were in their thirties and had joined armed groups in Algeria and Afghanistan, whereas the foot soldiers were in their twenties and had been drawn into violent extremism by recruiters for militant Algerian organizations in France.[33] Furthermore, whilst some of the lead figures came from Algeria's pious middle class and had received some formal education, the younger recruits typically hailed from working-class environments, having only received rudimentary education.

The network reflected how the GIA in Algeria combined experienced jihad veterans with youth gangs. The man who set up the terrorist cells in France, Touchent, was a shadowy figure who entered France in the late 1980s. Touchent's name surfaced in several investigations into FIS and GIA cells in Europe, but he always escaped prosecution.[34] Touchent's background is obscure, but he has been described as educated and sophisticated. A Moroccan who infiltrated GIA networks in Europe on behalf of security services said Touchent distinguished himself from the young recruits he supervised by being older, charismatic, "elegant" and "European," mastering several languages and participating in the production, translation and dissemination of propaganda.[35] While building the terrorist network, Touchent coordinated with the Algerian Afghanistan veteran Rachid Ramda.

Ramda was born in El Ogla, East Algeria, in 1969, and grew up in a traditional and educated middle-class Berber family. He studied architecture at the École Nationale Polytechnique in Algiers (one of his brothers was educated as an architectural engineer while another brother was a computer scientist). He claims to have been recruited to FIS by his literature teacher who was among the movement's founding members. In 1989, prompted by a documentary he watched about the suffering of Afghan refugees, he quit his studies and traveled to Peshawar, Pakistan, where he worked as an aid worker with several non-governmental organizations, including Doctors without Borders.[36]

In Peshawar, Ramda emerged as a lead figure among the Algerian foreign fighters, and came to act as the deputy of his old friend and the GIA's founder Qari Said, and as a facilitator in establishing guesthouses and training camps.[37] After Said traveled from Afghanistan to Algeria in 1991 and set up the GIA, Ramda took over as leader for the Algerian foreign fighter contingent. In 1993 or 1994, while violence was escalating in Algeria, Ramda traveled to London where he joined the GIA propaganda efforts and engaged in recruitment for the training camps in Afghanistan, before being arrested following the France attacks. While Ramda has denied being involved, French prosecutors presented him as a central facilitator and proved that Ramda was in frequent phone contact with Touchent and other members of the network in the run-up to the attacks, and that he had also transferred money to the terrorists.[38]

In February 1994 Touchent met a man named Safe Bourada. Bourada was a second-generation Algerian immigrant born in Lyon and a former member of the French Socialist Party who had turned to militant Islam. He worked as a social worker, and Touchent, whose persona and "great organizational capacity" impressed Bourada, persuaded him to start recruiting for the GIA.[39] Bourada was an entrepreneur-type who maintains that he rediscovered religion through "reading, thinking and reasoning."[40] He assisted Touchent in setting up a GIA logistics cell in Lyon, and introduced him to the twenty-four-year-old French-Algerian Khaled Kelkal, whom he had just recruited.

Kelkal was born in Algeria in 1971 and grew up in the Lyon suburb of Vaulx-en-Velin. His parents were poor work immigrants to France and moderately religious. Kelkal was a misfit who had serious problems integrating and hated life in the suburbs. He dropped out of high school and became involved in criminality. While in prison, a cellmate taught Kelkal Arabic and how to pray and introduced him to the Quran.[41] Outside jail, Kelkal came into contact with Bourada, who connected him with Touchent and the GIA. Thus, as opposed to the organizers Ramda and Touchent, who had become jihadis in

Algeria and Afghanistan, Bourada and Kelkal were "homegrowns" who connected with the GIA and embraced militancy while in France. Touchent stayed in an apartment in Chasse-sur-Rhône from April 1995 while completing the preparations for the attacks. He decided to place Kelkal, who had been assigned to execute the attacks in Paris, in charge of the operational terrorist cell in Vaulx-en-Velin. Touchent then made Kelkal recruit other Algerian youths and childhood friends for the cell.

The recruiter Bourada organized a support cell in Chasse-sur-Rhône, which included Algerian, French-Algerian and French radicals, some of whom had trained at the Khalden camp in Afghanistan. The main function of Bourada's cell was to provide shelter, false documents and weapons for Kelkal's attack crew, and it was never proved that Bourada's crew ever planted bombs.[42] In June 1995 Touchent informed Bourada that Zitouni had sent an "emir" from Algeria and a "mujahid" from Afghanistan to assist the French network.[43] Bourada then ordered a recruit named David Vallat to go to Istanbul and hand over a passport in the name of Ahmed Besbes to the "emir," Boulaem Bensaid. Bensaid entered France via the Netherlands and Belgium in July 1995. Bourada himself traveled to Italy and accompanied the Afghanistan veteran Smaïn Aït Ali Belkacem to France and the city of Lille, which became home to the third cell in the network, and was to be headed by Belkacem.[44]

The Lille cell was set up in July 1995 at a meeting inside a McDonald's restaurant during which Touchent introduced Belkacem to two members of the GIA's gunrunning network in Europe referred to as Mohamed Drici and Ali ben Fattoum. A few days after the McDonald's meeting, Touchent introduced Belkacem to Kelkal and his cadre in the Ternay Park near Lyon. Belkacem was an explosives specialist who was tasked with educating Kelkal's gang in bomb-making. Two other GIA activists, Khaled K. and Moustapha B., helped Belkacem to gather bomb-making materials. The terrorists rented two apartments for use as safe houses and bomb factories, one in Boulevard d'Ornano (eighteenth arrondissement) and one in Rue Félicien-David (sixteenth arrondissement). The former apartment was close to the mosque in Rue Myrrha where Sheikh Abd al-Baqi Sahraoui's murder took place. Kelkal's cell also organized a training camp for physical and mental preparation in the woods outside Lyon.[45] When all necessary preparations were finalized, Touchent passed the leadership on to Bensaid and went underground—before bombs started to go off in Paris.

It is believed that Touchent made it to Algeria but was shot and killed by Algerian security forces in 1997. After Kelkal was killed and his cell rendered harmless, the cell headed by Bensaid and Belkacem in Lille started preparing attacks. In November 1995, French police intercepted a phone call in which Bensaid instructed his cadre to bomb the Wazemmes flea market in the city. The Lille cell was then intercepted and its members apprehended. Bourada, the recruiter, managed to escape to the UK, where he was arrested, extradited back to France and convicted of terrorist offences. Bensaid and Belkacem were sentenced to life in prison in 2002.[46]

Mixed motives

Because Zitouni ordered the attacks in France, his statements are a central indicator of what motivated them. The dissent in the GIA's advisory council when Zitouni laid out the plans illustrated the disagreements within the group about exporting jihad abroad. Most Algerian jihadis wanted to prioritize the struggle against the regime, but those with experience from Afghanistan were more internationally focused. Although Zitouni never went to Afghanistan himself, his statements suggest that he belonged to the internationalist camp.

This was likely due to his radicalization having occurred among GIA's Afghan-Arab segment. Zitouni was recruited and mentored by GIA's third and fourth emirs, the Afghanistan veterans al-Afghani and Ghousmi. It was al-Afghani who initiated the group's campaign of violence against foreign (especially French citizens) inside Algeria. Al-Afghani also stepped up the group's threatening rhetoric aimed at the French authorities. For example, when the GIA attacked a housing complex for foreign workers in the fall of 1994 and killed five French citizens, al-Afghani took the opportunity to accuse France of "disgusting crimes" in Algeria and demanded that the country ended its support for the regime, paid compensation to Muslims who had suffered losses in the war, evacuated all French citizens from Algerian soil and ensured the honor and legal rights of Muslims living in in France—very likely a reference to the arrests of Islamists supporting armed groups in Algeria.[47]

In the same vein, Zitouni issued multiple statements which illustrated how he saw deterrence of the far enemy, France, as part of the Algerian jihad. According to Zitouni, "the un-Islamic regime's oppressive practices which are backed by France were never seen except during the French occupation over 132 years and which is still continuing today. France is now a full partner in Genocide by paying mercenaries and rewarding its agents and financing arms deals."[48] When fighters from the Green Battalion under the name "Those Who

Sign in Blood" kidnapped and killed four Catholic priests in Tizi Ouzou, Zitouni portrayed the ordeal as revenge for the GIA fighters who had died in the December 1994 Air France hijacking. According to Zitouni, the killing of the priests "came after four soldiers of the same GIA battalion [Signatories in Blood] were killed during a heroic battle on French crusader soil."[49] He further stated that the hijacking aimed to force France to end its "unconditional political, military and economic aid" to the Algerian government.[50]

In addition, Zitouni put forward demands for the release of Islamist prisoners both in Algeria and internationally, such as the GIA leaders Layada and Dr Ahmed al-Wud, FIS Sheikhs Abbas Madani and Ali Belhadj inside Algeria, the radical preachers Salman al-Awda and Safar al-Hawali in Saudi Arabia, and the religious guide of the Egyptian Islamic Group (IG), Omar Abd al-Rahman, who was imprisoned in the United States in 1993 charged with involvement in terrorist plans in New York.[51] Stepping up the threats against France, on 19 August 1995, after the killing of FIS's Sheikh Sahraoui, and before the attack on the Paris metro, the GIA published a personal letter from Zitouni to President Jacques Chirac inviting him to Islam. Zitouni later stated that Chirac's refusal to adopt the Islamic faith showed he was "totally ready to sacrifice more French nationals and let their blood flow."[52] Zitouni then addressed the French people, announcing that "We are continuing today ... our holy struggle and military strikes, and this time in the heart of France and its largest cities, to prove that nothing will stand in our way as long as our actions are for the sake of Allah."[53]

There was a contradiction between Zitouni's goal of internationalizing the national conflict and his desire to be in charge of the Algerian jihad. Zitouni had been recruited and radicalized by the Afghan-Arabs al-Afghani and Ghousmi, who were close to al-Qaida, and he fiercely opposed the idea that foreign fighters should be involved in Algeria, leading him to enter into open conflict with bin Laden and his allies. When bin Laden proposed that his network should take on a bigger role in Algeria during a meeting with a GIA emissary in Khartoum, the latter threatened to kill him. This led bin Laden to end his longtime support for GIA and the conflict grew deeper when GIA murdered a delegation from the al-Qaida-affiliated LIFG, which went to Algeria to offer support in the war on the regime.

Similarly, whereas Zitouni's terrorist campaign in France was consistent with al-Qaida's emerging ideas of global jihad, the GIA's violence against Muslims in Algeria was unacceptable to al-Qaida. A similar conflict over the killing of Muslims would later occur between al-Qaida's central organization and the organization's branch in Iraq. There also lies a contradiction in the fact that although GIA had built extensive networks outside Algeria, Zitouni maintained that the GIA was not reliant on foreign support. In a statement dated January 1995 he underlined GIA's independence from supporters abroad, saying that "jihad in Algeria ever since its beginnings did not rely on any foreign help whatever the source, in order to stay independent in making its decision in the field and in order to keep that decision only with mujahidin."[54]

However, Zitouni's expressed antipathy toward outside interference must be understood in the context of the internal wars that were brewing among Algerian Islamists during his emirate from September 1994 onwards. At the time of the attacks in France, the insurgency was deteriorating on many levels. GIA violence had escalated dramatically, and infighting among the Islamists had reached unprecedented levels. By late 1995, armed groups had destroyed hundreds of schools, killed hundreds of schoolteachers, many of the francophone Westernized secular elite, intellectuals, journalists, authors, state officials, more than 100 religious leaders and more than ninety foreigners.[55] The GIA began targeting anyone they believed to be regime collaborators, including other insurgents and members of the organization itself. Zitouni justified the murder of the LIFG-envoys, for example, by accusing them of cooperating with the regime.

This resulted in the loss of support from influential activists in Europe, such as Qatada and al-Suri. Even more critically, at the national level GIA's emir accused the Algerianists of engaging in secret negotiations with the security apparatus. Under this pretext Zitouni's death squads assassinated Algerianist leaders Mohammed Said and Abd al-Rasaq Rajam. These murders led to a rebellion within GIA and its members started to defect en masse, particularly the Algerianists, who formed one anti-GIA group dubbed the Islamic League for Preaching and Jihad (LIDD).[56] The GIA was then caught in the cross-fire, targeted by the regime, defector groups and FIS's armed wing, the Islamic Salvation Army (AIS). The GIA defectors stressed their Salafi creed as opposed to the takfiri praxis of Zitouni, and most of them gathered under the aegis of the GSPC and the Protectors of the Salafi Call. After fierce clashes, fighters from LIDD eventually killed Zitouni in July 1996. Zitouni was replaced by a member of the Green Battalion, Antar Zouabri, who headed the organization until it was dissolved in 2002. He took GIA's violence to a new level in what became known as the "era of slaughter."[57] Zouabri and the Green Battalion continued to organize bogus Islamic courts against dissenters. In the end, no-one within the GIA trusted each other and no-one was safe from being ambushed and executed by comrades-in-arms.

When exploring the chain of events that led to terrorist attacks in France, it should be noted that the bombings were ordered by a newly appointed and controversial leader, who clung to power with his back to the wall and burned bridges in the process. Whereas GIA's supporters in Europe were skeptical of Zitouni and condemned GIA's extremism in Algeria, they admired the operation in France.

The GIA media cell issued a special edition of *al-Ansar* magazine celebrating the bombings and Zitouni's letter to Chirac, while calling for "hundreds, if not thousands" of martyrs like Kelkal.[58] Moreover, al-Suri, who befriended GIA's founder Qari Said and the group's fourth emir Sherif Ghousmi in Afghanistan, has since boasted of how he contributed to the decision to launch attacks on French soil. Al-Suri claimed he advised Ghousmi, who was GIA's emir before Zitouni (and mentored him), that it would be "beneficial" to strike the French at home "to draw France into an openly declared support for the Algerian regime, a support which existed, but only in secrecy," adding "this will unify the Islamic Nation around the jihad in Algeria as it unified the Islamic Nation in Afghanistan against the Soviets."[59] Abu Hamza al-Masri, who supported the GIA almost to the bitter end, has also expressed admiration for the attacks in France, describing them as "most certainly justified Islamically and part of the war done by the believers against the enemies of Islam."[60] Hamza characterized the GIA's international operations inside France as "hard work," and as a positive effort in making the Algerians overlook the "shortcomings" of the GIA in other respects, likely referring to the group's atrocities against Muslims and Islamists inside Algeria.[61]

As he had been mentored by Afghanistan veterans who were influenced by al-Suri and other internationalist jihadis, Zitouni was surely aware that the France attacks would gain popularity beyond Algeria. He may therefore have hoped the attacks would galvanize outside support and unify the Algerian Islamists, as suggested by al-Suri. The focus on Muslim prisoners in Zitouni's statements suggests he was more concerned with the group's international support networks than he expressed in the statement released in early 1995. Although he wanted to appear independent, he knew the group could not survive without outside support. Also, he had ordered the attacks in France months before he entered the conflict with bin Laden and GIA supporters in Europe over the killings of Islamists in Algeria. Revenge for the GIA networks in Europe may have been a key motive for the attacks. There were multiple crackdowns on GIA cells in Europe in the time leading up to the campaign in France, and the GIA had threatened to retaliate.

With regard to the internal dynamics of the network behind the attacks, it was dominated by experienced jihad entrepreneurs, from Zitouni at the top of the chain, via organizers Touchent and Ramda, to the bomb-instructors Bensaid and Belkacem. However, the network also involved misfits and drifters who were recruited in France, with little or no experience and less obvious reasons for joining jihadism. The entrepreneurs had been socialized within militant organizations pursuing ideological and strategic aims in Algeria and elsewhere, whereas the latter sympathized with the GIA, but were also driven by grievances related to their lives as immigrants, or by their social connection and loyalty to charismatic recruiters, such as Touchent and Safe Bourada. Kelkal, who assumed a lead role in the execution of the attacks, fits most of the criteria for a misfit.

An interview Kelkal gave to a German sociologist from the time before he joined militancy suggests that grievances such as being an outsider in France contributed to his radicalization. He voiced strong frustration over the hardships of becoming integrated in his hometown of Lyon, for example, stating "there was no place for me, because I said to myself: complete integration is impossible, I can't eat pork. And they had never seen an Arab in their class— frankly you're the only Arab they said—and when they knew me they said: 'you're an exception.' But they always found it easier to talk to each other."[62] The feeling of being an alien led Kelkal to search for a purpose, as indicated by his statement that "there's no coherence in my life, just a little bit of that, and another piece of that. No, what I need is to have principles, even to respect something."[63] While many immigrants experience similar frustration and seek meaning, Kelkal became involved with the wrong people who could exploit his vulnerability and channel his anger into political violence. The case of Kelkal exemplifies how the GIA benefited from homegrown radicalization among immigrants in France. It also demonstrates that homegrown radicalization was part and parcel of jihadism in Europe from the outset. Whereas the first jihadi attacks in Europe were ordered from Algeria to further GIA's objectives at home, they were part of the emerging globalization of jihad, which would have a profound impact in Europe.

The GIA's international networks continued to shape the threat in Europe for years to come. The vicious circle of attacks and counter-measures triggered multiple other cells composed of ex-GIA members linked to al-Qaida. In 1996, for example, a Belgium-based GIA offshoot known as the "Roubaix Gang" initiated several heavily armed robberies, engaged in armed clashes with Belgian police and attempted to launch terrorist bombings. This gang was composed of young Algerians, Moroccans and French converts. The Frenchman Christophe Caze was the entrepreneur, and it also involved another convert, Lionel Dumont. Converts have always been part of Europe's jihadi phenomenon. Caze was a former Catholic and medical student who had spent time as a foreign fighter in Bosnia in the early 1990s, where he forged ties with jihadis linked to the GIA. One of these jihadis was the Canadian-Algerian Fateh Kamel, who became part of the Roubaix Gang in Belgium but escaped prosecution. Like many former GIA members he later joined al-Qaida and became involved in plans to bomb Los Angeles International Airport in 1999.[64]

Dumont was a journalism student and ex-soldier who had spent time in Bosnia as a foreign fighter. He was also believed to have forged ties with al-Qaida while spending time in Japan after escaping from a Bosnian prison.[65] In March 1996, members of the Roubaix Gang placed a car-bomb on the streets of Lille, three blocks from where leaders of the G7 were to meet. French police discovered the bomb device and rendered it harmless. The same day, police tracked down members of the gang inside an apartment in Lille. Four of them were killed in the ensuing police raids. The leader, Caze, initially managed to escape, but was shot dead by police the next day.

In addition to triggering off-shoots such as Caze's gang, those arrested for their roles in the GIA's bombings of Paris gained status as political prisoners and martyrs among Islamists in Europe. An example is the case of Rachid Ramda. Ramda was arrested and imprisoned in Britain in 1995, and continued to maintain his innocence before being extradited to France in 2006 where he was sentenced to ten years in prison. He has been eulogized by extremists in Europe and cited as a source of inspiration by individuals convicted of al-Qaida-linked terrorist offences in Europe.[66] Furthermore, people involved in the bombings of 1995 would work as recruiters behind bars, and several were implicated in terrorist plans upon their release.

This was the case with Bourada who (as with other terrorists discussed in this book) was obsessed with avenging his arrest. After being released in 2003, he was rearrested as part of a cell plotting attacks on the French security services.[67] There were also examples of people who escaped prosecution for the attacks of 1995 and surfaced in al-Qaida-linked plots at a later stage. One man operating at the fringes of the GIA cell in Lille, Fouhad Sabour, spent time in the UK and training camps in Afghanistan before taking part in a plot to bomb the Christmas marketplace in Strasbourg, which will be discussed in the next chapter.

Overall, there is a pattern whereby those involved in GIA attacks in France would later join al-Qaida's networks. This was also the case with Farid Mellouk who escaped the crackdowns on the Vaulx-en-Velin cell, and was not apprehended until March 1998 in a Belgian counter-terrorism raid code-named "Operation Lock."[68] At that time Mellouk was in charge of a support cell for al-Qaida. Most members of this cell hailed from the Middle East and many of them had undergone training in Afghanistan. Interestingly, the investigation into Mellouk's cell uncovered a sixty-page manifesto of the MICG, which would later organize international recruitment networks for jihad in Iraq, and provided operatives for the 2004 Madrid bombings. Thus while attacks in France were an all-Algerian operation, in the following years former GIA operatives started showing up in multinational cells linked to al-Qaida.

The pattern whereby GIA-members in Europe would team up with al-Qaida must be understood in the context of shifts in Algerian jihadism caused by GIA's extremism at home. The infighting among Algerian jihadis, which coincided with the attacks in France, opened a window of opportunity for al-Qaida to gain influence in Algeria and recruit among Algerians in Europe. When the GIA disintegrated under Zitouni and Zouabri, defectors were absorbed by the GSPC and the Protectors of the Salafi Call.

The GSPC emerged as the main jihadi force inside Algeria, and the group also came to dominate Algerian networks in Europe. The group was founded at the end of 1998 and issued its first statement under the name "The Blessed Group" in April 1999. In an effort to restore the shattered image of the Algerian jihad, the group distanced itself from the GIA, focused on combating the regime and sought rapprochement with al-Qaida. The first leader of the group was Abu Musab Abd al-Mujid. He was replaced by a former paratrooper in the Algerian Army, Hasan Hattab. The group initially received support from al-Qaida and Islamists in Europe who had rejected the GIA. An arrested Algerian jihadi testified that he had observed Hattab in phone contact with bin Laden and that it was al-Qaida's emir who had ordered the name change from "GIA in the second zone," or "The Blessed Group," to "The Salafi Group for Call and Combat" (GSPC).[69]

The connection between GSPC and al-Qaida and the presence of GSPC support cells in Europe created fears that the organization could replicate GIA's campaign. However, it soon transpired that Hattab was ambivalent towards global jihad and wanted to prioritize national matters. Accordingly, under Hattab's reign, the GSPC's activities in Europe were confined to support activism and the groups did not engage in terrorist plots.[70] When al-

Qaida launched 9/11, relations between Hattab and bin Laden reached a conclusion. Hattab viewed the attacks as being counter-productive and distanced himself from al-Qaida. Between 2001 and 2003 it seems there was only minimal interaction between GSPC and al-Qaida.[71]

Hattab's successor Nabil Sahraoui, on the other hand, wanted to re-connect with al-Qaida and reached out to the organization on 11 September 2003 by announcing that GSPC stood by bin Laden, al-Qaida and the Taliban in the war against the United States and its allies. However, while reaching out to al-Qaida, Sahraoui also underscored the idea that the struggle in Algeria took precedence over the far enemy, and the GSPC did not plot attacks in the West during his reign either.[72] When Sahraoui was killed by security forces in June 2004, the leadership was passed on to Abdelmalek Droukdel who continued the path of integrating GSPC and al-Qaida.

Under Droukdel's leadership the group established ties to al-Qaida's Iraqi branch (AQI), sent fighters to Iraq and took part in recruitment for the Iraqi jihad in Europe. Toward the end of 2006, Droudkel reiterated GSPC's support for al-Qaida and swore an oath of allegiance to bin Laden, and in January 2007 GSPC formally changed its name to al-Qaida in the Islamic Maghreb (AQIM). Although many terrorists surveyed in this book had connections to GSPC/AQIM, very few plots have been attributed to the group. The second phase of jihadi terrorism in Europe, which is the topic of the next chapter was dominated by ex-GIA members who had trained with al-Qaida in Afghanistan or the Caucasus, and members of the Jordanian group which would become al-Qaida in Iraq.

4

TOWARDS GLOBAL JIHAD IN EUROPE (2000–3)

In 2000–3 European security services uncovered a number of plots in France, Italy, Germany and the UK by North African and Middle Eastern terrorists linked to al-Qaida. This chapter examines four of these plots: a plan to bomb the Christmas market in Strasbourg in 2000, a plan to bomb US targets in Europe in 2001, a plan to strike Jewish targets in Germany in 2002 and a plan to attack the Russian embassy in Paris the same year. These cases epitomize the jihadi threat in Europe before the Iraq war in 2003.

The chapter explores how the cells emerged and how they fit into the wider jihadism phenomenon at the time. I surmise that the threat situation in Europe in 2000–3 was characterized by al-Qaida's effort to subcontract affiliates for global jihad. All of the cells grew out of support networks in Europe assisting mujahidin in Afghanistan, Chechnya and other places. The cells usually had dual ties to al-Qaida in Afghanistan and groups in North Africa or the Middle East. Many were former GIA, or linked to GSPC, and had spent time with militants in Algeria as well as Afghanistan. While plotting attacks in Europe they interacted with al-Qaida, directly or via middlemen, and some received instructions from bin Laden.

Most of the terrorists were immigrants to Europe, in their twenties or thirties. Algerians dominated the picture, but there were also Tunisians, Moroccans, Jordanians and Palestinians. One parallel to the GIA's networks of the 1990s was that the foot soldiers included socio-economic outcasts, whereas entrepreneurs included the lower middle-class and educated people. Some of the terrorists had fought jihad in their home countries, but others lacked combat experience. They were typically recruited from extremist networks in Europe, and then channeled to training camps in Afghanistan. In the camps they were indoctrinated and received training before being deployed to Europe.

While there were many parallels to the GIA, the new threat involved more nationalities and operated more in accordance with al-Qaida's vision of global jihad. For example, whereas the GIA wanted to hurt France, these cells focused more on the United States and Israel. Moreover, while the GIA emphasized France's interference in Algeria affairs as a motive, the cells of 2000–3 focused more on international causes. At the same time, the cells were not all about global jihad. The terrorists had stakes in insurgencies in their home countries and seemed torn between national and global aspirations. Because the terrorist cells analyzed in this chapter had tangible ties to al-Qaida, I first recount some milestones of the organization's global jihad as they relate to the case studies. I also present some background to the groups and networks the cells erupted from to use in my case study analyses.

Global jihad kicks off

At the turn of the millennium al-Qaida was at its most potent as a terrorist organization and managed to engage the United States in a dynamic of attack and counter-attack. The enmity towards the United States was nothing new in al-Qaida, but the declaration of global jihad took it to a new level. Al-Qaida had been attacking the United States since the early 1990s. While in Sudan, for example, bin Laden had sent his military commander Mohammed Atef with a group of fighters to engage US forces supporting UN peace-keeping in Somalia, and the organization trained the Pakistani-Kuwaiti Ramzi Yousef, whose terrorist cell launched the first attack on the World Trade Center (WTC) in 1993.[1]

Whereas bin Laden was always opposed to American interference in Muslim affairs, he regarded the placing of US troops in Saudi Arabia as an act of war and would use any opportunity to support anti-US violence, anywhere. When al-Qaida returned to Afghanistan in 1996, the organization had defined the United States as the main enemy. In 1996 it declared war on Americans around the world before declaring global jihad against "Jews and Crusaders" in February 1998.[2] The declaration was followed by the bombings of US embassies in East Africa and the war ship USS *Cole* outside Yemen. The Clinton administration responded by firing Tomahawk missiles at camps in Afghanistan. The missiles killed some twenty to thirty fighters, but missed bin Laden.

While the United States contemplated new strategies to combat al-Qaida, the organization began preparing for 9/11. The main planner was the Pakistani-Kuwaiti Khalid Sheikh Mohammed (KSM), who was the uncle of the entrepreneur of the first WTC attacks in 1993 (Ramzi Yousef). KSM had been a foreign fighter in the Afghan jihad under the warlord Abd al-Rasul Sayyaf. He met bin Laden then, but did not join al-Qaida. After leaving Afghanistan, KSM fought in Bosnia before taking up international terrorism, first on his own and later with al-Qaida. Following the first WTC attacks, KSM stayed with his nephew in the Philippines who was preparing new attacks on America, notably the plot known as "Bojinka" to down a dozen US-bound airliners from East Asia.[3]

Whereas Yousef was rounded up in Pakistan in February 1995, KSM escaped and re-connected with bin Laden. During a meeting in Tora Bora in May 1996, KSM presented an early version of the 9/11 plot to bin Laden and Mohammed Atef. They rejected the plan at first, but invited KSM to join al-Qaida. KSM initially declined and stayed a freelancer but maintained contacts with al-Qaida through Abu Zubaydah who acted as a facilitator of training camps in Afghanistan at the time.[4] KSM joined al-Qaida in 1998 and was put in charge of the organization's media committee.[5] In 1998 Mohammed Atef persuaded bin Laden to reconsider KSM's idea of hijacking airliners in the United States, and passed on responsibility for external operations to the Baluchi.[6]

The 9/11 operation was complex, time-consuming and costly (estimated at between 400,000 and 500,000 USD).[7] The plan involved the recruitment of a number of Saudis as well as Arab immigrants to Europe. The recruits were trained in Afghanistan and prepared for operating in a Western environment. The specifics of the operation were kept a secret between bin Laden, Atef and KSM, but rumors of a major attack inside America started spreading in the training camps and reached the Taliban. According to former Pakistani President Pervez Musharraf, several members of al-Qaida's advisory council opposed the plan on strategic and religious grounds, as did Taliban's emir, Mullah Omar.

However, by August 2001 bin Laden had managed to turn the council around and received its blessing.[8] The Taliban, on the other hand, tried to hamper the attack plans by issuing a general warning to the United States about a possible al-Qaida attack.[9] Like most terrorist cells addressed in this book, the European element of the 9/11 plot, the "Hamburg Cell," emerged partly within Europe and partly outside. The cell members were recruited in

Germany and trained in Afghanistan from 1999. Core operatives, such as Mohammed Atta, went through a radicalization process while attending the al-Quds Mosque in Hamburg. According to the 9/11 commission report, the terrorists originally wanted to join jihad in Chechnya, but were persuaded by an Egyptian al-Qaida associate to attend training camps in Afghanistan instead.[10] While at the camps they were chosen as operatives for the world's most devastating terrorist attack.

Although 9/11 must have demanded much of his attention, KSM also prepared other attacks, some of which were to take place in Europe. For example, he is thought to have prepared the Britons Richard Reid and Sajjid Badat to bring down transatlantic airliners in 2001[11]—Reid's operation failed, whereas Badat bailed out. It is further believed that KSM's most ambitious plan besides 9/11 was to hijack airliners in Eastern Europe bound for Heathrow and crash them into the terminal buildings in suicide missions. It has since been alleged, however, that this plot was invented by the CIA to justify the waterboarding of KSM at Guantanamo.[12]

From support network to terrorist cell

As well as plotting attacks in Europe on its own, al-Qaida also relied on friends to introduce global jihad in the region. Two such friends who maintained networks in Europe were the former GIA fighter Abu Doha and the Jordanian jihadi Abu Musab al-Zarqawi. Although these militants had close relations with al-Qaida, they were not part of the organization; nor were they entirely focused on global jihad. Rather, they were semi-independent and prioritized national or regional struggles, Doha in Algeria, and al-Zarqawi in Jordan and the Levant.

The Algerian-based Doha network was a GIA spin-off set up at the Khalden camp in Afghanistan. The network operated across the Middle East and North Africa, and maintained cells in multiple European countries, such as the UK, France, Germany, Belgium, Italy and Spain. Members looked to Qatada for religious guidance. Before it became involved in international terrorism, Doha's network in Europe concentrated on supporting groups in Algeria and their camps in Afghanistan.

Doha was born in Constantine in northeastern Algeria. Little is known about his background. What seems certain is that he joined GIA in the early 1990s and later defected, before ending up as an organizer of Algerian guesthouses and camps in Afghanistan. Doha also obtained political asylum in the

UK in 1994, where he joined the circles of Qatada and Hamza in London. From among their followers he recruited the UK branch of his network, which gathered regularly in an apartment near Finsbury Park Mosque. This branch was headed by Doha himself and another Algerian named Rabah Kadri.[13] Key supervisors of the network in other European countries were the France-based Yacine Aknouche and Mohammad Bensakhria in Germany. The latter headed a cell in Frankfurt focused on gunrunning. Bensakhria was an Afghanistan veteran and old comrade of Doha's, and the two of them spent time together in Khost and Jalalabad.[14] Doha-affiliates from different countries traveled regularly to London for meetings.

The original functions of the network were to channel money, weapons, equipment and recruits to Afghanistan and Algeria, as well as sheltering jihadis traveling through Europe en route to conflict zones. While overseeing these activities, Doha shuttled back and forth between Afghanistan, Europe, the Middle East and North Africa. According to US court hearings, in December 1998 Doha reached a deal with bin Laden in Kandahar according to which his cadre would execute global jihad attacks in exchange for money. For this purpose Doha recruited operatives from Europe and offered training at the Khalden camp where trainees were allowed to propose ideas for terrorist projects, which Doha would in turn present to al-Qaida's leadership.[15] From 1999 onwards Doha began to disperse trained terrorists tasked with staging attacks on US and Jewish targets in Europe, the United States and the Middle East.

In Europe the network plotted an attack against the Christmas marketplace in Strasbourg as well as attacks with bombs or poisons in the UK, France and Italy. Doha also recruited another ex-GIA member, Ahmed Ressam, for an attack against Los Angeles International Airport, which was intercepted in December 1999. Some sources allege that members of Doha's network were also involved in plans to attack tourist sites in Jordan in 1999 in concert with members of the Tawhid group, which will be discussed shortly. Doha was arrested at Heathrow Airport in February 2001 while trying to escape to Saudi Arabia. Because of his Algerian background, Doha has been portrayed as a leading GSPC figure. However, given the GSPC's focus on Algeria between 1998 and 2003, and Doha's role in international terrorism, he must have been closer to al-Qaida.

The other affiliate which ran errands for al-Qaida in Europe was al-Zarqawi's Tawhid group. The origins of Tawhid can be traced to the Salafi-jihadi movement which formed around the theologian Abu Mohammed al-Maqdisi in Jordan in the early 1990s. This movement produced several high-profile jihadi leaders and thinkers, such as al-Maqdisi himself, London-based Qatada, and al-Zarqawi.[16]

Born in 1966 in the city of Zarqa, al-Zarqawi was a misfit who entered the world of criminality and spent time in prison after being convicted of multiple felonies. In jail he became a born-again believer under the influence of Tablighis. In 1989, the twenty-three-year-old Jordanian traveled to Afghanistan to become a mujahid where he is said to have trained in the Sada camp under the guidance of al-Qaida's Mohammed Atef.[17] Al-Zarqawi did not meet bin Laden during this stay, but he did encounter his countryman, al-Maqdisi, who became his mentor. Upon returning to Jordan he became part of an activist group surrounding al-Maqdisi, which aimed to topple the monarchy and proclaim an Islamic state.[18] The group looked to al-Maqdisi and Qatada in London as its ideologues. Shortly afterwards, the Jordanian authorities accused the group of plotting attacks on a cinema and other targets in Jordan, and arrested its members. The subsequent trial, known as the "Bayat al-Imam case," received much media attention and made al-Zarqawi a household name in jihadi circles. When he traveled to Afghanistan again after being granted an amnesty in 1999, he was invited to have a sit-down with bin Laden and another al-Qaida commander, Saif al-Adel, in Kandahar.

Based on what they had learned about al-Zarqawi, they wanted to discuss his potential membership in al-Qaida. However, bin Laden concluded that al-Zarqawi was too extreme, partly due to his sectarian hatred of Shias. Al-Qaida instead proposed mutual cooperation between the two organizations and supported al-Zarqawi in setting up a camp in Herat on the Iranian border. Al-Zarqawi named the camp "al-Tawhid wa'l-Jihad" (monotheism and jihad) and wanted it to be the base of a special group for people from the Levant.[19] The camp quickly grew in size, attracting Syrian, Jordanian and Lebanese recruits. The aim of the group was to topple the regimes of the Levant and also to launch attacks against Jews and Americans in the region. Relations with al-Qaida were coordinated through monthly meetings, which were sometimes held in Kandahar and sometimes in Herat.[20]

Tawhid was set up as a hierarchical organization with al-Zarqawi as leader and al-Maqdisi and Qatada as religious authorities. In terms of enemy perception, Tawhid differed from al-Qaida by prioritizing fighting Jordan and Israel over the United States.[21] The group was also shaped by al-Zarqawi's intense antagonism towards Shias. This hatred translated into extensive sectarian violence when al-Zarqawi joined the Iraqi jihad, and it also placed a strain on his relations with al-Qaida.[22] Al-Zarqawi was wounded in the chest during the invasion of Afghanistan, but managed to escape to Iran with a group of fighters. From Iran, he zigzagged countries in the Middle East before settling in Iraq in mid-2003, by some accounts on advice from al-Qaida's Saif al-Adel.[23] From Herat, and later from Iraq, he oversaw international support networks in the Middle East and Europe. These networks also transformed into terrorist cells when needed.

The group was involved in international terrorism right from the start, mainly in the Middle East but also in Europe, as is discussed subsequently. In 2000, Jordan disrupted a plot to bomb US and Israeli tourists, which involved members of Tawhid and also had links to Doha's network.[24] Members of Tawhid were further tied to an attempted assassination of the leader of the Jordanian anti-terrorism unit with a car bomb in March 2002. One of Tawhid's most high-profile attacks in this period was the kidnapping and murder of the US diplomat Laurence Foley in Amman in October 2002. Then, in November 2003, Tawhid was implicated in suicide bombings against Jewish and British targets in Istanbul. These attacks were planned in cooperation with al-Qaida and local Turkish militants (IBDA-C and Turkish Hizbullah), but were overseen by a Tawhid-member and confidant of al-Zarqawi named Luayy Sakka.[25]

With the invasion of Iraq, Tawhid would come to play a central part in efforts to recruit foreign fighters for the Iraqi jihad. Recruitment networks for Iraq proliferated in Iran, Lebanon, Turkey, Syria, Iraq, North Africa and Europe.[26] Over time this effort came to involve contacts and cooperation between multiple Middle Eastern and North African jihad groups, including Tawhid, Kurdish-Iraqi Ansar al-Islam (AI), Lebanese Fatah al-Islam (FAI), the GSPC, as well as Moroccan, Libyan and Tunisian militants. In 2003–4 Tawhid emerged as major terrorist threat in Iraq. It specialized in large-scale suicide bombings aimed primarily at US/Western targets and Shias, such as car bombings of the UN headquarters in Baghdad in August 2003, and one aimed at the Shia leader Mohammed Baqir al-Hakim, killing scores of people. During the summer of 2004 the group staged a campaign of beheading hostages, which were videotaped and distributed online in the same way as ISIS/IS has been doing since 2014. The beheading campaign by al-Zarqawi's group in 2004 magnified its profile and was mimicked by jihadis in Europe, for example by the murderer of Theo van Gogh in 2004.

In October 2004, al-Zarqawi swore allegiance to bin Laden and took al-Qaida's brand name. Soon, however, relations between al-Zarqawi and al-

Qaida soured. Al-Qaida was opposed to al-Zarqawi's excessive sectarianism and his prioritization of the regional battlefield over global jihad. Al-Zarqawi was also very independently minded and he refused to become a tool for al-Qaida. In some ways there were strong parallels between Tawhid's leader and GIA's Zitouni. However, there was an important difference between GIA's terrorism in France and cells emanating from al-Qaida-affiliated networks such as Doha's and al-Zarqawi's. Although GIA drew inspiration from international jihad, it acted autonomously and prioritized national issues. The cells of the new millennium were the product of longtime cooperation and compromises with al-Qaida in Afghanistan and Europe. More than the GIA, they were a hybrid between national, regional and global driving forces, something which affected the way the cells emerged and behaved.

Frankfurt cell

In December 2000, German counter-terrorism police disrupted a terrorist cell in Frankfurt. This cell was planning to bomb revelers at the Christmas marketplace outside Notre Dame Cathedral in Strasbourg, France, on New Year's Eve. The terrorists planned to set off bombs made out of pressure cookers filled with bolts and nails and the peroxide-based explosive TATP with the aim of killing and maiming as many French people as possible. The cell was composed of the four Algerians—Salim Boukhari (thirty-one), Fouhad Sabour (thirty-seven), Aeroubi Beandali (twenty-six) and Lamine Marouni (thirty-one)—and was set up by Doha with support from al-Qaida at Khalden. The terrorists were recruited from Doha's network in the UK, Germany and France, and were sent for training in Afghanistan in 1999. Their training involved ideological indoctrination, physical and weapons training (described by one cell member as "heftier than the military"), and instructions on how to make bombs and the poisons ricin and cyanide.[27]

After being assigned to execute an attack in France, the cell members gathered in Frankfurt in October 2000 and started preparing. Doha himself acted as the principal entrepreneur and oversaw the plot from London. The attack cell nurtured contacts with Doha-affiliates in the UK, France, Italy, Belgium, Spain, Germany and other countries. In particular, the members of the cell were in frequent contact with a gunrunning cell headed by Mohamed Bensakhria in Frankfurt, and one of al-Qaida's support cells based in Milan, supervised by an Egyptian known as El-Sayed.[28] The Frankfurt plotters were detected as a result of a joint effort by the German, French and Belgian intelligence services, who traced a bag of weapons which had been smuggled from Belgium to an apartment in Sigmund Freud Straße no. 55, Frankfurt. MI5 intercepted phone calls from the operational cell's entrepreneur, Salim Boukhari, to Doha in London, in which the former asked for more money to realize the plan. Boukhari later picked up a fake credit card provided by Doha in the name of C. Aman from London (Claude Aman was one of his many aliases).[29]

This illustrated how the cell received outside funding, but it also shows that they were operating on a tight budget. During police raids investigators recovered chemicals suitable for producing TATP, laboratory equipment and training manuals from Afghanistan. The chemicals had been collected from separate pharmacies in Frankfurt, Stuttgart, Cologne, Berlin, Hamburg and other cities under the pretense that they were gathering materials urgently needed for hospitals in Africa.[30] Police also confiscated cash, false passports, computers, encrypted discs and weapons, including homemade detonators, rifles with telescopic sights, Scorpion submachine guns, a hand grenade, pistols, revolvers, silencers and large amounts of ammunition. Prosecutors contended the cell had been organizing a weapons transport to Algeria, in addition to planning an attack in Strasbourg. On 10 March 2003, in Frankfurt, Boukhari and the other members of the cell were convicted of conspiracy to commit murder by planting a bomb, and of weapons violations.

In most respects, the members of the Frankfurt cell resembled the terrorists responsible for the 1995 attacks in France. However, there was a major difference in that the cell was linked to al-Qaida via Doha, and originated in Afghanistan rather than Algeria. Moreover, whereas the GIA attacks also involved cross-border contacts, the Frankfurt cell was more transnational, conceived in Afghanistan, further developed in the UK and Germany, and was supposed to mount an attack in France. There were similarities between the organization and command structure of the GIA and the Frankfurt cases. Both networks involved compartmentalized cells, which were supervised and supported by organizations based in Afghanistan and Algeria respectively, and involved top-down processes of recruitment, radicalization and training. The top-down nature of the Frankfurt cell was reflected in the cell's internal command structure and how it followed advice from training courses in Afghanistan.

The cell leader, Boukhari, brought a notebook with him from Afghanistan which contained instructions on counter-surveillance and how to assemble bombs, detonators and poisons.[31] The plotters used aliases and fake IDs, and took multiple security measures such as hiring apartments on the first floor in case they needed to escape. They rented two apartments in Frankfurt and a third in the city of Baden-Baden on the French border for the purpose of reconnaissance and escape.

Reconnaissance was conducted by Boukhari and Fouhad Sabour in Strasbourg on 22 December 2000. During the trip they videotaped the marketplace, the nearby cathedral and other sites in the city, even asking police officers for directions to the cathedral while posing as tourists. In what became part of the evidence against the men, they also filmed the car journey between France and Germany chanting *nasheed*. Like the GIA, who sent bomb instructors to France, Doha had a bomb-maker named Merouane Benahmed sent from France to Germany to help out with the explosives. Benahmed, a former GIA member who had spent time as a foreign fighter in Afghanistan and Georgia, would become implicated in another plot to bomb the Russian embassy in Paris, as will be discussed later.[32]

Given the cooperation between Abu Doha's network and al-Qaida, and the latter's explicit prioritizing of U.S. and Jewish targets, it might seem a bit odd that some of the Doha-linked cells chose other targets, French civilians in the case of the Frankfurt cell.[33] However, there are many examples in al-Qaida's history of the organization issuing general guidelines while leaving decisions at the operational level to cells. According to some sources there was disagreement between Doha and the Frankfurt plotters over the target selection.[34] In light of Doha's purported deal with al-Qaida to focus on Jewish and US targets it seems likely that he would have proposed attacking such targets, whereas some of the cell members preferred to strike at the French public, and ultimately won through. If true, this exemplifies how the terrorists' personal enemy perception may affect a cell's behavior, even though it operates on behalf of an organization. As I shall discuss subsequently, another Algerian-based cell linked to Doha ended up targeting the Russian embassy in Paris after assessing different targets, including Jewish and American ones.

The overall picture of the terrorists' backgrounds resembled those who were members of GIA cells. With the exception of the French-born Sabour, the cell members were first-generation immigrants to France, Germany and the UK. Apart from Aeroubi Beandali, who was orphaned as a child, they all came from ordinary family backgrounds. Like the entrepreneurs of the GIA network in the 1990s, the man described in the verdict as the cell's diving force, Boukhari, was well educated when compared to the other cell members who had a basic education and survived by doing odd jobs or engaging in crime. The typical pattern was that the cell members first became radicalized over the war in Algeria, and that this radicalization was exacerbated by grievances related to being Muslims in Europe. However, they were finally pushed into militancy by their interactions with Doha's network and their training in Afghanistan. Three members of the cell were recruited individually by Doha's network in France, Germany and the UK, and all four cell members met each other for the first time at the Khalden camp. While Doha supervised the Frankfurt cell from outside, Boukhari was the entrepreneur within.

Born in 1971 in Algeria, he grew up with his parents, two brothers and four sisters, while his father worked on the railways. Boukhari completed high school and attended higher education in mathematics before going to France to continue his studies. After failing to obtain a permit of stay he traveled to the UK where he started to train as a chef. He was unable to complete this training because he failed to obtain a permit to remain in the UK and was expelled back to Algeria. Boukhari returned home when the national insurgency was escalating.

In an interview with the BBC he claimed to have sympathized with FIS, but that he had not joined FIS or the GIA.[35] He soon returned to the UK on a falsified Italian passport, married a Christian British woman in 1995 and subsequently obtained a permanent residence permit. While in London Boukhari was recruited by one of Doha's associates named Noureddine and started to mix with other network members while attending the sermons of Qatada. Noureddine, who had trained in Afghanistan, persuaded Boukhari to attend the camps and prepare for jihad in Algeria. He also showed Boukhari videos of atrocities against Muslims in Algeria, Palestine and Chechnya which made him receptive to the call for jihad. In 1998 Boukhari divorced and remarried a British woman who was an Islamist. With the help of Noureddine and Yacine Aknouche from Doha's network, Boukhari then traveled to Afghanistan via Pakistan in the fall of 1999. In addition to functioning as the cell's operational leader, Boukhari was also involved in the cell's efforts to produce explosives. He explained to the BBC how he had been involved in testing detonators at the camps in Afghanistan.[36]

The other lead figure, Fouhad Sabour, was not as educated as Boukhari, but had a past with the GIA's French network. Born in Romans-sur-Isère to Algerian parents in 1965, Sabour had two brothers and his father worked in construction. He attended a technical high school, and trained as a car-mechanic, although he never completed his training. He survived working odd jobs in France until he left for the UK in 1995, where he became acquainted with GIA activists. He then returned to France where he joined Smaïn Aït Ali Belkacem's GIA network in Lille. Sabour was arrested and interrogated by

French police between June and December 1996. After being released, he traveled to Bosnia and Pakistan together with a fellow militant. In 1999 he was convicted in absentia to three years in prison by a French court for involvement in the Metro bombing of 1995, as well as the subsequent attempt to bomb the TGV railway line near Lille. At that time Sabour was at the Khalden camp in Afghanistan undergoing training with the other cell members.[37]

A third member of the cell, Aeroubi Beandali, fits the description of a misfit who was recruited from criminal networks. His pathway to militancy seemed to be driven more by social grievances than Boukhari and Sabour's. His criminal connections likely explain why he was put in charge of financing and acquiring weapons. Beandali was born in Tiaret, Algeria, in 1975. His parents died in a car accident when he was two, after which his aunt took care of him. Beandali attended a Quranic school, but later enrolled in an ordinary state school. At one point he experienced a traumatic episode when he was beaten by a teacher. After dropping out of school he started training as an electrician, but never completed the training.

He arrived in Germany in 1992 as an asylum seeker, where he received a temporary permit of stay. Because the German authorities lacked the requisite documentation to return him to Algeria, Beandali drifted around several German cities. He used and dealt in drugs and was involved in petty crime. He was convicted of multiple felonies, including theft and assaults. Beandali claims a former Algerian Army officer persuaded him to change his life by showing him videotapes of massacres of women and children by the Algerian Army during the civil war. He was drawn to radical Islam as a result of his shock and horror at seeing these images and began to search for "the truth" in radical mosques.[38] At one point he encountered a member of the Doha network who advised him to look for answers in Afghanistan. He took out all his savings and traveled to Pakistan in November 1999. He subsequently attended Algerian guesthouses and camps in Pakistan and Afghanistan, where he met the other members of the Frankfurt cell.[39]

The last member of the cell, Lamine Marouni, was also a misfit and a "born-again-believer" who went from a troublesome life as a petty criminal to an even more troublesome but self-righteous existence as a jihadi terrorist. Born in Algeria in 1970, Marouni lived in Sheffield, UK, during the eight years prior to his capture in Frankfurt. Marouni was far from pious before embracing radical Islam. He was a known smoker and drinker, and he also dealt drugs. After mixing with extremists in London, his friends say he began to act as a fanatic and intimidated people to make them become more orthodox.

After shaving his head Salafi-style he became known as "Amin the skinhead."[40] He also tried to recruit a friend for training in Afghanistan with a view to joining the jihad in Algeria. Marouni functioned as a foot soldier in the cell, but he also smuggled manuals from Afghanistan, such as one containing instructions on how to produce the poisons ricin and cyanide.[41]

The terrorists seemed to have had mixed motives. At first they tried to convince the court that they had planned to bomb an empty synagogue in Strasbourg as a spontaneous reaction to Israeli transgressions in Palestine, but all evidence pointed to an attack on the Christmas market. Moreover, one cell member, Beandali, admitted that the marketplace was the intended target. Overall, the leaders, Boukhari and Sabour, came across as more ideologically committed and globally oriented than the foot soldiers Marouni and Beandali. For example, whereas the misfit Beandali expressed regrets about his involvement, the entrepreneur Boukhari never admitted to anything. Also, in his interview with the BBC from prison, he called for continued jihad. A twenty-minute reconnaissance video recorded by Boukhari and Sabour in Strasbourg contains statements indicating a dogmatic hatred of non-believers.

When filming people at the Christmas marketplace, Boukhari said: "those are the enemies of God, running around ... they are running and walking, have you seen this enemy of God? He was in fear." Directing the camera towards the crowds encircling the Christmas tree he continued: "these are God's enemies! They dance and are happy. Must they, if God wills [in sha Allah], burn in hell."[42] Their chanting of jihad hymns in the car when going from Frankfurt to Strasbourg to make the recording also demonstrated their affinities with the ideas and culture of jihad.[43] In the BBC interview recorded after the invasion of Iraq, Boukhari expressed grievances related to different contexts. He complained about having been harassed by French police, raged over atrocities against Muslims in Chechnya and Afghanistan and stressed that Iraq was the main battlefield. When describing his own path to militancy he said he had initially dreamt about joining jihad in Chechnya. He ended the interview by proclaiming that he was still a "mujahid," and that "it's the duty of every Muslim to get the Americans and the British out of Iraq."[44]

Beandali testified that his radicalization was driven partly by personal problems as an immigrant, and partly by France's involvement in Algeria. He claimed the cell aimed "to punish France for its policy of support for the Algerian government," which he accused of being guilty of "slaughtering" Muslims.[45] He also downplayed the cell's terrorist intent by saying its main purpose was to ship weapons to Algeria. While talking about his radicalization he told the court how he had transformed from "an irreligious drug dealer on the streets of Germany" into an Islamist extremist, and how he changed back on 11 September 2001. About his arrival in Germany in 1992 he said, "I was a man who loved the joys of life and was very happy," and continued, "I had no relationship to religion and lived in the European style: alcohol, women and hashish."[46] Beandali dated the turning point to 1998, a year before he traveled to Afghanistan, and emphasized the importance of the videos of atrocities in Algeria shown to him by the former Algerian Army officer. Beandali considered these videos "evidence of massacres of women and children by Algerian troops." In analyzing his own reaction to the images, he said, "I was much shaken and decided to change my life, which had previously been devoted to my own wellbeing, to focus on my own country."[47]

Like the other cell members, Lamine Marouni emphasized the Algeria–France dimension. During interrogations and the trial he declared he wanted to avenge the killings of women and children in Algeria and that he held France responsible for the atrocities there. Although Marouni was a misfit and reformed criminal just like Beandali, he seemed to be more extreme and committed. For example, he did not excuse his involvement and showed contempt for the court by saying "I am only in touch with my God. I do not want any contact with unbelievers."[48] While all of the terrorists emphasized radicalization over the situation in Algeria, there was no evidence of involvement by groups in Algeria, or that specific events in Algeria triggered them.

As for claims that harassment by French police contributed to radicalization, it is certainly true that France introduced tough measures against Algerian Islamists both before and after the attacks of 1995. These targeted the support networks of the GIA, the GSPC and the FIS, and forced radicals underground or to relocate to other countries in Europe, as well as Algeria and Afghanistan. In 1998, for example, French security services rounded up scores of GSPC-activists to forestall terrorist attacks during the soccer World Cup to be held in France. It can hardly be ruled out that French counter-terrorism affected the radicalization of the plotters in terms of strengthening their enmity toward France, but also by pushing them into the arms of terrorist recruiters in London. At the same time, the terrorists' antipathy towards France seemed to be rooted primarily in France's Algeria policy, and predated any encounters they may have had with the French security services.

Whereas all cell members expressed grievances about Algeria and France, statements by the cell's entrepreneur, Boukhari, about the situation in Chechnya, Palestine and Iraq proved that the most influential cell member had a global outlook on jihad. Considering how Boukhari stressed the plight of Palestinians as a justification, it is also relevant that the plot coincided with the second intifada after Ariel Sharon's visit to the Temple Heights of Jerusalem.

Because of the Frankfurt cell's ties to al-Qaida via Abu Doha, the terrorist plot should probably be understood as a product of the spiraling enmity between al-Qaida and the West at the time. After the East Africa bombings, the United States began targeting terrorist funding worldwide and intensified the hunt for al-Qaida personnel. The Americans also reached deals with Middle Eastern and North African regimes to have terrorist suspects extradited, or to gain access to them in foreign prisons. For its part, al-Qaida prepared attacks on US and Israeli targets worldwide. Plots by Doha's network to bomb Los Angeles Airport, Israeli tourists in Jordan and the market in Strasbourg were part and parcel of this development. The Frankfurt case demonstrated how the center of gravity for jihadi terrorism in Europe was shifting from Algeria to Afghanistan, and how al-Qaida exploited splits in Algerian jihadism to its advantage.

With the GSPC focusing on Algeria, internationally oriented Algerians in Europe were drawn into al-Qaida's orbit and recruited for global jihad. The situation was ideal from al-Qaida's vantage point as the Algerians had extensive networks in Europe which could be exploited for support activities and attacks. From the Algerians' vantage point, al-Qaida offered infrastructure for training in Afghanistan, and a framework for targeting the West in general and France in particular. The Algerian-based cells seemed to prefer to target France directly, or international targets inside France. Another Algerian-based terrorist cell was uncovered immediately prior to 9/11. This cell was linked to al-Qaida and Doha's network, and was led by an archetypal entrepreneur who would have a profound impact on the evolution of global jihadism in Europe from the late 1990s until the present day.

The network of Djamel Beghal

In the summer of 2001, US and European security services jointly dismantled a terrorist network led by the Algerian Djamel Beghal (thirty-seven), which was preparing suicide attacks on US targets in France and Belgium. The terrorists had close ties to radical preachers in London and some of them had met with bin Laden in Afghanistan. As part of the jihadi scene in London they mixed with Doha's network. However, Beghal was the entrepreneur of a network distinct from Doha's, although it had a similar relationship with al-Qaida in

Afghanistan. Core members of Beghal's network attended the Derunta camp in Jalalabad in 2000, and their stay in Afghanistan was facilitated by the Palestinian Abu Zubaydah, who put them in touch with al-Qaida.

Based on US intelligence, Beghal was arrested at Dubai Airport on 28 July 2001 while traveling to Morocco. When interrogated by United Arab Emirates officials, Beghal admitted to being in charge of a cell preparing attacks against the US embassy and the US Cultural Center in Paris. He told interrogators that al-Qaida had ordered the attacks and transferred money to a bank account in Morocco to finance the operation. He further said that a Tunisian national, Nizar Trabelsi (thirty-one), was going to launch a suicide attack on the US embassy. According to Beghal, the plan was that Trabelsi would forcefully enter the embassy with explosives strapped to his body, while a mini-van packed with explosives would detonate outside the building.[49] When Trabelsi was arrested by Belgian authorities in Rotterdam shortly afterwards he gave a different version of the plot. He admitted preparing an attack, but claimed that the target was the canteen at the US airbase at Kleine Brogel, near the Dutch border. Trabelsi was later convicted by a Belgian court in a trial against twenty-three Islamists accused of involvement in plans to attack Kleine Brogel, and of providing aid to the Tunisian al-Qaida members who killed the Northern Alliance leader Ahmad Shah Massoud in a suicide attack in Afghanistan on 9 September 2001.

Following Beghal's arrest in Dubai, French anti-terrorism police raided apartments in Chilly-Mazarin, Essonne, and arrested several of Beghal's co-conspirators, such as Nabil Bounour, Jean-Marc Grandvizir and his brother-in-law, Johan Bonte (twenty). Another accomplice, the French-Algerian IT-student Kamil Daoudi (twenty-seven), managed to escape to the UK where he was arrested in Leicester and extradited to France. In the Netherlands police arrested the Frenchman Jerome Courtallier, two Algerians, Abdelghani Rabia and Adel Tobbichi, and one Dutch-Ethiopian, Saad Ibrahim, and charged the men with providing cloned credit cards, fake passports and driving licenses to Beghal's network.[50] Jerome Courtallier's brother, David, was also arrested and charged with involvement in the terrorist ring. The investigations also led to the arrest of six militant Islamists in Spain suspected of providing logistical support to Beghal's terrorist network and the GSPC in Algeria.[51] French police confiscated helicopter manuals and aeronautical charts showing air approaches to Paris, which suggests that the terrorists also had plans to attack France from the air. Also, like the 9/11 pilots, several of Beghal's contacts had been taking flying lessons.[52] Furthermore, police secured fake passports and maps of the US embassy in Paris.

While investigating the apartment and several premises visited by Trabelsi in Brussels, Belgian police retrieved an Uzi submachine gun and a recipe for bomb-making. The police in Belgium also seized chemicals suitable for bomb-making in an Egyptian snack bar Trabelsi and other North African extremists had frequented. Explosives experts assessed that the chemicals were sufficient for manufacturing a bomb powerful enough to blow up a building. Investigations also revealed that Beghal and other members of the network belonged to Qatada's following in London and interacted regularly with the preacher. Further inquiries revealed multiple ties to armed groups in North Africa, the Middle East and the Caucasus, and to al-Qaida in Afghanistan.

As noted, the Palestinian jihadi Abu Zubaydah was believed to have been the middleman between Beghal's network and al-Qaida. Born in Saudi Arabia in 1971, Zubaydah joined the armed struggle against the Communists in Kabul in 1991. He was injured in a mortar blast in 1992, and in 1994 he was assigned to the role of coordinator, recruiter and fundraiser for the al-Qaida-affiliated Khalden training camp. Pervez Musharraf described Zubaydah as a high-ranking al-Qaida member and a recruiter of terrorist operatives.[53] Inquiries into Zubaydah's case, after he was captured by the Americans, suggest he had a more passive role as a facilitator of camps and had ideological differences with bin Laden.[54] In any event, different sources portray how Zubaydah assisted recruits traveling from Europe to the training camp, some of whom were later implicated in international terrorist plots.[55] In the case of the Beghal network, the claim that he acted as a messenger between the terrorists and al-Qaida seems to be well founded. In the UK, Beghal cooperated closely with the Leicester-based Ibrahim Benmerzouga (thirty-one) and Baghdad Meziane (thirty-eight), who were convicted of financing terrorism in 2003.[56]

Beghal and other members of the network supposedly met several of al-Qaida's top brass in Afghanistan, including bin Laden, al-Zawahiri, Abu Khabbab and Abu Hafs al-Mauritani.[57] French security officials dubbed Beghal's network "al-Takfir wa'l-Hijra" (Excommunication and flight). This was a reference to an extreme sect in Egypt in the 1960s known as the Society of Muslims (Jamat al-Muslimun) but dubbed al-Takfir wa'l-Hijra by the Egyptian press. The group excommunicated the state and fled into the mountains, from where it waged jihad on the regime and assassinated a state official before the authorities cracked down on the organization. The name was used in reference to Beghal's network because they were known to excommunicate worshippers at the mosques they frequented who did not accept their orthodox and militant version of Islam. However, the label caused some confusion as it led some to believe al-Takfir wa'l-Hijra was an independent and particularly extreme and dangerous terrorist group, although it did not differ much from other al-Qaida affiliates.[58]

Beghal and his accomplices prepared suicide attacks on US targets. Their modus operandi was in tune with al-Qaida's. At the same time, an attack on US interests inside France enabled the terrorists, most of whom were Algerians, to deal a blow to their archenemy. However, there was some confusion about where the attacks were to happen. The designated suicide bomber, Trabelsi, maintained he was supposed to execute a suicide car bomb attack codenamed "victorious" (*muntassir*) against the canteen of the US air base at Kleine Brogel, and that he acted on al-Qaida's orders and received money from the group. He also specified the time of the attack (between 12:00 and 13:00 during lunch time at the base), what car he was going to use (a Mercedes) and the potential casualties (between fifty and seventy Americans). Trabelsi further admitted to having obtained information about the routines at the base from an insider. Trabelsi denied the allegations that the US embassy in Paris was the target and said he did not even know where it was located.[59]

It has been speculated that Trabelsi lied so as not to be tried in Belgium because he believed the courts there would be more lenient towards him, but such claims are hard to verify. With regard to Beghal's confessions from Dubai, it should be noted that he retracted them after arriving in France and claimed that UAE police officers had beaten the confessions out of him. Although medical examinations conducted in France supported his claims of physical abuse, the case against him rested on much more than the confession in Dubai.[60] French intelligence had also picked up signals suggesting that the terrorists had assessed other targets in France, such as the US consulate in Marseilles. However, a common feature of terrorist planning involves assessing a range of ambitious targets before settling for a realistic option.[61]

Like the Frankfurt cell, Beghal's network was well organized and acted according to their training from Afghanistan. There was an internal hierarchy among the terrorists and they fulfilled different functions. Beghal was the overall leader, functioning as recruiter, organizer and ideologue. The IT student Kamel Daoudi was Beghal's protégé and confidant, and due to his technical expertise he was also placed in charge of the cell's online communications. Trabelsi was something of an outsider in the cell and had a conflictual relationship with Beghal. However, he was still assigned with crucial tasks such as scouting for targets and assembling weapons, and, ultimately, with launching a suicide mission.

The terrorists used aliases and fake documents, and they moved around so as to avoid attention. However, while acting secretively in operational matters, the terrorists also exposed themselves to the risk of detection by frequenting mosques, mingling with well-known radicals such as Qatada and taking part in recruitment efforts at Finsbury Park Mosque. Beghal and his accomplices were further involved in a variety of criminal activities such as credit card fraud and trafficking of stolen cars, which could also have jeopardized their plans. Given their links to al-Qaida, the timing of the operation was somewhat curious as it coincided with the final preparations for 9/11. It has been speculated that the plot was a diversion to draw attention away from the Hamburg cell. However, considering that al-Qaida had other terrorist projects pending in Europe that were meant to add to the 9/11 effect, the plans by Beghal and his crew may very well have been part of this broader scheme.

The terrorists' individual backgrounds paralleled those of the GIA and Frankfurt cells. Apart from Trabelsi, the terrorist plot involved Algerian immigrants, French-Algerians and French converts. They were all in their twenties and thirties and survived by working odd jobs, engaging in criminality or receiving welfare. As seen in the previous cases, the entrepreneur and his protégé were more educated and resourceful than the foot soldiers. The terrorists' radicalization revolved around preachers in Europe and training camps in Afghanistan. Central members had joined GIA off-shoots in France and Britain before linking up with al-Qaida. Parallel to the GIA and Frankfurt cases, senior activists recruited among marginalized youths, some of whom were criminals and drug addicts. The plot also exemplified how terrorists exploit their social networks by recruiting among friends and relatives who might be considered trustworthy and can be manipulated more easily than strangers. As for the terrorists' motives, as seen in the previous cases, members of Beghal's network expressed grievances about Algeria, Bosnia, Palestine, Chechnya and Europe. After their stay in Afghanistan they had adopted the position that attacks on US interests in Europe were the best way to address their grievances.

The overall entrepreneur of the cell, Beghal, demonstrates the importance of charisma in recruitment. He was characterized by different sources as highly intelligent, knowledgeable and likeable.[62] Beghal was born in Bordj Bou Arreridj, Algeria, in 1965. Raised in a traditional family among nine siblings he excelled in school and went to France to pursue computer studies in 1987.[63] In France he came to live in the Parisian working-class suburb Corbeil-Essonnes. As he had mastered the French language and married a French woman, with whom he had three children, he was seen as an immigrant who had integrated well. He earned a living through odd jobs and temping, something that caused him to become frustrated because he was ambitious. Struggling with political grievances over the situation for Muslims in Algeria and elsewhere, Beghal gradually embraced an orthodox and militant version of Islam between 1994 and 1997. In 1994 he was known as a religious seeker and follower of Tabligh in Paris. Beghal's radicalization accelerated after he moved to London and came under the influence of Qatada in 1997, with French security services identifying him as an operational terrorist as early as the following year.

Beghal was arrested for the first time during French police raids against GIA cells in 1994, but was released shortly afterwards. Between 1994 and 1997 he preached in radical mosques and centers in Paris, and collected money for Muslims in Bosnia and Chechnya.[64] In 1997 Beghal again caught the attention of the French domestic security intelligence service (DST) during investigations into Algerian-based support networks composed of former GIA members. In the same year he moved his family to Leicester and became a student under Qatada in London. Being part of Qatada's congregation at the Four Feathers Youth Club, he also frequented Finsbury Park and listened to Hamza's sermons. According to French judicial papers, Beghal also drew inspiration from the Moroccan preacher Mohammad al-Fizazi, seen as religious guide by many Moroccan extremists—although Beghal denied this in court.[65] In Leicester, Beghal gathered his own entourage of GIA sympathizers and in London he mingled with a multinational crowd of Algerian, Tunisian, Libyan and Moroccan al-Qaida associates. By 1998 Beghal had become a highly active jihadi recruiter, and a prime example of how interpersonal relationships and personality factor in when people are drawn to extremism.

Members of Beghal's network expressed strong admiration for his communication skills, enthusiasm and knowledge of Islam.[66] Several said it was Beghal who had converted them to Islam, or made them re-discover their faith. He was also a skilled organizer, always on the move, giving orders, making appointments, moving money, people, documents and messages.[67] After a network had formed around Beghal, members in turn started recruiting in mosques, or on the streets. While reaching out to potential recruits, Beghal's men were also known to intimidate fellow Muslims. People who frequented Finsbury Park at the time told *The Guardian* that the group surrounding Beghal was feared for being extreme and violent. There was a rumor that they had executed a Muslim in Afghanistan, for example, after accusing him of apostasy, and a so-called 'snuff movie' of the killing was said to have circulated among the worshippers at Finsbury Park.[68] Beghal's travel patterns illustrate the transnational character of his network. He traveled extensively in Europe, Saudi Arabia and Morocco, and in 2000 he moved his family to Jalalabad and spent time in Derunta with the co-conspirators. In early 2001 Abu Zubaydah was said to have passed a mission on to Beghal from al-Qaida to form a terrorist cell and prepare attacks on US targets in Europe. According to a French security official cited by *The New York Times*, Zubaydah gave him three symbolic gifts—a toothpick, prayer beads and a flask of incense—from bin Laden as a sign that the operation had his blessing.[69]

When setting up the terrorist network Beghal relied on a protégé, the twenty-seven-year-old IT-student Kamel Daoudi, whom he came to know while staying in Paris. Daoudi was born in Algeria in 1974 and raised in France from the age of five. Enraged by developments in Algeria and the treatment of Arabs in France, Daoudi embraced militant Islam in an intellectual manner on the one hand, but also seemed emotionally frustrated, humiliated and unstable.[70] His father, an immigrant to France, was a hospital worker who supported his wife and children in Algeria before he brought them to Europe in 1979. Daoudi lived up to his father's ambitions for him to excel in school and he received good grades.[71] He took classes in French, English, Spanish, Arabic, Latin and ancient Greek and flirted with the idea of becoming an anthropologist or a paleontologist, but pragmatism led him to choose a technical education instead.

At school, French children made fun of the intelligent youngster because of his name and Arab background. At one point he dreamt about becoming a fighter pilot, but due to his poor eyesight he decided to study for a qualification in aeronautical engineering at a French university. He encountered Beghal during his studies and, like the other members of the network, he became fascinated by his persona and knowledge of Islam. Beghal and Daoudi developed a close relationship, and the latter would become entrusted with important tasks such as encrypting online communications from a Parisian cyber-café, reconnaissance and bomb-making.[72] Daoudi also lived together with Beghal in his Paris apartment, as did other recruits from time to time.

Whereas Beghal was able to seduce intellectuals such as Daoudi, he also resonated with different kinds of people, such as a professional soccer-player turned criminal, Nizar Trabelsi, who was to play a key role in the plot. Born in Sfax, Tunisia, in 1970, Trabelsi stood out in Beghal's group. He was a talented footballer who played for the Tunisian national team in his youth and in 1989 he signed a contract with the German club Fortuna Düsseldorf. He played with several German and Belgian teams before his playing career went into decline and came to an end in 1995. Trabelsi earned a decent income, and at one point he owned his own restaurant. According to his teammates and coaches, he came across as a kind, shy and moderately religious person who did not talk about politics. At the same time, he was known to have problems fitting in and was hassled for being Arab and Muslim.[73]

Faced with racism and a failed marriage, Trabelsi started underperforming as an athlete, which resulted in cancelled contracts. He found comfort in drugs and became involved in crime. Between 1994 and 1998 the former athlete was charged with several felonies, including cocaine trafficking, in Germany, Belgium and the Netherlands owing to his involvement in a criminal network. In 1996 Trabelsi met the al-Qaida-associated Baghdad Meziane in Düsseldorf, who was also known as "Abu Abdallah from Leicester."[74] It was Meziane, a good friend of Beghal and a follower of Qatada, who introduced Trabelsi to militant Islam. In 1997 Trabelsi came to know Beghal and he too became fascinated by his eloquence and knowledge of Islam.[75] Trabelsi soon joined Qatada's congregation in London with the other members of the network and traveled extensively in Europe and the Middle East. He interacted with extremists in Germany, Belgium, Netherlands and the UK, and he also traveled to Saudi Arabia, Yemen, Pakistan and Afghanistan. He attended the Derunta training camp with Beghal and the others in 2000, bringing along his second wife, who was staying at a separate camp set up to accommodate the wives and children of trainees.

During the trial in Belgium Trabelsi told the judges he had met bin Laden in Afghanistan and expressed strong admiration and love for the Saudi. He claimed that bin Laden had personally helped him to be listed as a suicide bomber, even though "the list of martyrs was full."[76] Trabelsi further claimed to have visited bin Laden's house in Jalalabad on two separate occasions, staying several days each time, and he also boasted about having played soccer in bin Laden's courtyard. Despite his encounters with bin Laden, Trabelsi was an outsider in Beghal's group. He and his second wife were regarded as impure Muslims by the others. There were also conflicts between Beghal and Trabelsi over the latter's use of money and mixing with Afghans. During the trial Trabelsi seemed less committed than Beghal and Daoudi: he excused his actions before the court and even offered to become an informant.

The other recruits targeted by Beghal were also misfits and drifters, such as the sons of a French butcher and former Catholics, David and Jerome

Courtallier and Beghal's brother-in-law Johan Bonte. The Courtalliers were handsome, athletic and adventure-seeking young men from the French Alps who excelled in sports and were popular with the girls. After their father's business collapsed and their parents divorced, they started to abuse drugs and soon found themselves in a troubled situation with poor prospects for the future. Friends advised David Courtallier to travel to the UK to make a fresh start. After moving there he started frequenting radical mosques.

In 1997 both of the brothers lived in Leicester, UK, and David Courtallier was later living in the apartment of Beghal in Paris, where he met the other people involved in the terrorist network. After being urged to do so by his new friends, he eventually traveled to Afghanistan for training. On his journey to militant Islam, David Courtallier also spent some time in Morocco where he met people who later became associated with the terrorist attacks in Casablanca in 2003 and the Madrid attacks in 2004, such as Jamal Zougam, the brothers Abdelaziz and Salaheddin Benyaich, and Abd al-Karim al-Mejati.[77] Although the Frenchman Johan Bonte appears to have played a lesser role in Beghal's network, he exemplifies how family bonds can often be exploited in jihadi recruitment. He began to mix with other jihadis via his sister who was married to Beghal, and he was soon running errands for terrorists.

The statements attributed to members of Beghal's network did not differ much from those made by the Frankfurt plotters. The terrorists expressed a mixture of grievances over the suffering of Muslims in Algeria, Palestine and other places, and the injustices suffered by Muslims in Europe. The main difference was that the members of Beghal's network made direct references to interaction with al-Qaida and focused more on international matters in line with the latter organization's focus on global jihad. Trabelsi joined the network at a time of personal crisis and was seduced by Beghal and bin Laden.

When interviewed by Belgian radio in prison, the Tunisian said he loved bin Laden "like a father." His defense lawyer said Trabelsi was "under the spell, hypnotized, impressed by Osama bin Laden's piercing eyes and simple life."[78] Elaborating, the lawyer pointed out how Trabelsi's father had abandoned him at an early age, and how the Tunisian saw bin Laden as a father figure. Trabelsi himself said, "I am guilty; I will have to pay for it. What I did is not good, but I had no choice."[79] When talking about his relationship with bin Laden he said, "I don't care about everything he has done—September 11 and all that. I had good relations with him. He helped me and gave me advice."[80] Trabelsi also stressed injustices in Palestine, symbolized by the killing of a child in Israeli military operations, as a motive. Describing the plan to bomb Kleine Brogel he said:

The plan was that I would break through the gates at the Kleine Brogel army base in a Mercedes delivery van carrying a 100-kilogram bomb and crash into the canteen. It would happen between 12:00 and 13:00. Between 50 and 70 American soldiers would be eating there at that time. I would place a photo of a Palestinian child killed by the Jews on the van's dashboard to remind myself of why I was doing it.[81]

However, during the trial he also denounced his own actions, and, using a soccer metaphor, he said that "there will be no second half" to his life as a terrorist. He tried to reassure the court in the following way: "I would not do it again. Violence is not the answer. Look how the Americans reacted after 11 September. Fortunately I can think clearly again. I was a machine then. Even my wife's tears could not move me."[82] Somewhat paradoxically, he also declared, "I love Islam, I love Muslims and I love all human beings, except the Americans."[83]

Unlike Trabelsi, Beghal denied everything in court and revealed nothing about his personal motives. Leaks from his interrogations in the UAE and France indicate that he downplayed his own role in the conspiracy and described himself as a pawn in the hands of al-Qaida. He said that the attack orders came from bin Laden via Zubaydah who told him "that the time to act had come" and that his mission was to stage a suicide attack against the US embassy in Paris. He further said that his main role was to "observe, collect information and assess the extent of the surveillance in place around the embassy."[84] While the French authorities had faced severe criticism for building parts of the case against Beghal upon interrogations that may have involved torture, Beghal's legal defense failed to produce information countering compelling evidence from the wider investigations and testimonies by Beghal's accomplices putting him at the center of the events.

As for Beghal's protégé Kamel Daoudi, his prison memoirs provided a unique glimpse into the jihadi radicalization process. The young computer engineering student expressed hatred toward the Algerian Army for cancelling the 1992 elections and repressing the Islamists. He raged about France and other Western nations' support for the Algerian regime and injustices against Muslim immigrants in France. He said that during the conflict in Algeria he "started to worry about religious and political questions."[85] He criticized the French authorities for doing "everything possible to ensure than Algeria would not be an Islamic state. It backed an illegitimate and profoundly one-sided regime by sending weapons, helicopters and even the Foreign Legion."[86] Daoudi interpreted the eviction of his family from an apartment in a middle-class area, and relocation to a gritty suburb, as another sign of a French conspiracy against Muslims.

In the memoir Daoudi convincingly portrayed his radicalization as an intellectual process, which involved reading "the great contemporary writers of political Islam."[87] He said that "massacres committed by the Algerian army were the last straw for me."[88] He also traveled to Algeria to see the suffering of Algerian Muslims for himself. Using typical al-Qaida rhetoric, Daoudi linked the war in Algeria to injustices against Muslims in Bosnia, Iraq, Kosovo, Afghanistan and Palestine, and blamed it all on the Christian–Jewish Crusader alliance "influenced by atheism."[89] According to Daoudi, "the West hated us because we were Arabs and Muslims."[90] While speaking the language of al-Qaida, Daoudi denied having ties to the organization. He maintained that "Al-Qaida did not assign me the task of committing any kind of terrorist attack in Europe or elsewhere."[91] Daoudi concludes the memoirs by stating:

> my ideological commitment is total and the reward of glory for this relentless battle is to be called a terrorist. I accept the name of terrorist if it is used to mean that I terrorize a one-sided system of iniquitous power and a perversity that comes in many forms. I have never terrorized innocent individuals and I will never do so. But I will fight any form of injustice and those who support it. My fight will only end in my death or in my madness.[92]

In contrast to Daoudi, statements by other misfits and drifters linked to Beghal indicated more coincidental and superficial reasons for joining jihad. Referring to the dead-end life in his home village, the French convert David Courtallier said "I couldn't see a way out," and he seemed to have been driven by a combination of boredom, a lack of options and a desire for adventure rather than ideology.[93] When describing his journey to training camps in Afghanistan, Courtallier said "going there was going to be great ... I had never traveled ... I was taken care of totally." Recalling his first mosque visit, he said "it was impressive, all these people in the process of finding themselves. There was a serenity that showed on their faces." While Courtallier may have embraced the ideology once he was part of the network, his statements still represent something different from the step-by-step intellectual process seen in the radicalization narratives of Daoudi and Beghal.

The terrorist network overseen by Djamel Beghal resembled the Frankfurt cell in terms of the Algerian connection. The war in Algeria was an individual motive for cell members, and some of them had engaged in support activism for the GIA or GSPC. At the same time, the links to al-Qaida were stronger and the attack plan was more consistent with al-Qaida's ideology. Notably, as with the other cells discussed in this chapter, the terrorists emphasized injustices and racism against Muslims as factors in their radicalization. Another aspect of the case worth highlighting is the cell's appointment of one member in charge of online communication. While the GIA used the Internet for propaganda, there does not appear to be any evidence that GIA cells used online communications for operational purposes. Nor does there seem to be any evidence that the Frankfurt plotters used online communication, as is perhaps best exemplified by the reliance of the cell-leader, Boukhari, on a notebook from Afghanistan for operational advice. The Internet would gradually take on a more significant role in terrorist cell activities from the mid-2000s onwards.

Beghal's terrorist network was made up almost exclusively of Algerians, who were drawn to jihadism in Europe in the 1990s and early 2000s. Beghal himself would continue to influence patterns of jihadi terrorism in Europe from behind bars in the Fleury-Mérogis Prison near Paris.[94] The charismatic terrorist became a role model for delinquents who surfaced in terrorist investigations. Moreover, shortly after his release in 2010 he was implicated in a plot to free the GIA terrorist Smain Aït Ali Belkacem, for which he is still serving time. However, from 2001 onwards other segments of al-Qaida's networks would contribute to global jihad in Europe. An interesting example was a plot by a Jordanian terrorist cell to attack Jews in Germany. What makes this case particularly relevant today is that the plot belonged to Tawhid, which later evolved into the Islamic State (IS).

Tawhid

In 2002 Germany was the scene of a plot by Jordanian jihadis. On 23 April 2002 German anti-terrorism police arrested nine individuals in Germany's Ruhr region on suspicion of plotting attacks against Jewish targets in Berlin and Düsseldorf. The cell belonged to Tawhid. In contrast to the Frankfurt cell and Beghal's network, there were few indications that al-Qaida was closely involved in the plot.[95] Although Tawhid cooperated with al-Qaida, al-Zarqawi had his own ambitions in the Levant, and may have embarked on international terrorism on his own.

The members of Tawhid's German cell were Mohammed Abu Dhess (thirty-six), Shadi Abdullah (twenty-seven), Ashraf al-Dagma (thirty-three), Ismail Shalabi and Djamel Moustafa (twenty-nine).[96] They had all been involved in a support network for Tawhid in Germany. This network was linked to the group's camp in Herat. It was also linked to other Tawhid cells in Europe and the German branch of a broader support network for al-Qaida and the Taliban in Europe. When interrogated, one member of the cell named several Tawhid members in the UK and Ireland.[97] There had also been contacts between members of the German Tawhid cell and people linked to the 9/11 Hamburg cell. Moreover, several of the plotters had spent time in al-Qaida-run camps in Kandahar, or Tawhid's camp in Herat.

The plot in Germany was overseen by al-Zarqawi from Iran when he spent some time there during the spring of 2002 after fleeing Afghanistan. The legal case was based upon interrogations, testimonies and surveillance such as phone conversation transcripts, but the police also confiscated jihadi propaganda, computers, forged travel documents, forgery equipment and weapons. In October 2005 Mohammed Abu Dhess, Ashraf al-Dagma and Ismail Shalabi were convicted and sentenced to six to eight years in prison. In late November 2003, Shadi Abdullah was sentenced to four years in prison. Abdullah was treated more leniently because he had cooperated as a witness. Djamel Moustafa was sentenced to five years in prison for his support. Tawhid's German network was supervised by Mohammed Abu Dhess, and was originally fundraising and trafficking false documents for jihadis in Afghanistan. The network spanned multiple cities including Krefeld, Beckum, Munich, Nurnberg, Duisburg, Essen and Hamburg. Before the German counter-terrorism crackdowns, the network had generated some 150,000 euros.[98]

Investigations uncovered some interesting aspects of the group's relationship with al-Qaida. According to one member of the cell, the funds collected in Germany were to be channeled to Afghanistan via al-Qaida contacts. The man in charge of this insisted that most of the funds should go to al-Qaida and that the Taliban should also receive its share. The money was to be sent to Afghanistan via a hawala contact in Duisburg, and divided into three parts: 50 percent for al-Qaida, 25 percent for Tawhid and 25 percent for the Taliban.[99] Reflecting the fact that Tawhid was not part of al-Qaida, al-Zarqawi was furious when he heard of this demand and refused to agree to it.

Tawhid pursued its own agenda beyond its relationship with al-Qaida, and it needed funds to ignite jihad in Jordan and terrorism against Israeli interests in the Middle East. Judicial documents describe Tawhid as a hierarchical organization, and the terrorist cell in Germany also had a fixed structure with the entrepreneur Mohammed Abu Dhess as leader, his protégé al-Dagma as second-in-command—while the misfits and drifters Shadi Abdullah and Ismail Shalabi played subordinate yet operationally significant roles. Abdullah, for example, was tasked with gathering weapons, and he also conducted reconnaissance and was involved in discussions about targets.

It is believed the cell had decided to assassinate a Jew through the use of a silenced pistol in Berlin, and to execute an attack with hand grenades or a pressure cooker bomb against a Jewish-owned restaurant/discothèque in Düsseldorf. There was no concrete evidence that the attacks would involve suicide bombers. However, in a bugged phone call between Abu Dhess and al-Zarqawi on 18 October 2001, the former offered himself up as a martyr.[100] Interestingly, al-Zarqawi replied that Dhess was too important to be martyred at this point, exemplifying how jihadis pragmatically safeguard organizational capacities and entrepreneurs.

While preparing, the terrorists used aliases, communicated in codes, employed falsified travel documents and other IDs, and undertook reconnaissance of targets. According to the cell's code-language, "apples" meant hand grenades, and potential targets were spoken of as girls who were suitable for marriage. References to marriage are commonly used by jihadis when talking about their operations, the most famous example being the 9/11 attacks which were spoken of as "the big wedding," and there have been several examples of this in Europe. As for the timing of the plot, it should be noted that the original plans seem to have predated the invasion of Afghanistan in which German troops participated. According to judicial documents, the plans were finalized between 7 and 12 September 2001 in a meeting between Dhess and al-Zarqawi in Tehran.[101] In the wake of the invasion of Afghanistan, al-Zarqawi also asked the cell to acquire forty false travel documents and a Moroccan passport for himself, probably with the intention of facilitating the relocation of members of his group from Afghanistan to other countries. The cell in Germany acquired the requisite documents on the black market with money from one of al-Zarqawi's contacts in Saudi Arabia.

The cell started preparing for an attack shortly after the 2001 meeting with al-Zarqawi in Iran. By January 2002 the terrorists were assessing targets and Abdullah undertook reconnaissance of the Jewish Museum in Berlin, as well as a Jewish-owned café and discothèque in Düsseldorf, the latter of which was frequented by gay people. Over the following months Abdullah, Shalabi and Moustafa worked to obtain weapons and fake documents from criminal networks in Germany and Denmark. The travel documents were transported to al-Zarqawi inside Iran via a courier in February 2002. Yet by early April 2002 al-Zarqawi had started to become irritated by the slow progress and ordered Dhess to speed things up. In a parallel to what happened with the Beghal network, fierce infighting occurred between the entrepreneur Dhess and Abdullah—the latter of whom fits the description of a misfit. The two, who were longtime friends, started quarreling over the target selection and the leadership of the cell. Al-Zarqawi ultimately had to mediate between the them, and sent Ashraf al-Dagma from Iran with new instructions.

The Tawhid cell reflected the fact that jihadi terrorism in Europe was no longer confined to North Africans. The first example of this, which also occurred in Germany, was the 9/11 Hamburg cell. The cell was Arab-based but multinational, including Egyptian, Lebanese, Yemeni, Moroccan, Saudi and other nationalities. However, multinational cells would become more common in Europe after the invasion of Iraq in 2003. The members of the Tawhid cell were Jordanian immigrants to Germany in their late twenties or thirties. They hailed from ordinary if troubled family backgrounds. In Europe they lived unassuming immigrant lives, surviving on welfare, odd jobs or petty crime. It seems that all of the members of the terrorist cell started to embrace militant Islam in Germany before they visited training camps in Afghanistan.

Like the Beghal network, the Tawhid case exemplified the role of entrepreneurs and social ties in recruitment. The leader, Dhess, reached out to old friends and social misfits when setting up the cell. Dhess was born in Jordan in 1964.[102] In his hometown of Irbid he was known for being a basketball player and the lead singer in a band, in which Abdullah was drummer. He first traveled to Germany in 1992, but, as he could not obtain the necessary permits, he returned to Jordan shortly afterwards. In 1995 Dhess and Abdullah traveled together to Europe. Abdullah applied for asylum in Belgium and stayed there while the application was pending. Dhess applied for asylum in Germany under the pretense that he was an Iraqi refugee. After obtaining a permit, he lived on social welfare in Beckum and Essen, where he first began to mingle with Islamists. He married a Czech Muslim woman and was gradually absorbed into militancy. Seeking out militant networks and radical preachers he traveled to Belgium, Austria, Syria, Iran and the UK. In the UK Dhess joined Qatada's following, and it seems likely that he was in the UK when he joined Tawhid and became tasked with coordinating the group's German network.

The story of Dhess's comrade, Abdullah, clearly shows how jihadi networks offer opportunities for people in personal crisis. It also indicates how loyalty and companionship between friends matter in recruitment. Abdullah was born in Jordan in 1976 and his family hailed from Palestine.[103] Abdullah's father worked in construction and his mother was a housewife. After finishing elementary school he began training as a hairdresser. He then shifted to training as an automobile technician, but quit after suffering an electrical shock. He subsequently traded in used clothes, and played drums in Dhess's band. Abdullah fought with his parents over his failure to complete his education or get a proper job, in contrast to his successful brothers. He said the main reasons he left Jordan were his parents' disappointment with him and that he felt (socially unacceptable) sexual attractions toward younger men. If the latter is true, he would be the only known example of someone with homosexual tendencies joining jihadi cells in Europe, which is somewhat surprising as Islamist extremists are fiercely opposed to homosexuals and call for them to be executed.

In 1995 Abdullah traveled to Europe with Dhess and filed for asylum in Belgium. While the application was pending Abdullah developed a serious drug and alcohol problem. When he failed to obtain asylum, Dhess invited him to Germany, where he filed another asylum application. In Beckum, Dhess introduced Abdullah to a group of Islamists gathering at a secretive underground mosque at the premises of a mysterious scrap-dealer who functioned as one of Tawhid's recruiters. However, the addict did not seem to be ready to take up religion at first, and did not join this group.

He drifted around as a homeless person and continued to use and deal drugs, but in 1998 he received help from followers of a Tablighi mosque in Krefeld, kicked the habit and concentrated on Islam. He was offered food and housing from a mosque on the condition that he followed religious classes. In 1999 he went on pilgrimage to Mecca together with other worshippers at the mosque, and traveled from there to Afghanistan via Pakistan. Abdullah told investigators that in Mecca he met with bin Laden's son-in-law, Abdullah al-Makki, who persuaded him to go to Afghanistan and provided him with the necessary contacts to do so. Abdullah described al-Makki as a skilled recruiter, emphasizing the way in which he gradually introduced recruits to violent ideology.[104] Abdullah spent time in training camps in Afghanistan between December 1999 and August 2001 before joining Dhess's German cell.

The record of Abdullah's interrogations, published by Peter Bergen, provides a detailed account of what European recruits would experience in al-Qaida's camps.[105] He described a system designed to socialize the recruits into jihadi life and thinking, and how veterans handpicked recruits from European countries for international terrorism. Abdullah said that he first enrolled at al-Qaida's "Airport camp" in Kandahar. At this camp he received paramilitary training and was indoctrinated by well-known al-Qaida leaders, including bin Laden, Mohammed Atef, Saif al-Adel, Ramzi bin al-Shibh (one of the organizers of 9/11), and others. He also claimed to have met the twentieth hijacker who was supposed to have taken part in the 9/11 attacks, Zacarias Moussaoui, at the camp. Abdullah further explained that he first met al-Zarqawi in Kabul in March 2000. The reason for the meeting was that Abdullah had been told to convey a message to al-Zarqawi from Dhess in Germany, and Abdullah claimed that the two of them developed a "close, trusting relationship."[106] According to Abdullah, in May 2001 he was ordered by al-Zarqawi to team up with Dhess's cell for an operation in Germany.

As in the previous cases of jihadism in Europe, the Tawhid cell acted on orders from leaders based abroad. The other members of the cell had similar backgrounds to Abdullah and were drawn into Tawhid's networks by recruiters and friends. One of them, Ashraf al-Dagma, was born in 1969 in Gaza. Married, and later divorced, al-Dagma was not a pious Muslim when he first went to Germany in 1994. He applied for political asylum on the grounds that he was being persecuted by the PLO. Al-Dagma soon became involved in crime, and dealt cocaine and heroin at the Zoo Station in Berlin. He was eventually arrested and decided to change his life, re-discovering Islam while inside jail. When he was released he moved from Berlin to Beckum, Westphalia, where he worked as a cleaner and a waiter. In Beckum he joined the underground mosque of the scrap-dealer and Tawhid recruiter, in which he met the other cell members.[107]

The Tawhid cell issued no statements, and only Abdullah offered a full confession. The court questioned his reliability as a witness on the basis of psychiatric assessments, and was concerned that he may have overplayed his own part in the cell and his interaction with al-Qaida.[108] However, in most respects Abdullah's account was consistent with what Nizar Trabelsi of Beghal's network said about his stay in Afghanistan. Moreover, Abdullah was deemed trustworthy enough to be used as a key witness in several trials against suspected terrorists in Europe, such as Mounir al-Mutassadeq, an affiliate of the 9/11 Hamburg cell.[109]

Similar to the case of Djamel Beghal, the Tawhid cell's entrepreneur Mohammed Abu Dhess seemed to be more committed than his accomplices. While Abdullah, like Nizar Trabelsi, made confessions, excused his actions and denounced terrorism, Dhess acted more like Beghal. He denied that the cell ever planned an attack against Jews in Germany, adding that although he hated the Israeli system he did not "hate Jews as Jews."[110] However, the fact that Dhess offered himself as a suicide bomber in a phone-call with al-Zarqawi leaves little doubt about his commitment.

As opposed to Dhess, Abdullah talked at length to interrogators about his radicalization.[111] He described grievances related to his upbringing in Jordan, his life as an immigrant in Europe and his experiences as a recruit in Afghanistan. With regard to Jordan he emphasized how his family was poor and that he had troublesome relationships with other family members. As for immigrant life in Europe he stated that his dream of a new life outside Jordan culminated in feelings of emptiness. Moreover, he complained that his drug habit made him spend all his money. However, it was Abdullah's stay in Afghanistan and the interaction with al-Qaida and Tawhid that channeled his frustrations towards violent objectives.

The German Tawhid plot seems to have reflected the enemy perception and ambitions of al-Zarqawi. However, it is perfectly conceivable that al-Qaida was involved in the process, encouraging and supporting the plans. The organization certainly facilitated the training of Tawhid personnel and influenced the radicalization of cell members, such as Abdullah. Unlike in the Beghal case, there was nothing to suggest that the cell considered striking US targets, something which was a priority for al-Qaida at the time. Al-Zarqawi was known to prioritize jihad against Jordan, followed by Israel and then Shias. His group did not focus on the United States until it was reinvented as al-Qaida's branch inside Iraq. Most plots by Tawhid before the invasion of Iraq targeted Jordan, and if Tawhid in Germany acted independently, one might ask why it did not aim for Jordanian interests in Germany, such as the embassy in Berlin.

One possible explanation is that Tawhid could harm Jordan at home and regionally, whereas Israeli targets were easier to harm internationally. Another possible explanation is that Tawhid had made a compromise with al-Qaida. Tawhid still depended on cooperation with al-Qaida and attacks on Jews would serve the interest of both groups, hurting common enemies, while strengthening the impression that global jihad had reached Europe. However, considering al-Zaqawi's personal ambitions, his reputation for hardheadedness and his dissatisfaction with having to share money with al-Qaida, it could very well be the case that the plot in Germany was all Tawhid, and an opportunity to elevate Tawhid's international status and garner support for his goal of bringing down the Jordanian regime and extending jihad in the region. The fact that the cell does not seem to have considered a strike against German institutions or German society as a whole also points to the idea that the terrorists were primarily driven by factors related to the Middle East.

At the time of the plot, there was actually ample reason for jihadis to target Germany—the German authorities had implemented new anti-terrorism laws and had cracked down on jihadi networks as part of the 9/11 investigation.

Moreover, Germany had decided to deploy troops as part of ISAF. As noted earlier, Tawhid's plans to launch an attack in Germany are likely to have been finalized before the invasion of Afghanistan, but the cell could still have changed targets to send a political message to Germany if this was a priority. The decision not to target Germany or German society as a whole, or strike at US targets, which had the highest priority for al-Qaida at the time of the plot, supports the theory that this was al-Zarqawi's project rather than al-Qaida's. Furthermore, it cannot be ruled out that international events contributed to the terrorists' determination to kill Jews. In March 2002 the Israelis launched Operation Defensive Shield in response to the Intifada, and the month before the interception of the German cell Israeli fighter jets bombed targets inside Palestine, killing hundreds of Palestinians and wounding more than 1,000.

Overall, like the Frankfurt cell and the Beghal network, the Tawhid case reflected an internationalization of jihadi actors that had been focusing nationally and regionally. At the same time, although Tawhid was linked to al-Qaida, it pursued a different agenda, where Americans and Europeans were secondary to the regional enemies, and the groups seem to have been in a kind of marriage of convenience based upon compromises. Tawhid benefited from training camps in return for money and other services, and was perhaps inspired by bin Laden's focus on international terrorism without buying fully into global jihad. A similar duality characterized the final case to be addressed in this chapter, an Algerian, Abu Doha-linked terrorist cell uncovered in France in late 2002. However, this cell was a more clear-cut case of the transnationalization of jihad.

Chechen network

In December 2002 French police dismantled an Algerian terrorist cell plotting bomb attacks against the Russian embassy on boulevard Lannes in the sixteenth arrondissement, Paris. The terrorists had extensive international connections and were linked to the networks of Doha and al-Zarqawi, al-Qaida, Algerian groups and Chechen mujahidin. The first arrests were made in squatter apartments in the French suburbs and in the village of Cerbère on the Spanish border.

The core conspirators were Merouane Benahmed (twenty-nine), Menad Benchellali (twenty-nine), Noureddine Merabet (twenty-eight), Nabil Bounour, Mohamed Marbah and Ahmed Belhout. Benahmed was the cell's entrepreneur and leader. His protégé and second-in-command, Merabet, was arrested in Cerbère while on his way to alert an affiliated cell in Barcelona about the French counter-terrorism operations. Around the core cell members were a substantial number of associates (friends and family) who were involved in jihadi support activities. Some of these associates had a history in jihadi activism and connections to jihadi groups and training camps abroad, whereas others were novices in the field. French investigators dubbed the terrorist plotters the "Chechen network" because of their ties to Chechnya.

The core members of the cell were veterans of the GIA and its spin-offs in Algeria who had fled to Europe and formed support networks, attended training camps in Afghanistan and the Caucasus, and eventually began to plot an attack in Paris. The cell received support from two associates of Doha named Said Arif and Mabrouk Echiker (known as Moutana). The latter was based in Frankfurt, and his subsequent death in Chechnya would become a motivating factor for the cell. The plotters also received support from a militant based in Spain named Mohamed Tahraoui. Tahraoui headed a support cell in Barcelona, which was part of Doha's network, and there were regular contacts between the Barcelona cell and the operational terrorists in France. Arif coordinated contacts between the terrorist cell in Paris and other members of Doha's network in the UK and Afghanistan.

According to the French verdicts, individual members of the Chechen network also forged ties to al-Zarqawi's Tawhid network and the al-Qaida-handler Abu Zubaydah.[112] Benahmed's group in Paris initially focused on supporting training camps in the Caucasus. One important function of the group was to gather money for families of martyred Chechen mujahidin.[113] The funds were accumulated primarily through criminal activities such as the trafficking of falsified documents, electronics and stolen cars. The vehicles were stolen in Spain and Germany, and smuggled to North Africa for sale.

According to the verdicts, Benahmed's cell also supported jihadi groups in Algeria and Afghanistan, but Chechnya was its main focus in the time leading up to the arrests. The physical evidence against the Chechen network included, among other things, falsified documents, bank notes comprising 21,095 euros, 4,380 USD and 116 riyals, one unused NBC protection suit, one sender–receiver device believed to be a detonator in-the-making, chemicals suitable for the manufacture of TATP and bottles of butane gas. Police also confiscated diverse electronic equipment suitable for bomb-making, texts attributed to the GIA, FIS and another group in Algeria known as the Protectors of the Salafi Call, as well as documentaries about al-Qaida's attacks in Bali and the injustices committed by Israel in Palestine.[114]

The Chechen network's target selection differed from past patterns of jihadi terrorism in Europe. Because the cell involved ex-GIA members and was linked to al-Qaida, one would have expected that they would either target France or the United States (like the Frankfurt cell and the Beghal network)—rather than Russia. However, the cell had in fact assessed other targets and attack methods, including attacks with toxic gases on US, Jewish or French targets. For example, there had been suggestions of striking Chatelet metro station, a Naf-Naf shop, the Eiffel Tower and police stations.[115] Witnesses also described how the plotters had talked about attacking "unbelievers" in general, without specifying any nationality.[116] However, as will be discussed later, a number of events took place in the run-up to the plot which made the terrorists bent on harming Russia.[117]

Perhaps as a result of having trained with al-Qaida personnel in Georgia during 2001, the cell members were security conscious, using fake documents and aliases, routinely shifting meeting places, and hiding their views and activities from family members. However, while taking some security precautions, the plotters also exposed themselves to unnecessary risks which jeopardized their plans. Three central members of the cell (including the cell's leader), were arrested at Barcelona airport for stealing a laptop, calculator and travel documents from an American tourist, for example.[118] As will become evident throughout this book, similar recklessness was observed in numerous jihadi cells in Europe, which at the very least shows how jihadis in Europe were not exactly risk averse.

The genuinely transnational nature of the Chechen network is reflected in the cell members' travel patterns. Benahmed and his accomplices traveled extensively in Europe and the Muslim world (the UK, France, Spain, Italy, Austria, Germany, Algeria, Turkey, Afghanistan, Georgia, Saudi Arabia), and during the summer of 2001 members of the network attended training camps in the Pankisi Valley of Georgia with the intention of joining the jihad in Chechnya. These camps had originally been set up by the Saudi leader of the Arab foreign fighters in Chechnya, Emir Khattab, and were run by his deputy Abou Walid al-Ghamdi after Khattab was killed.

Encounters and events at the camps in Georgia appear to have influenced the terrorists' decision to strike in Paris. Two Jordanian al-Qaida associates at the camps, known by the aliases Abu Hafs and Abu Atiya, paid special attention to recruits from Europe and instructed them to return home and prepare terrorist attacks on US and Jewish targets in Italy, France and the UK.[119] Abu Hafs fought and acted as a trainer under Khattab during the 1990s, and he is further believed to have acted as an envoy of bin Laden in Chechnya and Georgia.[120] Abu Atiya has been portrayed as Abu Hafs's assistant who was in charge of the camps in Georgia when the latter traveled in Chechnya. At some point, Abu Atiya is also alleged to have forged ties to al-Zarqawi and Tawhid, and started to work as a representative of Tawhid in Georgia.[121] However, part of this deal was that Abu Atiya was granted autonomy with regard to organizing international attacks on Russian targets. In Georgia, Abu Hafs and Abu Atiya instructed recruits from Europe in the use of toxic substances, and committed themselves to supply international terrorist cells with explosives. After 9/11, the United States and Russia placed pressure on Georgia to shut down the camps in Pankisi and to stop foreign fighters from entering Chechnya. Many of those who were obstructed returned to their respective countries determined to harm Russian interests on the international arena instead.[122]

As part of this development, Benahmed's group returned to France from Georgia between September and November 2001. In March 2002, Benahmed, Benchellali, Merabet, Tahraoui and Arif attended a coordination meeting for North African jihadis (the Doha network) held in Barcelona. According to one witness, the purpose of this meeting was to "establish the goals of the Islamists' movement in Europe."[123] The possibility cannot be excluded that the final decision to launch an attack in Paris was taken at this meeting, because shortly after, in April/May 2002, Benahmed's cell started making concrete preparations.

The terrorists' radicalization pathways were similar to those of previous Algerian jihadis in Europe, but stood out as almost all of them had actual fighting experience from Algeria. Key members of the cell hailed from the same city of Chlef, west of the capital Algiers. They defected from the GIA during the reigns of Zitouni and Zouabri and joined the rival armed group dubbed the Protectors of the Salafi Call. In 1999 they migrated via Morocco to France, Spain and other European countries and meshed with networks composed of GIA defectors who had forged ties to al-Qaida's camps in Afghanistan. Like many other ex-GIA, several members of the Chechen network had spent time in the Khalden training camp in Afghanistan between 1997 and 1998, several years before they took up training again in Georgia.

The cell was composed of Algerian migrants in their twenties and thirties. Following the familiar pattern among Algerians, they were from poor backgrounds and pursued criminal activities to cover living expenses and fund jihad. As with the members of Beghal's network, the members of Benahmed's group were married with children. Numerous cases in the history of jihadi terrorism in Europe illustrate that there is no contradiction between being a family man and partaking in high-risk activities. This also applies to foreign fighters who bring their wives and children to conflict zones. Benahmed's wife was arrested and charged with complicity in the plot but was later acquitted. While Benahmed was the leader of the Chechen network, witnesses said he received guidelines from someone in Georgia.[124] This was likely a reference to Abu Hafs or Abu Atiya, who is believed to have persuaded the cell to launch an attack in France. Witnesses described Merabet as Benahmed's right-hand man.[125]

Benahmed was born in Algeria in 1973. Claiming "it was the guerilla or death," he joined the GIA as a youth and became a local emir.[126] He soon earned a reputation as an explosives expert.[127] When the GIA became too extreme under Zitouni, Benahmed defected and joined the Al-Furqan Battalion, which was merging with the Horror Battalion. These former GIA battalions had declared war on the mother group and took the name the Protectors of the Salafi Call to underline the idea that they were the true Muslims while the GIA had deviated from the straight path. Wanted by the regime for involvement in terrorism and by the GIA for assassinating GIA fighters, in 1999 Benahmed migrated to Spain, together with fellow fighters from Chlef, including Tahraoui and Belhout.

They all applied for political asylum. During the summer of 2000 Benahmed went to Germany under the cover of researching business opportunities.[128] It is believed that he tutored the Frankfurt cell on how to assemble bombs for their planned attack in Strasbourg while on this trip. In 2001 Benahmed settled in La Courneuve with his wife. He had spent time in France, Algeria, Spain, Morocco, Italy, Austria, Germany, Turkey and Georgia before he was arrested in Paris. The case of Benahmed is yet another example of the power of charisma in recruitment. One of his co-conspirators affectionately described him as "intelligent, with efficient speaking skills, having certain influence on the others, and all authority to take decisions."[129] His wife described him as being stern in religious matters and as hating non-believers.

Merabet, Benahmed's protégé, was born in Chlef, Algeria, in 1974 and finished high school before migrating to France. He left France after being arrested for violating immigration legislation and drugs offences, and stayed in Germany between 1994 and 1999, where he filed an asylum application. When the request was turned down, he returned to Algeria and became involved in the trafficking of stolen cars. In a parallel to the case of Dhess and Abdullah of the Tawhid cell, Benahmed helped his old friend from Chlef, Merabet, to return to France using fake documents.[130] Merabet trained as a member of Benahmed's group in Georgia in 2002 together with Benahmed, Moutana, Marbah, Benchellali and Arif, with the aim of fighting the Russians in Chechnya. In Georgia, Merabet met face-to-face with Abu Hafs and Abu Atiya as well as the main Chechen warlord Shamil Basayev.[131] Under the auspices of Abu Atiya, Merabet prepared some toxic agents, which he smuggled into France via Turkey.[132] Back in Europe Merabet shuttled between Spain, France and Germany engaging in support activities and attack preparations. Merabet was also in charge of trafficking stolen cars from Europe to Algeria, which was the main source of the network's income.

Benchellali was born in Lyon in 1973. He was the only homegrown element in Benahmed's cell, and he was a trusted operative. According to the case files, in addition to taking part in decisions, he was responsible for "everything related to chemical material."[133] Moreover, the French-Algerian was Internet-savvy and said to be a frequent visitor to jihadi websites. Benchellali was known to be secretive about his religious and political convictions, and took measures to ensure his own security, such as wearing fake glasses to alter his appearance.[134] From the mid-1990s Benchellali traveled to a number of different countries as part of his religious awakening, as is often the case when individuals seek to become jihadis. He went to Sudan, Syria, Jordan, Saudi Arabia and Egypt for Arabic-language courses, religious studies and hajj. He also traveled to Italy, the UK, Switzerland, Spain and Turkey for different purposes, including business and criminal activities. In 1998 he gravitated towards London and the Four Feathers Youth Club, where he worked for a while as an assistant to Qatada.

Benchellali admitted he was familiar with Doha's network and that he had sent his brother Mourad Benchellali and his friend Nizar Sassi to Afghanistan for training via Doha's contacts in the UK. He denied having received training, but several witnesses placed him at camps in Afghanistan in 1999/2000. His brother Mourad and Nizar Sassi confirmed that Menad had put them in contact with Doha's deputy in London, Rabah Kadri, who vouched for them and helped organize the journey from London to Pakistan. Illustrating the close, direct connections to jihadis in London and training camps in Afghanistan, Mourad and Nizar said that a reference to Kadri ensured that they were welcome at the Algerian guesthouse in Jalalabad, which was reportedly supervised by an ex-GIA member known as Abu Jaffar.[135]

Benchellali also exemplifies how jihadism runs in families and involves siblings, wives and, occasionally, the parents of terrorists. Menad's father, mother and brothers Mourad (twenty-three) and Hafez were also ardent extremists who took part in recruitment and fundraising for the camps in Afghanistan and Chechen mujahidin. Mourad was part of the Chechen network and attended training camps in Afghanistan, where he was captured by US forces during the invasion and detained at Guantanamo before being extradited to France. His father, Chellali Benchellali, acted as a radical imam at the Abou Bakr Mosque in Vénissieux, Rhône. Interestingly, among Menad's mother's belongings investigators retrieved a letter linking her son to Beghal, thereby illustrating the overlap between European jihad networks and Beghal's centrality in them.[136] After Menad was arrested for his part in the embassy plot, members of his family grew increasingly extreme and in 2004 several of them were arrested for planning and preparing attacks with biological agents inside France.[137]

The Chechen network differed from past cases in that the terrorists cited three specific motives. The first was to avenge the "elimination of the members of the Chechen commando who took a Moscow theatre audience hostage."[138] This was a reference to the Chechen terrorists, led by Movsar Barayev, who took the audience hostage at the Dubrovka theatre in October 2002. Barayev was the nephew of Arbi Barayev, a warlord heading the Special Purpose Islamic Regiment from his stronghold near Grozny. Arbi was killed in June 2001 and replaced by Movsar. In a much-criticized counter-terrorism operation, Russian Special Forces pumped an unknown type of gas into the theatre and killed forty terrorists and more than 100 hostages.

The second stated motive was the death of Emir Khattab in April 2002, who is believed to have died after being poisoned by Russian agents.[139] The third motive was the death of Mabrouk Echiker (Moutana), who was killed by Russian forces in Chechnya. The aforementioned Moutana was a close associate of Benahmed's cell and a member of Doha's network based in Frankfurt, who had managed to cross the border into Chechnya and joined the combat there. According to one witness, during conversations in one of the squatter apartments used as a meeting place by the cell, Benahmed put forward the idea of avenging Moutana by attacking the "Russian consulate" (embassy).[140] Chechnya was a frequent topic of debate in the group meetings, with the plotters describing the Russians as "infidels" and "bastards."[141]

However, witness accounts also suggest that the terrorists had numerous grievances related to multiple conflict zones, including Palestine. Benahmed, for example, once stated he had learned the art of making explosives with the firm intention of striking the "Russians in Chechnya and the Israelis in Palestine," when in reality he had developed the skill when he was involved in fighting for the GIA in Algeria.[142] The terrorists were said to have talked very passionately during their meetings about Israeli transgressions in Palestine.[143] This was likely related to the ongoing Intifada and the Israeli response, which infuriated Muslims worldwide. Moreover, they frequently discussed the situation in Algeria and criticized the FIS, the members of which they described as "unbelievers."[144] The enemy perceptions of the terrorists also involved general hatred towards Western "countries of unbelievers," in which Muslims were religiously permitted to engage in criminal activities such as theft and fraud.[145] One sign that the cell members shared al-Qaida's vision of global jihad is that they expressed strong admiration for bin Laden.

However, while thinking and acting as global jihadis in some ways, the plotters took a special interest in Algeria. Benahmed's wife told interrogators that he held GSPC-leader Hassab Hattab in high esteem even though he opposed al-Qaida's vision of global jihad and called upon Algerians to prioritize the national struggle.[146] Yet the Algerian jihad was in disarray in the early 2000s, something that may have contributed to pushing Benahmed's group towards global jihad. In February 2002, government forces killed Antar Zouabri, putting an end to the GIA. At the same time, the anti-GIA groups GSPC, Protectors of the Salafi Call and the militant FIS clashed in conflict while being infiltrated by the security services and losing on the battlefield. Hattab had been alienated from al-Qaida by 9/11, bringing to the surface the rifts between nationally and internationally oriented groups. Although members of the Chechen network admired Hattab, by interacting with al-Qaida and Chechen mujahidin they came to prioritize the international dimension.

The Chechen network is a fascinating example of the hybrid threat in Europe before the Iraq war. It illustrated how jihadism was in a process of transnationalization. The terrorists had been radicalized over events in Algeria, took part in support networks for international jihad in Europe and spent time in training camps in Afghanistan and Georgia. They expressed grievances related to Algeria, Palestine, Europe and other places, but Chechnya soon crystallized as the main motive. In Europe and the training camps they interacted with global jihadis who called for terrorism in the West. While first assessing French, American and Jewish targets, the terrorists ended up targeting Russia, triggered by Dubrovka and the death of their friend, al-Moutana. Whereas the Frankfurt and Tawhid cells exemplified how al-Qaida affiliates retained autonomy and pursued special interests, the Beghal and Chechen networks are examples of how cells adopted al-Qaida's way of thinking. The crackdown on the Chechen network coincided with the US preparations for the Iraq war, a development which opened a new phase in the history of jihadi terrorism in Europe. The jihad in Iraq became the number one cause for networks in Europe from that point on. As I will discuss subsequently, with Benahmed behind bars, members of his network who were not prosecuted now joined a Europe-wide effort to recruit for Iraq.

As stated at the outset of this chapter, I regard the cells discussed here as products of al-Qaida's effort to ignite global jihad. The cells operated broadly within al-Qaida's framework, but still maintained some autonomy. Although the number of jihadi incidents in Europe increased in 2000–3, only a small number of plots targeted European countries directly. Apart from the Frankfurt cell and other plans by Algerians to target France, most of the plots were aimed at the United States/NATO, or Israeli targets, and in the case of the Chechen network, a Russian one. The relative absence of plots targeting Europeans may have had something to do with the ideological disagreements concerning legitimacy addressed in Chapter Two. This began to change, however, when European countries took part in the invasion of Iraq. The Iraq war signified a shift from Europe functioning primarily as a support base, to a situation where European countries became targets of strategic and retaliatory attacks. During the build-up to the war, the number of plots in Europe increased before reaching an unprecedented level in 2004, when the region also saw the most deadly attacks by jihadis so far: the bombings of commuter trains in Madrid.

5

THE IRAQ EFFECT (2003-5)

The invasion of Iraq breathed new life into European jihadism. In the period from 2003 to 2005, the number of plots increased, resulting in several deadly attacks. What characterized the rising threat was that the terrorists were motivated primarily by the Iraq war, and sought to deter Europeans from further involvement in the country. Another feature of the threat after the invasion was that more nationalities became involved in the terrorist networks and that many of them had been born and bred in Europe. Some of the cells emanated from the networks of al-Qaida and affiliates, whereas others were grass root initiatives.

Some of the cells consequently had a top-down character, whereas others were more bottom-up. In this chapter I will take a closer look at two cases, the Madrid bombings and the murder of Theo van Gogh. Both of these terrorist acts primarily involved people from Moroccan backgrounds. What is interesting about these cases is that they are both similar and dissimilar, and serve to illustrate continuities and discontinuities in the threat. The main organizers of the Madrid bombings had been involved in jihadism in Europe for a long time and had extensive contacts in the region and overseas, whereas the murderer of van Gogh had vaguer ties to organized jihad. Yet the cells emerged in similar fashions, carried forward by entrepreneurs, and launched attacks in line with al-Qaida's vision of global jihad. Before moving on to the case studies, I discuss some of the factors which were shaping militant Islamism in Europe at the time of the invasion and occupation of Iraq.

The new generation

The Iraq war was a catalyst for a new generation of jihadis in Europe, composed of people born and raised in the region who had little experience of armed struggles. Many originated from North Africa and Pakistan, some from the Middle East, but there were also European converts among them. The new generation was recruited and socialized by jihad veterans in radical mosques, or online—via an ever-growing body of pro-al-Qaida websites. The recruits forged ties with entrepreneurs in Europe who were working on behalf of al-Qaida and likeminded groups in Af-Pak, Iraq or other places.

Investigations revealed that the Internet was used more actively than before in the formation of cells. Although the Internet did not replace face-to-face interaction with radical preachers, group socialization or training camps, it clearly supplemented existing recruitment routines. Exploitation of the Internet was a necessity for extremists, as radical mosques had been shut down or had come under close surveillance after 9/11 and the terrorist plots in Europe. However, the new generation was also a product of al-Qaida's need to recruit new manpower due to its losses in the War on Terror. The organization gradually adapted its propaganda to resonate with the young Muslims of the West by offering translation of ideological texts, statements and terrorist manuals to Western languages, and addressing causes which had a special appeal to European Muslims, such as the ban on headscarves in France. Young Western recruits with little history in jihad also represented strategic assets for al-Qaida and its affiliates because they were better suited for moving beneath the radar of the security services than ex-GIA members and other seasoned mujahidin.

With the rise of the new generation, there were also certain changes in the socio-economic make-up of the networks. Until this stage there had been an overrepresentation of poor, under-employed immigrants mixing in criminal environments. The new generation also included jobless delinquents, but because they were homegrown, more of them had at least some level of education, better chances to gain an income and rights to social services. This meant that they were generally better placed to finance attacks by themselves without attracting too much attention.

Within Europe's jihadi sub-culture the new generation let themselves become influenced by senior activists who lectured on atrocities committed against Muslims in Afghanistan, Pakistan, North Africa, the Middle East and other parts of the world. However, the Iraq war emerged as the number one mobilizing cause. The recruits were absorbed into an emerging support network for the Iraqi jihad, which focused on propaganda, fundraising and recruitment of foreign fighters.

Because many terrorist plots in Europe following the invasion of Iraq involved young Europeans, it was initially alleged that their radicalization had little or no connection to international jihadism. However, investigations revealed that the new generation eagerly pursued international contacts with al-Qaida-linked actors in Af-Pak, Iraq or elsewhere, online or through travel. Motivationally, the new generation seemed driven primarily by the war in Iraq, while Afghanistan fell into the background. The European jihadis also voiced more concrete grievances related to Europe than their forerunners. Whereas discrimination had been a factor in the radicalization of many terrorists in Europe in the past, the entrepreneurs of the cells now looked to frame European "injustices" against Muslims in ideological terms.

Injustices against Islam

From 2003 onwards, several terrorists in Europe specified anti-terrorism laws and counter-terrorism arrests, more restrictive immigration policies, anti-Islam discourses and insults against Islam as justification for their actions. Al-Qaida's propaganda had also begun to focus more on injustices committed against Islam in the West. By doing so the organization added to the vicious circle in which jihadi terrorism led to xenophobia, a rise in anti-Islamic sentiment and racism, which in turn marginalized Muslims and made them susceptible to extremist recruitment. Al-Qaida's focus on issues such as the ban on headscarves in France also served a concrete ideological objective, as the ability to practice Islam is one condition for the covenant of security between Muslims and Western host states. By highlighting hindrances on practicing Islam in Europe, al-Qaida fed the argument that security pacts were now invalid. Such attempts to manipulate the new generation into decentralized action were part of al-Qaida's struggle for survival. In another bid to regain strength, European jihadis were forming prison networks and mobilizing behind bars.

Jihadism behind bars

The disruption of al-Qaida's networks in Spain and Germany, and subsequent crackdowns on affiliated networks, such as Doha's, Beghal's and al-Zarqawi's, were a hard blow to European jihadism. Moreover, the arrests of the al-Qaida-affiliated preachers Qatada and Hamza, and the closure of the Finsbury Park

Mosque, placed a strain on recruitment. However, although counter-terrorism arrests weakened the networks temporarily, the propaganda effect of the arrests was vigorously exploited. Imprisoned preachers and terrorists were held up as martyrs by the new generation.[1] Many of the imprisoned Islamists were able to continue their activism inside jails, recruiting fellow inmates and smuggling out statements that were published online by followers on the outside.[2]

Jihadi figures and ideologues also highlighted counter-terrorism arrests as violations of covenants of security, implicitly calling for revenge.[3] Although the authorities began to separate extremist prisoners from others to avoid the contagion of radicalism, these counter-measures were circumvented in various ways. Brandon's fascinating survey of jihadism inside British jails exemplifies how imprisoned preachers, such as Qatada and Hamza, innovatively communicated with fellow prisoners, even by preaching through the pipes between cells.[4]

Al-Qaida's plans for Iraq

Although the new generation drew inspiration from al-Qaida, it had become more difficult for European extremists to interact with the organization after the invasion of Afghanistan. However, in 2002–4, al-Qaida gradually re-established its central leadership and rudimentary training facilities in Af-Pak. In the process, it brokered alliances with Pakistani groups (discussed in the next chapter). A recruitment network was soon established for Europeans who wanted to train with al-Qaida and affiliated groups in the lawless Afgan-Pakistani border region, an opportunity the new generation exploited.

In fact, although Iraq emerged as the most important motivation for jihadi terrorism in Europe, very few of the terrorists had ever set foot in the country and most had instead trained in Af-Pak. This may seem like a contradiction, but in the world of transnational jihadism there does not need to be a one-to-one relationship between where people train, where they fight and what they fight for. Moreover, al-Qaida and its affiliates in Af-Pak took a strong interest in Iraq and made plans to exploit the conflict.[5] In a letter from al-Zawahiri to al-Zarqawi (the then leader of al-Qaida's Iraqi branch) in 2005, he referred to the war in Iraq as the "greatest battle of Islam in this era," one which presented the opportunity to establish an emirate in the "heart of the Islamic world."[6]

In the letter al-Zawahiri proposed an incremental strategy by which mujahidin were first to expel the Americans prior to establishing an Islamic emirate, and then to extend the struggle to Syria, Jordan, Palestine and Egypt before attacking Israel. Al-Zawahiri cautioned that such a strategy would require time, fierce fighting and political endeavors. He stressed the need for popular support among the country's Muslim masses and avoiding unnecessary conflicts among the Sunnis, with the Iraqi Shias and with the Iranians—something which was never of great concern to al-Zarqawi's group and its off-shoot ISIS. Al-Qaida's hopes for Iraq were also reflected in the organization's propaganda, and Iraq became the dominant theme on pro-al-Qaida websites from 2004 onwards.[7]

The war in Iraq also shaped al-Qaida's alliance politics and its allocation of resources. According to Taliban commanders, al-Qaida made a decision to prioritize Iraq over Afghanistan in the fall of 2003. In November, a meeting was held between al-Qaida and the Taliban in Khost, during which the former said it would re-deploy one third of about 1,000 fighters to Iraq. Al-Qaida also informed the Taliban that it would reduce its monthly support from 3 million to 1.5 million USD, but vowed that it would never end its support completely.[8] By transferring funds and fighters to Iraq, al-Qaida was aiming to take the lead of the insurgency through al-Zarqawi.

In his letter to al-Zarqawi, al-Zawahiri expressed his disappointed with the Taliban's failure to rally popular support, implicitly criticizing al-Zarqawi's targeting of Shias and competing Sunnis in Iraq.[9] While supporting and attempting to control al-Zarqawi, another sign of al-Qaida's eagerness to take the lead in Iraq was that the organization initiated an alliance with the Kurdish-Iraqi Ansar al-Islam/Ansar al-Sunnah movement, which emerged as a strong force in the insurgency.[10] Al-Qaida also renewed its cooperation with the North African groups GSPC and the MICG. As I will explore in greater detail below, these groups became very active in recruiting fighters for the Iraqi jihad from Muslim countries and Europe.

Drumming for jihad in Europe

As will become clear in this chapter and the next, the increased threat in Europe from 2003 onwards was strongly linked to Iraq and its ability to inspire affiliates and sympathizers to strike at European countries which had joined the war. Although al-Qaida's networks in Europe were weakened by arrests, the organization retained a substantial following in the region and was successful in appealing to the new generation. In order to convince European citizens of the legality of attacking their countries, al-Qaida jumped over a number of ideological hurdles.

As discussed in Chapter Two, Europe held a marginal place in jihadi thought and attacks in countries where Muslims had protection were ideologically controversial. Al-Qaida talked little about Europe before the late fall of 2002.[11] However, from then on the organization started to threaten specific countries frequently. In October 2002, for example, al-Zawahiri issued a statement in which he made threats against Germany and France.[12] Germany had contributed to ISAF in Afghanistan and had cracked down on jihadis domestically, but did not support the invasion of Iraq. France had sent troops to Afghanistan, but was also opposed to the invasion of Iraq (France is a special case because of the Algeria dimension, however). In November 2002, bin Laden issued a general threat against all US allies.[13] In May 2003 al-Zawahiri issued a threat against the US, UK, Australia and Norway for killing "our brothers in Iraq."[14] Then, in October 2003, bin Laden mentioned Spain, the UK and Italy, and said al-Qaida would attack them at "the appropriate time and place."[15]

However, despite the fact that individual European countries which supported the invasion were mentioned by al-Qaida, "Europe" as a collective term was hardly used in statements until "The First Letter to Europe's People," released one month after the Madrid attacks.[16] In subsequent years, jihadi threats against Europeans became commonplace, and the publication of the Muhammad cartoons added to this trend. When calling for global jihad in Europe, al-Qaida stressed how the domestic and foreign polices of European nations had converged in a crusade against Islam. In February 2004, for example, al-Zawahiri portrayed the ban on veils in French schools as "a new sign of the enmity of the western crusaders against Muslims even while boasting of freedom, democracy and human rights ...", which was equivalent to "the burning of villages in Afghanistan, the destruction of houses over the heads of their inhabitants in Palestine, the massacre of children and the theft of oil in Iraq."[17] By making such issue-linkages, al-Qaida sought to communicate the idea that security pacts had become invalid, making attacks justifiable.

Recruitment for the Iraqi jihad

In addition to the increase in threats, support and recruitment networks for the Iraqi jihad also began to proliferate in Europe. These networks combined veterans and the new generation, and the mobilization involved both organized, top-down processes and grass root activism from the bottom-up. European security services uncovered recruitment networks in France, Italy, Germany, Belgium, Spain, Netherlands, the UK and the Scandinavian countries, funneling fighters from Europe to Iraq via Turkey and Syria.[18]

Recruits were typically sent to Iraq's neighboring countries under the pretext of attending religious studies or language courses.[19] No-one knows for sure how many recruits entered Iraq from Europe in the mid-2000s, but estimates vary between a few hundred and several thousand, the former of which is probably the most realistic.[20] Studies of foreign fighters in Iraq suggest the number of Europeans was very limited compared to Arabs.[21] For example, one survey of suicide bombers in Iraq registered only fifteen out of 102 individuals coming from Europe.[22] In interpreting this ratio it should be emphasized that Europeans were overrepresented among the suicide bombers. Jihadis in Iraq were known to use Europeans for suicide missions due to their lack of fighting experience and language skills. This was also a reason why recruitment from Europe dried up throughout the 2000s, as recruits dreamt of fighting as guerillas rather than being blown up on arrival.

The recruitment of Europeans to Iraq created fears of terrorist "blowback" in Europe by people with combat training. However, until recently, only a few plots in Europe have involved people with experience from Iraq, and overall the number of plots in Europe linked to Iraq is small compared to plots linked to Af-Pak.[23] After Europeans started to travel to Syria in greater numbers from 2012 there have been several incidents involving links to Syria and Iraq, as will be discussed in Chapter Nine. However, thus far, Iraq has primarily been a motive rather than a place where terrorists train for jihad in Europe.

The Iraq war had two main effects on the threat in Europe. First, it made some European Muslims bent on punishing their home countries for interfering in Muslim affairs. Second, it strengthened cooperation between al-Qaida in Af-Pak and regional jihadi groups in the Middle East and North Africa. Groups in different places found common cause in deterring Western powers from operating in Iraq. Support networks for Iraq became a venue for veteran entrepreneurs to interact with the new generation. They also became a venue for replenishing old alliances among jihadi actors. For example, in an interview, one European security official told me that a reunion between central al-Qaida and GSPC was facilitated by such networks from 2004 onwards.[24] The mobilization over Iraq reinvigorated networks in central parts of Europe and it also contributed to an increase in jihadi activism in Scandinavia (accentuated by the Danish Muhammad cartoons from 2005).

Different sources indicate that al-Zarqawi played a key role in supervising recruitment for Iraq in Europe. It is not clear if this was initiated by him, or if he operated on behalf of al-Qaida. In any event, recruitment networks for Iraq came to involve several close affiliates of al-Qaida, such as the Kurdish-Iraqi

Ansar al-Islam, the MICG and the GSPC. Individually, the different groups remained mainly concerned with national and regional matters, but cooperation over Iraq led to internationalization, and created opportunities for al-Qaida entrepreneurs to recruit for international operations.

Ansar al-Islam was founded by Abu Abdullah al-Shafi and Mullah Krekar in Kurdish Northern Iraq in December 2001. The group grew out of the Islamic Movement of Kurdistan (IMK) and fights for an Islamic state in the Kurdish enclaves. Al-Zarqawi was said to have spent time in the group's camps in 2002–3, while supervising Tawhid and networking internationally.[25] Ansar al-Islam oversaw an extensive support network in Europe spanning Germany, Italy, the UK, Norway, Sweden and the Netherlands, and the branches in Italy and Germany were particularly active in funneling fighters to Iraq.[26] Only two vague plots have been attributed to Ansar al-Islam in Europe: a plot to assassinate the Iraqi prime minister on a state visit to Germany and a plan to bomb a military hospital treating American soldiers, also in Germany.

Another group involved in the recruitment networks for Iraq was far more active in pursuing attacks in Europe. MICG has been portrayed as a superstructure for the terrorist cells behind the suicide bombings in Casablanca in 2003 (al-Salafiyyah al-Jihadiyyah and al-Sirata al-Mustaqim). MICG was founded in Peshawar, Pakistan, in 1993 and copies of its manifesto were confiscated in investigations of cells linked to al-Qaida and the GIA in Belgium and Italy in the late 1990s.[27] The manifesto called for jihad against the Moroccan Kingdom, specifying the army, the police and the security services, but it also contained international aspirations. The group claimed to have brothers in "all Islamic groups" and condemned the kingdom's lack of support for the Palestinians. The manifesto also condemned Jews and Christians in general.[28]

According to the indictment of the Madrid bombers, MICG mirrored the structure of al-Qaida and was funded through donations and crime. The group had offices in Kabul and Kandahar and a training camp in Jalalabad before the invasion of Afghanistan. It was also said to look to Ibn Taymiyyah, Qatada and Mohammed al-Fizazi for religious guidance.[29] One segment of the group operated out of Agadir in Morocco, whereas the city of Maaseik in Belgium was its main hub in Europe.[30] This city also produced the first female suicide bomber from a Western country, Muriel Degauque.[31] According to security officials, MICG ran cells in the UK, Italy, France, the Netherlands, Spain, Germany, Saudi Arabia, Morocco and Turkey, as well as in Af-Pak.[32]

While overseeing recruitment networks in Europe, al-Zarqawi is thought to have relied on middlemen, one of whom was the Germany-based Algerian

Abderrazak Mahdjoub. A veteran of jihad in Bosnia and the Caucasus, and a longtime agent of al-Qaida in Germany, Mahdjoub was arrested in Hamburg in November 2003. He was extradited to Italy, where he was charged with facilitating an Ansar al-Islam network funneling fighters to Iraq via Syria.[33] Another central activist in this network was the Kurd Mullah Fouad, who functioned as a gate-keeper to Iraq from Damascus.[34] The network was multinational and stretched from Southern Europe to Scandinavia. After Mahdjoub was arrested, an Ansar al-Islam member named Lokman Amin took over his role as a recruiter for Iraq in Germany until he too was arrested in 2005.[35]

During an investigation into jihadi networks in Morocco in 2005, information surfaced of a third purported middleman between al-Zarqawi's network and recruitment networks in Europe, an Algerian known as Khaled Abu Basir al-Jazairi.[36] Al-Jazairi was allegedly working on an ambitious plan to reunite GSPC and al-Qaida in Pakistan, and establish an al-Qaida branch in the Islamic Maghreb (AQIM), equivalent to al-Qaida's branch in Iraq (AQI).[37] He was also said to have worked on restructuring al-Qaida's Saudi networks and establishing an al-Qaida branch in Europe, combining networks in Belgium, France, Spain, the UK, the Netherlands, Denmark and Germany. While a clear-cut al-Qaida-branch in Europe never materialized, the other aims have been fulfilled, although I have found no additional sources regarding al-Jazairi's role in it. In Belgium, central recruiters for Iraq included, among others, the MICG members Mustapha Lounani, Abdel Salam al-Kharaz (brother-in-law to the leader of the Madrid bombers) and Abdelqadir al-Hakimi.[38]

In Spain, central recruiters included MICG members and brothers Mohammed, Youssef and Maymoun Belhadj, as well as MICG members Hassan and Lahoucine al-Haski. Several of the MICG members in Spain and Belgium were linked to the Madrid bombers. In France, two activists named Said al-Maghrebi and Farid Benyettou became key recruiters for Iraq. Benyettou was a self-appointed preacher in what became known as the 19th Network (after the nineteenth arrondissement, Paris), which sent several young Frenchmen to the conflict zone, some of whom would become implicated in subsequent terrorist plots in France.[39] However, the pattern according to which terrorist plots in Europe would emanate from support networks for Iraq was established firmly by the first lethal attacks executed by jihadis in Europe after the GIA's terrorism: the Madrid bombings and the murder of Theo van Gogh. Both cases illustrated the motivating effect of Iraq and the crucial role of network entrepreneurs in cell formation.

M-11

One year after the invasion of Iraq, 11 March 2004 (M-11), a North African-based terrorist cell with ties to al-Qaida and the MICG bombed four commuter trains during the busy morning rush hour in three different station areas in Madrid.[40] The attacks occurred three days ahead of the Spanish parliamentary elections, and prompted a chain of events that led to the fall of the conservative government and the withdrawal of Spanish troops from Iraq. The socialist opposition party had listed the withdrawal of Spanish troops from Iraq on its electoral manifesto and the terrorists targeted Spanish voters in order to affect the outcome of the elections. Ten bombs exploded inside the trains, causing the deaths of 191 people and injuring more than 1,800. The terrorists escaped and went into hiding, preparing new attacks. On 3 April 2004 Spanish police surrounded seven suspects inside an apartment in the suburb of Leganés. Besieged, the suspects made phone calls to their families and radical preachers before they blew themselves up in a collective suicide mission. This was the first suicide attack by jihadis in Europe, and caused the death of one Spanish special operations agent.

From the rubble of the apartment and other hideouts investigators retrieved bomb devices and other weapons, written and videotaped statements, computer files containing training manuals, bomb-making recipes, propaganda and ideological texts by jihadi ideologues and al-Qaida figures. On the day of the bombings, an email claiming responsibility for the attacks, signed "Abu Hafs al-Masri Brigades," was sent to the Arabic-language newspaper *al-Quds al Arabi* in London (Abu Hafs al-Masri was the warrior-nickname, or *kunya* of bin Laden's trusted military commander Mohammed Atef who was killed during the invasion of Afghanistan). Two days after the attacks a man telephoned a Spanish TV station and led journalists to a videotape which had been left in a waste bin. The videotape displayed hooded gunmen—one of whom presented himself as the "military spokesman for al-Qaida in Europe"—making statements I will discuss subsequently.

The scale of the operation and the references to al-Qaida prompted an intensive search for links to the organization, but it would take many years before such a connection could be established. What did not take so long to find out was that the terrorists had extensive international contacts in Europe, North Africa and the Middle East, and that several of those involved had taken part in recruitment for the jihad in Iraq. Core members of the terrorist network were closely linked to the militant community in London, and were followers of Qatada. A number of its leading figures were also linked to the

MICG. However, it took nearly six years before it transpired that al-Qaida's section for external operations may have had a hand in the bombings. A recent study by Fernando Reinares makes a strong case for the link to al-Qaida.

The cell placed thirteen bombs onboard different trains at Alcalá de Henares station and then left the scene. All trains departed from, or passed through, this station. The explosions were timed according to railway timetables. This prevented higher casualties, as one of the trains was delayed by two minutes. Two trains were supposed to be bombed simultaneously inside the Atocha station, bringing down the station building and maximizing the lethality of the attacks. Three bombs failed to explode and were detonated by Spanish bomb squads. Another device inside a blue bag believed to be the luggage of a victim was brought to a police station. The bomb was discovered when a cellphone inside the bag rang. The bag contained approximately 10 kilograms of the plastic dynamite Goma 2 ECO, 640 grams of bolts and nails, a copper detonator and a mobile telephone.

The cellphone functioned as a remote control, as the copper detonator was to be set off by its vibrating alarm function.[41] The cellphones used in the attack were supplied by the Moroccan salesman and jihadi Jamal Zougam, who was a central member of the terrorist network. The explosives originated from a mine in Asturias, Northern Spain. The Spanish drug addict Jose Emilio Trashorras had obtained the dynamite through contacts working at the mine.[42] Trashorras supplied 200 kilograms of the explosive, of which 130 kilograms were used on 11 March. Together with members of the terrorist cell and some criminals, Trashorras transported the explosives, inside haversacks, into Madrid using buses during January and February 2004. The terrorists gave Trashorras a Toyota Corolla and 25 to 30 kilograms of hashish for his services.[43] The rest of the explosives were destined for follow-up attacks in case the government did not respond to the cell's demands.

A video statement pieced together from the apartment in Leganés contained threats of new attacks if Spanish troops remained in Iraq. Documents retrieved from the attackers' homes indicated plans to attack Jewish centers, synagogues and a children's school, as well as railways and foreign tourists.[44] There was also one actual attempt to strike again. On 2 April railroad workers detected a bomb device on the tracks of the high-speed railway between Madrid and Seville. It was made out of the same explosive and constructed in the same way as those used on 11 March. The bombs were assembled at a farmhouse near Morata de Tajuña, near Chinchón, a quiet area outside Madrid, close to Alcalá de Henares. At the farm, investigators confiscated more detonators and dynamite. The farmhouse functioned as a meeting place and preparations base in the lead-up to the attacks. According to the investigation, the attacks were financed mainly through selling hashish, ecstasy and stolen cars.[45]

The terrorists were first-generation immigrants from Morocco, Algeria, Egypt and Tunisia who were living in Spain. Most of them were misfits and drifters who lacked qualifications, were underemployed and survived via temping, business ventures or crime. However, the entrepreneur of the attack cell and other lead figures had received some higher education. All of the terrorists were men, born between 1960 and 1983, with the majority aged between twenty-three and thirty-three.[46] As is relatively common for jihadis, several were also married with children. Patterns in recruitment and radicalization were characterized by a triangular interaction between local Spanish networks, regional contacts (London in particular) and international contacts in conflict zones. Senior activists in the Madrid network reached out to young immigrants, educated them in militant Islam and showed them videos of atrocities committed against Muslims in Bosnia, Chechnya and Palestine.

Many among the broader network from which the cell emerged had spent time among mujahidin in Af-Pak or North Africa, and they were part of the sub-culture around radical mosques and preachers in London and Madrid. M-11 also exemplified the function of social ties, family bonds and group processes in drawing people into extremism, as many of the terrorists were old comrades and kin hailing from the same area in Morocco, and had been radicalized together. In the now familiar fashion, the entrepreneurs went through a step-by-step process of ideological radicalization, whereas foot soldiers were caught up in terrorism swiftly and more coincidentally.

The terrorist cell emerged from different groups frequenting mosques and Islamic centers in Madrid. The main groups were the "Madrid Group" headed by Mustafa Maymouni, the "Lavapiés group" headed by Jamal Zougam, a group headed by Moutaz and Mouhannad al-Mallah and Rabei Osman El Sayed Ahmed (known as Rabei Osman, or "the Egyptian"), and Jamal Ahmidan's group of common criminals. Individuals and clusters of people within these groups had links to al-Qaida or affiliated groups in Europe and internationally. The Algerian Allekema Lamari had formerly been a member of a GIA cell in Valencia, and most of the Moroccans involved in the attacks were part of MICG. The Moroccans in the network interacted frequently with key organizers of MICG's European network in Belgium, such as the al-Haski brothers.[47] There were also links between the MICG members in

Spain and Belgium and the network that executed the suicide bombings in Casablanca in 2003. While MICG's part in the attacks at the very least implied an indirect link to al-Qaida, it later transpired that one of the Moroccans involved with the Madrid bombers, Amer Azizi, was likely an agent of al-Qaida's section for international operations.[48]

Al-Qaida did not claim responsibility for M-11, unlike 9/11 and the London bombings, but the organization has often been elusive about its exact role in terrorist attacks. The cell that executed the Madrid bombings combined members from the "Madrid group" and Jamal Ahmidan's gang of criminals. The seven people who blew themselves up in the city of Leganés, Rachid Oulad Akcha, Asrih Rifaat Anouar, Sarhane Ben Abdelmajid Fakhet, Jamal Ahmidan, Mohamed Oulad Akcha, Allekema Lamari and Abdennabi Kounjaa, were believed to have placed the bombs onboard the trains.[49]

The origins of the terrorist cell can be traced to an al-Qaida financing cell in Madrid which was supervised by the Syrian jihad veteran Abu Dahdah and Amer Azizi. This cell had a close relationship with Qatada in London, and members frequently traveled to the British capital bringing money that was to be sent to international jihad zones, and attended religious meetings.[50] In Madrid, Dahdah's followers frequented the Abu Bakr (Estrecho) and the M-30 mosques. The cell was mainly focused on supporting jihad in Bosnia, Indonesia and Chechnya, and sent a number of foreign fighters to Bosnia. The Spanish judge, Baltasar Garzon, claimed that money from Dahdah's cell had also been used to fund 9/11. Dahdah's cell was dismantled in late 2001 as part of the investigations into the Hamburg cell.

Before he was arrested, Dahdah participated in a series of meetings at a Moroccan-owned restaurant called al-Hambra, by the Navalcarnero River, in the Syrian al-Mallah brothers' apartment in Virgen del Coro Street, and in the apartment of Sarhane Ben Abdelmajid Fakhet (the Tunisian).[51] During these gatherings, attendees discussed the plight of Muslims worldwide, often focusing on Palestine and Chechnya, in addition to watching propaganda movies and singing jihadi hymns. A key organizer of the meetings was Amer Azizi. He had been recruited by Dahdah in the mid-1990s and was later sent to training camps in Afghanistan, where it is believed that he forged ties to al-Qaida, MICG and the LIFG. According to members of the Madrid network, upon his return from Afghanistan Azizi had become increasingly strict in religious matters and more militant than he had been before he had left.[52] While people in the militant Islamist community in Madrid in the 1990s looked upon Dahdah primarily as a fundraiser, Azizi was seen as someone "with ideas" who functioned as a recruiter and coordinator of activities.[53]

Together, Dahdah and Azizi were said to have recruited the Moroccan Moustafa Maymouni by showing him propaganda movies inside Azizi's apartment.[54] Along with the Syrian al-Mallah brothers, Maymouni assumed a leading position among jihadis in Madrid after Dahdah had been arrested. However, on a journey to Morocco in May 2003, Maymouni was arrested because of his ties to the perpetrators of the Casablanca attacks, and subsequently the Tunisian Sarhane Ben Abdelmajid Fakhet emerged as a lead figure in the network from which the M-11 terrorist cell emerged. As for the purported al-Qaida handler, Azizi, he left Spain amid the investigations into Dahdah's cell. He is believed to have traveled in the Middle East before relocating to Pakistan. According to a protected witness in the M-11 case, Azizi stayed in touch with the cell leader Fakhet by email during 2002 and 2003. In 2009, information emerged suggesting that Azizi had been among those killed in a 2005 CIA drone attack in Miran Shah, South Waziristan, Pakistan. The attack targeted the leader of al-Qaida's section for external operations at that time, Hamza Rabiyyah al-Masri.[55]

While circumstantial evidence suggests Azizi initiated and oversaw M-11 for al-Qaida, it was Fakhet who was the entrepreneur inside Spain. Fakhet was furious about the invasion of Iraq and Spain's contribution, and had begun to talk about an attack in Spain from the spring of 2003 onwards.[56] According to sources, Fakhet first asked Azizi to supply experienced terrorists from Morocco, but Azizi replied that Moroccan groups had no-one to spare because of the crackdowns following the Casablanca bombings.[57] Consequently, Fakhet had to recruit operatives from within Spain. It is believed that he received help from the former member of EIJ, Rabei Osman, to assemble the cell. He had been an explosives expert in the Egyptian Army before joining jihad and was believed to be operating as a recruiter for al-Qaida in Italy.

Based in Milan, Rabei Osman spent time in Spain during 2002 and 2003 interacting with people who became involved in the attacks, and he was also very active in spreading propaganda and recruiting online.[58] By the summer of 2003 Fakhet and Osman had gathered the needed manpower by recruiting from Jamal Ahmidan's criminal network. Fakhet's group, by now an active terrorist cell, became more secretive and encapsulated, withdrew from the mosques and gathered in apartments, in the streets, by the river and in a car park.[59] Ahmidan organized the meetings, but Fakhet acted as the leader. In October 2003 the cell stepped up its preparations. They bought cars and renovated the farm in Chinchón which had been rented by Maymouni in October

2002 and later bought by Fakhet.[60] Members of the cell spent much time at the farm, preparing mentally and physically, doing sports and assembling the bomb devices (they also made test explosions).[61]

With Azizi's connections to al-Qaida in mind, various communications by the Madrid bombers showed that they identified strongly with the organization. They signed statements "Ansar al-Qaida" (supporters of al-Qaida), for example, and consumed texts and audio-visual materials by al-Qaida's ideologues.[62] Investigators retrieved texts from the terrorists' computers written by classical thinkers such as Ibn Taymiyyah, Mohammed Ibn Abd al-Wahhab, Sayyid Qutb and Abdullah Azzam, as well as texts and audio-visual material produced by contemporary pundits such as bin Laden, al-Zawahiri, Qatada, Abu Mohammed al-Maqdisi, Hamza, Abu Basir al-Tartousi and a number of ideologues from Saudi Arabia, Morocco, Syria and Kuwait, including the aforementioned Mohammed al-Fizazi.[63] The cell seems to have been particularly fond of texts by the Saudi ideologues Abd al-Aziz al-Jarbu and Nasir Bin Hamad al-Fahd, which contained justifications for suicide attacks and jihad in Western countries.[64] Interestingly, in terms of assessing the influence of ideologues on jihadis in Europe, a key member of the network, Muhannad al-Mallah, told interrogators that Qatada had the same position in Europe as al-Qaida had in the world and that he was "the person in Europe calling for jihad, recruiting members, giving them missions to fulfill."[65]

While the M-11 cell may have been working for al-Qaida and inspired by global jihad, the terrorists' individual stories also suggest that their radicalization involved grievances related to their countries of origin and Europe. The entrepreneur of the terrorist cell, Fakhet, was born in Tunisia in 1968 and went to Spain on a scholarship to complete a doctorate in economics in 1994. At first an eager student, and not religiously devout, when confronted with some kind of personal crisis around 1999–2000 he grew increasingly conservative.[66] Fakhet then left his studies, began working in a travel agency and spent most of his spare time in the M-30 and Estrecho mosques, where he was approached and recruited by the leader of the "Madrid Group," Moustafa Maymouni. He subsequently married Maymouni's sixteen-year-old sister and gradually assumed a leading position within the group. At first he would rarely speak during the meetings, and instead listened quietly to what the others were saying.

According to witness accounts, the other members of the group respected him greatly because he was so educated.[67] This observation is interesting because militant Islamists are often portrayed as zealots who oppose education and critical thinking, whereas in reality many of the lead figures are not only knowledgeable about Islam but possess an academic background as well. Fakhet soon began to give passionate speeches about the injustices suffered by Muslims. In the words of one witness, Fakhet spoke with "much emotion and enthusiasm," and "could even cry with emotion."[68] Crying over the demise of Muslims tends to be seen as a sign of commitment and sincerity or even masculinity in jihadi circles, and it is not uncommon for radical preachers to burst into tears.[69] Fakhet spent a great deal of time on jihadi websites and downloaded numerous propaganda films which he used in recruitment.[70] It is also believed that he was the main author of all statements attributed to the M-11 cell.[71]

The Madrid cell's second-in-command and Fakhet's protégé, Jamal Ahmidan, played a key role in planning, financing and executing the attacks, in addition to functioning as a recruiter.[72] Ahmidan, known as the "Chinese" because of his physical appearance, was born in 1976 in Algeria to Moroccan parents. Like some of the other Moroccans he recruited, Ahmidan grew up in Tetouan, a city in Northern Morocco.[73] This is a parallel to the Tawhid and Chechen network cases, which involved the recruitment of childhood friends. Friends and kin share experiences and references, something that strengthens group identity, interpersonal communications and trust within jihadi networks. Ahmidan was an immigrant to Spain, a drug trafficker and leader of a criminal group, who spent time in Morocco from time to time in connection with his smuggling or family visits. He was married and had one son, who was in the custody of his grandmother.

It is believed he first connected with jihadis when he was imprisoned in Spain in the mid-1990s. He had been shown videos of mujahidin fighting in Chechnya, and his brothers told a journalist that after this he began to talk frequently about jihad and they described him as obsessive about the suffering of Palestinians. A prison official in Spain wrote a report on Ahmidan during one of his stays in jail which claimed that he dreamt of going to Israel to kill Jews. In 1999, Ahmidan began to mix with Dahdah's network in Madrid. As part of his religious awakening Ahmidan changed his Westernized appearance and started to wear white Islamic robes. He also wanted his son to attend a Quranic school at the M-30 mosque. Indicating some talent for leadership, while detained in an immigrant deportation center in Madrid he was said to have set himself up as an imam and gathered a group of followers among the illegal aliens. It seems Ahmidan continued his criminal activities up until the attacks, likely as a means to generate money for the jihad in Iraq and the attacks in Spain.[74] Ahmidan has been described as conflicted, having second thoughts about his criminal dealings and seeking redemption through militant Islam. In the time leading up to the attack he had become obsessed with the war in Iraq and eulogized al-Qaida.[75]

Several of the criminal misfits Ahmidan recruited for the cell hailed from his hometown of Tetouan, including Abdennabi Kounjaa (b.1975). Kounjaa became one of the foot soldiers in the cell, and took part in the preparations as well as the attacks themselves. He was married with two children who stayed behind in Morocco. From his belongings police retrieved a martyrdom testament addressed to his family, in which he quoted Ibn Taymiyyah, talked passionately about jihad and incited his children to join the ranks of the mujahidin.[76] Kounjaa was described as troubled and strongly religious, yet he had also been involved in criminal activities frowned upon in Islam. The criminals of the M-11 network exemplified how the radicalization of jihadis combines social dimensions with religious–political ideology.[77]

Although the terrorist network was dominated by Moroccans, some of its members belonged to other nationalities. The only Algerian, Allekema Lamari (b.1965), was an architecture student who left Algeria for Spain during the civil war, where he took part in support networks for the GIA.[78] It is not known exactly how he joined jihad, but it is believed that his brother had been killed fighting for the GIA, so it is possible Lamari was a member of the GIA on arrival in Spain, tasked with organizing support activities. The case of Lamari indicates that Spanish counter-terrorism efforts may have affected the terrorists' motives. Lamari was arrested in Valencia in 1997 as part of a crackdown on suspected GIA cells. He was convicted of membership in a terrorist organization and received a lengthy prison sentence. After being released in 2002, Lamari was said to have become obsessed with avenging his imprisonment. An intelligence report quoted in the M-11 indictments said that Lamari's only objective after he got out of jail was to cause a terrorist attack in Spain which would kill as many people as possible. He talked about derailing trains and starting forest fires. He re-connected with jihadi networks in Madrid and became a member of Fakhet's group.

The provider of cellphones for the detonators, Jamal Zougam (b.1973), hailed from a poor background in Tangiers and went to Madrid with his mother and half-brother for economic reasons in 1983.[79] Zougam frequently traveled back to Tangier to visit his father. During these visits he frequented radical mosques, and attended the sermons of Mohammad al-Fizazi, who during the 1990s had given lectures at the famous al-Quds mosque in

Hamburg frequented by the 9/11 terrorist cell. He was recruited by Dahdah's network in Madrid and was investigated in connection with Dahdah's arrest in 2001. As part of Dahdah's network, Zougam participated in jihadi support activities and interacted with Qatada in London. He was a close friend and work companion of Amer Azizi and part of the meetings staged by Fakhet in the run-up to the attacks. Zougam was known to have some personal problems and a bad temper that some believe contributed to his radicalization.

The M-11 terrorists had grievances related to a number of Muslim countries, Europe and international politics, but it was Iraq that consumed them from the time of the invasion in 2003. According to witnesses, during meetings group discussions were focused on the battle against regimes in Muslim countries. Fakhet would call for the "infidel" governments in Algeria, Tunisia and Morocco to be overthrown, saying that they were worse than the "original unbelievers" and the Jews because they portrayed themselves as Muslims when they were not.[80] He also spoke passionately about injustices in Palestine and Chechnya, showing members of his group videos of "Jews killing children in Palestine" and "how the Russians killed women and children in Chechnya."[81] However, this focus began to shift in 2003, when the Iraq invasion became the focus of his attention and he began talking about attacking Spain for sending troops to Iraq.[82]

The terrorists' public statements indicated strong inspiration from al-Qaida and anger over Iraq. On 14 March 2004, a man with an Arabic accent called the Spanish television station Telemadrid with a tip-off about a videotape in a trash can near the M-30 mosque. The tape displayed a man in an Arab robe (who was in fact the cell leader, Fakhet) carrying a machine gun and presenting himself as Abu Dujana al Afghani, "the military spokesman for al-Qaida in Europe."[83] Abu Dujana called the attacks "a response to the crimes that you have caused in the world and specifically in Iraq and Afghanistan," and threatened more attacks "if God wills it."[84] Using typical al-Qaida rhetoric, he stated "You love life and we love death," and, "If you don't stop your injustices, more and more blood will flow and these attacks will seem very small compared to what can occur in what you call terrorism."[85]

Another videotape recovered from Leganés also addressed the Spanish government and demanded a quick pullout of Spanish troops from Iraq. Another indicator of the strategic aim of M-11 and Iraq as the main motive was a forty-two-page document posted on the Internet message board "Global Islamic Media Front" in mid-December 2003. The document, entitled "The Jihadi Iraq" (Iraq al-Jihad, in Arabic), demonstrated that there was an ongoing strategic discourse among jihadis prior to the attacks on how to pressure the Europeans to withdraw from Iraq. The text, which is believed to have been authored by the newly established al-Qaida on the Arabian Peninsula (QAP), identified Spain as the country most likely to pull forces out of Iraq if they suffered "painful blows" close to the general elections.[86]

The authors anticipated that an attack on Spanish interests would lead to victory for the socialist party, which had promised to withdraw Spanish soldiers in its election manifesto. The text analyzed the domestic political landscape in three countries that contributed to the invasion and occupation of Iraq—the UK, Poland and Spain—and concluded that the Spanish government was the most likely to give in to demands for pulling out of Iraq. According to one source, Fakhet had obtained the document and may have drawn inspiration from it, although I have not found any confirmation of this in legal documents.[87] In addition to the strategic documents, several threats had been posted on the Global Islamic Media Front against Spanish interests outside Iraq as a response to the country's participation in the US-led invasion coalition. It was believed that these threats were also put forward by QAP, the forerunner of AQAP and the al-Qaida branch having closest ties to the central organization.

Moreover, a speech by bin Laden, issued on 15 April 2004, provided clues that the attacks were inspired or initiated by al-Qaida. In the speech, bin Laden offered European countries a "truce" if they pulled out of Iraq.[88] The speech proved that the M-11 had al-Qaida's blessing, and was within the organization's strategic framework. It addressed "our neighbors north of the Mediterranean," and said the attacks were consequences of European interference in Afghanistan and Iraq. Bin Laden appealed to "The European people" to pressure their governments to accept the truce within a three-month deadline. It would start "with the withdrawal of the last soldier" from Muslim lands.[89]

This speech marked a new tendency for al-Qaida to talk of Europeans as one entity. Also, as will be discussed in the next chapter, extremists linked to al-Muhajiroun in the UK interpreted this speech as an annulment of the covenant of security between Muslim immigrants to Europe and their governments—in effect a declaration of war. M-11 bore signs that the jihadi threat in Europe was becoming increasingly aimed at Europeans rather than Americans or Jews, and fueled by the war in Iraq. Like previous jihadi plots in Europe the attacks were therefore motivated mainly by international events, and al-Qaida may have had a hand in initiating them, although the exact details of its involvement remain unknown. The attacks also involved strategic thinking in line with al-Qaida's vision of global jihad. At the same time, hatred towards Muslim regimes and especially the native country of most of the M-11 terrorists had also fueled their radicalization, and it should be noted that several of the terrorists, such as Lamari, hated Spain because they had been arrested, or because of the arrest of the kingpin of Madrid's jihadi community, Abu Dahdah, in 2001. According to Reinares, Dahdah's arrest had been a major factor in the radicalization of the leader of the operational cell, Fakhet.[90]

From an ideological vantage point, by invading Iraq and arresting jihadis, Spain had broken two out of the three conditions for a covenant of security with Muslim citizens, the third being insults against the Prophet Muhammad and Islam. Violation of the latter condition would become a justification for another jihadi attack toward the end of 2004—the brutal killing of the filmmaker Theo van Gogh in the Netherlands. This case resembled the Madrid attacks in some ways, but it also represented something new and different.

The murder was carried out by the leader of an extreme group of al-Qaida-sympathizers formed inside the Netherlands. Like the M-11 network, the group was dominated by people of Moroccan origins, but they were born and bred in the Netherlands. As with the M-11 case, members of the Dutch group had been radicalized over the Iraq war. However, the case differed from past patterns of jihadism in Europe in that the terrorists had weaker ties to organized international networks. Also, while all previous jihadi plots in Europe involved grievances and motives related to the countries in Europe where the terrorists lived and operated, in the case of the Hofstadgroup this was a much more dominant feature. Finally, while M-11 was political and strategic in nature, the Hofstadgroup and the murder of van Gogh was more about revenge and religious fanaticism. The case was seen as the blueprint for the homegrown threat in Europe, although this needs to be problematized.

Hofstadgroup

On 2 November 2004 a twenty-six-year-old Dutch-Moroccan, Mohammed Bouyeri, shot, stabbed to death and tried to decapitate the filmmaker Theo van Gogh while he was riding his bike on Linnaeusstraat near the Oosterpark, Amsterdam. The assassin approached the victim, stepped off his own bike, drew an automatic pistol and shot van Gogh several times. The filmmaker stumbled off his bike but managed to cross the street heading towards a public building for shelter while begging for mercy. However, Bouyeri was determined to go through with the killing. Beforehand he had written an answer to the filmmaker's final pleas in the five-page letter written in Dutch he pinned to the victim's body: "There will be no mercy for the wicked, only the sword will be raised against them."[91]

The killer followed van Gogh across the street and shot him repeatedly. He then sat down and slit his throat and attempted to decapitate him with a butcher's knife while a female passer-by was screaming, urging him to stop. Ignoring the woman, Bouyeri stabbed a smaller knife through one of the letters he had brought with him, and into van Gogh's chest. After the brutal execution, Bouyeri walked slowly away from the murder site and headed for the Oosterpark. Police from a nearby police station tracked him down, and a shootout ensued in which one police officer, the assassin and a by-passer were wounded. This was the second terrorist assassination by jihadis in Europe, the first being the GIA's murder of the FIS-linked imam, Abd al-Baqi Sahraoui, in 1995. The murder of van Gogh was also one of the first plots in Europe by an individual instead of a group. Previous cases include failed plots by the al-Qaida-connected solo-terrorists Richard Reid and Sajjid Badat to down transatlantic airliners with shoe bombs in 2001, and the murder of Sheikh Sahraoui in Paris in 1995 may also have been an act of solo-terrorism by Khaled Kelkal.

However, although Bouyeri made most of the preparations for the slaying on his own, he was hardly a lone wolf. Investigations revealed that the assassin was part of an al-Qaida-inspired terrorist group, which had been dubbed "Hofstadgroup" by Dutch police because it was based primarily in The Hague (Hofstad). It transpired that members of the group had planned a variety of terrorist attacks in the Netherlands including assassinations of politicians and bombings of public places and buildings, such as the premises of the General Intelligence and Security Service (AIVD) and Schiphol Airport.[92] The Hofstadgroup was considered the prototype for homegrown terrorism by the new generation of jihadis in Europe.[93] The reason for this is that most members were Dutch, had been radicalized inside the Netherlands and had relatively limited interaction with jihadis internationally compared to other cells uncovered in the region. Moreover, some of the group's members seemed better integrated than terrorists operating in Europe in the past, and their radicalization seems to have been shaped by internal Dutch affairs to a large extent, involving grievances over immigration policies, criticisms of Islam and the mocking of Islamic symbols in public discourses.

However, while the Hofstadgroup was indeed a Dutch phenomenon, the homegrown element may have been overstated.[94] On my reading of the

149

sources, the group was very much a product of longstanding, transnational jihadi networks in Europe, which generally involved both a local European and an international dimension. The radicalization of individual members of the Hofstadgroup was not confined to the Netherlands. Nearly all members of the group originated from Morocco, and several were linked to members of MICG in Europe or Morocco through family ties or otherwise.[95] Members of the Hofstadgroup interacted with MICG contacts and other jihadis internationally, online and through travels, and drew inspiration from ideologues in London, and at least three members of the group are thought to have spent time with mujahidin in Af-Pak.[96]

Finally, although events inside the Netherlands were the main triggers for the murder of van Gogh, the Iraq war and the involvement of Dutch troops in Iraq were also major motives for van Gogh's killer and the Hofstadgroup more generally. While the way in which the terrorist cell formed shares certain similarities with previous cases, there was one important difference: the Internet was used much more actively as a meeting place and recruitment tool than ever before. Members of the group were Internet-savvy and employed websites and discussion forums extensively for the purpose of spreading propaganda and recruiting other young Dutchmen for jihadism in the Netherlands or abroad.

The group formed around two entrepreneurs, a Syrian jihad veteran and Mohammed Bouyeri, and it focused on supporting international jihad, mostly the jihad in Iraq after the invasion. Despite having emerged in the Netherlands, the formation and radicalization of the Hofstadgroup was clearly part of the Iraq effect in Europe. However, while the Madrid bombers would use their attacks as a crowbar to pressure Spain out of Iraq, the murder of van Gogh served a different purpose. It was the first jihadi attack in Europe to avenge insults against the Prophet Muhammad and Islam, justified by reference to a verdict by Ibn Taymiyyah. The murder was an omen of what was to come after *Jyllands-Posten* published Muhammad cartoons in 2005. Theo van Gogh was a descendant of Vincent van Gogh. He was a filmmaker, a TV producer and talk show host. He was also a provocateur, known for publicly ridiculing fundamentalists of any religion.[97]

The killer conducted reconnaissance of the victim's daily routines several weeks before the attack. He decided to strike in the morning while the artist was on his way to work at a film production company in the southern part of Amsterdam. Bouyeri had handpicked the exact spot for the crime, an open space near the District Council's office. He had acquired a semi-automatic

Croatian pistol and two different knifes, a machete for decapitation and a filleting knife for attaching a letter to the corpse justifying the murder. Another letter, which he carried in his pocket and which was addressed to his family, was a martyrdom testament entitled "Baptized in Blood."[98] Bouyeri wanted to die as a martyr in a shoot-out with the police. He admitted this was the plan while he was being brought to the hospital, and said to the policemen during trial that "I shot to kill you and be killed."[99]

Jihadis have to justify their suicide mission because suicide is generally forbidden in Islam. By reference to how the first Muslims used to charge into enemy lines fighting until death, a death in a shoot-out with first responders would be religiously justified. The same logic is applied to so-called Fedayeen attacks, when attack crews execute guerilla-style terrorist attacks where they fight until death (Mumbai). Moreover, a pre-recorded martyrdom video was circulated among Dutch extremists showing Bouyeri declaring that he had executed van Gogh and had become a martyr.[100] Because the assassin was obsessed with the invasion of Iraq and the Dutch military contribution, the attack method may have been inspired by a series of abductions and beheadings in Iraq in the months before van Gogh's murder. Videos of beheadings conducted by al-Zarqawi's group in Iraq were posted on pro-al-Qaida websites on an almost daily basis during the spring and summer of 2004.[101] The killer had downloaded such videos, as well as other clips and pictures of executions and torture.

Theo van Gogh was not Bouyeri's first choice as a target. The letter pinned to his chest was entitled "Open letter to Hirsi Ali" and threatened the female Dutch-Somali liberal politician, Ayaan Hirsi Ali.[102] The latter was a self-proclaimed "ex-Muslim" and member of parliament representing the right-wing populist party Volkspartij voor Vrijheid en Democratie (VVD—People's Party for Liberty and Democracy).[103] Hirsi Ali and another high-profile member of VVD and fierce Islam critic, Geert Wilders, had been threatened repeatedly on extremist websites prior to the slaying of van Gogh, and both of them continued to receive death threats in the wake of the assassination. The death of the filmmaker made Wilders an even more determined opponent of Islam, and subsequently he made the short film "Fitna" presenting Islam as a violent religion.[104]

Hirsi Ali had contributed personally to van Gogh's provocative works. She had written the script for van Gogh's latest short film, entitled "Submission," which dealt with domestic violence in Islam.[105] The film showed Quranic texts projected on a veiled woman, who is visibly naked beneath a fully transparent dress. During the murder investigation one witness said that extreme Muslims in the Netherlands had been collecting money for someone to kill van Gogh and Hirsi Ali. Moreover, the investigation also revealed that several members of the Hofstadgroup had posted death threats against the Dutch-Somali woman and other Dutch politicians online. Because the letters attached to van Gogh addressed Hirsi Ali, the artist likely functioned as a medium to harm the politician who was under heavy police protection. The "Open Letter to Hirsi Ali" also threatened other Dutch politicians who voiced criticisms against Muslims in the Netherlands, as well as politicians from Jewish backgrounds, such as VVD's leader Jozias van Aartsen, and the Jewish mayor of Amsterdam Job Cohen.

The Internet was a main communication platform for the Hofstadgroup. Online, Bouyeri and the other members accessed and spread propaganda, discussed ideological questions and jihad training, and issued death threats. Members of the organization administered several MSN groups such as "Muwahhidin/dewaremoslims," "5434" and "taweedwljihad" (likely a reference to al-Zarqawi's group in Iraq), and they also posted messages and tried to recruit on mainstream discussion forums for Moroccan youths. One sign that there was a distinct group identity among the Dutch jihadis is that their cyber-communiqués and propaganda bore the signatures: "Lions of the Tawheed," "Polder Mujahideen" or "Mujahideen of the lowlands."[106]

Although the Hofstadgroup was hardly as organized as the GIA or the M-11 terrorists, there was a hierarchy among the members and they fulfilled different functions. Bouyeri and a Syrian jihadi named Radwan al-Issa were leaders and religious authorities in the network, while another group member was in charge of money and coordinated online communications. Its members were security conscious and took precautions to avoid monitoring, such as coding electronic messages, removing SIM cards from cellphones during meetings and hiding their identities online. Another technique used by the group to confuse the security services was to communicate in Berber dialects, making eavesdropping more challenging.[107]

During 2004 the group also managed to recruit a mole inside the Dutch AIVD, a Moroccan translator and interpreter named Othman ben A., who provided the group with information about investigations that had been launched against members.[108] Other signs that members of the Hofstadgroup aspired to become foreign fighters or terrorists are that they acquired weapons and bomb-making materials, and that three of them sought to attend training camps in Af-Pak. Moreover, plans circulated among the group's members to attack the headquarters of the AIVD and Schiphol. These plans were amateurish and in an early stage of development, but were taken seriously by the security services because several members of the Hofstadgroup had access to Schiphol, working there as salesmen, cleaners or security guards. Van Gogh's killer, Bouyeri, had also applied for work at Schiphol, but he was rejected because he had a police record for violent behavior.

The Hofstadgroup can be traced back to between fifteen and twenty Islamists who came to know each other at the al-Tawheed Mosque in Amsterdam and the al-Sunnah Mosque in The Hague in 2002. At first a loosely connected religious community, around the time of the invasion of Iraq a distinct group formed and some members traveled to Pakistan to join jihadi camps, after which members of the group started to make plans for attacks in the Netherlands. The Hofstadgroup had been under surveillance for some time before the murder of van Gogh, and several members had been arrested on terrorism charges but were released due to a lack of evidence.

A Syrian named Radwan al-Issa came to act as spiritual leader for the group. With the exception of al-Issa, one Algerian, two Chechens and a Dutch-American, most members and associates of the group hailed from Moroccan backgrounds. Socio-economically, the militants were young and outwardly assimilated students, workers or unemployed. Several of them had criminal records and several were married with children. Unlike previous jihadi cells in Europe, the Hofstadgroup was not entirely male but also included wives and girlfriends. The women were not at the core of the group, but they were extreme too, and participated in the group's online propaganda and other support activities.[109] Moreover, after most male members of the group had been arrested by the end of 2004, the women posted death threats against Dutch politicians and public figures online.[110]

Although the group formed and radicalized in the Netherlands, some members connected with and were influenced by jihadis abroad. Investigations revealed contacts and interaction between the Dutchmen and other militants in Belgium, Spain, Portugal, Switzerland, Pakistan, Afghanistan, Morocco and Saudi Arabia. The exact natures of these contacts are poorly understood and may have been underestimated. For example, there were indications that the travels by three members of the group (Jason Walters, Ismail Aknikh and Zacaria Taiby) to Af-Pak may have involved interaction with MICG and other al-Qaida affiliates.

It would not have been surprising if MICG, which was known to be present in Af-Pak while running recruitment networks for the Iraqi jihad in Europe, had taken an interest in Dutch-Moroccan visitors to Pakistan and saw them as an asset. This theory is supported by the fact that one of the Dutchmen, Ismail Aknikh, stopped by Barcelona on his way back from Afghanistan to the Netherlands in the summer of 2003, where he held a meeting with a central MICG member in Europe known as Abdeladim Akoudad.[111] Akoudad was believed to be a coordinator within the European recruitment network for Iraq until he was arrested in Spain in October 2003, following a request from Morocco, which wanted to have him extradited and tried for being involved in the Casablanca attacks. At the time of his arrest, Akoudad was in possession of the phone numbers of several members of the Hofstadgroup, and it turned out he had been in frequent phone contact with one of them, Samir Azzouz.[112] These were the actual links between the Dutch jihadis and MICG. Moreover, information from investigations in Spain and Switzerland revealed more links between the Hofstadgroup and MICG. In Switzerland an Algerian MICG member known as Mohammed Achraf was arrested. Achraf had overseen a terrorist cell that planned to bomb the Madrid High Court in the late fall of 2004. He had called Bouyeri several times and he also wired money to Hofstadgroup members in the period prior to the van Gogh murder.[113]

The investigations uncovered that two other members of Achraf's terrorist cell had links to the Netherlands and the Hofstadgroup. Another indication of the Hofstadgroup's international dimension is a trip to Portugal by some members of the group in June 2004. Just before the Euro 2004 championship soccer tournament, hosted by Portugal, three members of the Hofstadgroup (Noureddine El Fatmi, Mohammed el-Morabit and one other) traveled to the north Portuguese city of Porto and stayed with a person who, according to Portuguese security officials, supported the Dutch jihadis with logistics.[114] In Portugal they collected money from Lisbon international airport, transferred by the group's alleged moneyman, Ahmed Hamdi. In the apartment of their Portugal-based accomplice, they visited jihadi and other prohibited websites, leading Portuguese surveillance teams to believe they were planning an attack on prominent guests visiting Portugal in connection with the soccer tournament. The Portuguese authorities took no chances and decided to arrest the Dutchmen and deport them to the Netherlands.

In addition to travel and face-to-face interaction, the group also drew inspiration from online jihadism. For example, Mohammed Bouyeri was strongly influenced by Hamza in London. He downloaded many of the preacher's texts and speeches and translated parts into Dutch, and the Hofstadgroup distributed London-produced propaganda movies online. However, while the

Hofstadgroup had links to transnational jihad, these were not as strong and direct as in the previous cases. Jihadis in Europe had come under pressure after 9/11, and the Madrid attacks added to this. It had become harder for the new generation to seek out famous preachers in London and travel to conflict zones undetected. Jihadis would still want to mingle with preachers and travel abroad, but security risks had to be factored in. This could be one explanation why the group relied so much on a local Syrian preacher and Bouyeri in religious matters, even though neither of them had formal qualifications in teaching Islam.

The Syrian Radwan al-Issa acted as the main theologian for the Hofstadgroup, whereas Bouyeri emerged as an ideologue over time. Al-Issa was the entrepreneur of the broader extremist milieu from which the Hofstadgroup emerged. He traveled to the Netherlands from Germany in 1998 after his asylum application had been rejected. Al-Issa had been impious in Germany—he visited discotheques, drank beer and watched porn movies. He was also arrested for possessing drugs. Al-Issa's real identity was unknown, as he had stolen the identity of a jailed Muslim Brotherhood member in Syria.[115] In the Netherlands he re-discovered Islam and started to educate himself in jihadi thought online. In a remarkably short space of time, the Syrian felt sufficiently competent to give lectures on the Quran to Dutch Muslim youths. He toured immigration centers in Germany and the Netherlands spreading the jihadi gospel, and set himself up as imam at an underground mosque inside an Internet café/phone center in Schiedam.

At this center he was approached by Bouyeri and El Fatmi. They were so impressed with his charisma and religious knowledge that they invited him to Amsterdam, where he gave lectures at the al-Tawheed Mosque, and later in Bouyeri's apartment in Marianne Philipsstraat. Al-Issa traveled back and forth between the Netherlands and Germany using fake documents. In October 2003 he was arrested in Schiedam for violation of immigration laws and he was also suspected of being involved in terrorist plans together with another member of the Hofstadgroup, Samir Azzouz. The terrorism charges against both Azzouz and al-Issa were eventually dropped because of a lack of evidence, but al-Issa was incarcerated because of the immigration offences.

In prison he received several visits from Bouyeri, who had become a loyal follower of the Syrian. After being released, al-Issa fled the Netherlands with the help of the Hofstadgroup members Rachid B. and Achmad al-A. Al-Issa then traveled to Syria via Turkey and Greece, and it is believed that he was arrested and incarcerated in a high security prison in Damascus in April 2005.

According to members of the Hofstadgroup, al-Issa was highly charismatic and was admired and feared at the same time. One member of the group described his knowledge of Islam as "five times higher" than that of Bouyeri, who was also considered very knowledgeable about Islam within the group.[116] In order to ensure group cohesion al-Issa was said to have introduced a rather odd practice of feeding members of the group breast milk drained from his Surinam wife to symbolize that they were his sons.[117]

Al-Issa's protégé, Bouyeri, was born and raised in an area called Overtoomse Veld outside Amsterdam. The suburb, which is populated mainly by Moroccan and Turkish immigrants, has been referred to as "Saucer city" because of the high concentration of satellite dishes used to watch television channels from the immigrants' homelands. Bouyeri and his three sisters were all born in the Netherlands. He attended a Quranic school as a child and his family has been described as moderately religious. He went to a local college, and did relatively well in school. After college he studied accounting and information technology at a technical educational institute in the town of Diemen, south of Amsterdam. While studying he spent much time with friends on the streets of his hometown, drinking beer and doing soft drugs.

Bouyeri was known to have problems controlling his temper and was repeatedly arrested for violent behavior. Between 1997 and 2004 he had five encounters with the police, and in 2000 he spent twelve weeks in prison after threatening to stab a Moroccan boy who had an affair with his sister, and for resisting arrest. It was reportedly inside prison that Bouyeri began to re-discover Islam. According to Bouyeri's friends, he was very angry and frustrated with political affairs such as the conflict in Palestine.[118] They also cited 9/11 as an inspiration and radicalizing factor. Moreover, some explained how the death of his mother from cancer contributed to the young man's growing rage.

Personal crisis and a family tragedy have often contributed to the radicalization of jihadis in Europe, as shown by the stories of Tawhid member Shadi Abdullah and the Courtallier brothers associated with Beghal's terrorist network. After growing increasingly religious Bouyeri started to wear traditional Islamic robes, grew a beard and took an interest in social activism and community work. He started to study social work instead of IT, and volunteered at the local community center named Eigenwijks and its youth center Oostover. At this time, Bouyeri acted as a devout idealist activist, staging several events for youths, and writing for the center's bulletin *Over 't Veld* (Over the fields). The chairman of the community center described Bouyeri as highly intelligent with a talent for leadership.[119] He aimed to establish a new immigrant youth centre, and lobbied relentlessly for support for the project in the

Dutch parliament and the Amsterdam City Council. However, in December 2002 it became clear that the center would not receive the necessary financial support, and Bouyeri blamed the politicians for the failure of the project. He dropped out of college and became more and more absorbed in religion, first on his own and later as part of the community at the Amsterdam Tawheed Mosque. At Eigenwijks he used one of the center's computers to visit jihadi websites, and he gradually grew more militant. He was a staunch supporter of the Palestinian Hamas movement, studied the group's suicide missions in detail and he hated the Americans for the invasion of Iraq.[120]

After a fierce conflict between Bouyeri and colleagues at the community center, because he advocated the segregation of sexes at the center, he left his job and moved to Amsterdam, where he frequented the al-Tawheed Mosque and the group surrounding al-Issa that became the Hofstadgroup. Bouyeri soon emerged as a leader within the group and offered his apartment as an underground mosque. Being an intelligent student, ideological texts seem to have played an important role in Bouyeri's path to militancy. He downloaded, read, translated and distributed texts by Sayyid Qutb, Ibn Taymiyyah and Hamza. The expert witness in the trial, Rudolph Peters, alleged that Bouyeri found religious justification for murdering van Gogh in Ibn Taymiyyah's text "Al-sarim al-Maslul ala Shatim al-Rasul" (The drawn sword against the insulter of the Prophet).[121] When operating online, Bouyeri used the alias Abu Zubair. On the MSN group "Muwahhidin/dewaremoslims" and other outlets he posted translations of ideological texts, propaganda and death threats.

Another core member of the Hofstadgroup was the illegal immigrant Noureddine El Fatmi (twenty-two). In his home, police found a martyrdom testament which he said had been drawn up by Bouyeri. El Fatmi lived in The Hague and in Bouyeri's apartment in Amsterdam. He worked for a phone company in Schiedam, and was involved mainly in gunrunning and recruitment. Witnesses said he tried to impress women by showing them violent movies from Palestine, Chechnya and other conflict zones, and that he eulogized al-Qaida. El Fatmi also told one witness that the aim of the Portugal trip in 2004 had been to procure weapons. El Fatmi fled to Morocco one day before van Gogh's murder but kept in touch with members of the group in the Netherlands. After returning in June 2005, he was arrested, together with his wife Soumaya S., in possession of a machine gun and a silencer, suspected of plotting the assassinations of Dutch politicians.[122]

A third key figure was Ahmed Hamdi. He was said to have begun his journey to militancy in connection with marital problems that coincided with him joining the study circle of al-Issa. After joining the Syrian's following, Hamdi became more devout and started to wear Islamic robes. He was married with two children and worked at Schiphol's duty-free zone. He is believed to have managed the finances of the Hofstadgroup and was also considered the group's computer specialist. The other members of the gang used to visit his house in northern Amsterdam to go online. On his laptop investigators found several articles about the terrorism threat to Schiphol, indicating that he had done some research into a possible attack. In 2004 Hamdi transferred money to the three members of the group who visited an accomplice in Portugal, money which was likely intended for weapons purchases. According to one source, he was also central in recruiting and obtaining sensitive information from the mole in the AIVD.[123]

One member of the Hofstadgroup, Jason Walters, differed from the others by not coming from a Moroccan Berber background, but rather being the son of an African American and a Dutch woman. Walters converted to Islam when he was sixteen years old. He was known to have experienced personal problems, and was harassed and exposed to racism at school. Walters connected with the Hofstadgroup at the al-Tawheed Mosque. However, he and his younger brother Jermaine had previously been expelled from the El Fath Mosque in Amsterdam for voicing extreme views. The two brothers had also imposed strict religious rules in the home of their divorced mother, who was intimidated and decided to move out of the house with her daughter.

After joining the Hofstadgroup, the brothers moved from Amsterdam to The Hague, which emerged as a main center for the activities of the group. Walters was very active online, and on several occasions he tried to recruit other youngsters for jihad via the Internet. In addition to being a follower of al-Issa, Walters was also fascinated by another radical preacher, Abdul Jabbar van de Ven, a Dutch convert in his twenties who gave lectures at al-Fourkaan Mosque in Eindhoven and acted as an online imam. Internet chats between Walters and another Hofstadgroup member suggest that Abdul Jabbar advised that attacking Dutch authorities was religiously legitimate. He also emphasized the need for Muslims to obtain military training, while at the same time urging the Dutch Islamists to be more patient and secretive about their training practices. Van de Ven advised them to begin preparing at home first, before going to the war zones in Chechnya, Afghanistan and Kashmir to train and fight with real mujahidin.

Jason Walters was among the three members of the group who traveled to Af-Pak for training, and may have interacted with the Pakistani jihadi outfit

Jaysh-e-Mohammed on the journey. Walters had also kept in touch with high-ranking members of the MICG and Ansar al-Islam according to sources in the AIVD.[124] In online chat sessions Walters explained how he enjoyed the camp experience and boasted about having learned how to use weapons and build bombs at the camp, adding he could disassemble a Kalashnikov blindfolded, and fire a pistol while doing a somersault. In a bugged phone call he offered a version of events in Pakistan, suggesting that there could have been a top-down element to the Hofstadgroup's terrorist actions. He said an emir at a training camp had sent him back to the Netherlands "to play a game."[125] Although Walters could seem like a mythmaker online, one European security official told me that Walters actually had crossed the border into Afghanistan and joined a training camp there, before flying back to the Netherlands from Jalalabad.[126] Walters' companion Ismail Aknikh may also have managed to cross the border to receive bomb-making training inside Afghanistan before traveling back to the Netherlands from Pakistan on 11 September 2003.[127]

The radicalization of the Dutch-Moroccan Samir Azzouz (eighteen) demonstrated how very young people may radicalize, a pattern that would become more common throughout the 2000s. Azzouz grew up in Bouyeri's neighborhood and came from a moderately religious family. By the age of twelve he had already become radicalized over injustices suffered by Muslims. He dropped out of elementary school and enrolled in an Islamic school in Rotterdam. He sympathized strongly with 9/11 and made an attempt to join the mujahidin in Chechnya at the age of sixteen.

In January 2003 he headed for the Caucasus with a schoolmate. They were stopped at the Ukrainian border by customs officials and then returned to the Netherlands. This journey may have been the first point of contact between the Hofstadgroup and MICG, as it is believed that it was en route to the jihad in Chechnya where Azzouz met one MICG member named Salaheddin Benyaich, the brother of one of the Casablanca bombers. Benyaich was also believed to be linked to Jamal Zougam of the M-11 cell and al-Zarqawi through the European support network for the jihad in Iraq.[128] After he returned to the Netherlands in October 2003, Azzouz was arrested by AIVD, together with other members of the Hofstadgroup (including al-Issa), suspected of plotting terrorist bomb attacks, but released. The plans seemed very amateurish and he had not acquired materials suitable for making efficient bombs. Azzouz was then rearrested in June 2004 in possession of more advanced bomb-making ingredients, as well as maps and floor plans of Borssele nuclear power station, Schiphol Airport, the Dutch Parliament, the

Dutch Ministry of Defense and other public buildings in The Hague. However, the evidence was again considered insufficient to keep him behind bars. Azzouz was married with one child and his wife was known to share his militant views, posing with a machine gun and swords on one family photo. When he was arrested again in connection with the van Gogh killing, investigators retrieved a martyrdom testament from his house, in which he called for his child to be raised in the spirit of jihad.

Bouyeri and the Hofstadgroup made no secret of their motives. They explained why they resorted to terrorism in letters pinned to van Gogh, in martyrdom testaments, online, during trial and in ideological texts. The most important motives related to Dutch immigration policies, the Iraq war and insults against the Prophet Muhammad, but they also expressed grievances related to Morocco and Palestine. Bouyeri, for instance, referred to the king of Morocco as the "whore" of US President Bush, and he lambasted Israel while eulogizing Hamas.[129]

The letter to Hirsi Ali contained references to al-Qaida's global jihad, as well as death threats against the female politician for leading a "crusade against Islam ... on the political arena of Holland."[130] It indicated that the murder was primarily motivated by injustices committed against Muslims in the Netherlands, and that it was part of a scheme to attack several Dutch politicians voicing anti-Islamic opinions and calling for tougher immigration laws. The letter staunchly criticized Dutch policies towards Muslims in general, as well as a concrete proposal by VVD to screen Muslim immigrants to make sure they did not sympathize with terrorism. The author of the letter (most likely Bouyeri) also expressed strong anti-Semitic views, arguing that Dutch politics is "dominated by Jews" and that Hirsi Ali was part of a "Jewish conspiracy" aimed at "terrorizing Muslims and Islam."[131]

While concentrating on the Netherlands, the language of the letter also echoed the godfather of the Afghan-Arab movement, Abdullah Azzam, and other jihad ideologues, stating: "There shall be no mercy for the unjust, only the sword shall be raised at them. No discussion, no demonstrations, no parades, no petitions; merely DEATH shall separate the Truth from the LIE."[132] The message to Hirsi Ali concluded by predicting the demise of the enemy on the individual, local, regional and global levels in prioritized order:

And like a great prophet once said: "I deem thee lost, O Pharaoh." (17:102) And so we want to use similar words and send these before us, so that the heavens and the stars will gather this news and spread it over the corners of the universe like a tidal wave. "I deem thee lost, O America." "I deem thee lost, O Europe." "I deem thee lost, O Holland." "I deem thee lost, O Hirsi Ali." "I deem thee lost, O unbe-lieving fundamentalist."[133]

During the trial Bouyeri praised the leader of the 9/11 cell Mohammed Atta and bin Laden, and his martyrdom testament was also inspired by al-Qaida's rhetoric. At the same time, the testament was written in a typical Dutch rhyming style. This illustrates how Bouyeri was familiar with Dutch traditions on the one hand, and how he wanted to become a mujahid and martyr on the other. It concluded by urging other Muslims to join jihad and conduct suicide operations. Bouyeri's online postings show how he was deeply affected by the war in Iraq and became markedly more aggressive in tone in the period coinciding with the invasion. He lambasted US troops in Iraq, saying they deserved to be beheaded.

According to one European security official, during the summer of 2003 Bouyeri stated online that "the Netherlands is now our enemy, because they participate in the occupation of Iraq. We shall not attack our neighbors but we will those who are apostates and those who are behaving like our enemy. Ayaan Hirsi Ali is an apostate and our enemy."[134] For Bouyeri, criticisms of Islam by van Gogh, Hirsi Ali and other Dutch politicians, and the invasion of Iraq represented different manifestations of the crusade against Islam. During the trial, Bouyeri highlighted how he was influenced by Ibn Taymiyyah's writ-ings on the death penalty for those who insult the Prophet Muhammad and stated that, "I was motivated by the law that commands me to cut off the head of anyone who insults Allah and his prophet."[135] While Bouyeri was the group's main ideologue, other members such as Walters and Aknikh also posted online messages, demonstrating their commitment to jihad and prais-ing the actions of Bouyeri. In one statement, signed "The Brigade of Islamic Jihad," issued after van Gogh's murder, they declared:

> We have, in accordance with the authentic Islamic manner slaughtered a lamb. From now on this will be the punishment that will be imposed, on anyone in this country who abuses and challenges Allah and his envoy. Oh, you Ayaan Hirsi, if Allah so desires it will be your turn tomorrow. Allah is the greatest of all and Islam will conquer ... It would be exceptionally pleasing to us if the Sharia were heralded by causing mister Wilders to be dashed to pieces from the Euromast ... moreover, we will make use of this event to rename the Euromast into a building for the execu-tion of these criminals, with the blood of mister Wilders ... hahaha, we, we, are the group of Mohammed B. with Theo van Gogh.[136]

In addition to their anger over anti-Islamic figures, the Hofstadgroup may have been seeking revenge for the counter-terrorism measures to which they had been subjected. Several members were furious with the AIVD for monitoring and arresting them, and planned to strike at the security services. At the same time, counter-terrorism measures had struck hard at their MICG contacts in Morocco and Europe in the wake of the Casablanca bombings and the Madrid attacks. Also, given Bouyeri's affection for Hamza, his arrest in August 2004 must have infuriated the short-tempered extremist. Bayeri's fervent ideology meant that there could no longer be a covenant of security between the Netherlands and its Muslims, as the country had taken part in a war in Muslim lands, and had arrested Muslims and insulted Islam.

In summary, the Hofstadgroup and M-11 were both part of a new jihadi threat in Europe motivated primarily by Iraq and directed against European countries involved in Iraq. The terrorist cells were linked to North African support networks in the region which by now were preoccupied with the jihad in Iraq. The new threat involved more nationalities than before, and more people born and bred in Europe, including converts. These developments must be seen, at least in part, as a result of messages by central jihadi thinkers suggesting European states had broken the covenant of security with their Muslim citizens.

The new threat would become more acute when the London-based radical preacher Omar Bakri Mohammed declared that the covenant of security between British Muslims and Britain was invalid. At the time, he headed the most potent group among Europe's new generation of jihadis, al-Muhajiroun, which had become dominated by British-Pakistanis nurturing close relations with al-Qaida in Af-Pak. This came to affect patterns of jihadi terrorism in the way Europe in the way that several major plots and attacks, involving al-Qaida-linked Pakistanis, would target the UK between 2004 and 2006. However, the involvement of Pakistanis in international jihadi terrorism from 2004 onwards was not caused only by events in the UK. It also had to do with changes in the relationship between jihadi outfits and the Pakistani state.

6

THE PAKISTAN AXIS (2004–6)

Before the invasion of Iraq, jihadi terrorism in Europe was dominated by North Africans. In the years following the invasion, the threat became increasingly multinational. Part of this development was the growing number of plots involving people from Pakistani backgrounds, and the deadly attacks in London on 7 July 2005. The near absence of Pakistanis in terrorist cells in Europe in the 1990s and early 2000s is something of a paradox given Pakistan's role in the Afghan jihad, the fact that most jihadi cells uncovered in Europe had links to Af-Pak, and that Pakistanis were central to the jihadi networks in London.

As discussed in Chapter Two, many Pakistani Islamists in Europe hailed from Kashmir and focused on supporting mujahidin there. Bakri's al-Muhajiroun and Hamza's Supporters of Shariah, for example, had close ties to Kashmiri groups and helped facilitate training in Pakistan for Britons. Bakri boasted that al-Muhajiroun had sent hundreds for training in Pakistan.[1] There was also a number of examples from the 1990s onwards of terrorist incidents in Kashmir and India involving British jihadis.[2] One such incident was a suicide truck bombing of an Indian Army barracks in Kashmir in 2000 by a twenty-four-year-old al-Muhajiroun member named Mohammed Bilal. This bombing is believed to have been the first suicide operation by a British jihadi, the second one being the bombing of the restaurant Mike's Place in Tel Aviv by two al-Muhajiroun members in 2003.[3] Although Pakistanis did not engage in terrorist plotting inside Europe until after the invasion of Iraq, as a general rule, there were a few exceptions. In 2001, for example, two Pakistanis assisted the "shoe-bomber" Richard Reid in Paris while he was preparing the attack on a transatlantic jet, and in January 2003 a group of Pakistanis was arrested in Italy suspected of plotting attacks on NATO targets in Italy, and the UK's top military commander, Sir Michael Boyce.[4]

However, from 2004 onwards, terrorist plots involving people from Pakistan became commonplace, although the threat was mostly confined to the UK. During the spring and summer of 2004, for example, two major terrorist plans were intercepted which involved British-Pakistanis linked to Bakri and Hamza in the UK and al-Qaida in Pakistan. The first case, which will be explored in detail in this chapter, was a plan to detonate truck bombs in London in March/April 2004. The second case was a plot to bomb public targets in the UK and financial institutions in the United States, which was thwarted in August 2004.[5] The latter incident was followed by the London bombings in 2005 and a plot to bomb transatlantic airliners in 2006, which will also be examined in detail.

While most plots involving Pakistanis took place in the UK, there were also incidents in Italy, Spain, Denmark and other countries. In September 2004, for instance, Spanish police disrupted a cell believed to be plotting attacks on Barcelona's Twin Towers,[6] and in 2008 a plan was uncovered involving suicide attacks on Barcelona's public transportation system by Pakistanis with alleged links to Tehrik Taliban Pakistan (TTP).[7] Furthermore, in 2009, US-based Pakistanis linked to al-Qaida were arrested for preparing attacks against the offices of *Jyllands-Posten* to avenge its publication of Muhammad cartoons.[8] From 2010 onwards, there have been multiple cases involving terrorists of Pakistani origin. These incidents will be commented upon in Chapters Eight and Nine.

In addition to the increase in Pakistani terrorist cells, Pakistanis continued to play roles as recruiters for training camps in Af-Pak throughout the 2000s. One example was the Germany-based Aleem Nasir, who was arrested in Pakistan in 2007 while trying to recruit young Germans for al-Qaida-affiliated groups in Waziristan.[9] People of Pakistani origin would also come to play vital roles as entrepreneurs within burgeoning jihadi networks in Scandinavia, which will be addressed in the subsequent chapters.

The Pakistani axis of jihadi terrorism in Europe was largely based upon cooperation between extremists in Britain and al-Qaida. Typically, a high-ranking al-Qaida figure would sit down with British recruits who had made their way to Af-Pak and convince them that they best served jihad by attacking at home. Interactions between al-Qaida and Pakistani jihadis were hardly a new development, nor were links between British-Pakistanis and groups in

Kashmir. Furthermore, there was nothing new about jihadi terrorists in Europe having spent time in Pakistan.

What was new, however, was the extent to which links to Pakistan came to shape the threat situation in Europe, and particularly in Britain. Key conditions were the re-consolidation of al-Qaida in Waziristan, intensifying conflicts between the state and Islamists in Pakistan, and radicalization among Pakistani Islamists in Europe. At this point in the history of jihadism in Europe, al-Qaida was using the opportunity to include European Pakistanis in global jihad. To be able to recruit and train them for international attacks, al-Qaida depended upon support from local groups. In order to obtain such support, the organization harvested goodwill from years of training mujahidin at camps in Afghanistan, maneuvering carefully among different groups and tribes, while igniting a terrorist campaign against the Pakistani state to create a common enemy.

Pakistani jihadis and al-Qaida

Although Pakistani jihadism is too multi-faceted to be treated in detail here, it is necessary to address those groups that were linked to terrorism in Europe, and some of the changes in the relationship between the Pakistani state and domestic jihadis that contributed to radicalization and internationalization. A nation founded on Islam, Pakistan has been haunted by sectarian and secessionist conflicts on the one hand, and external threats on the other.[10] Neither ethnically, geographically nor religiously homogenous, the country is populated by Punjabis, Kashmiris, Baluchis, Sindhis, Pashtuns and other groups. Most Pakistanis are Sunnis, while the minority adheres to Shia Islam, and the two communities have often clashed in violent conflict.

The interplay between internal conflicts and foreign pressures, combined with economic crises and poverty, has caused near constant problems of instability and terrorist violence in the country. Since Pakistan's birth, successive governments have engaged in border disputes with India and China over Kashmir and disputes with Iran over Baluchistan, while also interfering in the seemingly endless conflicts in Afghanistan. The enmity with India over Kashmir has resulted in three wars, and almost led to an exchange of nuclear missiles in 2002. The dispute with Iran has been less intense, but remains a challenge, mainly because Iranian authorities support Shia groups in the country, and accuse Pakistan of supporting Iranian Sunni extremists.[11] Pakistani policies towards Afghanistan have been shaped by a need to concentrate on the Indian archenemy. In order to do so, Pakistan has tried to ensure that its northern neighbor remains destabilized and weak, or a loyal, friendly ally.

Therefore, during the 1980s Pakistan's powerful Inter-Services Intelligence Directorate (ISI) cooperated with the CIA in supporting Afghan warlords. With backing from the ISI and diverse political parties and religious organizations, many thousands of Pakistanis joined the jihad in Afghanistan. The state support for the Afghan mujahidin and Pakistani foreign fighters led to close and enduring ties between the ISI and militant outfits in Afghanistan. The Pakistani military also began to fund and train armed groups emerging from the conflict with India, such as the deobandi Harakat-ul-Ansar (HuA)/ Harakat-ul-Mujahidin (HuM) and the Kashmiri Lashkar-e-Taiba (LeT).[12]

After the Soviet withdrawal, HuM and LeT concentrated almost exclusively on jihad in Kashmir.[13] Assisted by ISI, the groups set up camps in Pakistan-controlled Kashmir and engaged in guerrilla warfare and terrorist attacks against India in Kashmir and on Indian territory. It is believed that ISI supplied the groups with weapons, equipment, money and instructors. While enjoying state support on the one hand, the Kashmiri mujahidin also benefited from popular support and a reputation as "freedom fighters."[14] This attracted money from support networks and sympathizers abroad, including Europe. Throughout the 1990s, while propping up the mujahidin in Kashmir as buffers on the border with India, the Pakistani authorities continued to support the Afghan Taliban.

Islamic movements have played an important role in Pakistani civil society and political life. Like in the Arab countries, the Islamists offered social services neglected by the state, such as healthcare and education, and also ran political parties. The influx of Arab foreign fighters during the Afghan jihad was followed by money from Saudi Arabia and benefactors in the Gulf countries. The money went partly to mujahidin, and partly to facilitate the general spread of conservative Sunni Islam among Pakistanis. Aside from the proliferation of armed groups, the most visible manifestation of Saudi money and influences is the growth in the number of Islamic schools (madrasas) in Pakistan since rule of President Zia-ul-Haq (1977–88).[15] These schools, estimated at more than 12, 000 in 2009, provided recruits to the Afghan Taliban and came to function as recruitment grounds for different jihadi trends, including al-Qaida, Kashmiri mujahidin and, later, the Pakistani Taliban (TTP).[16]

While the Pakistani authorities managed to contain militancy in central parts of the country until the mid-2000s, the near absence of state governance in the areas bordering Afghanistan and India made these regions de facto

Islamic emirates, which were governed by warlords nurturing ties to the Afghan Taliban and al-Qaida. Before the invasion of Afghanistan in 2001, the Federally Administered Tribal Areas (FATA) and the North West Frontier Province (NWFP) functioned as recruitment grounds and gateways to the Taliban's and al-Qaida's Afghan camps. After the invasion, the areas emerged as rear bases for the warfare against ISAF and attacks against the Pakistani political leadership.[17] Unlike their Arab counterparts, Pakistani Islamists have rarely targeted their government. The Pakistani Muslim Brotherhood, Jamaat-e-Islami, and similar movements have worked peacefully through political activism and proselytizing for full implementation of Islamic law, but there was never an Islamist anti-state insurgency in Pakistan such as those in Egypt and Algeria. The main reason for this relative harmony was the mutual interests of the regime and the Islamists with regard to developments in Afghanistan and Kashmir.

Al-Qaida's declaration of global jihad in 1998 would alter this dynamic dramatically. After 9/11, when President Pervez Musharraf declared his support for the War on Terror, al-Qaida-linked jihadis initiated a terrorist campaign in Pakistan that included several attempts on the president's life, as well as attacks on state institutions and representatives.[18] The growing levels of anti-state violence led the government to respond via military incursions against al-Qaida and the tribes protecting the organization in FATA. The conflict reached its first peak with the Lal Masjid incident in July 2007, in which militants operating out of one mosque in Islamabad called for the overthrow of the government, engaged in violent demonstrations and set fire to a ministry building, as well as shooting at army guards.[19] The army subsequently besieged the mosque before storming it and killing many Islamists. Before the siege, Lal Masjid was a main destination point for young jihadi recruits from different parts of the world, including Europe, aiming to join training camps in the tribal areas bordering Afghanistan. One of these recruits would become involved in a terrorist plot in Denmark in 2007, as is discussed in the next chapter.

Although Pakistanis historically played minor parts within al-Qaida's Arab-dominated networks, there has been cooperation between Pakistani groups and al-Qaida dating back to the Afghan jihad.[20] However, there have also been ideological, cultural and practical obstacles to integration between Pakistani mujahidin and the global jihadis. Pakistani militants have generally focused on local issues, pursuing Pashtu nationalism, Kashmiri separatism or sectarianism rather than global jihad. Similar differences have inhibited integration between al-Qaida and the Afghan Taliban.[21] Because many Pakistani mujahidin are Pashtu-speaking Deobandi alumni from religious schools on the border with Afghanistan, they identify to a greater extent with the Deobandi Taliban than the Salafi al-Qaida.

Moreover, from al-Qaida's perspective, most rank-and-file members of armed groups in Pakistan lack the necessary language skills, education and travel documents to engage in international terrorism. This is why, for the purpose of international attacks, al-Qaida has been most interested in Pakistanis living in the West, primarily in Britain. However, as will become evident in the case studies below, the first contact points for British recruits in Pakistan were usually Kashmiri mujahidin rather than al-Qaida. There have also been quite a few examples of ad hoc cooperation between Pakistani jihadis and al-Qaida (via the Afghan Taliban or directly) during the 1990s and throughout the 2000s. The circumstances of the 1999 Indian Airlines hijacking in Nepal by members of Harkat-ul-Mujahideen (HuM) are a case in point.

HuM fighters hijacked the aircraft, carrying many Indian passengers, in Kathmandu and had it diverted to Afghanistan, aiming to negotiate the release of its leaders who were imprisoned in India. The Taliban facilitated negotiations from Kandahar airport, organized the exchange of prisoners and passengers, and escorted the hijackers from the scene, and some sources say the whole affair ended in an *iftar* party (*iftar* is the sunset meal during Ramadan when Muslims break the fast) organized by bin Laden to celebrate the success.[22] The hijacking and the release of the prisoners, one of whom was the British-Pakistani militant named Omar Saeed Sheikh, prompted the formation of a new group, Jaysh-e-Mohammed (JeM), which was portrayed as a Pakistani branch of al-Qaida and orchestrated the 2003 assassination attempts on Pervez Musharraf.[23]

The UK–Pakistan trail

The story of the London School of Economics' (LSE) student Omar Saeed Sheikh exemplifies how UK extremists were able to connect with Kashmiri groups and al-Qaida in Pakistan during the 1990s and how these ties provided a window of opportunity for al-Qaida when the organization relocated to Pakistan after the invasion of Afghanistan.[24] Sheikh was born in East London in 1973 to Pakistani work immigrants. His father was a wealthy businessman, and Sheikh was sent to attend elite schools in Pakistan and the UK. Described as charming, intelligent and caring, he enrolled at the prestigious LSE to study mathematics, economics, statistics and social psychology. Sheikh excelled in school and was also a gifted sportsman. His family was conservative and he joined the Islamic Society while at university.

Sheikh began to radicalize during an event called "Bosnia Week" at LSE, in which films of atrocities against Muslims in Bosnia were shown. He started to engage in activism in support of mujahidin in Bosnia, Kashmir and other places. In 1993 he joined his father on a business trip to Pakistan, where he connected with members of HuM and received paramilitary training at the group's camp called Khalid bin Waleed in southern Afghanistan. He went on to specialize in training in urban warfare, assault rifles, RPGs, surveillance, disguise, interrogation, secret writing and codes, instructed by soldiers in the Pakistani Army. Training with HuM, Sheikh befriended the group's leader Maulana Masood Azhar, who took the Briton as his protégé and soon asked him to join him in mediating between conflicting Kashmiri mujahidin inside India. Sheikh wanted to accompany Azhar, but was prevented due to a lack of travel documents. As it happened, Azhar was arrested by Indian security forces and imprisoned, after which HuM staged several hostage-takings with the intention of freeing the leader. In 1994 Sheikh participated in the abduction of a group of Western backpackers in India for this purpose. The operation failed, and he was arrested by Indian security services and ended up being incarcerated together with Azhar and other HuM fighters.

HuM subsequently organized new kidnappings, aiming to negotiate for the release of the imprisoned leaders. One was the abduction of foreign tourists (Germans, Americans, Britons and one Norwegian) in Kashmir in 1995 by a HuM front dubbed al-Faran. After a lengthy negotiation and rescue operation the hostages were all freed, except for the Norwegian Hans Christian Ostrø, who was decapitated and dumped in the mountains.[25] A few years later, in December 1999, HuM fighters hijacked Indian Airlines Flight IC-814 while it was taking off from Kathmandu Airport. The latter operation was effective, and after the killing of one Indian passenger, negotiations led to the release of Azhar, Sheikh and another HuM prisoner in exchange for the 154 passengers.

After staying for a while with al-Qaida and the Taliban in Afghanistan, Sheikh and Azhar returned to Pakistan, where the latter announced the formation of JeM at the Binoria mosque in Karachi. Azhar acted as a leader for the new group, while Sheikh functioned as his deputy. Azhar later became the leader of the Jammu and Kashmir faction of the Taliban, and at one point he was affiliated with the sectarian anti-Shia group Sipah-e-Sahaba. While Azhar became caught up in sectarianism, Sheikh grew closer to al-Qaida. Under the command of 9/11 planner KSM, he took part in al-Qaida's abduction and slaying of the American journalist Daniel Pearl in January 2002. He also helped facilitate the suicide attacks on the Indian parliament in 2001 by terrorists linked to JeM and LeT.

The following case studies demonstrate how British-Pakistanis who became involved in terrorist plots in the UK followed in Sheikh's footsteps, establishing contacts with Kashmiri mujahidin before moving on to al-Qaida. After the invasion of Afghanistan, al-Qaida and Taliban started to use FATA and NWFP as a sanctuary and operation base, as did likeminded movements from neighboring countries Uzbekistan, China and Iran. Amid the War on Terror the relationship between Kashmiri militants and the state gradually soured. JeM, which had a longtime affiliation with al-Qaida, embarked on a terrorist campaign against the regime. LeT (and its front-organization Jamaat-ud-Dawa) was banned by the regime, following US pressure after several high-profile attacks on India, nearly causing inter-state war. The group's activities in Kashmir were restricted, and from around 2006 it started taking part in the insurgency in southern Afghanistan, operating out of FATA and NWFP. This led to a closer relationship between LeT, al-Qaida, Taliban and other groups operating in the tribal areas.[26] Due to the close ties between British jihadis and Kashmiri LeT and JeM, access to al-Qaida became easy.

Waziristan and Europe plots

From around 2003, the vast majority of terrorist plots in Europe had links to al-Qaida and its affiliates in Waziristan and NWFP. Al-Zawahiri had been in charge of al-Qaida's alliance-building in Af-Pak, which aimed to secure the organization's leadership and sustain its capability to fight ISAF and engage in acts of international terrorism.[27] In order to achieve this, it was necessary for al-Qaida to obtain the support of local tribes and armed groups in FATA and NWFP.

In negotiations, al-Zawahiri relied upon a combination of economic incentives and inter-marriages between al-Qaida leaders and daughters of clan leaders and warlords. As well as securing the protection of tribes, such as the Mehsud and Wazir clans, al-Zawahiri and al-Qaida also needed to nurture relations with a number of Pakistani and Afghan groups which had operated in the border zone for many years, most importantly the Taliban-linked Haqqani network, a militant outfit named Tehrik Nifaz Shariat Muhammadi (TNSM), JeM and LeT, and later the Pakistani Taliban (TTP) emerging from around 2007.

Moreover, al-Qaida had to relate to multiple foreign groups that were present in the FATA. Some of these groups, such as LIFG and MICG, were longtime allies, which like al-Qaida had been pressured out of Afghanistan. Other groups, such as the Islamic Movement of Uzbekistan (IMU) and Islamic Jihad Union (IJU), and the East Turkestan Islamic Movement (ETIM), had also been pressured out of Afghanistan, but they had been closest to the Taliban, and came to compete with al-Qaida over resources in Pakistan.[28]

While al-Qaida was re-inventing itself in Waziristan in 2001–3, the organization's section for external operations continued to prepare attacks in the West. When KSM was arrested in Rawalpindi in March 2003 leadership was transferred to Hamza Rabiyyah al-Masri. With the help of Pakistani groups, al-Masri set up training facilities in the Shakai Valley, South Waziristan. Sources indicate that these camps were the location for meetings between al-Qaida and British-Pakistanis recruited for attacks in the United States and the UK. In August 2003, for example, al-Masri, al-Qaida's chief of internal operations at the time, Abu Faraj al-Liby, and another high-ranking al-Qaida figure known as Abdul Hadi al-Iraqi, held meetings with a jihadi named Mohammed Noor Khan, to discuss international attacks.[29] In April 2004, al-Masri and al-Liby sat down with an Indian jihadi named Dhiren Barot to discuss a plot to bomb financial institutions in the United States and public sites in the UK. In August 2004, UK, US and Pakistani security services jointly intercepted a British-Pakistani terrorist cell supervised by Barot. A few months earlier another cell with links to al-Qaida in Pakistan had been dismantled in Britain. This cell, which was dubbed the "Crawley group" because its members hailed from Crawley, a town in West Sussex, is the first of three cases I use to explore the Pakistani axis of jihadism in Europe. They all illustrate an intricate interplay between UK extremists and actors in Pakistan, facilitated by entrepreneurs.

Crawley group

In late March 2004, UK, US and Canadian security services disrupted an al-Qaida-linked plot to explode truck-bombs at a shopping center, a nightclub or gas installations in London.[30] The counter-terrorism operation was code-named "Crevice," and the cell was composed of young British-Pakistanis and one British-Algerian. The terrorists received support from accomplices in Pakistan, the United States and Canada. Because the entrepreneurs of the cell held meetings with al-Qaida in Waziristan and because the war in Iraq was a strong motivation, the plot had a global jihad dimension.[31] However, this cell and the other cells discussed in this chapter also illustrate how the extremist sub-culture of London and mobilization over jihad in Kashmir were driving the radicalization of British-Pakistanis.

All of the terrorists had been affiliated with al-Muhajiroun and Omar Bakri, who took a special interest in Kashmir, but also preached that attacks on European countries that violated the covenant of security were justified. The wannabe bombers had gathered approximately 600 kilograms of fertilizer for bomb-making, and had undertaken reconnaissance of potential targets when the security services intervened. The plot resembled M-11 in that the Iraq war was a central motive. Yet at the same time, it differed from the M-11 as the terrorists were second-generation immigrants who had lived most of their lives in the UK—a feature shared with the Hofstadgroup.

The Crawley group grew out of a UK-centered but transnational support network for international jihad. Plotting explosions in London, cell members received aid from two Pakistani immigrants to the United States and Canada, Mohammed Junaid Babar (twenty-seven) and Momin Khawaja (twenty-nine). The former was involved in facilitating training in Pakistan, whereas the latter built detonators for the cell. Babar and Khawaja were both convicted in the United States and Canada for supporting terrorism. The leader of the group, Omar Khyam (twenty-four) and four of his accomplices, Jawad Akbar (twenty-two), Salahuddin Amin (thirty), Waheed Mahmood (thirty-three) and Anthony Garcia (twenty-seven), were sentenced to life in prison in April 2007.

The evidence against the plotters included bomb-making materials and recipes, surveillance data (photos, audio-recordings, hard-discs and electronic storage devices), as well as information from the interrogation of the terrorists and witness accounts. Police secured training manuals and propaganda material from the terrorists' belongings. On Garcia's computer, for example, police discovered lesson five of the so-called "al-Qaida training manual," entitled "Means of Communication and Transportation."[32] On other computers and storage devices investigators retrieved violent movies showing the execution of a Russian soldier in Chechnya, as well as executions conducted by the Taliban and the Iranian regime.

The terrorist plans were typical of al-Qaida at the time, including transnational networking, training in Af-Pak and the intent to cause mass casualties. The investigations revealed that the group planned to use fertilizer bombs. Fertilizer is a popular bomb-making material in jihadi circles and has been used by many al-Qaida affiliates, such as the cell behind the first World Trade Center bombing in 1993. Unlike other al-Qaida attacks at the time, however, the Crawley terrorists do not seem to have planned suicide missions. They instead sought to construct a remote-control detonator which would set off the bombs using encrypted radio transmissions.[33] Also, core members of the cell had made travel arrangements to go to Pakistan on 6 April, likely after an attack was to have taken place.[34] Their co-conspirators in the UK, the United States, Canada and Pakistan mainly communicated with each other online and they also used the Internet to download propaganda and training manuals, and to search for bomb-making recipes and information on potential targets.

The Crawley group does not seem to have decided on the exact target(s) at the time of the arrests, but surveillance material and witness accounts presented by the public prosecutor illustrated how they assessed different possibilities. The terrorists' discussions on target selection provided an interesting glimpse into the mindset of jihadis in Europe and their balancing between pragmatism and symbolism. According to one witness, during training in Pakistan, Omar Khyam declared he wanted to strike at pubs, nightclubs or trains.[35]

Another member of the cell, Jawad Akbar, talked about attacks on civilian infrastructure, such as gas, water or electrical supplies. As shown in Chapter Two, there have been very few plans to target civilian infrastructure by jihadis in Europe. The reason why the group considered such attacks was likely because one of the members, Waheed Mahmood, worked for a sub-contractor of a company called Transco (now known as National Grid Plc.), which operates electricity systems and gas networks in the UK. Mahmood had stolen CDs containing information about the company's vulnerabilities, which were found in Akbar's possession.

However, while Akbar brought up infrastructure in group discussions, he also proposed mass casualty bomb attacks against public sites, and considered such attacks more likely to succeed. For example, he had also talked about striking "the biggest nightclub in central London," adding that "no one [in a nightclub] can put their hands up and say they are innocent—those slags dancing around," and that "I think the club thing you could do but the gas would be much harder."[36] Mahmood came up with several ideas such as poisoning burgers at football stadiums, but maintained that attacking a shopping center was the easiest way to success, stating "a little explosion at Bluewater [a large shopping center in Kent]—tomorrow if you want ... I don't know how big it would be we haven't tested it but we could tomorrow—do one tomorrow."[37]

Shortly before the arrests several members of the group participated in discussions about the Madrid attacks and expressed their admiration as well as their criticisms of the operation. Mahmood reportedly stated that: "Spain was a beautiful job weren't it, absolutely beautiful man, so much impact."[38] During a discussion in Khyam's car, another plotter expressed some reservations, suggesting that the bombings should have been carried out in June to hurt the tourist industry. In addition to the plan to poison burgers at a football stadium, the group had initially fantasized about buying a radioisotope bomb from the Russian mafia, but in the end they settled for more conventional plans.[39] They bought fertilizer from an agricultural merchant, and stored it at a self-storage facility in Hanwell, near Heathrow Airport. British agents had the storage under surveillance and had replaced some of the fertilizer with other substances, thereby rendering it harmless.

Another aspect of the group's activities that was illuminated during the trial was the terrorists' training in Pakistan. While some information about al-Qaida's camps in Afghanistan had surfaced from investigations, at the time of the Crawley case little was known about training in Pakistan, and though both the M-11 and the Hofstadgroup involved a Pakistan dimension, details were murky. The investigation of the Crawley plotters revealed that all of them attended provisional training in houses and backyards in Kohat, Malakand, NWFP, Pakistan, during June and July 2003. On their way to Malakand they also spent time in Lahore, where they paid several visits to al-Muhajiroun's offices in the city.

The training activities in Malakand were attended by a number of people that would become involved in the subsequent terrorist plots in the UK discussed in this chapter. The training in Malakand was supervised by the ringleader Omar Khyam and the US-based al-Muhajiroun member and al-Qaida-affiliate Mohammed Junaid Babar, who hired an Afghan explosives expert to instruct them in bomb-making. According to intelligence leaks, at the end of the training, Khyam, Babar and the Pakistani-Canadian Momin Khawaja traveled to South Waziristan where they met with two al-Qaida commanders known as Abd al-Hadi al-Iraqi and Abu Munthir al-Maghrebi.[40]

Al-Iraqi was one of al-Qaida's top military figures with responsibility for operations in Afghanistan, but at the time of the Crawley case he was also involved in the activities of the section for external operations, which was headed by Hamza Rabiyyah al-Masri.[41] Al-Iraqi is a former Iraqi Army officer who climbed the ranks of al-Qaida in the late 1990s. He was apprehended in Turkey while on his way to Iraq during the fall of 2005, and later detained at Guantanamo Bay. A senior counter-terrorism official told the press that al-Iraqi had stressed that the UK should be the main battleground for al-Qaida in Europe. Al-Iraqi was linked to several cells operating in Europe between 2003 and 2005, including the 7/7 cell. He was said to have overseen the training of Western recruits in the South Waziristan Shakai Valley, who were to be dispatched to their home countries as "sleepers."[42] In a video published by al-Sahab in August 2005, al-Iraqi appeared while talking to a group of trainees including Britons, a Frenchman (with a North African accent) and one Australian. The video shows training in the manufacturing of bombs and firing of missiles, and in one sequence it refers to a "chemical crew."[43]

During their training in Kohat, members of the Crawley group learned how to handle handguns and AK-47s and staged test explosions of small fertilizer bombs. They also discussed ways to smuggle bomb ingredients and detonators from Pakistan to the UK via Belgium, as well as the possibilities of utilizing other kinds of bomb ingredients, such as urea (jokingly stating that if urea worked as a bomb-making ingredient, it would be one less ingredient to smuggle into the UK).[44] The focus on training showed that the Crawley plotters aimed at some level of professionalism. In fact, Khyam urged the others to "be professional" and security conscious, and to avoid mixing with too many people.[45]

The activities of the cell in the UK and Pakistan show how the cell members stressed the need to be conscious of their own security, and acted according to established counter-surveillance techniques. They used false names, coded their communications and disposed of laptops and mobile phones on a regular basis. Furthermore, when visiting Pakistan the plotters dressed and acted as tourists in order to avoid attracting attention. Members of the cell said they had been told to hide their religious convictions as a security precaution by al-Iraqi. According to the same logic (for security reasons), Mahmood suggested sending a recent convert to Pakistan for the purpose of smuggling bomb ingredients back to the UK, as he would be less likely to be spotted by the security services.[46]

This suggestion illustrates how al-Qaida-affiliated terrorists see in converts a tactical advantage, something which is also confirmed by the fact that several converts have risen in the ranks of al-Qaida, and that the organization has used them for international operations on several occasions. Another aspect of the Crawley cell's security strategies was that the terrorists sought secure ways to communicate online. Conspirators in the UK and accomplices abroad kept in touch via several different Internet cafes. They would write messages to each other in the draft messages of Yahoo email accounts, which they accessed with shared passwords. In this way no messages were actually transferred between accounts, making it more challenging to monitor communication.[47]

The Crawley cell emerged from among the followers of Bakri and Hamza. Bakri confirmed to the UK press that the plotters had been members of al-Muhajiroun.[48] However, it was indicated that they had been part of a group of some forty individuals who left Bakri's organization in 2000 on the grounds that the group was too moderate and had forbidden its members from violating the covenant of security with the British state.[49] Subsequently, Omar Khyam, the US-Pakistani Mohammed Junaid Babar and a Pakistani jihadi based in Luton referred to as Mohammed Qayum Khan, cooperated in establishing ties to Kashmiri mujahidin, the Afghan Taliban and al-Qaida. Mohammed Qayum Khan, a part-time taxi driver, was in charge of an al-Qaida-linked support network centered on Luton, which took orders directly from al-Iraqi.[50] In January 2004 all central members of the Crawley group and some of their international contacts gathered in London in preparation for the attacks.

Socio-economically, the Crawley plotters were a good example of how British-Pakistani jihadis tended to be more educated and generally better off than their North African counterparts. Most members of the cell hailed from the middle class, some of them had established successful businesses, and they were students and workers. All of them had some level of education and several had received higher education. Several had been involved in religious and social activism. There were also a few talented athletes among them. According to the familiar pattern, their radicalization differed from one person to the next, but they shared anger over the situation in Kashmir and the invasion of Iraq, and interacted with jihadi networks in the UK and internationally.

The entrepreneur, Khyam, was born in Britain in 1981. He came from a secular family and became increasingly religious and politicized as a teenager. Khyam studied at the University of North London (now known as the London Metropolitan University). He obtained good grades, excelled in sports and was elected captain of the school's cricket team. However, while being outwardly Westernized and wearing designer clothes, he developed a strong interest in conservative Islam and started to spend more and more time in the local mosque in Langley Green. After his father left the family, Khyam took his place as the man of the house and imposed stern religious practices, such as forbidding his brother from interacting with girls or watching impious TV programs. At eighteen Khyam joined al-Muhajiroun.

As a member of Bakri's group, like so many other terrorists discussed in this book, he was exposed to movies and images of atrocities against Muslims in Chechnya. He also attended Hamza's lectures at the Finsbury Park Mosque. Becoming increasingly religious, Khyam grew a beard and started to wear

Islamic robes. At one point he connected with Britons who had fought with Kashmiri mujahidin against the Indians and became determined to join jihad in Kashmir.[51] After traveling to Pakistan Khyam connected with Laskhar-e-Taiba (LeT). He trained in one of the group's camps from January to March 2000. In Khyam's words: "They taught me everything I needed for guerrilla warfare in Kashmir," such as using AK-47s, pistols, RPGs (rocket-propelled grenades), sniper rifles, climbing and crawling techniques, reconnaissance and light machine guns.[52]

His family in the UK strongly opposed his militant activities and trips to Kashmir, and with the help of an uncle working for ISI they managed to get him back to the UK. Reflecting the close relations between ISI and LeT at that time, the uncle was able to reach his nephew via radio contact with the camp. He ordered him to travel to the nearest city and return home. Still determined to become a mujahid, in 2001 Khyam traveled to Afghanistan to seek out the Taliban. While traveling between the UK and Pakistan, Khyam became further enraged by the War on Terror and particularly the invasion of Iraq. A security official with knowledge of the investigation described Khyam as a person who embraced militancy gradually and intellectually, and who was very active online.[53] In 2003, he borrowed some £16,000 from a bank and traveled to Pakistan. Via the al-Qaida contact in Luton, Khyam then connected with al-Iraqi who was the main organizer for the training of Western al-Qaida recruits in Waziristan.

The oldest of the terrorists, Waheed Mahmood (thirty-two), also had a lead role in the Crawley cell. Few details were known about his personal motives, but witness accounts and surveillance data revealed he was extreme. He was the one saying to the others, for example, that the Madrid attacks were a "beautiful job" and suggesting the Bluewater shopping center in Kent as a target.[54] He did not give statements during trial, and destroyed his computer when he knew he was going to be arrested. Married with children and working in the gas industry, Mahmood first encountered Khyam at al-Muhajiroun meetings in Luton, and the cell used a house in Gujar Khan, Pakistan, owned by Mahmood's family as a meeting place on trips to Pakistan. His brother was also part of Bakri's following and would later join the jihad against the Assad regime in Syria.[55]

Salahuddin Amin has been described as the cell's facilitator, and one of the links between the plotters and organized jihadi networks. He was born in Pakistan and arrived in the UK when he was sixteen. Around 1999/2000 he became involved in support activism for jihad in Kashmir. In the UK he studied product design engineering and worked as a taxi driver. He was recruited by a jihadi named Aftab who had trained in Pakistan and was later killed in Afghanistan. Aftab showed Amin videos that accelerated his radicalization. He joined a radical mosque in Luton where he met the other members of the cell. In 2001 Amin moved to Pakistan and worked for his uncle's business. While in Pakistan he was contacted by the Luton-based Mohammed Qayum Khan, who asked Amin for help in sending funds and equipment to Afghanistan.[56]

A fourth convict, Jawad Akbar, was born in Pakistan and grew up in Italy where his father worked in the wine industry. The family settled in Crawley when he was eight. Akbar had been working in shops at Gatwick airport, but it was while studying mathematics, technology and design at Brunel University that he joined an Islamic study group, and came in touch with extremists. He met Khyam through his cousin Nabeel Hussain and grew increasingly radical by watching videos of atrocities against Muslims in Pakistan, before joining training camps in the country with other members of the Crawley group.[57]

Anthony Garcia differed from the other terrorists. He came from an Algerian background and dropped out of school when he was sixteen. Garcia was a fan of basketball and rap-music, and wanted to become a male model. He drifted between odd jobs and did not act religiously. He drank and smoked, and wore designer clothes. It was his brother Lamine Adam who introduced him to political Islam in the late 1990s, and the brothers attended meetings about the situation for Muslims in Kashmir. Garcia claims he was deeply affected by movies showing the atrocities committed by Indian forces against women and children in Indian-controlled Kashmir.[58] In 2002 he met Khyam (also via his brother Lamine), and he later joined the training organized by Khyam in Pakistan.[59] It was Garcia who had procured the fertilizer meant to be used in the planned bombings in late 2003.

The Canadian-Pakistani Mohammed Momin Khawaja (twenty-nine) was arrested by Royal Canadian Mounted Police in Ottawa shortly before the British counter-terrorism operation on 29 March 2004. Born in Canada, Khawaja was educated as a computer programmer. He has three brothers and one sister.[60] He is the son of an academic who has voiced anti-Western sentiments. Khawaja worked as a software consultant for the Canadian government and was in charge of building remotely controlled detonators for Khyam's cell. He was in regular email contact with Khyam informing him about the progress of the detonators, attended training in Malakand during the summer of 2003 and visited the plotters in the UK in February 2004.

Khawaja had passwords for the Yahoo email accounts used for intra-cell communication, and he was also very active on blogs spreading jihadi messages.[61]

Mohammed Junaid Babar was born in Pakistan, but raised and educated in New York, and was a member of al-Muhajiroun. He interacted with other al-Muhajiroun followers in New York and regularly accessed audio-visual speeches and texts by Hamza and Bakri online. Between 2001 and 2004 he lived in Pakistan and worked at al-Muhajiroun's office in Lahore. In Pakistan he organized training for British jihadis in Malakand. He also traveled to London, mixing with al-Muhajiroun and engaging in fundraising for the battle against ISAF in Afghanistan.[62]

Statements attributed to the Crawley plotters reflected the tendency seen in M-11 and the Hofstadgroup for jihadi terrorists in Europe to employ al-Qaida-inspired rhetoric and to focus on global issues. Unlike the former, the Crawley group did not issue communiques, or record martyrdom testaments. According to the public prosecutor, the cell was initially driven by an urge to join jihad in Afghanistan. Mohammed Junaid Babar quoted Khyam as saying he wanted to attack inside the UK because the country was "unscathed" and "needed to be hit because of its support for the U.S."[63] He also referred to UK participation in Iraq as "the final straw."[64]

Khyam himself told the judges that by 1998 he was ideologically committed to freeing Muslim lands from occupation, reaffirming that he still believed in that cause. Commenting on 9/11, Khyam stated: "I was happy. America was, and still is, the greatest enemy of Islam."[65] He then described the invasion of Iraq as a "war against Islam." Talking about his 2001 visit to the Taliban, Khyam said he met "amazing people, people who loved Allah, they were soft, kind and humble to the Muslims, harsh against their enemies. This is how an Islamic state should be."[66] Jawad Akbar expressed general hatred towards unbelievers and was quoted as saying "we know Allah hates the Kufs [kuffar]."[67] In a bugged phone call Mohammed Junaid Babar argued that the "U.K. should be hit because of its support of the U.S. in Afghanistan and Iraq," because "British soldiers are killing Muslims" and because "nothing had ever happened in the U.K."[68]

Developments and events in Pakistan clearly influenced the radicalization of Khyam and his accomplices, pushing them towards global jihad. During Khyam's first visits to Laskhar-e-Taiba and the Taliban in 2000–1, Pakistan was a sanctuary for jihadis from which they could support and partake in guerilla war and terrorism against India, or ISAF and the new government in Afghanistan. The resurgence of al-Qaida and affiliated groups in Waziristan broke the delicate balance that had been maintained in Islamist–state relations inside Pakistan. Al-Qaida brokered deals with Pakistani tribes and militant outfits with the dual aim of igniting an insurgency against the Pakistani government while at the same time using Pakistan as a launching pad for jihad in West. While militant Islamist groups in Pakistan had previously been loyal, useful tools for the Pakistani state, from now on the country faced a terrorist threat from some of them, while others would begin to dabble in transnational terrorism on al-Qaida's behalf. The assassination attempts against President Musharraf by Jaysh-e-Mohammed and al-Qaida in December 2003 and the terrorist plot in the UK by the Crawley group were part and parcel of this, and may even have been linked. In fact, one of the terrorists, Mohammed Junaid Babar, admitted before the court to have been involved in two assassination attempts against President Musharraf.[69]

At the same time, jihadis in the UK had come under increased pressure after the Madrid attacks. By 2004, Qatada was behind bars, central support networks such as Doha's had been crippled by counter-terrorism arrests and the followings of Hamza and Bakri had been placed under tighter surveillance. Paired with British participation in the Iraq war, this situation forced UK jihadis who saw themselves as living under a covenant of security with the authorities to reconsider their status. According to jihadi ideology, they had to choose between leaving for a Muslim country, keeping a low profile to ensure their security or initiating jihad in Britain. As noted earlier, the members of the Crawley group seemed to have opposed the idea of a covenant of security between Britain and Muslims. Long before the invasion of Iraq they had begun to distance themselves from al-Muhajiroun and sought out jihadis in Pakistan, precisely because Bakri had imposed restrictions on his followers in terms of waging jihad in the UK. Khyam's reference to UK participation in Iraq as the "final straw" may have referred to his belief that a covenant of security was no longer valid.

While there were many commonalities between the Crawley group, the Madrid bombers and the Dutch Hofstadgroup, such as the triggering effect of Iraq, there were also some differences signifying new patterns of jihadism in Europe. First and foremost, the radicalization of the plotters was rooted in Pakistan rather than North Africa and, second, the case signaled that global jihadis were more bent on punishing Britain than they had been in the past, and would rely on British jihadis to do so. Although the terrorists were enraged by the Iraq war, they chose to go to Pakistan instead of Iraq to join the jihad. The main reasons for this were likely pragmatic. They were part of jihadi networks in the UK with strong ties to Pakistan, and it was easier for them to go there than to Iraq undetected, simply because they had contacts and family in the country, and because they knew the language and customs. While members of the Crawley group may initially have wanted to join the jihad against ISAF in Afghanistan, the contacts they made with al-Qaida in Waziristan led them to become part of a global jihad offensive against Britain instead. Khyam and his cadre were intercepted, yet another cell connected to the same network managed to launch multiple suicide attacks on the London Underground and a bus on 7 July 2005, causing mass casualties.

7/7

The year after M-11, London became the scene of the first successful mass casualty suicide attacks in Europe when al-Qaida-linked terrorists bombed the underground subway system and a bus. The perpetrators of the 7 July 2005 London bombings (7/7) were three British-Pakistanis and one British-Jamaican: Mohammad Siddique Khan (thirty), Shehzad Tanweer (twenty-two), Hasib Hussain (eighteen) and Jermaine Lindsay (nineteen). The terrorists blew themselves up in suicide attacks on the trains and a bus during the morning rush hour. The attacks killed fifty-six people and injured more than 700.[70]

Early in the morning, three of the attackers drove from the northern city of Leeds to Luton train station. In Luton they teamed up with the fourth member of the cell, loaded explosives from the car trunks into rucksacks and took a Thameslink train to King's Cross station in Central London. At King's Cross, three of them (Khan, Tanweer and Lindsay) jumped on different trains and detonated their bomb devices in simultaneous suicide attacks at about 8.50 a.m. Because one of the trains was running late, the fourth attacker, Hussain, went out of the station area. He then walked around for a while, visited a McDonald's restaurant and tried to call the other attackers on their cellphones. He detonated his bomb on a London double decker bus, the number 30, on Tavistock Square at 9.47 a.m., almost one hour after the other explosions. The picture of a wrecked red double-decker London bus became the signature of the attacks in the media and al-Qaida's propaganda.[71]

Like the Crawley group, the 7/7 bombers were followers of radical preachers in London, were part of the jihadi support networks in the north of the UK and had established ties with Pakistani jihadis and al-Qaida in Af-Pak. Members of the cell attended sermons by Hamza, Bakri and al-Faisal, and investigations revealed that there had been contacts between the leader of the 7/7 cell and the Luton-based Mohammed Qayum Khan, an associate and supporter of al-Qaida, with whom the Crawley group also interacted.[72] Furthermore, the entrepreneur of the 7/7 cell, Siddique Khan, and his protégé, Tanweer, attended the training sessions organized by Khyam and Mohammed Junaid Babar in Malakand, NWFP, in 2003. They later received training in bomb-making, and recorded martyrdom videos under the supervision of al-Qaida personnel in Waziristan between November 2004 and February 2005.

In a video published by al-Sahab in July 2006 featuring Tanweer's martyrdom testament, al-Zawahiri took credit for the attacks and said al-Qaida had trained the attackers.[73] A collection of martyrdom biographies written by a Saudi jihadi going by the name of Abu Ubaydah al-Maqdisi dated 2006 contained information supporting al-Zawahiri's claims. In the biography of Hamza Rabiyyah al-Masri, who acted as chief of al-Qaida's external operations from the death of KSM until 2005, it was claimed that he personally had been involved in "preparing the men" who "tore away the dignity of the Crusaders" in Britain.[74] In the biography, al-Masri was described as the "engineer of the foreign operation."[75] Moreover, after the killing of bin Laden in 2011, leaked intelligence indicated that Khan and Tanweer had met with bin Laden's courier Abu al-Kuwaiti in Abbottabad, Pakistan (the town where the al-Qaida leader was captured and killed), who functioned as a middleman between the bombers, al-Iraqi and bin Laden.[76]

The 7/7 attacks resembled other plots attributed to al-Qaida involving peroxide-based explosives and suicide bombers. The terrorists used the homemade explosive HMTD (hexamethylene triperoxide diamine), and TATP (triacetone triperoxide), and the bombs were set off by push-button detonators. Recipes for HMTD are available online, but the explosive is difficult to work with and requires practice. The chemicals needed are ingredients in common household products, which can be bought from laboratories, pharmacies or industrial wholesaler chains. However, the chemical combinations are highly unstable and decompose continuously.

Being unpredictable and dangerous, HMTD earned the name "Satan's Mother." It is also time-consuming to make even small amounts of it. In order to assemble the devices, the group rented an apartment at Alexandra Grove as a make-shift laboratory. Because the explosives were so volatile, they had to store them in high-grade refrigerators. They even had to transport the devices to London inside coolers. Working in the laboratory they exposed themselves to unhealthy substances and took security risks. For example, the families of Tanweer and Hussain registered that their hair became lighter during the time they assembled the bombs. This was a result of the bleaching effects of the chemicals, which they themselves explained as an effect of chlorine from swimming pools.[77]

The reason why al-Qaida opted for peroxide-based explosives on several occasions was likely for security reasons. Ingredients for such bombs can be obtained from different sources, and it is hard to prove that possession of single ingredients imply terrorist intent. This was why the Frankfurt cell bought chemicals from different pharmacies under the pretense of collecting medical aid for Africa. Conversely, the Crawley group was detected partly because it employed the more common bomb ingredient, fertilizer—teaching al-Qaida a lesson for follow-ups in Britain. The 7/7 cell managed to pull off a complicated operation avoiding detection. The terrorists were well organized, determined and meticulous, as demonstrated by the test-run of the attack they made in the subway system on 28 June.[78]

The cell resembled the Crawley group and encompassed three British-Pakistanis and one Jamaican. The leader of the cell was a thirty-year-old, whereas his accomplices were very young. All of them came from middle-class backgrounds and had some level of education. All were outwardly Westernized, yet secretly mingled with extremists. At least two members (Khan and Tanweer) were known to have engaged in religious and social activism before becoming terrorists. As seen in previous cases, the length and speed of their radicalization varied between members. There are signs that the cell's leader embraced jihadism gradually from the mid- to late 1990s onwards, but that the process accelerated in conjunction with 9/11 and the invasion of Iraq.

However, the most important factor in translating their radicalization into terrorist actions was the journeys to Pakistan by lead members of the cell between 2001 and 2005. On these journeys they made contact with Pakistani mujahidin and al-Qaida, and from 2003 onwards it is believed that cell members interacted with al-Qaida commanders al-Masri and al-Iraqi in Af-Pak. A document which was uncovered in the investigation of a German al-Qaida cell in 2011 revealed that it was a British-Pakistani named Rashid Rauf who recruited and put the plotters in contact with al-Qaida. He also organized training for them and supervised the plot as a handler for al-Qaida's section for external operations. It also transpired that Rauf had been involved in the training of the leader of the cell that attempted to copy the 7/7 attacks on 21 July 2005 and the cell that planned attacks on transatlantic airliners from Britain in 2006, to be discussed later in this chapter.[79]

Khan was the entrepreneur of the cell. It was he who recruited the other members. Khan was born and raised in Beeston, Leeds, and was relatively successful both professionally and privately. His parents were work immigrants from Pakistan. He got married in 2001 and enrolled in business studies at Leeds Metropolitan University in 1996. While at university he started to work part-time as a community worker. He also met his wife at university. She was a British Muslim of Indian origin, and a social activist. Curiously, she was known to be concerned with women's rights and held anti-Taliban views. After his studies, Khan was employed as an advisor at the local Hillside Primary School. He worked there between March 2001 and November 2004, when he left after a period of frequent absences.

Khan was a committed worker and well regarded by his colleagues, as well as the pupils' parents. Youths looked up to him and saw him as a mentor and father figure whom they nicknamed "Buddy."[80] His work focused mainly on assisting disaffected children from immigrant families. Khan and his wife had one child, and they were expecting a second. They earned a decent income, and owned their own house and a car. However, the couple seem to have experienced a marital crisis after having their first child, and split up in May 2004.

In a parallel to the case of the Dutch-Moroccan terrorist Bouyeri, in 1997 Khan participated in a demonstration in Leeds arranged by the Kashmiri Welfare Association, a charity associated with the Hardy Street Mosque in Beeston. The group rallied against a decision by Leeds City Council to allow a housing company to build houses on a location which they had hoped could be used for a new community center. At the event, Khan gave an interview to a local paper, in which he passionately complained about problems for local youths and that the existing youth center was way too small.[81] From the mid-1990s Khan had also been a leading member of an anti-drugs activist group called the "Mullah Boys" which used to kidnap addicts, with the consent of their families, and have them locked up and "cold-turkeyed."[82] Continuing to act openly as a social activist, in 2002 Khan gave another press interview, in which he expressed pride about his achievements as a mentor for immigrant children. Like Bouyeri, he also expressed frustration that the city council was not providing sufficient funding for the renewal of his hometown.[83]

According to some sources, by this time (2001–2) Khan was already operating as a jihadi recruiter, was linked to members of the al-Muhajiroun organization and attended training camps in Pakistan. Khan also ran an Islamic bookshop in Leeds, and he established two local gyms with government funding. The first one was established in February 2000, in the name of the

Kashmiri Welfare Association. The second gym was set up in 2004 on Lodge Lane in Beeston, as part of the Hamara Centre charitable foundation's youth program. The latter had not been officially opened, but all the members of the terrorist cell worked out there in the months before the attacks. They also met at the bookshop run by Khan, and in the basement of a local mosque. Some witnesses said the meeting places were hubs where extremists lectured and in which young people could watch propaganda on DVDs, videos and online. One friend of Tanweer told the press he once saw Tanweer and Khan watching a DVD in the bookshop of an Israeli soldier killing a Palestinian girl. However, although vocal about social issues, Khan was not known to voice political opinions. Colleagues and friends noticed how he gradually became more religious, but he did not express extreme political views, and he publicly opposed 9/11.

Several radical preachers were known to have influenced Siddique Khan. Like Khyam and the other members of the Crawley group, Khan and the other 7/7 plotters attended the sermons of Bakri and Hamza, and members of the two cells interacted in the context of jihadi underground communities in London and Luton.[84] In November 2004 Khan recorded a farewell video to his daughter, which indicated that he wanted to die fighting as a mujahid in Afghanistan. However, al-Qaida in Pakistan had other plans for him.

Khan's protégé Tanweer was also raised in Leeds. His parents were immigrants, and he had three siblings. Tanweer's father went to the UK to study textile manufacturing. He built a business including a butcher's shop and a fish and chip shop, in which Tanweer occasionally worked. The Tanweer family was well-off and well regarded in the local community, and was seen as an immigrant success story.[85] The family was moderately religious and attended Friday sermons at the local mosque, but they rarely observed all prayers.

Tanweer studied sports science at Leeds Metropolitan University. He was an athlete and dreamt about becoming a professional cricket player. Tanweer has been characterized as an intelligent, skilled and social person who received good grades. Friends portray a handsome and lively person with a sense of humor. There are no indications he experienced social problems, or that he was exposed to racism. He was known to take care of his appearance; he was fashionably dressed, wore expensive sportswear and owned his own car, a Mercedes.

Like Khan, he was an idealist and social activist. He volunteered to organize sports activities for children at a local community center, and did social work for the Tabligh movement. A childhood friend said Tanweer never expressed political views, and that she had never seen him reading newspapers or watching the news. To her knowledge, Tanweer had not even attended demonstrations against the wars in Iraq and Afghanistan.[86] Other friends talk about Tanweer's political and religious awakening when he was turning eighteen. From this point on he distanced himself from British culture and started hanging out with Islamists.[87]

As seen in the radicalization narratives of multiple other jihadi terrorists in Europe, Tanweer's friends point to 9/11 as a trigger. However, it seems to have been his interaction with Khan that took him from radicalism to militancy. Tanweer knew Khan from his childhood, but they re-connected in context of radical mosques. Khan and Tanweer spent much time together in the two years before the attacks, sometimes with Lindsay and Hussain, and other times on their own. They attended lectures and sermons by radical preachers in Leeds, Luton and London. Khan, his accomplices and other youths who frequented the gyms, the bookshop and the basement mosque, organized physical activities such as white-water rafting and paintball games.

Khan and Tanweer went on a camping trip together in April 2003 and on a white-water rafting trip in June 2005. In November 2004 Khan and Tanweer traveled to Pakistan and stayed there until February 2005. In Pakistan, Tanweer stayed with his family in Punjab and went on trips with Khan, likely to seek out al-Qaida-affiliated training facilities.

The fact that only Tanweer accompanied Khan on this trip to Pakistan suggested that the cell leader trusted him more than the other members of the group, Hussain and Lindsay. Tanweer's relatives in Pakistan said Tanweer had changed his appearance and acted more religiously than he had done during past visits. He grew a beard and prayed five times a day. He also initiated discussions about religious issues and politics, and fiercely criticized UK policy towards the Kashmir issue, UK participation in Iraq and Afghanistan, and expressed admiration for bin Laden and al-Qaida. He referred to bin Laden as his personal hero, saying: "everything he did was right," that "America had made Muslims suffer all over the world" and "that India was committing great atrocities against the Muslims."[88]

The teenager Hasib Hussain had lived with his family in the Leeds suburb of Holbeck for his entire life. Hussain was a misfit with a troubled background who struggled at school and experienced social problems. He lived in the shadow of an older brother who was an excellent athlete and did well in school. Between 1998 and 2003, Hussain completed a course in business studies at Matthew Murray High Comprehensive School, graduating with mediocre grades. He enjoyed sports, but lacked talent.[89] His father maintained that his son never got into trouble. However, others said Hussain was rebellious, spent time drinking in pubs, smoked marijuana and got into fights with racists.[90]

Like other misfits in jihadi cells in Europe he had problems controlling his temper and had encounters with law enforcement. He had been abusive to a schoolteacher once, and was also questioned by police over an allegation of shoplifting. In 2002 his parents sent him to visit relatives living near Islamabad, Pakistan, hoping the trip could have a positive effect on the boy. The whole family went to Mecca for hajj the same year. Around this time Hussain became more religiously observant. He began to wear Islamic robes, grew a beard and prayed regularly. He read religious texts, said he wanted to become a cleric and voiced sympathies for al-Qaida and 9/11. Hussain was the childhood friend of Tanweer, and Khan was also an old friend of his family. He started to hang out frequently with Khan and Tanweer around the time of his religious awakening. Hussain's father seems to have had some reservations concerning his son's close relationship to Khan, fearing that something bad was going on.[91]

The fourth cell member, Jermaine Lindsay, alias "Jamal," was born in Jamaica in 1985 to a British mother and a Jamaican father who took no part in his son's life. Lindsay suffered from the lack of a father figure, and one of his stepfathers treated him harshly. Lindsay has been described as intelligent, artistic and into music. Friends describe him as being "fascinated by world affairs, religion and politics."[92] He was also a talented athlete and fitness fanatic, practicing martial arts and body-building. He converted to Islam shortly after his mother initiated a relationship with a Muslim in 2000. His sister said he changed markedly after his conversion and that she felt alienated from him. He took the name Jamal and began to study Urdu. He was said to have met and befriended Khan and the other cell members during his conversion process. Shortly afterwards, his schoolteachers became alarmed because he attempted to radicalize fellow pupils, handed out al-Qaida propaganda and announced that he wanted to fight British soldiers in Afghanistan.

Lindsay married the British convert Samantha Lewthwaite, whom he had met online, and the couple was expecting their second child. Lewthwaite told the press she knew nothing about her husband's terrorist activities and that she suspected he was having an affair because he was secretive about text-messaging and disappeared several times a week. She also publicly condemned the attacks in media interviews. However, Lewthwaite would continue to mingle with Islamist extremists in Britain, and later moved to East Africa where she is believed to have married a high-level al-Shabaab commander in Somalia and became part of al-Shabaab's networks in Somalia and Kenya. She has since been suspected of involvement in multiple terrorist plots in Kenya, including the attacks in the Westgate shopping mall in 2013, and is also known to have acted as a propagandist for al-Shabaab from Kenya.[93]

Lindsay was influenced by radical preachers in the UK and was observed together with Khan and Tanweer listening to Hamza on the streets of London after police closed Finsbury Park in January 2003. According to the official report on the London bombings, Lindsay was particularly interested in a radical preacher known as Abdullah al-Faisal, who, like Lindsay, was a Jamaican and a convert to Islam. Al-Faisal was born in St James, Jamaica, in 1963. He was raised a Christian by parents who were members of the Salvation Army, but converted to Islam at sixteen. Al-Faisal studied Arabic and Islamic studies for one year in Guyana, South America, before he traveled to Saudi Arabia in the 1980s, where he enrolled in religious studies at the Imam Muhammad Ibn Saud University, Riyadh.

He graduated in 1991, and in 1992 he settled in the UK and married a British woman with whom he had some children. He established himself as a preacher at a radical mosque in Brixton and emerged as a charismatic figure within Britain's jihadi sub-culture alongside Qatada, Hamza, Bakri and his protégé Anjem Choudary, and others. He was arrested and convicted of soliciting the murder of Jews, Americans, Christians and Hindus and stirring up racial hatred in 2003. After his release in 2007 he was deported to his native Jamaica.[94]

The London bombers stated very clearly what motivated the attacks and that they were part of a global jihad. The highly politicized video testament by Khan, released by al-Qaida's media production company al-Sahab one month after 7/7, stood in stark contrast to the way he was portrayed by family, friends and colleagues as a religiously observant but non-political person. On the tape, Khan stated:

> Our driving motivation doesn't come from tangible commodities that this world has to offer. Our religion is Islam—obedience to the one true God, Allah, and following the footsteps of the final prophet and messenger Muhammad ... This is how our ethical stances are dictated. Your democratically elected governments continuously perpetuate atrocities against my people all over the world. And your support of them makes you directly responsible, just as I am directly responsible for protecting and avenging my Muslim brothers and sisters. Until we feel security, you will be our targets. And until you stop the bombing, gassing, imprisonment and torture of my people we will not stop this fight. We are at war and I am a soldier.[95]

In tune with al-Qaida logic, Khan portrayed himself as a just warrior, fighting for Muslim brothers and sisters across the world. Tanweer's martyrdom testament was just as explicit about global jihad as Khan's. Addressing the people and government of Britain he said "What you have witnessed now is only the beginning of a string of attacks that will continue and become stronger until you pull your forces out of Afghanistan and Iraq and until you stop your financial and military support for America and Israel."[96] He further said that "Muslims suffer at the hands of the U.K. government," placing responsibility with the victims of attacks, "the non-Muslims of Britain," "those who have voted in your government," the "government that has openly supported the genocide of 150,000 Muslims in Fallujah," and "continues to oppress our mothers, children, brothers and sisters in Palestine, Afghanistan, Iraq and Chechnya."[97]

A martyrdom tribute for the third bomber, Lindsay, written by people who knew him and sympathized with the attacks, did not contain concrete references to political grievances. The tribute stressed Lindsay's religious commitment and willingness to become a martyr, and stated he had "no love whatsoever" for the world, and his "only goal in life was to implement Islam to its fullest and strive in the path of Allah to earn Allah's pleasure."[98] I did not find political statements attributed to the misfit Hasib Hussain, but he too was known to voice support for al-Qaida.

Although the terrorists talked about the global jihad and lambasted Britain for the war in Iraq, they had in fact been radicalized within British extremist networks with strong links to Pakistan before Iraq was invaded. Both Khan and Tanweer were involved in support activism for Kashmiri mujahidin and they connected with al-Qaida in Pakistan via Kashmiri groups. As discussed earlier, Pakistan's support of the War on Terror affected the jihadi landscape in the country and created opportunities for al-Qaida. The gradually deteriorating relationship between the state and Kashmiri groups facilitated closer ties between the latter, the Taliban and al-Qaida.

British-Pakistani extremists always had close ties to armed groups in Kashmir, supported them, and went to Pakistan to train and fight. And the enhanced relationship between these groups and al-Qaida improved the latter's ability to connect with European Pakistanis, especially in the UK. The recruitment of the Crawley group, the 7/7 bombers and the airliner plotters, to be discussed shortly, was part of this development.

The increased radicalization among young Pakistanis in the UK and other European countries was partly driven by events in Pakistan, such as incursions by the Pakistani Army in the Af-Pak border region, partly by Iraq, but the arrests of radical preachers and the closure of radical mosques in the UK also contributed. While the idea of a covenant of security may previously have prevented British citizens from launching attacks at home, now there was a notion among the extremists that such a pact, if it ever existed, was invalid. The statement by Bakri in January 2005, in which he called off the covenant, combined with bin Laden's ultimatum for Europeans to pull out of Iraq or face consequences, were further signals to the new generation of jihadis in Europe that time had come to retaliate. The plot to down transatlantic airliners departing from Heathrow must be understood in this context.

Airliner plot

With the arrest of Hamza in 2004, British authorities put an end to "Londonistan" in the form in which it had existed since the 1990s. The security services' first offensive against UK jihadis followed 9/11, and led to the arrest of Qatada and the disruption of Doha and Beghal's networks. There were also several raids on the Finsbury Park Mosque, which ultimately closed in 2003. The mosque was later reopened by moderate Muslims. After 7/7, UK counter-terrorism efforts reached unprecedented levels. Moreover, based on experiences from the Pakistan-linked cases in 2004–5, Britain's security agencies fully acknowledged the role of Pakistan's tribal areas in the training of terrorists for international attacks.

Because they had come under pressure, UK extremists began moving their activities underground, or online, while some radical preachers, such as Bakri, left the country. Bakri relocated to Lebanon promptly after the 7/7 attacks, from where he continued to guide his disciples via online chat rooms. In Bakri's absence, several spokesmen for the al-Muhajiroun spin-off al-Ghuraba, or the Saved Sect, issued threatening statements to the press, lionizing bin Laden and the 7/7 bombers. They justified the London bombings by saying that European governments had failed to respond to bin Laden's truce offer in 2004 and had arrested many Muslims, thus violating the covenant of security. They also called for new attacks, something that led to their arrests.[99]

In this situation, news broke about a new ambitious terrorist plot by al-Qaida-linked Britons. In August 2006 UK, US and Pakistani security services dismantled a terrorist network preparing suicide bombings of transatlantic airliners taking off from Heathrow. Most members of the cell were British-Pakistanis hailing from Walthamstow and High Wycombe, and a number of accomplices were arrested in Pakistan.[100] The British-led counter-terrorism operation, given the counter-intuitive name "Operation Overt," was launched in July 2005, when citizens of Walthamstow alerted police about the suspicious activities of a group of young Muslims gathering at a local mosque and in several rented apartments.[101] The suspects were put under extensive surveillance, including phone tapping, electronic room surveillance, surveillance of bank transactions and online communications. More than fifty people were monitored.

Prosecutors said the terrorists intended to smuggle explosives onboard the aircrafts inside hand luggage, camouflaged as sports drinks. The disclosure of the plot and the novel use of drinking bottles led to major changes in the security regimes of air travel, restricting travelers from bringing liquids past security. The evidence included bomb-making recipes, chemicals and equipment suitable for making the peroxide-based explosive HMTD (Satan's Mother), which was also used by the 7/7 cell. UK police searched sixty-nine houses, apartments, firms, cars and outside locations. Investigators confiscated bomb-making equipment, chemicals, electronic devices, diverse documents, more than 400 PCs, 200 mobile phones, and 8,000 removable storage media devices (CDs, DVDs, memory sticks). Investigators secured approximately 6,000 gigabytes of data, and ran thousands of analyses of fingerprints, DNA, handwriting and chemicals.[102] In addition to bomb-making materials, police confiscated eight martyrdom videos recorded by members of the cell.

The attack type was typical of al-Qaida's section for external operations as it targeted commercial airliners, was ambitious and innovative, and involved suicide bombers and mass casualties. Yet one of the main differences between the airliner plot and previous cases in Europe was the size of the cell. Even if only half of the fifty people monitored were involved and boundaries of cells are vague, this was by far the largest cell uncovered in Europe. A plausible explanation for the size was the scale of the operation, comparable to the 9/11 operation, which required manpower. The terrorists planned to bomb nine transatlantic passenger jets mid-air, simultaneously.[103] They intended to insert HMTD into sport drink containers, and set off the explosions using a converted battery as a detonator. Al-Qaida and its affiliates have targeted commercial airliners since the early 1990s, an effort that culminated in 9/11.

The scale of the plot and the explosives pointed to al-Qaida, and the terrorists seemed well organized and trained. According to one security official, operational security was "very, very good."[104] In the UK, the terrorists operated from different apartments and they established a bomb factory in one in Forest Road, Walthamstow, where they mixed chemicals. One sign that the cell received external backing was that the leader, Abdulla Ahmed Ali (twenty-seven), bought the apartment used as bomb factory with large amounts of cash.[105] Like the Crawley and 7/7 cases, investigations revealed links to Kashmiri groups and al-Qaida in Pakistan. The terrorists communicated extensively with contacts in Pakistan via coded emails and held meetings with al-Qaida in the tribal areas between 2003 and 2006. Communications from the UK to Pakistan read like progress reports, whereas emails from Pakistan to the UK were of a more instructional nature.[106] US officials soon indicated that the plot was overseen by al-Qaida's chief of external operations at the time, Abu Ubaydah al-Masri. Also, as in the Crawley and 7/7 cases, the terrorists obtained training via different contacts in Pakistan, including al-Qaida and other militant outfits. For example, one cell member said they had received bomb-making instructions from a Kashmiri mujahid named Jameel Shah.[107]

However, it was the aforementioned British-Pakistani Rashid Rauf who acted as a handler for the cell on behalf of al-Qaida. Rauf detailed his role as a recruiter, trainer and supervisor of the 7/7 attacks, the 21/7 copycat attacks and the transatlantic airliner plot in a document that surfaced in the investigations of an al-Qaida cell dismantled in Germany in 2011.[108] Interestingly, the document was encrypted and hidden inside computer files attached to a pornographic movie. In the document, Rauf described how he organized the training of British-Pakistanis for al-Qaida in Waziristan during the winter of 2004.

It was he who connected the leader of the airliner plotters, Abdulla Ahmed Ali, to al-Qaida's then chief of external operations, al-Masri. The latter persuaded Ali, who had gone to Pakistan to join jihad in Afghanistan, to undertake an attack in the West instead. Rauf also indicated that it was he who had come up with the idea to smuggle explosives in liquid form onboard planes after several other targets and types of attacks had been discussed. Moreover, Rauf claimed to have instructed the terrorists in the UK via email, phone calls and text messages. Rauf was arrested in Pakistan on the day of the counter-terrorism raids in the UK, but he mysteriously escaped from prison in 2007. According to some sources, he died in a US drone attack in Pakistan in 2008, but other sources indicated he may have survived and had a hand in several international plots by al-Qaida since, such as the plans to launch attacks in New York, Manchester and Denmark in 2010, which will be discussed in Chapter Eight.

Many of those implicated in the plot spent time in Pakistan in the years leading up to the arrests. Ali undertook many journeys to the country, one of which overlapped with the training of the 7/7 and 21/7 cells. Several members of the group also spent time as humanitarian workers in Kashmir after the earthquake in 2005. They traveled there via al-Muhajiroun's networks in Pakistan and were suspected of having met al-Qaida personnel who were in the region at the time.[109] Pakistani authorities arrested a number of people belonging to al-Muhajiroun's Pakistani network suspected of having facilitated the airliner plot. As mentioned earlier, al-Muhajiroun ran an office out of Lahore, which played a major part in the group's propaganda and was a contact point between activists in the UK and armed groups in Pakistan. This office was also involved in channeling money and relief workers from Britain to Kashmir in connection with the earthquake crisis. Several sources suggested that the circumstances of the earthquake provided an opportunity for interaction between the plotters and al-Qaida, and that money gathered for humanitarian purposes ended up in the hands of the terrorists.[110]

Most of the terrorists had been working or studying. Two worked as salesmen who sold the kind of sports drink that was supposed to be used to smuggle explosives onboard the aircrafts. Another member worked as a security guard at Heathrow Airport. The group also included a bio-medical science student with ambitions to join the police as a forensic expert, and one art student. Several of those arrested were married, two of them had children and one was about to become a father. Several had been associated with Tabligh and several had participated in Islamist activism in the past. The core members of the cell were radicalized first as followers of Bakri in the UK, and by mid-2003 they were part of the training sessions organized by the Crawley group in Malakand. There were a few examples of personal problems, problematic family backgrounds and criminal histories among the terrorists. However, the broader picture was of a group of well-integrated, well-behaved, compassionate young men from well-functioning and moderately religious families.

Several of the airliner plotters were described as having a lax attitude towards religion and living Western lives before becoming extremists. Several were ardent football fans and sport enthusiasts, and members of the group worked out together at a gym called Al-Badr. However, friends and relatives had noticed how they gradually turned devout, regularly attending mosques and religious meetings, and began dressing in a traditional Islamic way. One of them was said to have changed markedly after a visit to Pakistan.[111] When he came back he wore a beard and shaved his head Salafi-style. He had also become more physically fit, something that in retrospect made witnesses surmise he had attended training. The lead members had been followers of Bakri and Hamza, and mixed with al-Muhajiroun and its spin-offs. The cell emerged from exactly the same environment as the Crawley and 7/7 cells, and investigations revealed phone contacts between the leader of the airliner plot, Ali, and the leader of the 21/7 cell, Mukhtar Ibrahim.[112]

The cell's entrepreneur, Abdulla Ahmed Ali, was an engineering graduate who pursued business in Pakistan after he graduated in 2002. Ali, described as "intelligent, strong-willed and charismatic," grew up partly in Pakistan and partly in Britain, with five brothers and two sisters.[113] Married and having one child, Ali had become radicalized as a teenager after watching videos of atrocities against Muslims in Bosnia. For most people involved in jihadi terrorism in Europe, videos showing maltreatment of Muslims were a radicalization trigger. Growing increasingly religious, Ahmed Ali joined Tabligh in his teens and was involved in Islamist activism at university. In 2003 he joined a charity aiding Afghan and Kashmiri refugees. Ali was appalled by the conditions at refugee camps in Pakistan, and blamed the West for not providing aid. After becoming disillusioned with political activism and aid work, he grew increasingly radical and embraced jihadi thought.[114]

Ali's protégé and second-in-command with regard to the cell's activities in the UK, Assad Sarwar (twenty-four), was a misfit described as a failed student with low self-esteem who survived by working odd jobs. Within the terrorist cell, Sarwar was in charge of gathering and hiding the bomb-making materials, and during trial he admitted to having received bomb-making instructions in Pakistan. It is believed that it was Ahmed Ali who recruited him while he was involved in aid work for the Pakistani refugee camps. They first met in the UK and later spent time together in Pakistan. According to his lawyers, Sarwar admired Ali for his leadership abilities and described himself as a follower rather than a leading figure.[115] The group's martyrdom videos were found in his garage, but he had not recorded one himself.

A friend of Ali and Sarwar, Umar Islam (thirty-one), changed his name from Brian Young when he converted to Islam in 2001. After studying business at college he took a job as a postman, and joined Sarwar in charity work at the refugee camps in Pakistan in 2002. Umar Islam was one of those within the group who had recorded a martyrdom video, indicating that he had been designated as a suicide bomber.[116] Oddly enough, one year earlier he had helped shield the public and was looking for bomb devices during the London bombings on 7 July in his job as a ticket inspector on buses.[117]

Prosecutors characterized Tanvir Hussain (twenty-seven) as a central member of the cell. Like many jihadis in Europe, Hussain defied the stereotype of an

Islamist. He was described as fun-loving, into fashion and someone who had experimented with alcohol, drugs and women in his youth. He worked as a part-time postman, and was also into sports.[118] He assisted in procuring bomb-making materials together with Ali and Sarwar and took part in attempts to construct the bomb devices. He also conducted research on bomb-making recipes and communicated with Ali in Pakistan using code language.

The Islamist Waheed Zaman (twenty-four) was sentenced to life in jail for his involvement in the conspiracy in a 2010 re-trial. Zaman was an active follower of Tabligh and a biomedicine student at London Metropolitan University. At university he was elected head of the students' Islamic Society. Friends said he had an ambition to become a medical doctor, and portrayed him as pious, friendly and peaceful.[119] He was described as a supporter of the integration of Muslims living in the West. However, he was also known to have denied the involvement of Muslims in 9/11 and 7/7. Moreover, British media found jihadi propaganda and terrorist training manuals in portable buildings used as meeting places and a library by the Islamic Society headed by Zaman. Much of the propaganda was traced to al-Muhajiroun, which ran an office near Zaman's home.[120]

The background and radicalization of the man overseeing the plot from Pakistan for al-Qaida, Rashid Rauf, was almost identical to that of Omar Saeed Sheikh. Rauf was arrested near the city of Bahawalpur in Punjab just before the arrests in Britain on 10 August. The British-Pakistani baker's son grew up in Birmingham. He left the UK for Pakistan in 2002, shortly after his uncle was killed under mysterious circumstances, and he has since been suspected of involvement in the murder. In Lahore, Rauf spent time among al-Muhajiroun activists and mixed with people who had ties to the Kashmiri mujahidin and al-Qaida.[121] At some point he met Ajmad Hussain Farooqi, a leader within JeM and Laskhar e-Janghvi, two Kashmiri-based groups with strong ties to al-Qaida. As he was of Kashmiri origins and part of a family with a long history of Kashmir activism, Rauf was well received and in 2003 he married a woman who had family ties to the founder of JeM, Sheik Maulana Masood Azhar.[122]

Rauf's contact Ajmad Hussain Farooqi was a well-known terrorist alleged to have been one of the organizers of two attempted assassinations of Musharraf, as well as the murder of Daniel Pearl in 2002. In connection with the attempts on Musharraf, Farooqi was said to have cooperated with al-Qaida's third-in-command at the time, Abu Faraj al-Liby. It is further alleged that it was Farooqi who introduced Rauf to al-Liby and other al-Qaida commanders operating from the Af-Pak border zone.

Investigators retrieved six martyrdom videos from Sarwar's garage which left little doubt that the terrorists were acting according to al-Qaida's vision of global jihad. The terrorists' statements focused mainly on international matters, but there were also hateful characterizations of Britain and Britons, and signs that developments inside the UK had influenced their decision to attack their country. All of the videos contained praise to God and calls for martyrdom, references to al-Qaida and justifications for murdering civilians. The terrorists expressed anger over Western campaigns in Muslim countries, and in the manner of al-Qaida they also raged over Western support for un-Islamic regimes in Muslim countries and "so-called moderate Muslims."[123]

In Ali's video he was heard saying he was the leader of the group and that he had longed for martyrdom since he was a teenager. Ali stated, "I was over the moon that Allah has given me this opportunity to lead this blessed operation."[124] He further claimed that he wanted to guarantee paradise for himself, his family and friends, and "on top of this ... to punish and to humiliate the non-believers, to teach them a lesson that they will never forget."[125] Ali then underscored that "Sheikh Osama [bin Laden] warned you many times to leave our lands."[126] Upon being asked by the person recording the tape about the killing of innocent civilians, he compared potential targets with "animals" as opposed to the "Muslim nation" (*ummah*).[127]

Rather curiously, the purported second-in-command of the cell, Sarwar, did not record a martyrdom video himself. The convert Umar Islam, on the other hand, appeared on tape characterizing the group's actions as "revenge for the actions of the USA in the Muslim lands and their accomplices such as the British and the Jews."[128] He also echoed al-Qaida statements by saying "as you bomb you will be bombed. As you kill you will be killed," before saying, "If you think you can go into our land and do what you are doing in Iraq, Afghanistan and Palestine and keep on supporting those that are fighting against the Muslims and think it will not come back on to your doorstep then you have another thing coming."[129] Umar Islam then turned to the British people and criticized them for continuing to fund the army and supporting politicians, while being too busy watching television and sipping alcohol "to care about anything."[130]

In his suicide video, Waheed Zaman underscored that "the only solution to this current situation of the Muslims is by fighting Jihad for the sake of Allah until the enemy is fully subdued and expelled from our lands."[131] Zaman specified that the United States and the UK had been chosen as targets because they had invaded and built bases in Muslim lands, and because they supported the "accursed Israelis."[132] Zaman also emphasized he had not been "brainwashed," but rather was educated and "old enough to make my own decisions."[133] The statement by Tanweer Hussain focused on explaining how the group was targeting "economic and military targets" and not innocent civilians.[134] Hussain also told Western nations to stop "supporting the puppets and helping our enemies" so as not to feel the "wrath of the mujahidin."[135]

The statements taken from the terrorists' martyrdom testaments indicate that the airliner plot was motivated mainly by international events and global jihad. Notably, there were several developments in the time leading up to the plot that played into al-Qaida's narrative that Muslims and mujahidin were under attack from Jews and Crusaders all over the world. In June 2006, the leader of al-Qaida in Iraq, al-Zarqawi, was killed in US air strikes north of Baghdad. During the summer of 2006 Israel launched an offensive against Hizbullah in Lebanon, which included the bombing of Beirut that struck civilian targets and cost lives. In the UK, the extremist networks of which the plotters had been part were monitored closely after 7/7, and radical preachers and other entrepreneurs went in and out of jail, or had to flee the country. As noted, this situation led Bakri, who had been a main ideologue for the terrorists, to annul the covenant of security between Muslims and the British state in January 2005, long before the arrest of Ahmed Ali and his accomplices. Another event in Europe that also played into al-Qaida's narrative was the publication of cartoons of the Prophet Muhammad by *Jyllands-Posten* in late 2005.

The publication of the cartoons did not have a direct effect on the circumstances of the airliner plot, as the plotters were already radicalized and in training at the time of their publication. However, as will be discussed in the following chapter, the cartoons would come to dominate al-Qaida's discourse on attacks in the West from 2006 onwards, and were cited as a motivation by several terrorist cells in Europe. The publication of the cartoons in Denmark, and re-prints by multiple European media outlets in the following years were portrayed by al-Qaida as another sign that covenants of security were invalid.

In sum, the airliner plot was the last in a series of interlinked plots involving al-Qaida-affiliated Pakistanis trained in the tribal areas. The Pakistani axis involved ideological radicalization among European Pakistanis who had previously acknowledged the covenant of security and limited themselves to supporting jihad in Kashmir, but who now adopted al-Qaida's vision of global jihad. The radicalization was partly linked to the Iraq war, and partly to an escalating conflict between Islamists and the state in Pakistan, a conflict that was initiated by al-Qaida to create a common enemy with local Pakistani groups.

The terrorist plots discussed in this chapter were initially thought to signify a trend towards Pakistani jihadis becoming the vanguard of terrorist plotting in Europe, following the break-up of North African cells and networks. However, as will become evident in the following chapters, Europeans from diverse origins were seeking out Af-Pak to become mujahidin, some of them ending up as terrorists at home. The Pakistani axis should therefore be understood as a more general trend towards a diversification of the threat to Europe, implying multinational, transnationally operating cells of the new generation. These cells would connect with multiple groups in different conflict zones via online platforms. Many would seek out al-Qaida in Af-Pak, but they would also seek out affiliates of the organization in other conflict theaters.

7

THE NORTHERN FRONT (2005–8)

Following the London bombings, the number of terrorist plots by jihadis in Europe stabilized at a lower level than in the immediate aftermath of the invasion of Iraq. At the same time, there were several failed and foiled plots that were potentially large scale. One such incident was the airliner plot by British-Pakistanis. Another was a plan by the former GIA recruiter Safe Bourada to attack French security services and Orly airport when he was released from jail. The latter plan involved longstanding al-Qaida-affiliated networks in France, and there were also links to al-Qaida's Iraqi branch, although details were scarce regarding the group's exact involvement (the resilience of well-established networks and the role of jihadis released from prison in terrorism after their release is discussed in Chapter Nine). However, there were some incidents in the period from 2005 to 2008 that represented something new, and signified that the jihadi threat to Europe was growing increasingly diversified.

I have chosen five terrorist plots in Denmark, Germany and the UK to exemplify these patterns. The cases illustrate how jihadi terrorism in Europe was growing increasingly multinational, and how networks of the new generation exploited the Internet and social media to a larger extent than in the past. They also demonstrate that, although most jihadi terrorist cells in Europe have grown out of well-known local networks, plots could also be hatched by people from abroad, having lived in Europe for a short period of time with weak ties to local networks. The cases further show how jihadi groups beyond al-Qaida's central organization and closest affiliates were taking an interest in Europe as a place to launch international terrorist attacks. Furthermore, the cases show how the threat to Europe gradually came to involve a wider set of motivations based on grievances related to injustices against Muslims in Europe, insults against the Prophet and European counter-terrorism measures seemed significant—in combination with anger over the invasions of Afghanistan and Iraq, and the suffering of the Palestinian people.

Finally, until the mid-2000s, the threat had largely been confined to the UK and continental Europe, but now it was spreading north to more peripheral parts of the region. While terrorists continued to pose a threat to the UK and France, there was a resurgence of the threat in Germany, and a sudden rise in incidents in Denmark, something that would continue for years to come and also affected other Scandinavian countries. Although some of the plots uncovered in 2005–8 involved young Europeans who lacked a history in jihad and were primarily pursuing jihadism online, they should not be seen as having been detached from organized networks and mujahidin in conflict zones. All of the plots studied in this chapter had links to al-Qaida affiliates in Pakistan or Iraq. And although there were cells which did not emerge from local, European networks, the terrorists were still part of international efforts to support the Iraqi jihad.

The first two cases deal with the emergence of global jihadi terrorism in Denmark. The first Danish plot resembled models of homegrown, bottom-up terrorism, where young Europeans radicalized in the context of local networks and interacted with international jihadis online. The second plot emerged from the same network, but the terrorists connected with al-Qaida in Pakistan and were assigned with a mission. The two German cases involved connections to al-Qaida affiliates in Iraq, Lebanon and Pakistan, whereas the UK case may have been clearest example in Europe until then of involvement by al-Qaida's branch in Iraq. Moreover, the cases addressed in this chapter coincided with an unprecedented intensification of counter-terrorism efforts Europe-wide following the London bombings and the airliner plot, and also with the publication of cartoons of the Prophet Muhammad in Denmark. The latter development cannot be overstated as a driving force for jihadi terrorism in Europe, as it has had a profound impact on the threat situation in the region from 2005 until the present day.

Cartoons

The publication of twelve cartoons of the Prophet Muhammad by the Danish newspaper *Jyllands-Posten* in September 2005 gave al-Qaida ammunition in its efforts to justify attacks in Europe and recruit European Muslims. The cartoons led to widespread protests from mainstream Muslims and Muslim governments, as well as non-violent and violent Islamists, including the jihadis.[1] Danish politicians defended the publications on the grounds that the country's citizens had the right of free speech, and the subsequent refusal by the then Danish prime minster, Anders Fogh Rasmussen, to meet with and apologize before a delegation of protesting Muslim diplomats was followed by a series of increasingly extreme reactions. The situation deteriorated when a group of prominent Danish imams toured Muslim countries showing the most provocative drawings, claiming they reflected Western views of Islam. Violent demonstrations soon erupted in several Muslim countries, such as Egypt and Syria, which culminated in the arson attacks on the Danish and Norwegian embassies in Damascus. Norway had been drawn into the matter because a small Christian newspaper reprinted the cartoons, but protests against Norway were completely overshadowed by the reactions against Denmark, which ranged from official condemnation by Muslim states and boycotts, to violent protests, and ultimately threats from al-Qaida and further terrorist plots in Europe.

When the jihadis eventually responded to the drawings, their language was full of threatening vitriol. In a statement in April 2006, entitled "O People of Islam," bin Laden portrayed the cartoons as a worse crime than the bombing of the "villages that collapsed over our women and children."[2] The comparison resembled the language al-Zawahiri used when he condemned the ban on veils in French schools in 2003. In the April 2006 statement bin Laden went on to order "Islam's youths" to come forward and kill the cartoonists and punish the Danish government for allowing them to be published.[3] The cartoons were also condemned in threats by al-Zawahiri and a Libyan al-Qaida leader known as Abu Yehia al-Liby.

In view of the mobilizing effects of the Muhammad cartoons, on one level the time lag between them being published and al-Qaida's eventual reaction seems slightly strange.

However, it would have been problematic for al-Qaida to become too closely associated with protests by Arab regimes and clerics which the organization had declared to be its enemies. Al-Qaida's reaction needed to be independent from that of Arab dictators and mainstream Islam, and it had to be grounded in jihadi ideology. Thus, when addressing the cartoon issue, bin Laden referred to Ibn Taymiyyah's rulings on individual punishment of whoever insults the Prophet and Islam. Ibn Taymiyyah described insults against the Prophet as the gravest sin, one punishable by death, and stressed that it was the individual duty of every Muslim to carry out the death sentence. The Muhammad cartoons consequently emerged as a perfect recruitment tool for al-Qaida, partly because of the widespread resentment the drawings provoked among Muslim masses, and partly because of the clarity of the rulings of a well-respected Salafi scholar in the matter.

After the cartoons had been reprinted in the newspapers of several European countries in 2008, the jihadis' focus on the Muhammad cartoons reached unprecedented levels. In 2008, al-Qaida-associated terrorists bombed the Danish embassy in Islamabad, while in Europe itself al-Qaida's propaganda efforts led to several plots against the artists who drew the cartoons, as well as the offices of *Jyllands-Posten* from 2008 onwards. Some of these plots were linked to al-Qaida and its affiliates in Pakistan, whereas others involved individuals with ties to al-Qaida affiliates in other regions, such as the Somali al-Shabaab movement.[4]

However, while the publication of the cartoons certainly led to the emergence of plots targeting individuals and institutions involved in the cartoons, the cases discussed in this chapter also show how the cartoon issue was cited as a radicalization factor and motive for jihadis plotting attacks on other targets. For many jihadis, the Muhammad cartoons were seen as the last straw, which in addition to military campaigns in Muslim lands and the arrests of Islamists, had invalidated the covenant of security and legitimized attacks in Europe by European Muslims. As will be discussed in the next chapter, the cartoons further contributed to a rise in single-actor terrorist plots because in jihadi ideology it is the duty of every Muslim to seek to implement the punishment for people who insult Muhammad.

Although the cartoons were not the primary motive in the first major jihadi terrorist case in Denmark, the case is a perfect example of how the threat was spreading from core areas in Europe, and particularly the UK, to more peripheral parts of the region such as Scandinavia. The development had been exacerbated by the mobilizing effect of the Iraq war, the massive growth in online jihadism and the Muhammad cartoons. Jihadi networks in Northern Europe and Scandinavia formed around entrepreneurs with connections to mujahidin in conflict zones and international networks in Europe.

"Al-Qaida in Northern Europe"

A Scandinavia-centered but multinational terrorist network was dismantled in the fall of 2005 which was geographically dispersed, sociologically diverse and particularly Internet-savvy. The network, which came to be known as the "Glostrup cell" or "al-Qaida in Northern Europe," resembled the Hofstadgroup in that its members used social media for communication, propaganda and to issue threats. However, like the Dutchmen, the members of the cell also traveled between countries to interact on a face-to-face basis, and leading figures went to Bosnia for terrorist training.[5]

This was unusual for jihadi terrorists in Europe. While terrorists operating in the region in the 1990s and early 2000s were radicalized over the war in Bosnia, and some of them had spent time there as foreign fighters, the number of Bosnia veterans in terrorist cells in Europe is negligible when compared to the number of terrorists who have been to Af-Pak. Despite the fact that al-Qaida and its affiliates were active in Bosnia, there is little to suggest that global jihadis operated significant training bases there recruiting Westerners for international attacks. Hence the Glostrup cell differed from the common pattern by having links to Bosnia and Iraq instead of Af-Pak.

The Scandinavian-based network also signified how jihadism was no longer confined to European states with a history of enmity from jihadis, but now also expanded into the region's periphery. This was partly a necessity because the most significant networks in countries such as the UK and France were under increasing pressure following a number of high-profile plots and attacks. However, it was also a result of broader efforts to build jihadi support networks all over Europe from the early 1990s onwards. Scandinavian terrorist cells sprang from extremist communities that had been forming around radical preachers with a history in foreign fighting and support networks for international jihad.

The Glostrup cell was plotting an attack in Bosnia or Denmark, and the terrorists issued an online statement in the name of al-Qaida, while threatening attacks in Europe. This was the second example of a terrorist cell in the region using the al-Qaida label, the first one being the M-11 bombers. In October 2005, Bosnian anti-terrorism police acted on a tip-off from US intelligence and arrested two terrorist suspects, the Swedish-Bosnian Mirsad Bektasevic (eighteen) and the Danish-Turk Abdelkader Cesur (eighteen), inside the apartment of the former's uncle in Sarajevo. As they were being arrested the suspects attacked the police officers and aimed a gun at them before they were overpowered and placed in prison.

Police confiscated 20 kilograms of explosives, a suicide-belt with a detonator, and a martyrdom video announcing an attack in Europe to avenge the deployment of European troops to Afghanistan and Iraq.[6] Police also arrested two

Bosnian criminals and Islamists who had helped the Scandinavians acquire guns, explosives and other equipment, one of whom had an image of bin Laden tattooed on his chest.[7] Bektasevic and Cesur were sentenced to fifteen and thirteen years in prison respectively for planning terrorism. One of the Bosnian accomplices was sentenced to two years in prison. Further investigations revealed links to extremists in Denmark, the UK, Canada and the United States, some of whom maintained relations with al-Qaida in Iraq (AQI).

After the Bosnian raids, the Danish Police Security Intelligence Service (PET) took action against a group of extremists in the Copenhagen suburb of Glostrup. Subsequently, UK police arrested three individuals in London who were linked to the plotters in Bosnia and who had been involved in spreading online propaganda and fundraising on behalf of AQI. In addition, the UK suspects maintained contacts with a far-reaching network of terrorists plotting attacks in the UK, the United States and Canada. The Canadian terrorists, referred to as the "Toronto 18," were plotting truck bombings and shootings against public sites, the press, political institutions and politicians in Ontario, and the cell was disrupted in June 2006.[8] The US-based contacts had been discussing plots against military bases and oil refineries, and were preparing to go to Pakistan for terrorist training.[9]

Apart from the items seized in Bosnia, the case against the plotters was built upon online communication and cellphone traffic, propaganda movies, ideological texts, training manuals and bomb-making instructions, in addition to other surveillance data. A central piece of evidence was the founding statement of al-Qaida in Northern Europe, which was published on the pro-al-Qaida discussion forum "Ansaar" on 11 September 2005.[10] Core members of the network came to know each other online, but radicalization took part within extremist communities in Denmark and the UK under the guidance of radical preachers. The broader network was typical of the new generation of jihadis in Europe, involving young, second-generation immigrants who were followers of local preachers, as well as Bakri, Qatada and Hamza in London. In Denmark, four people were charged with terrorism offences, but only one of them, Abdul Basit Abu-Lifa (seventeen), was convicted and sentenced (he received seven years in prison). The other three were freed for lack of evidence (they are anonymized in the sources I cite).[11]

The exact target selection of al-Qaida in Northern Europe was never established fully. There were two main theories. One was that the Danes plotted to execute an attack in Denmark on 11 September 2005 using explosives and weapons smuggled from Bosnia. The other is that the Dane and the Swede who were arrested in Sarajevo were preparing suicide missions against European embassies or other military targets in Bosnia.[12] The theory of an attack in Denmark can be traced to the arrest of a well-known Bosnian criminal, Marinko Mitric, in Rostock, Germany, while carrying a bag of TNT. Mitric left Bosnia on 9 September on a bus to Denmark, which was to arrive in Copenhagen on 11 September. When news of Mitric's arrest was broadcast, members of the Glostrup cell frantically called each other and arranged a face-to-face meeting.

The Danish suspects' interest in Mitric, coupled with the issuing of the online threat communiqué on the same day, led investigators to believe Mitric was to hand the explosives over to the Danes who would execute an attack in Denmark that day. The investigation failed to produce evidence of this, and the trial in Denmark instead focused on how the group in Denmark had supported a plot to launch suicide attacks in Bosnia. The explosives, the suicide-belt and the video-statement retrieved from the apartment in Sarajevo suggested an imminent attack within Bosnia. On the martyrdom video the terrorists announced that they would attack a European country which had deployed troops to Iraq and Afghanistan. This could in principle have been achieved both in Bosnia and Denmark. However, the video recording showing the plotters in paramilitary clothing and preparing explosives indicated a sense of urgency to the operation.[13]

Although it has been rumored that jihadis have maintained secretive training facilities in Bosnia since the war in the 1990s, there were no indications that the Scandinavians had attended any camps there. Rather, sources say Bektasevic and his accomplices tried to set up their own training camp in the hills near to Sarajevo.[14] Although the Scandinavian terrorists were not trained from the top-down by an organization, by being part of the online world of jihadism they became security conscious and introduced counter-surveillance measures. They used aliases, communicated in code and accessed training manuals and bomb-making manuals to educate themselves. They also contributed to online jihadism by producing and disseminating propaganda.

The terrorists' radicalization narratives show how they embraced extremism at home but established extensive international contacts online and through travel. Sociologically, the case involved young, second-generation immigrants from Muslim backgrounds. They hailed from middle-class backgrounds and had some level of education (although several had dropped out of school). Several were described as Internet-savvy and into sports. Most members had been involved in extremism in the years before they became involved in terrorist activities.

The Danish Glostrup cell emerged from the followers of the Palestinian preacher Abu Ahmed at the Taiba Mosque in Nørrebro, Copenhagen.[15] Ahmed supervised his own study circle, teaching between fifty and 100 students. The group was called al-Tawhid (hereafter Tawhid), and ran its own website, which was administered by an activist using the Internet alias Abu Hudhayfah (who in reality was a Danish convert named Daniel). Although little is known of the extent and nature of Ahmed's ties to foreign jihadis, the Tawhid website was used to disseminate the propaganda of al-Qaida in Iraq. The site also published writings by Ibn Taymiyyah justifying jihad in non-Muslim lands.[16]

Ahmed is a Salafi, a Thai-boxer and self-declared preacher who has specialized in teaching young Muslim immigrants about the virtues of jihad in Danish. In his lectures he focused on injustices committed against Muslims in Denmark, lionized al-Qaida and justified jihad in the West. Ahmed was educated as an engineer and worked as a consultant for a Danish firm. In his spare time he worked as a martial arts instructor for Muslim youths.[17] In 2005, when the newspaper *Politiken* exposed the study circle, Ahmed and his followers were expelled from the Taiba Mosque on the grounds that they were too extreme and were generating bad publicity. Ahmed then relocated the Tawhid group to another Copenhagen mosque located in a street named Horsebakken, in which he continued to promote jihad to Danish Muslims. He later moved his activities to an apartment in Amager.

One aspect of the Glostrup case illustrated the role of jihad entrepreneurs in London vis-à-vis emerging networks in different parts of the region. The Danish extremists first caught the security services' attention in the summer of 2004 when a group of Ahmed's followers attended a conference hosted by Bakri in London. The conference was said to attract more than 1,000 Islamists from different countries, and the Danes received special treatment, being shown around London by Bakri's peers, and receiving personal lectures and visits from Bakri himself. They also went to dinner with the Syrian while in the UK.[18] The main organizer of the trip to London was a Pakistani Dane. It is believed he was the main recruiter and facilitator of the Glostrup cell and subsequent terrorist plots in Denmark, and he was known to have traveled several times between Denmark and Pakistan in 2005, 2006 and 2007. After the Danish excursion to London, the extremists from Glostrup continued to stay in touch with Bakri. For example, in a recorded phone call, one of the Danes, a young man of Syrian-Palestinian origin named Imad Ali J., asked Bakri how Qatada was faring in jail.[19]

Another ideologue and leader for the Glostrup cell was the Moroccan Said Mansour. Mansour went to Denmark as an asylum seeker in 1983. He married a Danish woman, had one child and became a Danish citizen in 1988. A new-born Muslim, Mansour embraced jihadism and established himself as a propagandist and fundraiser for militant groups. He opened a bookshop named al-Nur Islamic Information and ran his own support group named Soldiers of Allah.[20] Mansour mingled with a number of Egyptian jihadis who had taken refuge in Denmark in the 1980s, including a high-ranking member of the Egyptian IG named Talat Fuad Qasim. In the early 1990s, he also hosted IG's religious guide Omar Abdel-Rahman in Denmark on two occasions.

Over time Mansour developed ties to multiple jihadi groups (EIJ, MICG, GIA/GSPC and Tawhid) and disseminated their propaganda. He also developed personal relations with many jihadi leaders, including Abu Mohammed al-Maqdisi, Qatada, Bakri, Hamza, Dahdah and al-Zawahiri. Mansour was frequently in touch with Qatada and Bakri in London from a phone booth at Copenhagen's Central Station, and once received a visit from Madrid's jihadi kingpin, Abu Dahdah. Mansour also traveled frequently to London to mingle with the jihadi scene there.[21] He has been tied to a number of people linked to terrorist plots in Europe, Morocco and other places, and several active terrorist cells possessed propaganda produced by the al-Nur Islamic Information. Mansour was held in high esteem by Ahmed's Tawhid group, and he knew several members of the Glostrup cell personally. Mansour was arrested by Danish police in September 2005 and charged with inciting terrorism. He was sentenced to three and a half years in prison by a Danish court in April 2007.

Before he was arrested, Mansour came to know the Swedish-Bosnian Mirsad Bektasevic, alias Maximus, when the latter visited the Glostrup group in August 2005 and assumed a leading position among them. Bektasevic connected with the Danes via the online chat room PalTalk, which had become one of the main platforms for preaching and recruiting among Europe's new generation of jihadis. His first Danish contact was a close friend of Mansour named Elias Ibn H.[22] After winning the confidence of lead figures among the Danish extremists, Bektasevic soon emerged as the main entrepreneur in the group.

His radicalization path, however, was that of a misfit. He moved from Bosnia to Sweden with his mother and younger brother in 1994 after his father died in a car crash. They settled in Kungälv outside Gothenburg. As a teenager, he would play soccer and practice boxing, yet he later became involved in crime and dropped out of school after the ninth grade. He began to rediscover Islam after the funeral of a friend who had died from brain cancer. At the funeral he felt ashamed because he did not know any prayers—or even the opening verse of the Quran—and his friend's father yelled at him for being so ignorant.[23]

Bektasevic started to radicalize after attending the Ahl al-Sunna wa'l Jama'a Mosque in Gothenburg. Like other misfits and drifters, he expressed admiration for the sense of community at the mosque, and started to attend Swedish-language Quran classes. He gradually became more extreme. He grew a beard, began to wear Islamic robes and Palestinian scarves, stopped going to music classes, and refused to shake hands with women. He also gave up boxing and isolated himself in his room surfing pro-al-Qaida websites and discussion forums. Via discussions on PalTalk he connected with the group in Glostrup and a twenty-two-year-old British-Moroccan Internet jihadi in London named Younis Tsouli.[24]

Tsouli was the son of a diplomat to the UK who lived in West London and called himself irhabi007 (terrorist007) online. Tsouli administered the pro-al-Qaida Ansaar forum and was involved in several other online outlets for jihadism, such as "al-Ekhlas" and "At-Tibyan Publications." The Ansaar forum was used extensively by al-Qaida in Iraq to disseminate propaganda. Tsouli was also an able hacker who managed to penetrate US government websites and plant jihadi material there. At the time of his arrest he was designing a website which was to be dubbed Youbombit.com for spreading bomb-instructions.

Tsouli got in touch with al-Qaida in Iraq when he helped them spread the video in which al-Zarqawi beheaded the hostage Nicholas Berg—the start of the heinous campaign of beheadings throughout 2004 which elevated AQI's international profile. AQI was impressed by Tsouli and he started to work as a propagandist for the group. Tsouli's main contribution to the Scandinavian-based terrorist network was his help with designing the statement signed al-Qaida in Northern Europe. Tsouli was convicted in July 2007 together with two accomplices, British-born Waseem Mughal (twenty-four) and Tariq al-Daour (twenty-one) from the United Arab Emirates, all of whom received long prison sentences for supporting terrorism. In addition to the international contacts, Bektasevic also mingled with extremists in Gothenburg, known to be the main hub for Islamist extremism in Sweden, including a convert known as Abu Usama al-Sweid.[25] The convert, whose real name was Lennart, had gained notoriety when he called for the killing of a Swedish priest who had described the Prophet Muhammad as a pedophile for marrying his youngest wife.[26]

After chatting online with people like Tsouli in London and Copenhagen-based Elias Ibn H., Bektasevic decided to act on his militant convictions. His mother claimed her son had been brainwashed, and that the last time she had seen Mirsad before the arrests in Bosnia was when he had been picked up in a blue car by someone she described as looking like an Arab. At that time, Bektasevic was heading for Denmark where he stayed with the Glostrup group in Copenhagen before traveling to Bosnia. In Copenhagen he earned the respect of Mansour and started to act as an entrepreneur among young Danish extremists. Also, on one occasion the Swedish-Bosnian became involved in a sectarian gang fight between Ahmed's students and some Shias. It was Mansour who sparked the brawl by slapping an Iraqi Shia who was playing music from his car stereo outside the Taiba Mosque.[27] The incident is an interesting example of the fierce anti-Shia stances and moral policing among European Salafi-jihadis. In Sarajevo Bektasevic connected with Bosnian criminals and Islamists at a mosque named King Fahd, who helped supply weapons and bomb-making materials.[28]

Bektasevic's co-conspirator in Sarajevo, Cesur, was born in 1985 in Frederiksberg, but grew up in Avedøre, south of Copenhagen. He did not have a religious upbringing. He came from a somewhat troubled family background, but did well in school and enrolled in a course on business studies. In the wake of 9/11 he began to seek out extremist groups such as Hizb ut-Tahrir, before joining Ahmed's circle. He started to dress in an Islamic way and intimidated moderately religious family members and worshippers at the local mosque.

Cesur was among the group that traveled to the UK to attend Bakri's conference in London, but he was stopped at the airport and sent back to Denmark because he had forgotten to apply for a Danish passport. Although part of the Glostrup group, Cesur claimed he met Bektasevic only three times in a Copenhagen mosque before they traveled together to Sarajevo. It was originally another lead member of the network, Abdul Basit Abu-Lifa, who was supposed to be joining Bektasevic in search of weapons and training in Bosnia, but his father learned about his travel plans and confiscated his passport.[29] Cesur then stepped in as a replacement.

Abdul Basit Abu-Lifa (seventeen) was charged with being the main organizer of the cell's activities in Denmark, and was the only member of the group to be convicted (to seven years in prison for terrorist offences in Denmark). He hailed from a Palestinian and sternly religious family background and went to Islamic schools. Abu-Lifa had shown signs of extremism at a very early age and became radicalized as a young boy in conjunction with the War on

Terror following 9/11. He joined Ahmed's group and, despite being so young, he became an entrepreneur within the Glostrup group.

Elias Ibn H. (sixteen) hailed from a Moroccan background and grew up in Denmark. He was described as highly intelligent and a successful athlete—he has received several awards in karate in Denmark and once came third in the European championship. He grew up in a strictly religious family and was a close friend of Mansour, and a follower of Ahmed. His main contribution to the cell appears to be that he was the one to introduce Bektasevic to the group. He was also part of the delegation that visited Bakri in London in 2004.[30]

Another traveler to London, Imad Ali J. (eighteen), came from a Syrian-Palestinian background. Born and raised in Frederiksberg, Denmark, he dropped out of high school and started hanging out with Ahmed's group. In 2005 he traveled to Syria claiming he wanted to spend time with his family.[31] However, telecommunication data indicated that Imad Ali J. entered Iraq and that he made a phone call from Iraq to Denmark in January 2005. It is not known if he ever made contact with AQI or other groups in Iraq.

Another member of the group, the Danish-Bosnian Adnan A., had a background as a petty criminal and was suspected of functioning as a fixer and fundraiser for the group. He had downloaded propaganda, training manuals and bomb-making recipes, and it was alleged that he and Abdul Basit Abu-Lifa had prepared armed robberies with the aim of supplying the suicide bombers in Sarajevo with money. Adnan A. admitted to planning the robberies, but said that the funds were intended for the victims of the atrocities in Srebrenica in 1995 and the victims of the Tsunami in Asia in 2004.[32] Considering the Danish Islamists' relations to preachers and activists in London, it is noteworthy that the funding of jihad through robbing unbelievers, was portrayed as justified Islamically by Abu Hamza al-Masri before his followers in the UK and in speeches that were widely distributed online.

Statements attributed to the Scandinavian plotters indicated that they were focused on global jihad and furious over the invasions of Muslim lands and arrests of Muslims. In the videotape retrieved from Sarajevo, the wannabe martyrs used typical al-Qaida rhetoric:

> Allah is the greatest. Our brothers are preparing themselves for an attack. They are showing us the things they will use in the attack. Our brothers are ready to attack, and if Allah wills, they will strike the infidels who are killing our brothers; the Muslims in Iraq, Afghanistan, Chechnya and in other countries. This weapon will be used against Europe, against those whose forces are in Iraq and Afghanistan. Our two brothers have dedicated their lives to please Allah, to help their brothers

and sisters. They are Muslim. Their time will come. They are ready to strike, so don't believe we have forgotten you. We are here, and we are planning and we are ready. This message is for you.[33]

The fact that they issued an online statement entitled "Declaration of the Establishment of the al-Qaida Organization in Northern Europe" demonstrated that they held al-Qaida in high esteem and acted according to its ideology, regardless of whether or not they had direct ties to the organization. The first drafts of the statement were written by Abdul Basit Abu Lifa in early September. As he was struggling with the design and logos he contacted irhabi007 via the Ansaar forum for help. Tsouli then organized an online workshop, and through the joint efforts of the cyber-jihadis the statement was ready to be published on Ansaar early in the morning of 11 September 2005, possibly with the intention that this would coincide with an attack in Denmark.[34]

The statement declared war on all unbelievers as a means to fight injustices against Muslims "everywhere," specifying imprisonment and torture.[35] The statement ended by defining al-Qaida in Northern Europe as soldiers and protectors of Islam, raising the "banner of the holy warriors ... just like the holy warriors in Great Britain did" (a reference to the 7 July attacks in London).[36] The condemnation of atrocities against Muslims was consistent with the radicalization of the plotters, which was linked to the War on Terror, and especially the invasion of Iraq. For example, Maximus's radicalization picked up speed in connection with the invasion of Iraq, and through his contacts with Irhabi007.

Abdul Basit Abu-Lifa was also known to be fiercely opposed to the Iraq war. He once wrote school papers on the torture of Muslims in Abu Ghraib in which he explained how the United States was responsible for the current state of war between Muslims and non-Muslims. Elias Ibn H. had also been very outspoken about his support for al-Qaida, and had once threatened a classmate whose friend had been a soldier in Iraq. The immigrant from a Syrian background, Imad Ali J., was known to have voiced concerns over Muslim prisoners. The convert administrator of the Tawhid webpage, Hudhayfah, also applauded terrorism: online he justified the attacks against tourists in Sinai in July 2005 and defended the killing of Muslims who worked in Egypt's tourist industry. Interestingly, several members of the Glostrup group had expressed anger over the publication of the Muhammad cartoons on 30 September 2005, but they were all apprehended or under close scrutiny of the security services when the conflict over the cartoons escalated during the spring of 2006.[37]

The emergence of "al-Qaida in Northern Europe" coincided with the rise of al-Qaida's branch in Iraq and a series of spectacular terrorist attacks in that country, which seem to have inspired the Scandinavians. Because several members of the Glostrup group had family ties to the Middle East, they may have been predisposed to having intense feelings about the Iraq war, like many of the Pakistanis who had been radicalized over Kashmir. According to the same logic, Bektasevic's connection to Bosnia may have been the reason he selected that country as the place to train for jihad.

As for the Danish dimension, it was not surprising that the first jihadi terrorist plot in Scandinavia happened in Denmark. Denmark is a close ally of the United States and the country made a sizeable contribution to the wars in Iraq and Afghanistan. This had elevated Denmark in the hierarchy of al-Qaida's enemies before the dismantling of the terrorist network, and the country had received repeated threats from al-Qaida. Moreover, like the other terrorist cells discussed in this book, Denmark's first jihadi case did not emerge in a vacuum. Over previous decades significant numbers of North African Islamists obtained asylum in Denmark and set up support networks for jihadis. Investigations into international terrorist networks revealed various links to Danish Islamists. Mansour spread propaganda and raised funds for the GIA in the 1990s and held meetings with Spanish jihadis. Also, the investigation of Tawhid in Germany revealed that those terrorists obtained passports from a criminal Islamist in Denmark. In another incident, a Danish-Moroccan was convicted for involvement in the Casablanca attacks in 2003. Moreover, as will be discussed later in the chapter, extremists in Denmark and Sweden emerged as central nodes in the European recruitment networks for the Iraqi jihad.

Given the level of jihadi activism inside Denmark and the ties between Danish jihadis and their international counterparts, Denmark was bound to be affected by global jihad. However, the speed and intensity by which Denmark emerged as a target was determined by several factors, of which the Danish approach to Islamism and Islam in general seems significant. Although generally perceived to be a liberal society, often compared to the Netherlands, Islam was never well received in Denmark, and harsh criticisms of Muslims and Islam have flourished in public discourses.[38] In the wake of 9/11 and M-11, the situation grew worse, causing frustration among Muslim immigrants and extremists among them, making it easier for jihad entrepreneurs to recruit. Part of the spiraling fear of terrorism was the exposure of Ahmed's study circle and the arrest of Mansour in September 2005, something that put the country's extremists under pressure and may have contributed to the shift from support activism to terrorist plotting.

The publication of the Muhammad cartoons added to the tensions and led Denmark to become a reoccurring theme in al-Qaida propaganda. In the following years, the cartoons would contribute to a significant increase in jihadi activism and terrorist plotting in Scandinavia, as will be discussed further in the subsequent chapters. The first Danish terrorist case substantiated that radicalization over Iraq and online jihadism was making the threat to Europe more transnational and multinational. Young, European extremists made contact with counterparts throughout Europe and Muslim countries via discussion forums and chatrooms, and were influenced by ideologues and groups, such as AQI. However, the case also showed that, although the Internet contributed to radicalization, meetings with extremists locally, in the UK and Bosnia seemed crucial in pushing the Scandinavians from extremism to terrorism. There was little to suggest that the network received instructions from al-Qaida or its affiliates, but they were clearly inspired by global jihad and had indirect ties to AQI via Tsouli, and perhaps another affiliate of the group who traveled in Syria and made phone calls from Iraq. Although the plotters were aware of and angry over the cartoons, Bektasevic and his accomplices had taken the decision to strike before they were publicized.

The next Danish terrorism case, the Glasvej cell, which grew out of exactly the same radical environment as the Glostrup group, does neither seem to have been motivated solely by the cartoons, although the entrepreneur of the cell cited the publication as one reason why he left Denmark to join jihad in Afghanistan.

Glasvej

In September 2007 Danish police arrested eight Muslim men aged between nineteen and twenty-nine in Glasvej, a suburban area of Copenhagen, on the grounds they had been preparing bomb attacks in Denmark. Most of those arrested were acquitted, but two men of Pakistani and Afghan origin, Hammad Khürshid (twenty-two) and Abdolghani Tohki (twenty-two), were ultimately sentenced to twelve and seven years in jail respectively for preparing acts of terrorism. The convicts were among Abu Ahmed's disciples and friends with people implicated in the Glostrup case (including Cesur and Mansour). Danish police apprehended several people affiliated with the plotters. One of them, a Dane with a Turkish background, was later charged with terrorist offences, including having discussed with a Turkish contact to kidnap Danish soldiers in an unspecified country, aiming to swap them for the release of Muslim prisoners in Denmark, such as the convicts in the Glasvej case. He was aquitted after trial, however.[39]

The Glasvej cell differed from the Glostrup group in that one of the convicts, Hammad Khürshid, had established direct ties to al-Qaida in Pakistan and attended training in Waziristan. Evidence against the Glasvej plotters included, for example, monitored phone and online communications, room surveillance of Khürshid's apartment, recipes for making poisons and bombs, prepared TATP explosives and cellphone video-clips showing the convicts manufacturing explosives and threatening terrorist attacks. While Khürshid and Tohki were already part of a network of extremists that was being watched by the security services, what made Danish spies pay special attention to them was US intelligence that Khürshid had made contact with al-Qaida figures abroad. In March 2007 he took leave from his job as a painter in Denmark and traveled to Pakistan. During a visit to Lal Masjid (the Red Mosque) in Islamabad he connected with people who could arrange training Waziristan, and returned to Denmark with bomb-making instructions and the intention of launching a terrorist attack.

The specific target(s) of the Glasvej cell were never confirmed, but circumstantial evidence suggested that the terrorists prepared to launch suicide bombings against public sites. One of the reasons for this was that, in addition to explosives, from among the convicts' belongings investigators retrieved drawings believed to illustrate buses and trains. However, the members of the cell categorically denied having any intention of carrying out attacks in Denmark. Khürshid admitted to having ties to militants in Pakistan and both of the convicts admitted to having staged a small test-explosion of TATP, but maintained they had done this simply because it was fun to do.[40] Investigators also retrieved a martyrdom testament from a notebook belonging to Khürshid, a strong indicator that suicide attacks had been planned. When Danish intelligence learned about Khürshid's trip to Pakistan, agents secretly searched his luggage at the airport and installed cameras inside his apartment in Glasvej. Subsequently, cameras recorded Khürshid and Tohki sitting by a sofa table manufacturing TATP and conducting a test explosion in the stairway of the building in Glasvej. In addition to being filmed by investigators, the plotters made cellphone recordings of themselves making threatening statements and manufacturing explosives.

On one video-clip, which they entitled "The Making," Khürshid stated: "this is some of the explosives. We'll see you in a week."[41] He also sang jihad hymns calling for martyrdom. It is believed that the plotters had planned to upload the clip to YouTube as some kind of threat, but they did not know how to hide their identities. During the trial, Khürshid testified that the bombs were constructed according to a bomb-manual he copied during a visit to the Red Mosque in Islamabad.

The Red Mosque was a hub for militancy frequented by Kashmiri mujahidin and Pashtuns from clans in Waziristan, many of whom had established stronger ties to the Afghan Taliban and al-Qaida after the invasion of Afghanistan and the influx of al-Qaida and Taliban fighters to the Af-Pak border zone. In 2007 the mosque became the scene of a major stand-off between Pakistani jihadis and the army which ended in a bloody military operation and the closure of the mosque.[42] The battle of the Red Mosque became a catalyst for Pashtu–Pakistani Taliban groups joining forces in a movement called Tehrik Taliban Pakistan (TTP), which continued to battle the Pakistani state and cause a surge of terrorism inside Pakistan, which is still ongoing today. Through ad-hoc cooperation with al-Qaida, TTP militants would also become involved in international terrorism in Europe and elsewhere, a development which will be discussed in later chapters. The Glasvej cell was also the first example of an ethnic Afghan being implicated in a terrorist plot in Europe.

The plotters became extremists in the context of Ahmed's Tawhid group in Denmark. However, the plan to launch suicide attacks in Denmark likely stemmed from meetings between Khürshid and al-Qaida in Waziristan. Khürshid, the entrepreneur in the plot, was born in Denmark but raised in Gujrat, Punjab, Pakistan. He completed college in Pakistan before moving and settling in Copenhagen in 2003, where he lived with his older brother in an area named Mjølnerparken and worked as a painter and salesman; he was a religious seeker. He became part of Hizb ut-Tahrir's Danish branch, attended the radical mosque in Heimdalsgade and joined Ahmed's study circle.

There were also indications that Khürshid had connected with militant Islamists during a number of visits to see his family in Pakistan. Khürshid had been part of the jihad scene in Denmark for a long time. In 2005, together with other members of the Tawhid group, he participated in a mock video-recording depicting the beheading of Nicholas Berg by al-Zarqawi.[43] Khürshid was known to hold the Taliban and al-Qaida in high regard and regularly consumed their propaganda online. In 2006, Khürshid and his brother rented the apartment in a street called Glasvej (which gave the name to the terrorist case), and between March and May 2007 he likely received training from al-

Qaida in Waziristan. Before going to Pakistan in 2007, Khürshid held a meeting with the Pakistani Dane who organized the Danish excursion to Bakri's conference in London in 2004.[44] Given the previous patterns in Pakistan-linked terrorism in Europe, Khürshid may have sought to establish ties to al-Qaida in Pakistan via the Dane's UK contacts.

Before traveling to Pakistan, Khürshid requested leave from his job as a painter on the basis that he was depressed because his (non-existent) wife did not want to live in Denmark because of the Muhammad cartoons.[45] After visiting his family in Gujrat, he began frequenting the Red Mosque, where he met with a recruiter known as Hamza, who allowed him to copy recipes of poisons and explosives. Hamza then took Khürshid to Waziristan where he is believed to have received training and met with high-ranking al-Qaida figures. At the camp, the Pakistani-Dane made several video-recordings with his cellphone, showing mujahidin carrying weapons and expressing their intent to fight jihad.

US intelligence believed that Khürshid became part of al-Qaida's training program for Western recruits that were to execute operations for al-Qaida in their home countries, the same program that the Crawley group, the 7/7 cell and the airliner plotters had attended. At the time of Khürshid's alleged training, the program was presumably overseen by Abu Udaydah al-Masri, and US intelligence alleged that the Pakistani-Dane had been instructed personally by the Egyptian.[46] When he had returned to Denmark, Khürshid communicated with his handlers in Pakistan, which included an individual who was believed to function as an intermediary between the Dane and al-Qaida known as Muhammad Ilyaas Subhan Ali, or Abu Ali. The conversations were in code. In one tapped phone call the contact in Pakistan addressed Khürshid as "the sheikhs' sheikh" and predicted a great future for him within "the firm." Khürshid admitted during trial that "the firm" referred to a band of jihadis.[47]

Khürshid's accomplice, Abdoulghani Tokhi, was born in Kandahar, Afghanistan, in 1986. His family went to Denmark via Thailand as part of the UN's refugee program. The family settled in the Danish town of Avedøre. Tokhi came from a strongly religious family and attended Islamic schools in Afghanistan. After becoming radicalized at a young age, Tokhi dropped out of high school in Denmark, and like the other radical Islamists living in the Copenhagen area, he began to frequent the Taiba Mosque and Ahmed's underground mosque in Amager.

The aforementioned Pakistani-Dane who organised the trip to London was said to have been central to the inclusion of Tokhi into Copenhagen's extremist networks. After joining Ahmed's group he befriended Khürshid and several members of the Glostrup group, including Abdulkader Cesur who lived in the same neighborhood as Tokhi's family. When Khürshid returned from Pakistan he and Tokhi became close friends and went to the mosques and the gym together. Khürshid told Tokhi about his trip to Pakistan and the bomb recipes and soon, during the summer of 2007, they started to produce small amounts (ten grams) of TATP.[48]

Surveillance tapes and other evidence, such as cellphone video-recordings, confirmed the terrorists' adherence to al-Qaida's vision of global jihad. Investigators discovered a host of pro-al-Qaida propaganda videos on the convicts' cellphones and computers. One video showed some mujahidin in Pakistan shouting "death to America, jihad, jihad," and there was also propaganda imagery of the 9/11 attacks and the martyrdom videos of the nineteen hijackers. Khürshid and Tokhi were caught on camera by the security services watching al-Qaida propaganda films showing training camps in Afghanistan, while the former was also recorded boasting about his Pakistan journey and the people he had met in Waziristan.

During the trial, the terrorists tried to paint a more nuanced picture of their religious–political beliefs, denying having prepared an attack, adding that they were opposed to the killing of civilians. When evidence was put forward claiming that Khürshid had collected a bomb-making manual at the Red Mosque, Khürshid stated that he had been interested in explosives since his childhood. In court, Khürshid appeared confident, grinning towards family and friends. He mocked Danish society and culture, saying it was impossible to be a true Muslim in Denmark "with all the naked women, bustling around here."[49] He explained how he had wanted to go to Pakistan to train and then join the jihad inside Afghanistan.

Interestingly, and alluding to the radicalizing effect of Israeli policies in the Middle East, he also said that he and a Saudi Islamist whom he had encountered on one of his journeys to Pakistan had talked about going to Lebanon in 2006 to fight the Israelis, although this never amounted to anything. Khürshid said that he supported the Taliban and that he agreed with al-Qaida on some matters but not on others, such as the killing of civilians.

When confronted with records of conversations with his contacts in Pakistan in which attacks on Westerners were discussed, he sought to reassure the court by saying they were talking about possible attacks outside Denmark.[50] He stressed how he had wanted to join a legitimate armed struggle rather than international terrorism, saying the investigators would be unlikely to find any justifications for attacks against the West among his belongings.[51] Abdoulghani Tohki did not reveal a great deal about his motives for joining Khürshid's project. Despite attempting to reassure the jury that he too objected to the killing of civilians, he had downloaded a number of videos to his cellphone showing the execution of civilians by jihadis. He also told the court he had not been "dismissive to the idea of following Hammad to Pakistan and Waziristan," indicating that he also wanted to join jihad abroad.

The Glasvej cell was intercepted at a time when transnational jihadis were gradually re-focusing their attention back to Af-Pak after concentrating on Iraq. While the Iraqi jihad had dominated the jihadi Internet since 2003, online activists were now focusing on the battles against ISAF and the Pakistani government. Al-Qaida's leadership was by no means neglecting the Iraqi cause, but the organization was also talking more about developments related to Afghanistan and Pakistan in its public statements, especially after the death of al-Zarqawi in the summer of 2006. Given the Glasvej plotters' bonds to Afghanistan and Pakistan, the fact that Pakistan was becoming a frontline in the War on Terror during 2006 must have affected them.

The United States had stepped up its drone war on al-Qaida in Af-Pak and the Pakistani government had deployed army units to the tribal areas. The conflict between the army and al-Qaida-affiliated groups in Waziristan caused a surge in anti-state terrorism, and there was also a spike in sectarian violence against Shia Muslims. As with the UK-Pakistani jihadis, the deteriorating situation in Pakistan may have contributed to the radicalization of the Glasvej plotters. Moreover, given al-Qaida's focus on the Muhammad cartoons in Denmark from April 2006 onwards, as mentioned earlier, it is clearly significant that Khürshid referred to this issue as one of the reasons for leaving Denmark and joining jihad abroad.

The cartoons had already been cited as a motive in another terrorist plot uncovered in Denmark and would be referred to by multiple terrorists in Europe for years to come. In the fall of 2006, before the Glasvej plot and while the Glostrup case was pending, PET discovered another gang of extremists in Vollsmose, Odense, which was plotting attacks on Danish politicians and the editor of the culture section of *Jyllands-Posten* to avenge the cartoons of the Prophet.[52] The entrepreneur of that plot, the eighteen-year-old, Iraqi-born Ahmed Khaldhahi, had been radicalized via jihadi forums online and within an extremist community at a local mosque. Khaldhahi was infuriated by the Iraq war and the publication of the cartoons. On the pro-al-Qaida forum "al-Hesbah" he asked other extremists for advice on how to assassinate the cartoonists, and proposed the use of poison as one attack method. In the end,

Khaldhahi and his co-conspirators gathered fertilizer and produced TATP for an attack.

Although the plot was portrayed by Danish authorities as the most serious case in Denmark until then, and the main plotters received lengthy prison sentences, the Vollsmose case was highly controversial. The reason for this was because a police informant had played a role in instigating an attack. The informant also came up with a number of allegations about Khaldhahi's connections to Iraq, proposing that the cell was controlled by AQI. This was believed to be false. In any event, the cell in Vollsmose was the first of a series of Danish plots triggered by cartoons and insults against Islam.

The Glasvej case resembled the British-Pakistani networks. It involved a Pakistani entrepreneur who radicalized first in Denmark, but connected with jihadis his country of origin, pursuing a dream of becoming a mujahid. Also parallel to the UK cases, al-Qaida figures in Pakistan were believed to have persuaded the Dane to execute an international attack instead. Moreover, there were links between the Glostrup–Glasvej case complexes and networks in the UK, implying phone contacts, chat rooms, discussion forums and travel, such as the trip to London and interaction with Bakri in 2004. However, while al-Qaida likely held sway over the Glasvej plotters, they were also part of the local Danish extremist scene, which had already produced two plots mainly from the bottom-up.

The cartoons of the Prophet Muhammad continued to mobilize Danish extremists and caused them to grow more determined to strike at home. Being part of the new generation and influenced by Bakri, the Danish extremists did not feel they were bound by a covenant of security, and the Glostrup and Glasvej cases suggested they considered European participation in Afghanistan and Iraq sufficient justification. The cartoons removed any doubts they might have had.

Having looked at how the threat began spreading to Scandinavia, I now turn to two cases in Germany which illustrated how affiliates of al-Qaida in Waziristan and its branch in Iraq also affected the threat situation in Europe in 2005–7. The first case, an attempted bombing of trains in Cologne, was linked to al-Qaida in Iraq, whereas a second plot to attack American interests in Germany was traced to an Uzbek group in Waziristan.

Suitcase bombers

A plot to blow up passenger trains in Germany in 2006 may have been the first attempt by AQI to cause an attack in Europe.[53] On 31 July 2006, the Lebanese students Youssef Muhammad al-Hajdib and Jihad Hamad tried to blow up trains in Cologne. At 14.40 the students placed time-bombs inside suitcases onboard regional trains and went into hiding. The devices failed to explode and were secured by bomb-squads at 19.35 the same day. Almost three weeks later, on 19 August 2006, Al-Hajdib was arrested at a railway station in Kiel and prosecuted in Germany. He was sentenced to life in prison by a German court in 2008.[54] On 24 August Jihad Hamad gave himself up to Lebanese police in Tripoli.

The suitcase bombers were linked to Islamists in Germany, Scandinavia, the Middle East and possibly the UK. They also had family ties to members of a newly established Lebanese jihadi group and to the European recruitment network for AQI. The attackers received assistance from contacts in Lebanon and Germany in locating viable bomb recipes and collecting necessary equipment.

One Lebanon-based contact, the brother of Youssef Mohammed al-Hajdib, Saddam, later became a high-ranking member of the Lebanese-based Fatah al-Islam movement which seized control of the Nahr al-Barid refugee camp, which was besieged by the Lebanese Army from May 2007. Fatah al-Islam was formed by the Palestinian Shakir al-Absi, a former fighter pilot and an associate of al-Zarqawi, in Northern Lebanon in November 2006. It was alleged that the group received support from al-Qaida, even though al-Absi described the group's links to the organization as emotional and fraternal.[55]

Fatah al-Islam fought fiercely against superior forces until the Lebanese Army decimated the group in September 2007. According to sources, Saddam al-Hajdib had been observed celebrating with his brother after the attempted attacks in Germany. He was later killed in clashes with the Lebanese Army alongside nine other Fatah al-Islam members in the incident that ignited the battle at Nahr al-Barid. Further investigations in Lebanon led to charges being brought against Jihad Hamad and several other Islamists suspected of having had a hand in the plot to bomb trains in Cologne, such as Youssef al-Hajdib's cousin, Ayman Abdullah H., Khalil el-B., Saddam al-H. (the brother of Youssef al-Hajdib) and Khaled Khair-Eddin al-H., another cousin of Youssef. Jihad Hamad was sentenced to twelve years in prison by a Lebanese court.

In Germany, police also launched an investigation into a car dealer in Essen who had been associated with al-Zarqawi's German Tawhid networks and individuals involved in the plot to attack Jewish targets in Berlin and Düsseldorf in 2002.[56] The initial German investigations focused on the bomb devices, computer hard-drives, mobile phone data, DNA analyses and interrogations. From computers investigators retrieved images of bin Laden, a video of the beheading of Nicholas Berg entitled "The Emir of Slaughter," plus images of bomb devices and chemical powder.

In January 2008, an alleged al-Qaida-associated Syrian named Mohammed N. sent a threat to the German embassy in Beirut that there would be attacks on civilians in Germany in the subsequent months in revenge for the conviction of one of the Cologne bombers in Lebanon.[57] He was later arrested by Lebanese authorities and interrogated. The plan allegedly involved setting off a truckload of explosives smuggled into Germany from Russia. The Syrian said an operational team, dubbed "Jihad Islami" and composed of a Turk, a Saudi and one Australian national in Germany, was to carry out the attacks.[58]

Youssef al-Hajdib's brother, Khaled Ibrahim al-Hajdib, who was living in Sweden at the time, was in frequent contact with Youssef in the run-up to the attacks and paid him several visits. According to Swedish authorities, Khaled's home in Sweden was a meeting place for extremists.[59] Khaled traveled to Lebanon immediately after the attack in Germany. It is believed that he was involved in fundraising and recruitment for al-Qaida in Iraq from Sweden.

German investigators believed it was he who recruited his brother and Jihad Hamad, and that he proposed the attacks in Germany as an "initiation test" for AQI, and Lebanese officials claimed that Khaled was a member of the organization.[60] It is alleged that he set up the contact between Youssef and Jihad Hamad while they were studying in Germany. The students chatted online before they met up in Cologne. They were also in touch with other Islamists in Germany, some of whom were investigated but were cleared of charges in connection with the Tawhid case in 2002.

The Lebanese students had first discussed blowing up the landmark railway bridge at Hohenzollernbrücke in Cologne, but settled for a plan more likely to succeed: placing time-bombs onboard regional trains at Cologne's main train station. They constructed the bomb devices (made out of propane gas canisters containing petrol and diesel) and timers (made out of alarm clocks, batteries and flammable liquid in soft drink bottles) in Jihad Hamad's apartment in Cologne based on instructions they had downloaded from the Internet.[61]

Where the Hofstadgroup and "al-Qaida in Northern Europe" were good examples of how the Internet was being used in recruitment and propaganda, the plot in Cologne exemplified how jihadis in Europe tried but failed to obtain sufficient bomb-making skills online. The Lebanese students visited a number of extremist websites, and like Mohammed Bouyeri, they downloaded ideological texts justifying the killing of people insulting the Prophet

Muhammad.[62] The bombs were timed to explode simultaneously when both trains were inside the station area in order to maximize deaths. A similar modus operandi was chosen by the Madrid bombers, who planned to bring down the station building but failed to do so because one of the trains was running late.

The Lebanese train bombers failed because the bomb devices were poorly constructed. They used the wrong type of gas and the detonators malfunctioned. According to police experts, a successful detonation would have been the most lethal ever terrorist attack in Germany. The plot coincided with Germany hosting the soccer World Cup, but it is unknown if this affected the timing of the attack. If successful, the media effect would have been enormous, especially given the World Cup and the ongoing Israeli campaign in Lebanon. During the trial of one of the terrorists in Düsseldorf, the prosecution estimated that the attacks could have killed seventy-two people if the bombs had exploded.[63]

The cell was composed of well-educated, young Lebanese men from families that could afford to send their children abroad for education. It was one of the first jihadi plots in Europe involving terrorists from the Middle East. While most cells in the region had been North African-based, Germany had faced another threat from Middle Eastern jihadis back in 2002, when al-Zarqawi's Tawhid tried to attack Jewish targets in the country. Interestingly, there were some indirect links between the Lebanese suitcase bombers and the leader of that cell, Mohammed Abu Dhess.

Youssef al-Hajdib (twenty-one) was singled out as the leader of the cell, although the plot was overseen by his older brothers in Lebanon and Sweden. Another brother of his was living in Denmark and working as a taxi driver. Al-Hajdib went to Germany in 2004, two years before the bomb plot. He hailed from a sternly religious family and several of his eight brothers became jihadis. His father was enraged by the cartoons of the Prophet Muhammad and acted as a lead figure in the protests in Lebanon.

Al-Hajdib was a student at the University of Kiel and lived in student accommodation. He isolated himself from his German co-students and only interacted with people of Arab origins. In one radical mosque in Kiel, Youssef was said to have interacted with extremists who had ties to the jihadi scene in London.[64] At university, al-Hajdib grew increasingly extreme and openly voiced support for bin Laden. In a classroom discussion about the Muhammad cartoons he became very aggressive and intimidated a female teacher.

He also participated in demonstrations against the cartoons in Germany. When he was arrested after the failed bombings, al-Hajdib was on his way to

Denmark, and in his pocket police found the number of an Odense-based imam named Abu Bashar. Bashar was a lead figure among the Danish delegation of imams that traveled the Middle East to mobilize international protests against the Muhammad cartoons. Bashar denied any affiliation with al-Hajdib, but he had been the religious mentor of several of those arrested in the aforementioned Vollsmose plot to kill Danish politicians and the editor of the culture section of *Jyllands-Posten*. He was also known to have made threats according to which Denmark should expect terrorist actions as a response to the military contribution in Iraq.[65] Such kinds of threats were typical of extremist communities inspired by Bakri and his protégé Anjem Choudary in London, who specialized in pursuing their jihadi activism within the boundaries of European laws.

Al-Hajdib's co-conspirator Jihad Hamad (twenty) hailed from Tripoli in Lebanon. In his home country he had frequented a radical mosque in which the imam, Husam al-Z., had preached that those who insult the Prophet Muhammad should be punished by death. Hamad was a student in Cologne and lived in an area called Neu-Ehrenfeld. In Lebanon, Hamad's parents sent him to a Christian school and they advised him and supported him to go to Germany for higher education and to marry a German woman.

In Germany the young student lived with his uncle in Essen. A car dealer in the same town helped Hamad obtain a visa to Germany by inviting him to the country.[66] As mentioned earlier, it transpired that this car dealer was already known to German police because he had once assisted the leader of Tawhid's network in Germany, Mohammed Abu Dhess, to obtain an apartment.[67] This connection illustrated the small world of jihadism, and how individuals, cells and networks are often inter-linked across state boundaries and over time. According to German media, Hamad had also met with another affiliate of Tawhid, although details were murky.

After the attacks in Cologne, Hamad escaped to Lebanon where he was apprehended by Lebanese authorities and sentenced to twelve years in prison. Three alleged accomplices (Khaled Khair-Eddin el-H., Ayman Abdullah H. and Khalil al-B.) were tried but acquitted. Several of the suspects who were arrested and tried in Lebanon had been living in Denmark and some had obtained Danish citizenship.[68]

Statements by the suitcase bombers indicated that they were driven by grievances over events in the Muslim world and the West, and their backgrounds and contacts implied they had a longtime affiliation with Islamist extremism and bonds to militant groups in the Middle East. The investigation indicated that the plotters were pushed forward by the brother of one of them who was recruiting for al-Qaida in Iraq from Sweden. However, they also harbored personal anger over European participation in the War on Terror and the Muhammad cartoons.

The terrorists did not issue public statements, and as in most jihadi cases in Europe, the full extent of their ties to organized networks was unclear. However, leaks from interrogations, witness accounts and emails presented as evidence during their trials suggest they were motivated more broadly by the War on Terror, and triggered by the re-publication of the Muhammad cartoons in German newspapers and the death of al-Zarqawi in Iraq.

Al-Hajdib had sent an email to Hamad six weeks before the attacks in which he wrote that they had to be patient "until we have totally made it and passed the initiation test. Then we'll travel to Iraq together."[69] The concept of an initiation test is interesting as there have been several examples in the history of jihadi terrorism in Europe of terrorists making arrangements to travel to conflict zones after an attack was going to happen. The Frankfurt cell and the Crawley group are a case in point and I will also discuss other cases in subsequent chapters.

In the email from al-Hajdib to Hamad, the former also announced that they would receive a visit from his brother Khaled Ibrahim al-Hajdib, the purported AQI recruiter from Sweden, perhaps signifying that AQI wanted to play a role in the plot. It was not entirely clear from the sources I reviewed whether or not Khaled al-Hajdib spent time in Germany in the immediate run-up to the attempted bombings, however.

In trial, Jihad Hamad denied any intent to kill. He said he only wanted to warn people against insulting the Prophet. He also said he had been exploited by al-Hajdib—whom he portrayed as the brains behind the operation. Hamad also told interrogators that al-Hajdib was motivated by the Muhammad cartoons and the death of al-Zarqawi in Iraq in June 2006. Youssef al-Hajdib, on the other hand, accused Hamad of being the ringleader and operational planner of the terrorist plot. However, he confirmed that the plot was meant as retaliation for the re-printing of the Muhammad cartoons by German newspapers.[70]

The attempted attacks in Cologne thus coincided with major events that clearly affected the terrorists. In the Middle East, the Americans had killed the leader of the group the plotters aspired to join (AQI), and Israel was attacking Hizbullah and Lebanon, killing many civilians in the process. Furthermore, life as an Islamist in Europe was becoming increasingly difficult as a result of counter-terrorism efforts across the region, while tensions were rising over the cartoons of the Prophet Muhammad.

Because one of al-Hajdib's brothers would become a central member of Fatah al-Islam (FAI), which was established shortly after the train bombing attempts, it cannot be ruled out that the plot was meant as a means to launch the new group, in order to build a reputation and attract external funding. While the terrorists spoke of the plot as an "initiation test" for AQI, this does not necessarily contradict a wish to promote FAI.

Although the latter was an independent group, its leader had a long relationship with al-Zarqawi, and there seems to have been a certain overlap between the groups' membership bases. Plotting an attack in Europe to elevate a group's profile may also have been the rationale for a subsequent plot by an Uzbek-based al-Qaida affiliate to launch an attack in Germany, as will be discussed shortly.

Because the Lebanese suitcase bombers were living in Germany on student visas, they were in principle bound by a covenant of security. However, they had ties to extremist networks in Europe and groups in the Middle East who did not accept such a covenant due to European participation in Afghanistan and Iraq, arrests of Muslims and insults against the Prophet and Islam. Between the Tawhid plot in 2002 and the Cologne plot, German security services had cracked down on several active support networks linked to Tawhid and Ansar al-Islam, but there had been no serious terrorist plots in the country. Jihadis in Germany had focused mainly on recruitment for Iraq after the invasion, but the Lebanese suitcase bombers signified that Germany once again was facing a threat of attacks.

The plot differed from the other plots in the same period in that the homegrown element was less pronounced. The terrorists had entered Germany a relatively short time before the attacks, and seemed to have been radicalized on their arrival in the country. And although the exact nature of the terrorists' organizational affiliations was not fully uncovered, there was much to suggest they were linked to AQI's recruitment networks and primarily wanted to join the jihad in Iraq. Whereas the plot seemed to have been driven mainly by international events, the plotters did interact with extremists in Germany and Europe and drew motivation from German affairs, such as the republication of the Muhammad cartoons in the German press.

I will now examine another case in Germany illustrating the interplay between domestic networks and foreign terrorists. A major development with regard to Islamism in Germany, which I will explore subsequently, was the radicalization of Turkish immigrants. Turks make up one-third of immigrants to Germany but were rarely tied to German jihadism before 2007. The same was true for Turkish communities in other European countries. However, a terrorist plot uncovered in the fall of 2007 demonstrated that Germans of Turkish origin were finding their way to al-Qaida's networks, something that was commented upon by al-Zawahiri in a speech he gave in 2010.[71] A fascinating aspect of the German-Turkish plot, referred to as the "Sauerland cell," is that it is the first example of an ethnic European convert becoming the entrepreneur of a jihadi terrorist cell in the region.

Sauerland cell

The so-called Sauerland cell was composed of Turkish immigrants to Germany, and was led by a German convert. The Sauerland cell illustrated how transnational jihadism was becoming more ethnically diverse. The plot was the first example of a convert managing a jihadi cell in Europe. Another atypical feature of the Sauerland case is that the terrorists gave full confessions during trial in order to speed up the legal process and reduce their sentences. Other than their confessions, the German prosecution relied on surveillance data, bomb materials and diverse technical evidence, as well as pro-al-Qaida propaganda, including ideological texts justifying jihad.

The case made international headlines on 4 September 2007 when German anti-terrorism police arrested the members of a group in Oberschlehdorn, Westphalia, who were suspected of preparing car bomb attacks against US interests in Germany. The core members of the cell included German converts and Turkish immigrants Fritz Gelowicz (twenty-eight), Daniel Schneider (twenty-one), Adem Yilmaz (twenty-eight) and Atilla Selek (twenty-two).

The terrorists were in contact with and received training, support and instructions from a Pakistan-based Uzbek jihadi group called the Islamic Jihad Union (IJU). The IJU was established in 2002 as an offshoot of the Islamic Movement of Uzbekistan (IMU), with support from al-Qaida. IMU was based in Tajikistan until 1998 before the group relocated to Afghanistan. IMU fought mainly against the regime of Islom Karimov in Uzbekistan. The splinter group, IJU, adopted a more global approach to jihad. The IJU forged two main alliances on the Af-Pak border with the Arab-based group of the Libyan al-Qaida member Abu Layth al-Liby, and a group headed by the Afghan Taliban commander Jalaluddin Haqqani and his son Sirajuddin. The ties to al-Liby and al-Qaida made IJU more internationally focused than it had been initially.

In 2004 the group attacked US and Israeli embassies in Tashkent. IJU also began to recruit fighters from Europe and North Africa, offering training in

Pakistan. The group's leader, Abu Yahia Muhammad Fatih, stressed the multinational character of the group, claiming that it encompassed "believers from all over the world." He said that "many brothers" contributed with "financial, moral, scientific and operational" support, but without specifying whether or not the "brothers" included al-Qaida members.[72]

The German IJU cell had assembled large quantities of chemicals and military detonators, and the plotters had undertaken reconnaissance of a variety of targets. The anti-terrorism operation "Alberich" was launched in October 2006 when the US intelligence organizations NSA and the CIA informed their German counterparts about online communications between IJU handlers in Pakistan and the cell in Germany. Altogether, forty-five individuals were placed under surveillance.[73] The entrepreneur, Fritz Gelowicz, told the court that the cell planned attacks on different US targets including the Ramstein US military airbase, as well as several bars frequented by American troops, adding "we didn't want to kill two or three U.S. soldiers, but rather many."[74]

Inside a rental car (which had been bugged by spies), while on a trip gathering bomb-making materials, Gelowicz and Yilmaz talked about killing up to 150 people in the attacks. The alleged second-in-command, Yilmaz, denied any intention of launching mass casualty attacks and insisted during trial that the plotters only planned minor explosions at the Düsseldorf or Dortmund airports with the aim of disrupting traffic. He further argued that they wanted to minimize civilian casualties, especially the deaths of Muslims.

The IJU issued a communiqué on its Turkish-language website taking responsibility for the plot and claiming that the cell also planned an attack on "the Uzbek consulate" (likely referring to the Uzbek embassy in Berlin).[75] At the time of the arrests the terrorists were manufacturing improvised explosives based on Internet recipes in a cabin in Sauerland, Westphalia. Gelowicz told the judges that the attacks were supposed to be launched at the beginning of October, when Germany's parliament was to vote on a continued mandate for German forces in Afghanistan.

As with the London bombings, hydrogen peroxide was supposed to be the main component of the explosive. The terrorists had assembled twelve barrels, containing more than 700 kilograms of hydrogen peroxide, with a concentration of 35 percent. The detonators, believed to come from Syrian military stocks and obtained on the black market, were smuggled into Germany from Turkey by a German-Tunisian teenager, sown into a pair of sneakers.[76]

The plotters were well aware they were being monitored and implemented several counter-surveillance techniques, such as coding their communications, using multiple email accounts and listening to police radio. However, while protecting their communications, they also took actions that seemed irrational, or at least hazardous, given their terrorist plans. For example, the leader of the group gave an interview to a German magazine complaining about being persecuted by the authorities for no reason.[77] Moreover, in one incident, a member of the cell who was being tailed by agents, Attila Selek, walked up to their car and slit one of the front tires with his pocketknife. In another hazardous incident on New Year's Eve 2006, Gelowicz and Selek drove a car back and forth near the barracks of American soldiers in the town of Hanau, and were confronted by police officers.[78]

In the typical pattern, the Sauerland cell emerged from a local jihadi support network. This network supported jihad in Iraq, Afghanistan and Chechnya, and included both immigrants and naturalized Germans. The network spanned a number of German cities and different parts of the country. Gelowicz and Yilmaz told the court they had originally sought to join the jihad in Iraq. After failing to connect with a recruiter in Damascus, they considered going to Chechnya instead, but did not find the right contacts to get there. They instead came in touch with a representative for the IJU in Syria, who helped them gain access to a training facility run by the group in Mir Ali, Waziristan.

When they were training in Pakistan, the Germans inquired about the possibilities of joining operations against ISAF, but the IJU leaders told them to return to Germany and carry out attacks there instead as it would be "more use to the jihad."[79] Interestingly, the IJU handlers argued it was easier to inflict damage on US soldiers in Germany than in Pakistan and Afghanistan because it was possible to attack them while they were not on duty and off guard. Similar attacks against uniformed soldiers would become more common in Europe over time, as exemplified by the killing of French soldiers by Mohammed Merah in France in 2012 and the killing of a British soldier in Woolwich in 2013, to be discussed later. Gelowicz and Yilmaz reluctantly agreed to the mission proposed by the IJU.

Contacts between the Sauerland cell and IJU supervisors were direct and enduring. The organization facilitated training, supplied the cell with bomb-making manuals and gave instructions concerning the preparations and timing of an attack. Having previously operated mainly in Uzbekistan, in April 2007 the group announced online that it would step up its international operations.[80] Subsequently, after the disruption of the Sauerland cell, the organization claimed responsibility for the plot on a Turkish-language website.[81]

After the man alleged to be IJU's main link to al-Qaida, Abu Laith al-Liby, was killed by a US drone attack in Mir Ali in January 2008 (several IJU members were killed in the same attack), the group seems to have prioritized fighting coalition forces in Afghanistan in concert with Haqqani's armed group. In 2008, the IJU also assigned some of its Western recruits to fight inside Afghanistan. In March 2008, for example, the group declared that a German-Turk Cüneyt Ciftci had carried out a suicide attack on US and Afghan soldiers in Paktika.[82]

The members of the IJU terrorist cell in Germany came from relatively well-to-do, middle-class families and had received some level of education. Prior to becoming involved in the plot, the cell leader, Gelowicz, had been studying engineering, Yilmaz was working odd jobs and Schneider was unemployed after German military service. Living inconspicuous lives, for various reasons they gravitated towards Islamist extremism. At approximately the time of the invasion of Iraq, Gelowicz, Schneider and Yilmaz became part of a jihadi support network centered on Westphalia, which was dominated by Germans and Turks. The network involved around fifty individuals, many of whom had traveled to Pakistan for training. A forty-seven-year-old Pakistani named Aleem Nasir was convicted in 2009 for playing the role of recruiter, financer and facilitator within the network.[83] An Egyptian radical preacher acted as a spiritual guide for members of the network from a radical mosque in the German town of Neu-Ulm.

The jihadi bearing the unlikely name of Fritz Gelowicz was the entrepreneur of the terrorist cell. He was born in Munich and grew up in the southern German city of Ulm. Described by Guido Steinberg as "by far the most intelligent member of the cell," Gelowicz converted and radicalized within the context of mosques and support networks in Germany.[84] He hailed from an ordinary middle-class family by German standards. His father was an engineer, running a firm developing solar energy technology, and his mother was a medical doctor. Gelowicz's parents divorced when he was a teenager. Former schoolmates say the divorce was difficult for him, and some suggest he turned to religion as a way of dealing with it. His brother also converted to Islam, but, according to German authorities, he never dabbled in extremism.

Fritz studied engineering at Ulm University, where he joined an Islamic study circle. During regular meetings at the Turkish "Cafe Istanbul," members of this group were overheard legitimizing the killing of Christians, Jews and infidels. Gelowicz also became part of the extremist scene at a cultural center and radical mosque named MultiKultur Haus in Neu-Ulm. At the centre he befriended Yehia Yousif, an Egyptian medical doctor with ties to militant Egyptian Islamists, who acted as imam and charismatic leader among the extremists in Neu-Ulm. Yousif went to Germany in the late 1990s and obtained his doctorate in medicine from the University of Freiburg; he started to build a following in Neu-Ulm from around 2001 onwards. Under the influence of Yousif, MultiKultur Haus became a magnet for Islamists from all over Germany. However, after German authorities launched an investigation into the activities of the radical preacher he left the country, most probably for his homeland, or Saudi Arabia.[85]

Fritz soon lost interest in his studies and became absorbed into jihadism. During the winter of 2003–4 he sat some exams and achieved varying results, after which he took a leave of absence, which was to last for eighteen months. Like many other European extremists he enrolled in Arabic-language courses in Egypt and Syria, and undertook religious studies in Saudi Arabia. He also went on hajj to Mecca during this time, together with Selek and Yilmaz. According to US intelligence, in March 2006 the three of them spent time training with IJU in Waziristan on invitation from the IJU recruiter in Damascus.

The cell's second-in-command, Adem Yilmaz, was a Turkish national who went to Germany in 1986. He testified that he had embraced militancy in 2004 and had a strong desire to join the jihad in Iraq. He worked at Frankfurt airport between 1997 and 2007. Yilmaz seems to have functioned as a recruiter for the cell, while at the same time having responsibilities for the gathering of necessary equipment. For example, he recruited two activists, a German Afghan named Omid S. and a German-Turk named Huseyin O., for IJU's camps in Pakistan, and made them supply GPSs and night vision goggles that were to be transported to mujahidin in Pakistan.

Attila Selek and Daniel Schneider seem to have fulfilled subordinate roles in the plot. Selek was a German citizen of Turkish descent. He hailed from a conservative family and worked as a car painter and car salesman. Selek joined the extremist scene in Neu-Ulm around 2004 and traveled with Gelowicz to the Middle East and Pakistan. He received only three years in prison for complicity. Schneider is a German convert from a similar background to Gelowicz. He received a heavy prison sentence, but this was mainly because he attempted to shoot a police officer during his arrest.

The confessions of Gelowicz and Yilmaz provided a picture of committed global jihadis nurturing strong hatred for the United States and Israel. Their grievances could be traced both to Germany and global affairs. Neither Gelowicz nor Yilmaz showed any signs of remorse during the trial hearings. Yilmaz stressed how he remained a militant and was determined to become a martyr. Gelowicz told judges that he was motivated by US support for Israel and what he described as its war on Islam.[86] Their radicalization accelerated following the invasion of Iraq. Gelowicz generally blamed excesses in US counter-terrorism for his militancy.

Explaining how the United States "carried the war into my mosque," he told the judges about the CIA's kidnapping of a father who worshipped with him at the mosque in Neu-Ulm. The individual, a Lebanese national named Khaled el-Masri, was kidnapped in Macedonia in December 2003 and transferred to Afghanistan, where he was interrogated and abused. It ultimately transpired that the CIA had mistaken him for someone else, after which the agency dumped him in Albania with no apologies or compensation. Al-Masri has since sought vindication through lawsuits, albeit without success.[87] Gelowicz described the kidnapping as "the straw that broke the camel's back."[88]

During interrogations, Selek also condemned the Americans' use of torture, and claimed it disqualified the evidence presented against the plotters. Gelowicz characterized an attack against US soldiers in Germany as "targeted retaliation" and a protest against what "these pigs" (i.e. the American soldiers) were doing to innocent people in places such as the Abu Ghraib prison in Iraq.[89] Fritz believed their actions would "please detainees in Iraq, Afghanistan and also at Guantanamo," adding, "that was the most important thing to me." Similarly, Adem Yilmaz characterized the activities of the cell as "defensive jihad."[90]

Surveillance data clearly illustrated the cell's enmity towards Americans. In a conversation recorded during the summer of 2007, Gelowicz stated that "American targets are the most important; everything depends on those targets," adding one should "punch every American in the face."[91] Moreover, at one point German agents observed a member of the group and some of his friends trying to provoke fights outside a nightclub frequented by American soldiers stationed in Darmstadt. When they failed to provoke a response, they slit the tires of US-produced cars in the area. Also, in bugged conversations the cell's members discussed attacking a disco with "American sluts."[92]

Unlike the entrepreneur Gelowicz and his protégé Yilmaz, the misfits and drifters Schneider and Selek expressed some regrets about their actions. Schneider told judges he was happy he had been arrested, and that he considered the cell's terrorist plans to have been a mistake. Selek said he had been involved in planning "deeds that are not reconcilable with the Quran," adding that "when I went into jihad I didn't want to kill people. That is not the aim of jihad."[93] The radicalization of the terrorists involved factors related to Germany, the Middle East and Pakistan. They grew extreme amid the invasion of Iraq, were recruited by an armed group in Damascus and sent to Pakistan for training.

The Sauerland cell further exemplified the pattern whereby jihadi plots in Germany were not aimed at the public, and were usually aimed at US or Jewish targets. The only plot that has been aimed at the German public was that of the Lebanese suitcase bombers. They had likely been representing al-Zarqawi's group in Iraq, known to have a preference for Jewish and Shia targets, but also for extremism and indiscriminate terrorism with less apparent strategic rationales.

By the time of the Sauerland plot, Germany had strengthened its military presence in Afghanistan, had received multiple threats from al-Qaida and German security services were cracking down on jihadi support structures in the country, something which affected the Sauerland cell directly.

Possible explanations why the cell still preferred to target American interests include their personal hatred of the United States, but it could also be that the IJU, independently or in concert with al-Qaida, saw an attack on the German public as counterproductive at the time, as it could have strengthened German resolve in counter-terrorism. Conversely, an attack on American interests might have had the opposite effect.

Whereas al-Qaida in Iraq and its off-shoot Islamic State have gained a reputation for pursuing extreme violence for its own sake, al-Qaida always pursued a more strategic approach. Since the late 2000s, al-Qaida-inspired terrorism in Europe has become more discriminate, likely because the organization faced pressure and competition and needed to boost its legitimacy and support among a wider audience.

The Turkish dimension of the Sauerland plot was unprecedented in Europe. Turks and Turkey never played a central role in jihadism. Because of its large Turkish immigrant community, for a long time Germany was seen as an example which demonstrated that Turks were immune to al-Qaida. The invasion of Iraq, German participation in Afghanistan and the arrests of Islamists in Germany appear to have changed this pattern. In the time leading up to the emergence of the Sauerland cell, jihadi entrepreneurs in Germany, such as the above-mentioned Aleem Nasir and Yehiah Yousif, managed to mobilize German and Turkish extremists. A factor that may have eased their efforts is that al-Qaida began to translate its propaganda into multiple languages, including German and Turkish, and addressed young Muslims in the West in order to recruit them for global jihad. It has been argued that language was one of the main factors in IJU's success in attracting German Turks, because Uzbeks and Turks belong to the same language family.[94]

A final aspect of the Sauerland plot that contradicted past patterns of jihadism in Europe was the fact that it was led by an ethnic European. However, although ethnic Europeans had not headed an operational cell in the region, several Europeans and Americans had assumed leadership positions among transnational jihadis in the past. In fact, for unknown reasons, Germans showed special talents for climbing the ranks of al-Qaida. In the mid-1990s, for example, a German convert of Polish origin, Christian Ganczarski, was recruited by al-Qaida's networks and came to function as a courier and computer expert for bin Laden. He was subsequently implicated in an attack against German tourists on the Tunisian vacation island of Djerba, for which he was sentenced to eighteen years in prison by a French court.[95]

Similarly, the German-Moroccan Harrach Bekkay, who was linked to the Westphalia-based support network from which the Sauerland cell emerged, managed to connect with the inner circles of al-Qaida and became a spokesperson for the group. Bekkay was born in Morocco in 1977 and moved to Germany as child. He grew up in Bonn and studied economics at the University of Koblenz. Bekkay was recruited to the Westphalia network by the aforementioned Pakistani Aleem Nasir. With a letter of recommendation from Nasir he traveled to Waziristan via Turkey and Iran, where he managed to connect with leading al-Qaida figures and was trained by Abu Ubaydah al-Masri, the mastermind of the 2006 airliner plot in the UK.

A member of al-Qaida and protected by the Haqqani network, Bekkay was used as a recruitment tool in several al-Sahab propaganda productions targeting German youths and issuing threats against Germany. Bekkay was killed in 2009 while fighting inside Afghanistan. The stories of Fritz Gelowicz and Harrach Bekkay illustrate how al-Qaida and its affiliates were strategically recruiting converts as a means to stage attacks in Western countries on the one hand, and for recruiting among a Western audience on the other.[96]

In a broader perspective, the Sauerland case demonstrated how non-Pakistani groups besides al-Qaida in Af-Pak possessed the will and capacity to carry out attacks internationally. Like some of the North African and Pakistani networks discussed in previous chapters, IJU pursued different agendas, combating the regime in Uzbekistan, ISAF in Afghanistan and international terrorism. The Sauerland cell also demonstrated the multinational character of jihadism in Europe, being Turkish-based but led by a German. To conclude this chapter I examine an attack in Britain in the summer of 2007. The cell, which also involved links to AQI, nearly killed scores of people at a nightclub in Central London and at Glasgow international airport. The plot contradicted assumptions that the threat was becoming entirely homegrown. The cell also stood out in that it involved highly educated people, medical doctors and engineers, leading it to be dubbed the "doctors' cell."

Doctors' cell

The doctors' cell refers to a failed plot by an Islamist medic and an engineer to execute simultaneous car bomb attacks outside nightclubs in London in June 2007. While on the run from police the terrorists also attempted to stage a suicide mission by ramming a car filled with explosives into the terminal building at Glasgow airport. Fortunately, the car got stuck in the terminal door and the bomb failed to explode. One of the attackers then poured gasoline over himself and tried to set himself on fire in a desperate attempt to cause an explosion. There was no loss of life in the operation except one of the attackers, who died from his burns.[97] There were indications that the cell was linked to AQI, but the exact nature of these links was not clear.

The cell was composed of Kafeel Ahmed and Bilal Talal Abdul Samad Abdullah. A third person named Mohammed Jamil Abdelkader A. was suspected of supporting the cell, but due to a lack of evidence he was not convicted.[98] Abdulla was sentenced to a minimum of thirty-two years in prison in December 2008. On Kafeel Ahmed's computer, which was retrieved from the burning car in Glasgow, investigators found ideological and strategic texts, audio-visual material by bin Laden, al-Zawahiri, al-Zarqawi and al-Suri, as well as several texts by the Saudi ideologues Sulayman Ibn Nasir Al-Ulwan, Husayn ibn Mahmud and Hamud Bin Uqla al-Shuaybi.

Moreover, although the terrorists were not known to frequent radical mosques in the UK, they had been influenced by Qatada. The international character of the doctors' cell contradicted predictions that the threat was becoming Europeanized. The case also demonstrated how the Iraq war continued to motivate terrorism in Europe, despite the fact that al-Qaida and its affiliates had begun to pay closer attention to Afghanistan and Pakistan than Iraq after the death of al-Zarqawi. Similarly, the fact that the plot involved highly educated and well-to-do individuals who had embraced jihadism gradually and intellectually contradicted predictions that the threat to Europe was becoming dominated by socially disaffected and ideologically deprived second-generation immigrants.

The attack method was typical of al-Qaida-associated terrorism in Europe in the mid-2000s insofar as the terrorists aimed to kill as many people possible using bombs. However, the terrorists did not plan suicide attacks, unlike the 7/7 cell and the airliner plotters controlled by al-Qaida from Af-Pak. The doctors' cell initially sought to execute hit-and-run car-bombings with remotely controlled detonators. They opted for a suicide mission when the first attacks failed.

On 29 June 2007, two Mercedes packed with gas canisters, petrol and nails were placed in Haymarket on London's busy West End (near Piccadilly Circus), outside the Tiger Tiger nightclub (a popular club able to accommodate more than 1,700 people) and on Cockspur Street nearby. The car bomb in Cockspur Street was meant to kill people trying to escape from the explosion outside Tiger Tiger, and the bomb devices were to be detonated by cellphones. The reason why the bombs failed to explode was that the air inside the cars was too humid, and there was not enough oxygen for the petrol and gas to ignite. The investigations uncovered that the terrorists had pre-planned follow-up attacks because they possessed two other vehicles and additional bomb-making materials.[99]

The attackers prepared the mission from Scotland and drove the cars to London on the day of the attacks. After the failure of the attacks, the plotters hid in a hotel before returning to Glasgow the next day via Stoke. While on the run, they hastily prepared another vehicle for a suicide attack on Glasgow airport terminal. There, they rammed the car at full speed into the door of the terminal building. When the vehicle got stuck in the door, one attacker poured fuel over the car and himself. He desperately tried to cause an explosion while shouting "Allahu Akbar" (God is greater). He later died from his burns.[100]

The preparations for the attacks began in February 2007. The cell took many security precautions and was meticulous in terms of planning. This may have been because they had received terrorist training, although it could equally be the case that it simply reflected the fact they were intelligent and well educated. In any event, their security consciousness allowed the cell to fall under the radar of the UK security agencies, which were on maximum alert after the 7/7 attacks and the airliner plot.

Each of the terrorists owned a number of cellphones and they regularly changed between them. They bought five cars (Mercedes and BMWs), bomb-making materials (gas canisters, nails and screws, fuel, transistors), phones for the detonators, a satellite navigation device and a video camera. They also rented a house with a garage for the construction of the bombs and undertook reconnaissance of the attack scenes. Abdulla and Ahmed also kept in touch with each other online via emails and the Yahoo instant messenger service.[101]

From interrogations and witnesses, investigators learned that there had been several discussions between the terrorists about various purchases, such as whether they should rent an apartment or a house, and if they needed access to a garage.[102] They ultimately bought a house with a garage on 6 Neuk Crescent in Houston, Paisley, Scotland, which was used as a bomb factory.

The prosecution claimed that the discussions concerning the bomb factory proved that the alleged accomplice, A., was aware of the bombing plans, but this did not hold up in court. They also highlighted how, after every significant act of preparation, the bombers had contacted A.

After renting the house they covered the windows of the garage so that no-one could see what was going on inside. Several witnesses observed the plotters frequenting the garage and heard suspicious noises coming from inside. The terrorists obtained the bomb ingredients shortly before the attacks, between 29 May and 27 June, either by mail order, or from different shops and wholesale stores. Investigators recovered a laptop from the burnt car in Glasgow, and by analyzing the hard drive they found out that the plotters had conducted research on how to make petrol bombs online. They had also been using the Internet to research the nightclubs selected as targets. The cell undertook reconnaissance on several occasions in May. In addition to Haymarket and Cockspur Street they also scouted London's Old Bailey central criminal court, which had been the scene for the prosecution of high-profile jihadis such as Rachid Ramda of the GIA's network in the mid-1990s, Qatada, Hamza, Omar Khyam of the Crawley cell, and many others.

The purchasing of materials and equipment was financed from the plotters' salaries and savings, and by personal loans, including one provided by A. Although the plotters earned good salaries, money was short, and an issue of debate and conflict within the cell.[103] The plotters rented a room at a hotel in Forest Gate to be used during the escape from London back to Scotland, where they had two other vehicles ready for follow-up attacks. They were staying at the same hotel during the reconnaissance in May. From the hotel Abdulla sent an email to his employer, pretending to be his own sister, and informing him that he had been injured in a car accident. The purpose of this email was likely to confuse the investigation in case the terrorists needed more time to realize their objectives.

On the day of the attacks, leaving the cars near Tiger Tiger, the attackers hid their faces from CCTV cameras, Ahmed using an umbrella. While walking away from the scene they called the cellphones inside the cars to set off the explosions, before they jumped on rickshaws and met at Edgware Road. Staff at the club noticed gas inside the car and a strong smell of petrol, notified the police and started evacuating the club. The second car was detected by investigators after it had been ticketed during the evacuation of clubbers, and subsequently towed to a car park. From the cars police secured DNA, fingerprints and cellphones. The failed bombers spent one night in the hotel room before they traveled to Stoke, where they met up with A., before they continued to Glasgow and set a second attack in motion.

It is believed that the members of the terrorist cell met each other for the first time in Cambridge, UK, while they were studying, and in context of an Islamic charity and a prayer room attached to it. It is also believed they had established ties to AQI, and that they may have received orders and support from the organization. It is not entirely clear whether the cell was initiated inside the UK or abroad, but the men implicated in it had lived in the UK at the same time in the past, and were all working in the UK during the run-up to the attacks.

The terrorists hailed from well-to-do families from the Middle East and India, and they were considerably better educated than other jihadi terrorists in Europe. There was thus nothing to suggest that socio-economic hardship and experiences of social injustice had contributed to their radicalization.

The entrepreneur, Bilal Talal Abdul Samad Abdulla (twenty-nine), was born in the UK while his father was studying medicine. The family later returned to Baghdad and were said to maintain good relations with the Baathist regime. Abdulla was educated as a medical doctor in Baghdad. One of his classmates claimed he had been radicalized during a trip to Jordan in 2000. Abdullah was in Iraq during the invasion, and this, together with the killing of a Sunni dean at his faculty and his replacement by a Shia Muslim, was the source of considerable anger for him. He expressed a hatred of Shias, the US occupiers and strong sympathies for al-Qaida.[104] He went to the UK when he graduated in 2004 and enrolled in courses at Cambridge to qualify to practice medicine in the country. At university he mingled with members of Hizb ut-Tahrir.

While in the UK he continued to voice support for al-Qaida and browsed jihadi websites. He was known to have become very upset over the coalition forces' attack on Fallujah in 2004.[105] In 2006 Abdulla was employed as a junior surgeon at a hospital in Paisley. He was known to be a very orthodox Muslim who was knowledgeable about the Quran and had mastered classical Arabic. A relative in the UK said he showed religious passion when preaching at a mosque in Cambridge in the absence of the usual mullah.[106] The relative told the media that Abdulla had wanted to become a mullah rather than a doctor and that "I saw him praying one time and he had tears in his eyes."[107]

During a quarrel with a roommate in the UK, Abdulla showed him a video of beheadings by AQI as a veiled threat. He spent time in Iraq between May and July 2006. The prosecution believed that he interacted with AQI representatives during this stay and was assigned to execute a terrorist mission in the UK. US security officials told the media that Abdulla had joined an AQI cell in Baghdad. It was alleged that he had been too valuable a recruit to be used as a suicide bomber in Iraq because of his language and Western cultural skills, and that he was instead persuaded to strike in the UK to retaliate for Britain's military campaign in Iraq.[108]

The terrorist who set fire to himself in Glasgow, Kafeel Ahmed (twenty-eight), hailed from an Indian doctors' family. He studied mechanical engineering in India and Ireland before starting his PhD studies at Cambridge University in 2004. From 2004 onwards he traveled back and forth between India and the UK to visit one of his relatives who was in poor health. Ahmed was a Salafi and follower of Tabligh, and he had clashed with religious leaders at a mosque in Bangalore for trying to make fellow worshippers more conservative.

Ahmed entered the UK for the final time in May 2007 when the cell started preparations for the attacks. Because of his educational background as an engineer it is believed that Ahmed was responsible for constructing the bombs. Ahmed's brother, a medical doctor working in Liverpool at the time of the attacks, was first suspected to be involved, but later cleared.[109]

The man believed to have played a role as a coordinator and facilitator of the cell, Mohammed A. (twenty-seven), hailed from Saudi Arabia and was married with children. He has been described as religiously orthodox and highly talented, obtaining a scholarship from the University of Amman, Jordan, to study abroad. A. arrived in the UK in 2003. After going back to Jordan he arrived for a second time in 2005 and went on to work as a neurologist in several hospitals across the UK. A. met Abdullah and Ahmed in Cambridge and was in frequent contact with them up until the attacks.

Witness accounts, personal communications and martyrdom testaments cited in the case files left few doubts that the terrorists were committed global jihadis. The attackers seem to have wanted to avenge US and UK military campaigns in Iraq and Afghanistan and they were ready to sacrifice their lives in the process. Statements attributed to the terrorists, and propaganda in their possession, indicated that they identified strongly with al-Qaida in Iraq, and that the occupation of Iraq was at the very core of their motivation.

Communications between the plotters also suggested they might have received instruction from al-Qaida in Iraq. From confiscated hard drives, investigators retrieved a draft martyrdom testament by Abdullah which addressed "the leaders of the Iraqi jihad; bin Laden and the brothers or soldiers of jihad in Afghanistan, Chechnya, and Palestine."[110]

The testament specified the intent to kill as retribution for US and British warfare in the Muslim world. Moreover, a whole section of the text was dedicated to al-Zarqawi, the iconic leader of AQI who had died a year earlier.[111] Furthermore, in a letter uploaded to the draft messages folder on his Gmail account, Kafeel Ahmed explained to his brother Sabeel the reasons for his own death:

> this is the "Project" that I was working on for some time now ... Alhamdulillah [praise to God]. Everything else was a lie! And I hope you can all forgive me for being such a good liar!! It was necessary, just so that YOU know Alhamdulillah. Everything since last week was executed by me and my team (this is confidential) on behalf of our Amir (if you have sins then the plan was stalled mid-way). If they can't figure out who it was, then keep me alive as long as possible.[112]

The claims he had a team and acted on behalf of an emir fed the theory that AQI might have had a hand in the plot. The interrogations of A. also confirmed that Ahmed and Abdullah were focused on Iraq. Though the prosecution doubted his credibility, A. said that Abdullah had been trying to persuade friends to go to Iraq to fight.[113] He also said that Abdullah and Ahmed spoke to him about martyrdom and that he had a feeling they were preparing to leave for Iraq.

Computer files recovered from the plotters' hard drives contained a number of movies showing jihadi operations in Iraq, but there were also religious rulings by Saudi preachers on the legitimacy of suicide attacks and terrorism against Americans, as well as texts justifying jihad against Muslim regimes, including Abu Basir al-Tartousi's "A Verdict Regarding the Saudi Regime."[114]

Several developments in Iraq may have provided AQI with incentives to attack internationally. After the death of al-Zarqawi, Iraq witnessed a surge in violence which led the Bush administration to send more troops to the country, with 2007 becoming the deadliest year for US troops since the beginning of the war. Also in 2007, the British forces handed over the control of Southern Iraq to the Iraqis and started sending soldiers home. At the same time, central al-Qaida was concentrating on the battle against ISAF and the looming insurgency in Pakistan.

In this context, an attack in the UK by AQI might have been a strategy designed to increase international attention and support, and sway a Western audience to vote for parties promising withdrawal of troops from Iraq (like M-11). The US Democrats' election manifesto, for example, contained promises for a withdrawal from Iraq.

At the same time, as mentioned earlier, although AQI repeatedly threatened to launch attacks in the West, only a limited number of plots with some kind of connection to AQI occurred in Europe. The most high-profile incidents before the doctors' cell were Tawhid's plot in Germany in 2002 and the suitcase bombers in 2006. Sometime after the UK plot, the new leader of AQI after al-Zarqawi's death, Abu Hamza al-Muhajir, stated that the group was behind the doctors' cell, although the exact details of its involvement were never firmly established through the investigations.[115]

Contrary to most other plots in Europe, the doctors' cell did not emerge from a local extremist scene. However, the plotters had mingled with British Islamists and charities. Witnesses spoke of Ahmed's activism as an Islamist and head of the Islamic Society in Cambridge, and he also shared an apartment with members of Hizb ut-Tahrir. The terrorists had been studying, working and pursuing Islamist activism in UK from 2004, at a time when British authorities were intensifying their efforts to halt extremism.

By 2007, most radical preachers were behind bars, and there were ongoing legal proceedings against a number of terrorist suspects. One high-profile prisoner was Abu Qatada, who himself boasted about having influenced the purported facilitator of the cell, A. In a letter smuggled out of prison in 2009, the Jordanian explained how he had encountered Abdullah and A. in prison, and how they had impressed him. He also said that the latter had told him how he had been inspired by Qatada's audio-taped sermons.

In the same letter, Qatada fiercely criticized Britain's new terrorism laws on the grounds they allowed the country to "persecute" Muslims, specifying the bill of 2008 that gave authorities the right to impose restrictions on terrorist suspects who were not in prison. Alluding to his own case, as well as that of Hamza and other British prisoners, he also complained about the abuse of the prisoners and extraditions of Muslims to their home countries or the United States. Given the terrorists' interest in Qatada and other preachers, it can certainly not be ruled out that counter-terrorism arrests were a partial motive for striking Britain, particularly as the arrests of Muslims had been gaining traction as a motive for jihadi terrorism for some time.

The doctors' cell caught the security services by surprise. The case contradicted predictions about homegrown terrorism and demonstrated how the Iraq war continued to motivate attacks in Europe despite increased jihadi focus on Af-Pak. All of the cells studied in this chapter demonstrated that, while there were some changes in the social make-up of cells and their use of the Internet, much stayed the same. Cells were still connected to international groups and traveled to interact with mujahidin and obtain training.

At the same time, transnational jihadism was facing challenges and going through some changes in 2007–8 which would make its virtual component a more decisive factor. Drone strikes and incursions by the Pakistani Army in the Af-Pak tribal areas were taking a toll on al-Qaida. Some of its regional affiliates, such as the Iraqi branch, had also been severely weakened, and other affiliates, such as AQIM in Algeria and al-Shabaab in Somalia, were on the rise.

In 2009, al-Qaida's Saudi Arabian branch would also reinvent itself in Yemen and join jihad in the West. In this situation the leaders of global jihad were introducing new strategies in an effort to survive and sustain the struggle. Al-Qaida started to rely more on its regional branches outside Af-Pak, and put more emphasis on recruiting Western youths via social media. The organization also strengthened its focus on enemies such as Jews and military targets in order to appeal to a broader audience. Furthermore, al-Qaida and its affiliates also placed a renewed emphasis on old ideas within the network of "decentralized jihad," employing small independent cells or single-actor terrorists that were hard to trace to organizations. The impetus to implement such a strategy in the West was the publication of cartoons of the Prophet Muhammad.

8

DECENTRALIZATION (2008–10)

In 2008–10 the number of jihadi plots in Europe increased and reached a peak in 2010. This was an unexpected development because transnational jihadism was perceived to be in crisis due to the weakening of al-Qaida in Af-Pak and Iraq, and the crackdowns on cells and networks in Western countries. However, several developments contributed to upholding the threat, although the phenomenon was changing in nature.

First, al-Qaida's alliance-building in Af-Pak and the brewing Islamist–state conflict in Pakistan had drawn new actors into the global jihadi orbit. They included Pakistani groups, such as the Pakistani Taliban (TTP), groups from neighboring areas, such as the East Turkestan Islamic Movement (ETIM) from China, or even European groups, such as the German Taliban Mujahideen.[1] These groups (even the German one) pursued different agendas mainly related to Af-Pak, but they also became implicated in al-Qaida's international operations.

Also, while some of al-Qaida's regional affiliates, such as AQI, were in a difficult position, others were in a potent state, such as AQIM in Algeria and al-Shabaab in Somalia, or on the rise, such as al-Qaida in the Arabian Peninsula (AQAP). The latter was an off-shoot of al-Qaida's Saudi branch (QAP) which was defeated by Saudi security forces after a terrorist campaign in the kingdom in 2003–4.[2] AQAP was created by Saudi and Yemeni jihadis, with the Yemeni-American Anwar al-Awlaki as its religious guide, and would initiate a global campaign against American targets, which also involved Europe. Moreover, a small number of plots in 2008–10 involved people having some connection to AQIM and al-Shabaab.

Second, apart from relying on new allies among established groups, al-Qaida also began re-introducing the concept of "decentralized jihad" which had been developed by one of its main strategic thinkers, Abu Musab al-Suri, in the late 1990s.[3] Al-Suri prescribed the use of independent cells and individual attackers in situations where jihadis were unable to gain territorial control and set up emirates. The idea of leaderless resistance is usually traced to nineteenth-century anarchists and has also been promoted by American anti-communists and far-right extremists.[4]

The strategy is designed to secure the survival of a militant movement by removing ties between operational cells and the strategic leadership, enabling terrorists to wage a war of attrition against superior enemies. In accordance with this, al-Qaida leaders and spokesmen began to call upon young Muslims of the West to execute attacks on their own within al-Qaida's framework. Al-Qaida's branch in Yemen (AQAP) re-distributed al-Suri's ideas in its online English-language *Inspire* magazine, accompanied by propaganda and images designed to resonate with young extremists in Western countries.[5] As will become evident in this chapter and the next, *Inspire* magazine was downloaded by many cells and single actors in Europe since 2009.

Third, from 2008 onwards jihadis were increasingly employing the social media platforms YouTube, Facebook and Twitter for propaganda. In this way they managed to reach new and broader audiences than was the case with the more exclusive and frequently password-protected forums they had been using in the past. The immediate reason for this shift was that in 2008 intelligence agencies managed to shut down the main jihadi forums for several weeks. This led strategists among the cyber-activists to call for the use of social media and mainstream discussion forums instead.[6] The strategy proved to be a major advantage for a transnational movement in need of new recruits, and a formidable instrument to implement decentralized jihad. Al-Qaida and likeminded groups could instantly spread vast amounts of propaganda much more effectively than in the past, allowing them to reach its target group among young and social media-savvy youths in the West. They could also do so without running security risks.

Fourth, the publication of the cartoons in Denmark provided transnational jihadis with a tremendous propaganda and recruitment tool which was well suited for igniting a campaign of decentralized jihad in the West. The cartoons had caused uproar among Muslims far beyond the ultra-extreme audience that would normally support al-Qaida, and when bin Laden called for assassinating the cartoonists, even many mainstream Muslims refused to condemn this.

Muslims' love for their Prophet is difficult for Westerners to grasp, and may be compared to anybody's love for close kin and children.

This, coupled with the fact that the death penalty for anyone who insults the Prophet Muhammad finds support in theological texts written by acknowledged scholars who enjoy popularity beyond jihadism, created an explosive situation which the jihadis knew how to exploit. Al-Qaida and AQAP were using the cartoons and Ibn Taymiyyah's verdict in efforts to boost recruitment and to justify terrorism by sympathizers in the West. In addition, the Muhammad cartoons and the jihadi response inspired mentally challenged and unstable individuals to take matters into their own hands, and implement the death penalty on people they perceived as having insulted the Prophet.

With regard to operational patterns and how cells emerged, the plots in 2008–10 did not deviate drastically from those that emerged prior to this. However, although much stayed the same, there were some new features with regard to the terrorists' backgrounds and group affiliations, as well as the configuration of cells and their choice of weapons, tactics and targets. Plots would continue to target the jihadis' main European enemies, the UK and France, and the majority of cases still had some kind of connection to al-Qaida or its affiliates in Af-Pak. Likewise, most plots had a substantial homegrown element in that the terrorists had interacted with extremist communities and jihadi support networks in Europe, online or face-to-face before plotting attacks. Furthermore, most plots involved bombing in public areas, sometimes by the use of suicide bombers.

At the same time, an increasing proportion of plots were occurring in Scandinavia. The sudden rise in terrorist plots in Scandinavia was primarily linked to the cartoons or art projects by the Swedish artist Lars Vilks mocking Islam. However, it was partly also a result of the toughening of measures against Islamists in countries such as the UK, France, Germany, the Netherlands and Spain following plots and attacks. Scandinavia had a shorter history of jihadism and fewer incidents than core areas of jihadism further south in the region. There had been support networks for the GIA in Sweden, Denmark and Norway in the 1990s, and in the wake of 9/11 several investigations were launched against financing networks, and against recruiters and propagandists such as Said Mansour in Denmark and Mullah Krekar in Norway.

However, compared to their counterparts in countries such as France, Belgium, Germany, Spain and the UK which had long experience in countering Islamist extremism, the Scandinavian security services were not as vigorous in terms of the counter-measures they adopted. This led jihadis from other

European and Muslim countries to go to Scandinavia for sanctuary, or to set up support networks. This was likely also the reason why Scandinavian countries emerged as central nodes in the European recruitment effort for the Iraqi jihad, as exemplified by the case of the suitcase bombers in Germany, al-Qaida in Northern Europe and multiple investigations of extremists in Scandinavia with international links in Europe and conflict zones of the Muslim world.

In addition to a wider geographical distribution of terrorist plots, from around 2008 more plots came to involve assassinations of public figures, such as artists involved in the Muhammad cartoons, politicians or moderate Muslim leaders. There were also more incidents with links, some vague and some very direct, to al-Qaida's regional branches or affiliates in Yemen, Somalia and Algeria. However, the most substantial change was a significant rise in single-actor terrorism by extremists with varying ties to organized networks in Europe or abroad.

The sudden rise in single-actor plots started around 2008 and reached a peak in 2010, but would continue to affect jihadism in Europe for years to come. The single-actor terrorists came in different forms. Some of them were entrepreneur types who radicalized gradually and intellectually, whereas others were misfits and drifters, who joined jihadism more coincidentally. Some were recruited and instructed by organized groups from the top-down, whereas others had a bottom-up approach, reaching out to jihadi networks for training, advice and support; only in rare cases did the terrorists lack any ties to organized networks.

I now take a closer look at some cases which exemplify the continuities and discontinuities of the jihadi threat in Europe in 2008–10, exploring how it was affected by al-Qaida's alliances and strategies, social media and the Muhammad cartoons. I will first discuss incidents reflecting the continued threat from networks and cells supervised by jihadis in Af-Pak. I then address multiple cases of single-actor terrorism which illustrate the different types of the phenomenon and also exemplify the growing threat in Scandinavia and links to al-Qaida's affiliates in Yemen, Somalia, Iraq and Algeria.

Continued threat from Af-Pak

In January 2008, in a counter-terrorism operation dubbed "Cantata," Spanish police arrested a group of Pakistanis and two Indians suspected of plotting suicide bomb attacks on the subway in Barcelona on behalf of the Pakistani Taliban (TTP) and al-Qaida in order to avenge the Spanish participation in

ISAF.[7] It was alleged that the attack was planned to coincide with a visit to Europe by the then president of Pakistan, Pervez Musharraf, and that the subway was chosen as a target because it was hard to access for first responders and would maximize causalities. Ten Pakistanis and one Indian were sentenced to between nine and eighteen years in prison.

The cell was intercepted because one of the designated suicide bombers had second thoughts and alerted the security services. Spanish police raided several sites and confiscated computers and bomb-making materials (including chemicals and timers), in addition to ideological texts and propaganda. In a video circulated online, TTP's then leader Baitullah Mehsud took responsibility, specified that an attack was to happen in Barcelona and said more terrorists besides those arrested were prepared to attack. The investigation suggested TTP had planned to issue several demands if the attacks had succeeded, and if these demands were not met, there would be follow-up attacks in Germany, France, Belgium, Portugal and the UK, all of which had contributed to ISAF.

However, there were also indications of al-Qaida involvement. The entrepreneur of the cell, Mahroof Ahmed Mirza, had acted as preacher and another central member was Mohammad Ayub Elahi Bibi. A protected witness in the case, likely the individual who pulled out of the mission, testified to have received instructions from an al-Qaida handler based in Paris and that he had received training from al-Qaida in Waziristan. He also said he had been part of a support network for al-Qaida in France before becoming involved in the plot. In some ways the plot echoed the Sauerland cell in that a newly established al-Qaida affiliate in Af-Pak was going international to elevate its profile, with help from al-Qaida. More plots began to emerge from Af-Pak in 2009 and 2010 which were transnational and ambitious in accordance with al-Qaida's modus operandi.

In April 2009 UK police arrested twelve terrorist suspects in a series of raids across Northern England. Eleven were Pakistani nationals, and ten held student visas. Investigators believed they planned to launch suicide-bombings against shopping centers, a train station and a nightclub in Manchester during the Easter holidays. There were indications in the case that the attack was going to be launched sometime between 15 and 20 April 2009.[8] Interestingly, information retrieved from bin Laden's compound in Abbottabad in 2011 showed that al-Qaida's leader had been involved in the planning.[9] In raids, British investigators confiscated quantities of flour and oil that could be used in the production of peroxide-based explosive devices, as well as photographs that appeared to be surveillance of the potential targets.

The purported leader of the cell, Abeed Naseer, sent coded messages to an email address in Peshawar, sana_pakhtana@yahoo.com, believed to belong to Saleh al-Somali who was al-Qaida's chief of external operations at the time. This email address linked the Pakistanis in Manchester to another al-Qaida-affiliated cell in Norway disrupted in the summer of 2010, and the Afghan-American jihadi Najibullah Zazi plotting to bomb the New York Subway in September 2009, discussed shortly.

The entrepreneur of the Manchester cell, Abeed Naseer entered the UK first on a student visa in 2006, and spent time in Pakistan in 2007 and between September and November 2008. Evidence against the Manchester plotters was limited and most of them were released shortly after their arrest without being charged and were instead placed in immigrant detention centers. Ten people voluntarily returned to Pakistan, whereas Naseer and Ahmad Faraz Khan appealed to the Special Immigration Appeals Commission, which handles cases involving deportation of people believed to constitute a threat to national security.

Based on intercepted email correspondence and classified intelligence, the commission decided that the appellants were indeed linked to al-Qaida and constituted a threat, but they could not be deported due to the risk of torture.[10] The emails between the UK and Pakistan revolved around finding appropriate wives for the suspects, a common code for discussing targets among jihadis. Surveillance material and suspicious photographs of the Arndale shopping center in Manchester supported this interpretation.

The investigation of Najibullah Zazi and two accomplices who planned a suicide mission against the New York subway shed new light al-Qaida's continued efforts to strike in the West. The New York plot was linked to the Manchester cell and another cell in Norway. In 2008, Zazi and his co-conspirators traveled to Pakistan to join the Taliban against ISAF. In Peshawar they met an al-Qaida recruiter who took them to Waziristan where they sat down with Saleh al-Somali, the handler of the 7/7 cell and the airliner plot Rashid Rauf, and the Saudi-American Adnan Shukrijumah, who is believed to have been involved in the 9/11 operation and multiple subsequent plots by al-Qaida. According to sources, Shukrijumah belonged to al-Qaida's external operations section until his death in 2014.[11]

Zazi indicated to investigators that it was Shukrijumah who persuaded the cell to attack at home rather than joining the Taliban, arguing that the message to President Obama and the negative effect on the American economy caused by an attack in New York would best serve jihad.[12] The terrorists also learned how to make explosives out of hydrogen peroxide and organic substances (such as flour) and were asked to use the word "wedding" as a code for the attack—as with the 9/11 "big wedding" and the Manchester plotters who were ostensibly searching for girls to wed. Back in the US, the American plotters communicated with the same sana_pakhtana@yahoo.com email in Peshawar as did the Manchester cell and a third cell of the network,—in Norway.

In July 2010 the Norwegian police security service (PST) arrested the thirty-nine-year-old Uighur Mikael Davud and a thirty-one-year-old Uzbek, David J., on suspicion of plotting attacks for al-Qaida. In a simultaneous operation, German Bundeskriminalamt (BKA) arrested the thirty-seven-year-old Kurd Shawan Bujak while on a trip to Germany. Davud and Bujak were convicted of plotting attacks for al-Qaida in 2012, whereas David J. was acquitted of terrorism charges. In addition to a small quantity of hydrogen peroxide and other bomb-making material, investigators confiscated propaganda and a notebook containing names and emails. These included another alias of Saleh al-Somali, Abd al-Hafiz, and the sana_pakhtana@yahoo.com email.

An interesting detail illustrating the Af-Pak dimension, as well as the overlap between networks in time and space, was that the plotters possessed a passport photo of a UK-based terrorist fugitive, Ibrahim Adam, who was linked to the al-Qaida-led Crawley group intercepted in the UK in 2004, discussed in chapter six. Davud and David J. were discussing how to obtain a passport for Adam, who was killed by a drone strike in Waziristan in 2011. They also searched online for media sources about the German Sauerland cell, and referred to the terrorists as "brethren."[13]

The entrepreneur of the cell, Davud, whose original name was Muhammad Rashidin, was believed to have received training from al-Qaida in Waziristan during the winter of 2008/9, following a similar route to the area as members of the Sauerland cell (via Turkey and Iran). At the trial he vehemently denied having planned an attack in Denmark (which was the investigators' main theory) and maintained he had planned to bomb the Chinese embassy in Oslo as retribution for the deaths of family members persecuted by Chinese authorities in Xinjiang province.

He also maintained that he was acting on his own. This may have been a strategy to avoid terrorism charges, as to meet the Norwegian legal definition of terrorism at that time required a conspiracy between two or more people. The court saw no reason to doubt that Davud had suffered persecution in China and genuinely hated the Chinese regime. However, it did not believe the claims that he acted alone and plotted to bomb the Chinese embassy. The

Norwegian court considered Davud's Kurdish-Iraqi accomplice, Bujak, to be more trustworthy. He told interrogators that the cell had first planned to bomb the offices of *Jyllands-Posten* in Denmark before settling for a plan to assassinate Kurt Westergaard.[14]

The cell members went to Norway as refugees in the late 1990s and lived in different parts of eastern Norway before gravitating towards the capital. They worked periodically and ran small businesses. They were also part of religious communities in Norway and were known to harbor radical views, including voicing support for al-Qaida. However, whereas plots in Europe usually emerged from local networks, the investigation did not find any evidence that the plotters had been part of an extremist group in Norway.

Before the dismantling of the al-Qaida cell, Islamist militancy had been a marginal phenomenon in Norway, and there were few incidents linked to jihadism before the arrests of 2010. However, from 2009 a community of al-Qaida sympathizers had been emerging around a Norwegian-Pakistani reformed criminal, Arfan B., and the Kurdish-Iraqi Islamist, jihad-veteran and co-founder of Ansar al-Islam, Mullah Krekar. B. had previously been prosecuted for planning an attack against the US embassy and involvement in the shooting of the synagogue in Oslo in 2006. He was acquitted of the former but received a sentence for aiding and abetting the latter incident. According to patterns observed in Denmark, the Norwegian extremist community linked up with extremists in the UK and Muslim countries, and came to produce one of the largest foreign fighter contingents in Syria controlled for population. I will return to this development in the following chapter. However, although there was little to suggest that the Norwegian al-Qaida cell emerged from within, the trial generated interest among Norwegian Islamists and Arfan B. attended the court hearings and greeted the defendants before being escorted out of the court building.[15]

The Oslo–New York–Manchester case complex was classic al-Qaida and demonstrated how the organization remained bent on continuing its international operations in the West, either by sending terrorists from abroad or recruiting Muslims living in the West. The Norway plot demonstrated that, in addition to calling upon sympathizers to avenge the Muhammad cartoons by themselves, al-Qaida was taking concrete steps to do so on its own.

Another terrorist plot targeting *Jyllands-Posten*, which was intercepted in October 2009, pointed in the same direction. This plot was also the first example of US-based extremists planning an attack in Europe after conspiring with al-Qaida and its affiliates in Af-Pak.[16] The case further illustrated how jihadism is not solely a youth phenomenon, as the terrorists were close to fifty.

US authorities arrested two Pakistan-linked men who had prepared an attack on the offices of *Jyllands-Posten*.[17] One of them, Tahawwur Hussain Rana (forty-eight), was of Pakistani origin, and the other, David Coleman Headley (forty-nine), was an American citizen who had lived in Pakistan. Both men had graduated from a Pakistani military academy, and cooperated with another Pakistan-based army veteran identified as Abdur Rehman Hashim Syed. The terrorists first cooperated with Laskhar-e-Taiba, but it was a Pakistani militant known as Ilyas al-Kashmiri who ended up directing the plot.

Al-Kashmiri had ties to al-Qaida, but he also headed his own Pakistani-based group named Harkat-ul-Jihad al-Islami (HUJI). As discussed in Chapter Six, it was rare for Laskhar-e-Taiba to target the West. The group was most known for attacks in India, such as those in Mumbai in 2008. These attacks gave a name to a new jihadi terrorist tactic, involving multiple mobile attack teams, launching guerilla style attacks with handguns, grenades and small bombs in urban areas.

Such attacks are also referred to as Fedayeen operations, and include a martyrdom element in that the gunmen fight until death. After attacking the public at different locations, the Fedayeen teams in Mumbai besieged the Oberoi Trident Hotel, which also involved taking hostages. The attacks lasted for four days and were designed to exhaust first responders and maximize the media effect. The attacks are also believed to be the first example of terrorists using social media to communicate and monitor the moves of first responders.[18]

It transpired that the entrepreneur of the *Jyllands-Posten* plot, Headley, had been doing reconnaissance for Laskhar-e-Taiba in Mumbai on five occasions in the time leading up to those attacks. In early November 2008 he was then instructed by Laskhar-e-Taiba to do some reconnaissance of *Jyllands-Posten*'s offices in Aarhus and Copenhagen. In January 2009 he visited the offices posing as a businessman and filmed the interior and exterior of the buildings. However, at some point Laskhar-e-Taiba pulled out of the plans because the group was facing pressure after the Mumbai attacks. The army veteran Abdur Rehman Hashim Syed then put the cell in contact with Ilyas al-Kashmiri, who took charge of the operation—likely on behalf of al-Qaida.

Members of the cell were clearly inspired by al-Qaida, and had discussed an al-Sahab video in which the organization claimed responsibility for the attacks on the Danish embassy in Islamabad in January 2008, and called for additional attacks to avenge the cartoons. Al-Kashmiri provided Headley with a contact in the UK and Sweden who was supposed to provide manpower. Al-Kashmiri envisioned a Mumbai-style Fedayeen attack, and wanted the attackers to behead the hostages and throw the heads onto the streets to maximize the terror and provoke an overreaction from the Danish authorities against Muslims. Luckily, the plot was stopped at an early phase.

The plans to attack *Jyllands-Posten* attributed to Laskhar-e-Taiba, al-Qaida and HUJI signaled the continuing effect of the cartoons and illustrated how al-Qaida's affiliates in Af-Pak had brought a new modus operandi to the table. Since 2008 there have been an increasing number of plots which involved a Mumbai-style modus operandi. Despite the fact that no such attacks reached fruition in the time period explored in this chapter, the plans that were discovered were taken very seriously by the region's security services given the deadly nature of the attacks in India.

In September 2010, for example, news broke that European security services had disrupted a so-called "Europlot" to launch Mumbai-style attacks in Britain, France and Germany by a Pakistan-based network with links to al-Qaida and the Taliban. Information about the plot first surfaced in interrogations of an Afghan-German at Bagram Prison near Kabul. He claimed that while staying in Mir Ali, Waziristan, he had been sought for recruitment by an al-Qaida handler going by the name of Younis al-Mauretani for a team of terrorists that was being prepared to be sent to Europe to carry out Fedayeen attacks. The information was corroborated by three different sources within the German jihadi network, some of whom were linked to the German Taliban Mujahideen. Interestingly, a member of the 9/11 Hamburg cell who was still at large, Said Bahaji, met with people involved in the plans.[19]

Later, in December 2010, *Jyllands-Posten* was once again exposed to a Mumbai-style terrorist plan when five men were arrested in Sweden and Denmark for plotting a Mumbai-style attack on the newspaper's offices.[20] The Danish Police Security Service (PET) believed that the terrorists planned to storm the localities of the newspaper and kill as many people as possible. If they failed to get inside the building they planned to enter other buildings in the area and kill innocent civilians. It was also believed that the terrorists aimed to create a prolonged hostage situation. During arrests police seized a machine gun and plastic strips suitable to be used as handcuffs. Three of the suspects were Swedish nationals, one was a Tunisian citizen and the last was an Iraqi asylum seeker living in Denmark.

The leader of the group, Lebanese-Swedish Munir Awad and several of the others had been traveling to Pakistan mixing with German members of IMU and other militants. It also transpired that some of the terrorists had been in contact with a Stockholm-based Moroccan businessman alleged to have been the Swedish contact who should have provided manpower to David Headley's plot against the offices of *Jyllands-Posten*. This led the authorities to suspect that it was intended that Awad's cell would complete what Headley had begun for al-Qaida and HUJI. The pursuit of guerilla-style attacks by al-Qaida-affiliated groups in Af-Pak was a new pattern in 2008–10. Another new feature of the threat in this period was the rise in plots and attacks by jihadis acting alone.

Single-actors on the rise

From 2008 onwards there was a steep rise in plots by jihadi terrorists working on their own (from 12 percent before 2008 to 38 percent of plots in 2008–13). This change was caused by a combination of factors, but was ultimately rooted in strategies to circumvent counter-terrorism measures and facilitated by ideology. To deal with the pressure it was facing, al-Qaida re-worked Abu Musab al-Suri's vision of decentralized jihad, with the aim of enabling the new generation Western jihadis to engage in a war of attrition behind enemy lines. The general idea was to prompt young sympathizers who had no known record in jihadism and were able to avoid attracting the attention of the security services to execute small attacks. These attacks were to accompany the efforts of organized networks to execute ambitious, bigger attacks. The call for individual terrorism emerged as the main feature of jihadi propaganda aimed at followers in the West, with AQAP's *Inspire* magazine being at the apex of the campaign. The rise in single-actor plots in Europe was clearly linked to this propaganda.

However, before looking at some of the cases exemplifying the trend, it is important to conceptualize single-actor terrorism and mention some of its underlying causes. The literature on single-actor terrorism makes a distinction between "solo-terrorists" and "lone wolves."[21] The former operate alone but are linked to and may receive support from organized groups. Lone wolves operate alone and only draw inspiration from political movements. A good example of solo-terrorism is Richard Reid, who tried to bomb a transatlantic jet for al-Qaida in 2001, whereas the attacks by the right-wing mass killer Anders Behring Breivik in Norway in 2011 was the work of a lone wolf. Among solo-terrorists it is further possible to distinguish between those who are tasked "from above" by a group (top-down) and those who initiate something "from below," reaching out to organized groups for guidance and assistance (bottom-up).[22] While the distinction between solo-terrorists and lone wolves can be blurred, it must be kept in mind when exploring why more jihadis came to operate alone in Europe.

Research has yet to identify a common profile for terrorists who operate alone. However, characteristics such as social problems, loneliness and mental illness are more common among lone wolves than other terrorists. The latter do not systematically differ, socially and psychologically, from non-terrorists.[23] Also, whereas solo-terrorism is supposed to fulfill some strategic aim for organized groups (in this case upholding a threat level from the global jihadis), lone wolves tend to be driven by more elusive motives, mixing political grievances with personal ones.

Most jihadi single-actors in Europe have been bottom-up solo-terrorists, but some received directions from al-Qaida or its affiliates. However, there were also examples of terrorists resembling lone wolves. The majority interacted with local extremists, and many had spent time with mujahidin abroad. Most if not all drew inspiration from al-Qaida, although they rarely received operational assistance. Most were relatively normal, troubled young men, and there was only one example of a woman. Several were known to have experienced social and psychological problems, and at least one of them had been diagnosed with a disorder within the autism spectrum (Asperger's syndrome).

The fact that ties to organized networks were commonplace supports the idea that the increase in single-actors stemmed mainly from tactical adaption to counter-measures. As noted, individual attacks were called for by multiple pundits such as bin Laden, Abu Yahya al-Liby and Anwar al-Awlaki, and advertised in *Inspire* magazine. As I will discuss below, al-Awlaki also guided two single terrorists in Europe directly, and was cited as the main inspiration by the female lone wolf, the British-Bengali Roshonara Choudhry. That jihadis also managed to ground individualized terrorism in classical Islamic theology (as exemplified by bin Laden's reference to Ibn Taymiyyah in the speech from April 2006), is probably underestimated when assessing triggers for solo-terrorists and lone wolves.

In addition to strategy and ideology, the contagion effect of terrorism was probably a considerable factor. Lethal shootings, such as those at Fort Hood in 2009, were promoted widely in al-Qaida propaganda and jihadi social media. While most single actors caused limited numbers of casualties, some 70 percent of the plots in 2008–13 reached the execution stage. Moreover, some of the incidents, such as the shooting spree by Mohammed Merah in France in 2012, did cause multiple deaths and had a massive terrorizing effect through mainstream and social media. The plots to bomb transatlantic airliners by al-Qaida operatives Richard Reid and Sajjid Badat just after the millennium and the murder of Theo van Gogh stood out as rare examples of single actors among jihadi terrorists in Europe before 2008. The former plots were top-down solo-terrorism designed to add to the 9/11 effect, whereas the latter was largely a bottom-up project by a member of an extremist group with connections to foreign mujahidin.

Most cases in 2008–10 were bottom-up projects, but they did not emerge in a vacuum. Rather, they involved individuals who belonged to (more or less) organized extremist communities, offline and online. Usually this interaction went beyond mere inspiration in that that there were discussions of attacks, with encouragement or advice and instructions being received. At the same time, there were also clear-cut examples of top-down recruitment and supervision of singletons by foreign terrorists. Only one case seemed detached from extremist networks (Roshonara Choudhry).

There was no clear pattern as to the profiles of those who were agents for groups and those who were independent. However, the latter seemed to include more misfits and drifters, whereas the former were usually entrepreneur-like, educated and sternly religious. The exception was the lone wolf Roshonara Choudhry, who was resourceful and pious.

Bottom-up solo-terrorists

The nineteen-year-old convert Andrew Ibrahim was behind a bomb plot in Bristol uncovered in April 2008. He was clearly a misfit who found comfort and direction in radical Islam. After raiding his apartment police confiscated home-made explosives of the same type as those employed by the 7/7 cell (HMTD), and equipment for manufacturing detonators. In 2009, he was convicted of plotting a bomb attack against the local Broadmead Shopping Centre.

The son of a British mother and an Egyptian Coptic Christian father, Ibrahim was described as a shy boy, and as an "emo kid" with a strong interest in music. He used to dye his hair, had several piercings and was known to have a drug habit, even doing heroin at one point. In 2005–6 he converted to Islam and became a Salafi. As seen in many other cases, the conversion coincided with a life crisis, in this case the divorce of his parents, after which he dropped out of school, lived for a while in a hostel for homeless people, began to attend mosques and accessed sermons by radical preachers online. During trial, Ibrahim said he had seen himself as a "sad loser" and that being a jihadi made him "feel cooler."[24] While mingling with extremists, Ibrahim did not appear to have had any ties to organized militants, and while in prison he retracted his support for terrorism and cooperated with police in de-radicalization efforts aimed at youths. His mother also joined de-radicalization efforts in Britain.

A similar case occurred one month later, in May 2008, when a twenty-two-year-old convert, Nicky Reilly, attempted to detonate three bombs in a restaurant in Exeter.[25] Only one of the devices exploded while Reilly was preparing explosives in the restaurant's toilet. Suffering from Asperger's Syndrome and obsessive compulsive disorder, Reilly was the only known example thus far in the history of European jihadis with a psychiatric diagnosis (however, it should also be noted that medical records have rarely been made available).

Reilly was also affected by personal crisis and attempted to overdose at sixteen after feeling rejected by his father. He then converted during 2002–3 after he was dumped by his girlfriend and another attempt at suicide. He befriended local Kurdish immigrants and learned the Kurdish language. A Kurdish woman he met on the Internet was said to have encouraged him to carry out the bombing. He also interacted with and was influenced by Pakistan-based extremists and ideological material online. The online contacts were said to have instructed him on how to make the bomb and what target to strike.

Reilly eulogized the 9/11 terrorists and even took the name of one of them as his Muslim identity. He was strongly inspired by al-Qaida and longed for martyrdom, as illustrated by a martyrdom testament he left behind. In it he raged about US and British campaigns in Muslim countries, the arrest of Muslims in Britain and immorality among Britons. According to his mother, like Ibrahim, Reilly regretted his actions in prison.[26]

Whereas the Muhammad cartoons were not specified as a motive in the plots by Ibrahim and Reilly, another incident in September 2008 illustrated the power of insults against the Prophet in triggering plots by single actors. This terrorist plan involved forty-one-year-old Ali Beheshti, a British-Pakistani extremist and ardent follower of Abu Hamza, who tried to set fire to the home of the publisher Martin Rynja.

The motive for the attack was Rynja's willingness to publish a book entitled *The Jewel of Medina*, which gave a fictional account of the Prophet's youngest bride, Aisha. Beheshti poured diesel into the publisher's mailbox and attempted to set the house alight. He was helped by two accomplices, and the three men were ultimately jailed. Despite an extensive extremist past, like Andrew Ibrahim, Beheshti de-radicalized in jail with the help of a charity fronted by the activist Usman Raja, which uses religious knowledge as an antidote to extremism.[27]

Yet another case of bottom-up solo-terrorism occurred in October 2009 when the Libyan Mohammed Game attempted to break into the Santa Barbara military barracks in Milan and detonated a small ammonium nitrate-based explosive device at the entrance while guards tried to stop him. The attacker suffered serious fire wounds, and one guard suffered minor injuries.

Game was an immigrant to Italy who was married to an Italian woman and he also had children. He prayed at the Viale Jenner in Milan, which has served as the main hub for radical Islam in Italy and a support base for the Bosnian jihad during the 1990s. Game radicalized in connection with a personal crisis after the failure of his restaurant business. He was furious at Italy's participation in ISAF, and it is this which was the motive for the attack.[28] Game was not acting in isolation. He was part of an extremist circle and received assistance from an Egyptian and a Libyan accomplice in acquiring chemical materials and assembling a bomb.[29] However, while Game was known for extremism, he does not appear to have received any top-down guidance from international organizations.

The same may also have been true for the plot by a Chechen living in Belgium, Lors Doukaiev, to attack the offices of *Jyllands-Posten* in Copenhagen in September 2010, although elements of the case indicated that he may have been connected with and received support from Islamists.[30] The twenty-four-year-old, who was a former professional boxer and had lost one leg, accidentally set off an explosion inside a Copenhagen hotel and suffered minor injuries when preparing the explosives for the attack.

Investigators believed that he meant for the bomb, which was made out of TATP, estimated to equal the strength of a hand grenade and wrapped inside a Nintendo box together with metal bullets, to be sent as a mail delivery to *Jyllands-Posten*. At the same time, when he was arrested he was also in possession of a loaded gun and forty rounds of ammunition, implying that shootings may also have been part of the modus operandi. He maintained he had brought explosives and the gun to Denmark for personal protection and, just as curiously, he stressed to interrogators that no-one had taught him how to construct the device and that it was common knowledge for someone hailing from Chechnya.

The Chechen arrived in Copenhagen by bus on 7 September and had bought tickets for a bus heading to Belgium two hours after the explosion occurred on 10 September, something that indicated he was not going to launch a suicide mission. He used false names, bought equipment for the package bomb in Denmark and borrowed the computer of a Japanese tourist to search for the address of *Jyllands-Posten*. The investigation also uncovered a hard drive belonging to the plotter which contained videos of attacks on Western forces in Iraq and Afghanistan, speeches by al-Qaida leaders and videos glorifying the mujahidin in Chechnya and the leader of the foreign fighters, Emir Khattab. It also contained weapons manuals and recipes for bombs and poisons, some of which originated from right-wing extremist websites.

In interrogations, Doukaiev was highly elusive about his contacts with extremists and al-Qaida sympathizers in the German town of Bremen, which surfaced in an investigation in Germany. The Chechen had attended a baptism party together with German extremists. Doukaiev was never tied to well-known al-Qaida members, and would not talk about his Islamist contacts, but he was hardly a "lone wolf."

Whereas the bottom-up cases dominated the picture there were also examples where foreign terrorist groups manipulated single-actors into action online or otherwise. Several cases had links to AQAP in Yemen, but there were also examples of involvement by AQIM and AQI. There was also an incident linked to al-Shabaab, although the level of involvement was questionable.

Top-down solo-terrorists

One case which seems to have involved both bottom-up and top-down aspects was the Adlène Hicheur incident. In 2009 a thirty-two-year-old French-Algerian physicist exchanged emails with AQIM about executing attacks in France.[31] Although Hicheur was charged and convicted without having taken any active steps towards an attack, it is important to discuss the case because it was one of only a small number of plots in Europe that involved ties to al-Qaida's Algerian branch.

Despite the fact that AQIM vowed allegiance to al-Qaida and took the brand name in 2007, the organization continued to focus on North Africa and the Middle East. The group attacked Western targets and took Western hostages regionally, but it rarely operated attack cells in the West. Hicheur was arrested for having contacted AQIM online and discussing attacks on French businesses and military facilities with representatives of the group. The case was taken very seriously because the physicist was employed at a nuclear research center overseen by the European Organization for Nuclear Research (CERN), and possessed unique technical knowledge that could have been exploited by the terrorist group. Hicheur was sentenced to five years in prison, but released in 2012.

According to some sources, Hicheur was already on the radar of European security services before he contacted AQIM because he had interacted with a Belgian-based recruitment network for Iraq, centered on the female propagandist and jihad recruiter Malika al-Aroud.[32] France's experience with threats emanating from North African networks spanning France and Belgium likely affected the decision to have him prosecuted as soon as he began discussing attacks with AQIM.

The next example of a single-actor with ties to an al-Qaida affiliate was far more advanced and acute.[33] In December 2009 a Nigerian mechanical engineering student, Umar Farouk Abdulmutallab, managed to smuggle a homemade bomb device made out of PETN and TATP hidden inside his underpants onboard a US flight from Amsterdam to Detroit. He succeeded in causing a small explosion, but fortunately it only injured the terrorist and did not tear a hole in the aircraft.

The Nigerian came from a wealthy family and studied in the UK in the mid-2000s when he became involved in Islamist activism and was flagged by MI5 for mingling with extremists. At some point Abdulmutallab became fascinated with the Yemeni-American radical preacher Anwar al-Awlaki and followed his online sermons. Al-Awlaki would emerge as the main ideologue for AQAP when the group was established in January 2009. Later that very same year Abdulmutallab enrolled at an Arabic-language institute in Sana. He soon dropped out of the classes and attended radical mosques where he enquired about how to contact al-Awlaki.

After making contact, al-Awlaki talked with him for three days and persuaded him to launch an operation. He then met AQAP's infamous bombmaker Ibrahim Hasan al-Asiri and the current leader of AQAP, Nasir al-Wuhayshi, and the then editor of *Inspire* magazine, Samir Khan. After attending training and recording a martyrdom video, he was equipped with an advanced bomb and sent to Europe to initiate the attack.

Another plot intercepted in the UK in February 2010 resembled the "underpants bomber."[34] In this case AQAP and al-Awlaki recruited a Bengali Islamist working as a computer expert for British Airways at Heathrow Airport, with a view to smuggling a bomb or a suicide bomber onboard a transatlantic flight. The plot demonstrated the determination of AQAP in recruiting Europe-based militants for attacks on transatlantic aviation, which would harm Europe and the United States at the same time. This AQAP plot also illustrated the common pattern that jihadis in Europe were partly linked to militant movements and events in their original home countries, in this case Bangladesh.

The British Airways' worker, Rajib Karim, hailed from a wealthy Bengali family and studied electronics in Britain in 1998–2000, before returning home where he radicalized together with his brother Tehzeeb by consuming online jihadi propaganda and attending extremist study circles. They also supported a local al-Qaida affiliate known as Jamaat-ul-Mujahideen Bangladesh, which was fighting for the establishment of an Islamic state.

After this group was cracked down upon from 2005 onwards, Tehzeeb traveled to Yemen in 2009 where he joined and trained with AQAP. Rajib went to Britain instead in order to work and for his son to receive medical treatment. According to the prosecution, Karim was in contact with jihadi handlers abroad from 2007 onwards and acted as a "sleeper" who blended in so as not to attract attention. However, in 2009 he was activated through personal email contact with al-Awlaki. What was new about this contact was that it involved highly advanced encryption software that had been developed by jihadis after the Manchester–Norway–New York case complex, which was detected by monitoring emails and other electronic communications.

Another new feature of the case was that it involved a Bengali. Many Bengalis were involved in the UK extremist scene, but they rarely took part in attack-related activities before the case of Karim and there have been several examples of terrorist plots in the UK involving Bengali extremists in the period since. By the time Rajib Karim was arrested, he had singled out two Muslim baggage handlers as potential suicide bombers. He was sentenced to thirty years in jail.

Yet another case in 2008–10 raised questions about command-and-control by an al-Qaida affiliate, this time the Somali al-Shabaab movement. In January 2010 a Danish-Somali named Mohammed Geele broke into the home of one of the cartoonists who drew the most infamous cartoon in which the Prophet Muhammad had been depicted with a bomb in his turban, Kurt Westergaard.[35] Armed with a knife and an axe, Geele threatened to kill Westergaard who was forced to flee into his panic room, leaving his five-year-old grandchild who was visiting him behind. Westergaard was under police protection and officers quickly arrived at the scene, rendering the would-be-assassin harmless by shooting him in his knee and shoulder.

Besides underscoring the continued determination of jihadis to avenge the cartoons, the plot was the first in Europe to be linked to al-Shabaab, which joined al-Qaida's network and pledged allegiance to al-Zawahiri in 2012 (but without adopting the brand name). Al-Shabaab grew out of the Islamic Court Union, a jihad movement that seized power in Mogadishu in 2006 and was then defeated by invading Ethiopian forces. It has since fought the UN-backed government of Somalia, Ethiopia and launched terrorist attacks in Kenya. Elements within al-Shabaab have a long affiliation with al-Qaida dating back to the "Battle of Mogadishu" in the 1990s and the bombings of the American embassies in Kenya and Tanzania in 1998. Somalians have also risen in the ranks of al-Qaida, even supervising its external operations section (Saleh al-Somali). Yet al-Shabaab has rarely been tied to plots in the West, something that appeared to be changing from 2010 onwards.

The attacker, Geele, had spent time in Somalia on several occasions in the period since 2005–6, ostensibly for humanitarian aid purposes, and returned to Denmark for the last time before the attack via Kenya in September 2009. Several of his friends had died fighting with al-Shabaab and he and friends had been detained in Kenya for immigration violations, or suspicion of terrorist activities, during Hillary Clinton's visit to the country. Geele was obsessed with the situation in Somalia and highly supportive of al-Shabaab. He was also furious over the publication of the Muhammad cartoons and inspired by al-Qaida.

He accessed speeches by bin Laden online calling for attacks on the cartoonists, texts by Abdullah Azzam and searched for videos and information about AQAP. He was also connected to the extremist circle of al-Qaida sympathizers in Copenhagen from which the Glostrup group and Glasvej cell emerged, including the radical preacher Abu Ahmed and the propagandist Said Mansour. Geele clearly wanted to die in the attack. He had drenched himself in perfume, in accordance with jihadi mythology that the blood of martyrs smells of perfume and that they are the "perfumed ones" who will reach the highest levels of Paradise. As he was unable to reach Westergaard inside the panic room he calmly waited in the apartment without hurting the child, and when the police officers arrived he charged at them in the hope that he would be shot.

The modus operandi resembled that of Mohammed Bouyeri and other jihadis charging against "enemy lines" to avoid committing suicide in the sense prohibited under Islam. While Geele was linked to al-Shabaab, there was nothing in the case to suggest he received instructions from the group. Al-Shabaab spokesmen praised the attack, but did not claim responsibility in the way IJU did with the German Sauerland cell and TTP did with the foiled plot against Barcelona's subway. While it could not be established whether Geele received orders, it cannot be ruled out that he was on a mission from al-Shabaab's network in Kenya, or al-Qaida. Al-Qaida and its affiliates do not always claim responsibility for attacks, especially when they fail.

A final case which seems to have involved a substantial top-down aspect was the Swedish-Iraqi suicide bomber who blew himself up near a busy shopping street in Stockholm just before Christmas 2010. Only the bomber was killed, but two passersby were wounded. The attacker, twenty-eight-year-old Swedish-Iraqi Taimour Abdulwahab, does not seem to have been part of an organized network in Sweden, but had extremist contacts in Europe, and was likely commissioned by al-Qaida's Iraq branch.[36] Abdulwahab used fertilizer-based pipe bombs (which were quite advanced) and he had prepared a written martyrdom testament and one audio-recording stating he wanted to avenge Swedish military participation in Afghanistan and the mocking of Islam by the Swedish artist Lars Vilks.

The statements were sent via email to the security services and the press. Abdulwahab carried some explosives with him and had others placed in a car which was parked in a street where people would have fled from the scene. It was only the fact that the bombs went off prematurely that prevented mass casualties. The suicide bomber emigrated to Sweden with his family when he was ten. He later studied in Luton, UK, where he radicalized and was believed to have forged ties with extremists, possibly the network from which the British-Pakistani cells emerged (al-Muhajiroun with links to al-Qaida).[37] The events of 9/11 and anti-Islam extremism in the UK have been cited as possible triggers for his radicalization.[38]

He had also been traveling extensively in the Middle East in the time leading up to the attack under the pretext of doing business. Abdulwahab was very active in jihadi social media and expressed support for al-Qaida's Iraqi branch on his Facebook profile. Iraqi security sources later claimed that Abdulwahab had gone through a three-month training course organized by AQI in Mosul, with a view to preparing recruits for attacks in the United States, Europe or Britain.[39] Another feature of the case illustrating how Abdulwahab had connections in the jihadi underworld was the fact that international investigations uncovered links to an accomplice in Scotland, an extreme Islamist named Nasserdine Menni, who helped finance the attack.[40]

The final case I address in this chapter is an example of a single-actor terrorist who is hard to situate in patterns of jihadism in Europe before 2010 as it involved a highly resourceful woman without known militant connections.

Lone wolf terrorism

In May 2010 the British-Bengali female student Roshonara Choudhry stabbed the British Member of Parliament Stephen Timms.[41] The MP suffered serious wounds but survived the attack. The assassin had made an appointment to meet Timms at his constituency office, and when they greeted each other she stuck a knife into his stomach. This was the fifth example of a jihadi assassination plot in Europe after the GIA's murder of an FIS imam in 1995, a vague plot to murder a top British military official by a cell based in Italy in 2003, the murder of van Gogh and the attempt on Martin Rynja.

This tendency would continue as part of a trend towards more discriminate targeting, as will be discussed in the next chapter. While all of the previous assassination plots involved people who seemed to have been embedded in known extremist environments, or were acting on behalf of organizations, investigations failed to detect significant interaction between Choudhry and extremists either face-to-face or online. It became clear that she had consumed jihadi propaganda online and listened to the lectures of AQAP's ideologue, but only passively and without interacting. Choudhry cited the Iraq war and inspiration from al-Awlaki as a motive. There were indications she wanted to die a martyr, such as having cleared all her debts before the attack.

Like Rajib Karim, Choudhry is of Bengali descent and had been an accomplished student at King's College. She was also teaching at an Islamic children's school. She had been radicalized gradually and dropped out of her studies because King's College had given an award to former Israeli Prime Minister Shimon Peres and worked against Islamist radicalization. However, frustration over the war in Iraq combined with inspiration from radical preachers and websites appears to have pushed her over the edge. Timms was chosen as a target partly because he was on a list distributed by an American website named RevolutionMuslim.com detailing politicians who had voted in favor of the war in Iraq. However, Choudhry had also met Timms on a school trip a few years earlier, illustrating how personal experiences influence target selection. Inspiration from al-Awlaki seems to have played the most important role, however, and she expressed admiration for his charisma, religious knowledge and analysis.

While Choudhry had not been on the radar of the security services for mixing with militants, her trial mobilized massive support from former al-Muhajiroun (now Islam4UK) members surrounding Anjem Choudary, who staged rallies outside the court building. Whether the activists were simply expressing their support for her actions, or hailing her as one of their own, remains an open question. Interestingly, one source with knowledge of the investigation told me that interrogators had been surprised by Roshonara Choudhry's unsolicited insistence on acting alone. It was one of the first things she told the interrogators. There have been other examples where the terrorists claimed to act alone while being part of a group, and she may well have wanted simply to protect friends and/or kin. However, it could also mean she wanted to protect extremist contacts.

Solo-terrorism and assassination plots would continue to be a factor in the final time period I examine in this book, 2011–15. In November 2010 French police uncovered plans by extremists who had fought with the Taliban and al-Qaida to assassinate the rector of the French capital's main mosque and leading Muslim cleric, Dalil Boubakeur, and other such cases would follow. However, the threat from 2011 onwards involved much more than solo-terrorism assassinations. The phase was characterized by a continuing diversification of European jihadism. All of the trends explored in previous chapters—from the large-scale, top-down al-Qaida attacks to the small-scale assassination plots by independent homegrown sympathizers, were combined in an increasingly volatile and heterogeneous threat situation.

This was partly due to the evolution of jihadism inside Europe, and partly a result of developments in the international arena which affected transnational militant Islam. In Europe, networks faced a difficult operational environment. However, the new generation continued to pursue public activism balancing within the boundaries of laws, or anonymously via social media. The community surrounding Anjem Choudary in London played a vital part in upholding activism in Britain and setting up spin-off groups in other European countries.

Moreover, jihadi prisoners who had been released were continuously melting back into networks and continued to act as entrepreneurs. Entrepreneurs also continued to recruit within jails. In 2010 French authorities released Djamel Beghal, who led plans to attack US targets in Europe for al-Qaida in 2001 (Chapter Four). He was rearrested shortly afterwards for involvement in a conspiracy to free one of the men behind the attacks in Paris in 1995, Smain Ait Ali Belkacem, with the help of young Islamists he recruited in prison. This plot was an omen of a massive terrorist attack in Paris in January 2015, as will be discussed in the final chapter.

Internationally, the death of bin Laden and the Arab Spring led to disarray, internal conflict and competition among jihadis on the one hand, and opened new fronts and possibilities on the other. The civil war in Syria gave rise to a new actor, the Islamic State in Iraq and Syria (ISIS/IS), which by 2014 seemed to have eclipsed al-Qaida as the world's most dangerous terrorist organization. The jihad in Syria would become the primary destination for militant Islamists from all over the world and would attract an unprecedented number of foreign fighters from Europe. Some of them were veterans who had acted on behalf of al-Qaida in Europe, whereas most were from the new generation. A power struggle between al-Qaida and IS then led "old school" jihadis to side with al-Qaida while the new generation chose IS. This split would affect the threat situation in Europe and add to the heterogeneity.

A HETEROGENEOUS THREAT (2011–15)

In 2011, the number of jihadi plots in Europe declined to the lowest level since 2001. This, combined with the assassination of bin Laden in May and the advent of the Arab Spring, initially led to expectations that international jihadism was a spent force, and that the threat in Europe was fading. These expectations were shattered when al-Qaida survived the death of bin Laden, and the Arab Spring deteriorated into a jihad front and foreign fighter destination for European extremists. These developments were accompanied by a new upswing in plots and several ruthless attacks in the region.

This chapter examines terrorist cases in Europe from 2011 onwards and places them into their proper context. It also concludes the study by commenting on the current status of the jihadi threat in Europe and discussing policy implications. I will argue that from 2011 the history of jihadi terrorism in Europe was coming full circle. Influenced by instability in the Middle East and mobilization among European extremists, different trends of jihadism in Europe, which had been evolving since the 1990s, converged and created a volatile and heterogeneous threat situation.

Al-Qaida and regional affiliates in Af-Pak were continuing to pursue attacks in Europe. In some instances extremists in Europe connected with groups abroad for support, but attacked on their own. On other occasions people belonging to extremist networks in Europe acted on their own without interacting with foreign militants, and in rare instances plots were only inspired by online extremism. From 2013 onwards plots were also uncovered that had links to new actors emerging from the Syrian jihad, which had become the main rallying cause for jihadism by 2012.

The threat involved groups, solo-terrorists and lone wolves. The proportion of plots by single-actors increased to almost 40 percent in 2008–13, though group-based plots still dominated the picture. Terrorist plans gradually came to involve a broader repertoire of weapons and tactics. Bomb-plots were still the most common, but the use of handguns and Mumbai-style tactics were becoming a more popular modus operandi, and targeting had become increasingly narrow ever since the publication of the Muhammad cartoons. While the era of mass casualty attacks was by no means over, a higher proportion of plots were aimed at societal sub-groups rather than the general public. Jews, soldiers in uniform, individuals involved in the Muhammad cartoons or otherwise known to be anti-Islam, or Muslims opposed to jihadism, were particularly at risk.

Motivationally, the Muhammad cartoons and other "injustices" suffered by and "insults" against Muslims and Islam were gaining in significance when compared to the wars in Afghanistan and Iraq, or support of Israel's actions in Palestine. Several terrorist plans in this final phase were linked to imprisoned preachers and other entrepreneurs, and several plans involved people who had served time in prison for terrorist offences and had been released. This was not a new phenomenon, but it was a growing trend ten years after 9/11. The main reason for this was simply that many terrorists who had operated on behalf of the GIA and al-Qaida in the 1990s and early 2000s had rejoined extremist networks once they had been released.

The intensifying and diversifying threat after 2011 was also the result of successful efforts by European jihadis to sustain and widen recruitment among the new generation. These efforts exploited freedom of expression and social media. It also exploited the fact that al-Qaida's propaganda was increasingly portraying Europeans as enemies because of the invasions, cartoons and arrests of Islamists. In the Muslim world, the Arab Spring and the war in Syria were a game changer. The instability in the Muslim world created opportunities and new fronts for transnational jihadism.

After some initial disarray, Islamist foreign fighters were flooding into Syria. The development was at first encouraged by neighboring Turkey, the Gulf states and the West, who wanted the Iran-friendly Assad regime to be overthrown and replaced by a secularist or moderate Islamist opposition. It soon transpired that only the mujahidin had the capacity to challenge the Syrian regime without foreign military support, and soon al-Qaida-affiliated groups were controlling Northern Syria. A new and strengthened version of al-Qaida in Iraq, calling itself the Islamic state of Iraq and Syria (ISIS), then emerged as the main fighting force in Syria. It also captured swathes of Iraq and threatened Baghdad.

The Syrian jihad became the main focal point for extremists in Europe and scores of them traveled via Turkey to join the struggle in the ranks of al-Qaida-affiliated groups or IS. The situation was ideal for European extremists in need of a new cause, and a new place to train and fight. Before the Syrian jihad, Europeans were having difficulty traveling to Af-Pak and Yemen. Some Europeans made their way to Somalia, but most had a Somali background, and al-Shabaab remained focused on Somalia and neighboring countries and was not considered a major source of plots in the West.[1]

Western security services and their counterparts in Muslim countries were paying closer attention to foreign fighters than ever before, however, as the link to international terrorism was no longer questioned. As a result, many Westerners were captured in transit to jihad zones, or if they made it to the area they faced the danger of drone strikes, operations by Western Special Forces or army incursions by local regimes. Because Westerners attracted attention, they would often be easy targets, leading many to stay at home and pursue activism instead. The war in Syria changed this. The exodus of Europeans to Syria was so large that it exhausted intelligence capacities, and the West lacked a clear strategy to deal with this development. Finding a strategy was also complicated by the fact that many of those who traveled from Europe had not committed terrorist offences, and laws did not generally forbid foreign fighting.

Moreover, the conflict in Syria generated massive humanitarian efforts and many traveled to provide aid rather than fighting. Among those who went to fight it was also hard to distinguish between those joining jihadi outfits and those fighting with the Free Syria Army, a coalition of armed non-jihadi opposition groups, supported by the West and Muslim countries. However, whereas the conflict in Syria attracted many aid workers, most of those who went there to fight were jihad-oriented.

Syria and the new generation

With many members of Europe's longstanding support networks behind bars, it was the new generation of extremists that came to spearhead the mobilization over Syria. At the core of the mobilization was Anjem Choudary in London. After Bakri left the UK, Choudary had continued to build networks in Britain, and in the following years he also helped facilitate the establishment of networks in other countries modeled on al-Muhajiroun/Islam4UK, such as Sharia4Belgium, Shariah4Holland, Shariah4Austria, Forsane Alizza in France, Millatu Ibrahim in Germany and The Prophet's Ummah in Norway.[2]

These networks were built around committed activists who had been part of European jihad networks for a long time, and had spent time in conflict zones. However, most of the grass root activists were from the new generation. Among them, some came from families where parents and older brothers had been involved in extremism, whereas others had no extremist past. Like Islam4UK, its spin-offs also recruited converts and women. In the spirit of al-Muhajiroun, the spin-offs held a public profile, staged rallies and had a massive online presence on Facebook, YouTube, Twitter and other sites. Activists from chapters in different countries would visit each other and participate in each other's rallies.

The new generation networks were the strongest in European countries with a long history of jihadism, such as the UK, France, Germany, Belgium and the Netherlands. However, with the Muhammad cartoons as a backdrop, extremism was reaching unprecedented levels in Scandinavia. The region also saw an upsurge in terrorist plots, almost paralleling the threat to the jihadis' European archenemies, the UK and France, in 2008–13. Whereas Sweden and Denmark had hosted jihadi networks for years, and been nodes in the recruitment network for Iraq, jihadism was taking root in Norway from around 2009. Like the Danish Islamists, who were cooperating with Bakri and al-Muhajiroun in the mid-2000s, the Norwegians came to cooperate with Choudary and Islam4UK.

The rise of jihadi activism in Norway exemplifies how networks were dispersing. In 2009 there were violent demonstrations in Norway protesting against the Israeli incursions in Gaza, which involved young Islamists. The same year, the ex-criminal Norwegian-Pakistani Islamist, Arfan B., was released from prison after serving time for aiding and abetting shootings against the synagogue in Oslo.

He emerged as a network builder among young radicals who had taken part in the Gaza riots. They would soon start to attend lectures by Ansar al-Islam co-founder Mullah Krekar and a former deputy minister of health in the Taliban regime, who had gained asylum in Norway.[3] Inspired by Islam4UK, the extremists staged public rallies against the cartoons and Norwegian participation in ISAF, and voiced support for al-Qaida. They also maintained a major media profile, with spokesmen giving interviews and even staging a press conference.

With the arrest and prosecution of Mullah Krekar for issuing death threats against three Kurds and the former minister for immigration (and now prime minister), Erna Solberg, and the eruption of the war in Syria, the Norwegian extremist community grew and radicalized further, and developed closer ties to Islam4UK. In connection with the Mullah Krekar trial, Choudary visited the Norwegian extremists, who were now operating under the name The Prophet's Ummah, after its Facebook page and main mobilization platform.

The rise of Norwegian jihadism illustrated how Choudary and Lebanon-based Omar Bakri had a direct hand in establishing extremist communities in other countries based on the UK model. In addition to Choudary's visit to Norway, he as well as Bakri had been giving online lectures to the Norwegian extremists via PalTalk. Norwegian jihadis joined the fighting in Syria from the late fall of 2012, first in the ranks of al-Qaida's affiliate Jabhat al-Nusra, and later with ISIS/IS.[4] In an interview with Norwegian media in September 2013 Bakri boasted that he had helped 65 Norwegians across the border to Syria, although he is known to exaggerate.[5]

Reciprocal radicalization

One pattern worth highlighting in the growth and spread of networks inspired by Islam4UK is the reciprocal radicalization between Islamists and anti-Islamic extremists. There have been many examples where racism was a factor in the radicalization of individual terrorists, such as Nizar Trabelsi of the Beghal network and Hasib Hussain of the 7/7 cell. The Hofstadgroup also targeted anti-Islam activists such as Theo van Gogh, Ayan Hirsi Ali and Geert Wilders, and the murder of van Gogh triggered attacks on mosques by anti-Islam forces in the Netherlands. Furthermore, the Muhammad cartoons were seen by jihadis and mainstream Muslims alike as an anti-Islam campaign. In the late 2000s there were several developments in Europe that made it easier for al-Qaida to sell the narrative that Europeans were leading a campaign against Islam.

Amid the growing threat from jihadism, the youth riots in Paris in 2005 and the violent reactions to the Muhammad cartoons, people on the far right and the far left, including liberals and feminists, as well as people opposed to feminism, found a common cause in anti-Islam, or anti-jihad. This hybrid movement gave rise to extremist groups such as the English Defence League (EDL), established in 2009, which uses anti-Islamic rhetoric and calls for all Muslims to be deported from Europe. The most extreme expression of this trend was Anders Behring Breivik, who bombed the Norwegian government quarters and massacred children at the political youth camp of the immigration-friendly Norwegian Labor Party in 2011, with the aim of sparking a civil war between Europeans and Muslim immigrants.[6]

Although Breivik had psychological issues, he represented a growing anti-Islam sentiment in Europe which was reflected in media and public discourse, and affected Islamist radicalization as well as the actions of terrorists. From the late 2000s and increasingly after 2011 there were violent rallies involving Islamists on the one hand and anti-Islam demonstrators on the other in several European countries. In the UK, Islam4UK clashed with the EDL. In Germany, radical Salafis such as Millatu Ibrahim clashed with German anti-Islam demonstrators. These incidents were accompanied by an increase in hate-crimes against Muslims, and terrorist incidents targeting anti-Islam extremists, such as a plot in the UK to attack an EDL rally, and plots in Germany to attack anti-Islam politicians.

The Syria effect

However, whereas factors inside Europe contributed to the region's sustained extremism, factors external to Europe contributed to a greater extent. After some initial hesitation following the death of bin Laden, al-Qaida's new leader Ayman al-Zawahiri began to exploit the Syrian uprising. Al-Qaida and its affiliates began to focus on Syria in propaganda and positioned themselves vis-à-vis the Syrian rebel groups. The organization established bonds with and leadership over the main jihadi fighting faction, Jabhat al-Nusra, and other outfits such as Ahrar al-Sham. Al-Qaida and other groups in Af-Pak, such as TTP, also contributed resources and fighters to the anti-Assad struggle. The Syria struggle would further attract fighters from al-Qaida branches and affiliates in other regions, such as AQIM in Algeria and al-Shabaab in Somalia.

With the Arab world's security apparatuses severely weakened following the revolts of the Arab Spring, exiled jihadis were returning to their home countries and creating networks and training camps. Jihadis were also obtaining weapons from the caches of the Libyan Army after the fall of Gaddafi in Libya, the Syrian Army in areas taken by the insurgents or the Iraqi Army when the jihadis pushed into Iraq. While the war was raging in Syria, transnationally operating jihadis would initiate guerrilla wars and terrorist campaigns across the Middle East and North Africa in Egypt (Sinai), in Libya and Algeria.

For a short while it seemed as though the global jihad against the West was falling into the background and had become less of priority due to more pressing matters on the jihadis' home turfs. However, a statement by al-Zawahiri in September 2013 strongly suggested otherwise. In the statement he confirmed that the jihad in Syria held highest priority for al-Qaida. Yet at the same time he also underscored that "all Mujahid brothers must consider targeting the interests of the western Zionist–Crusader alliance in any part of the world as their foremost duty."[7] The continued growth of attack-related activities in Europe despite the heavy jihadi involvement in multiple conflicts across the Muslim world pointed in the same direction.

The Syrian jihad became a magnet for foreign fighters from Europe, and as of 2015 some 3,000 to 5,000 Europeans were believed to be fighting alongside groups in Syria.[8] This number is unprecedented. No other international jihad front had ever attracted as many recruits from Europe. Many Muslims traveled from Europe to support the Afghans in the 1980s and many also participated as aid workers and mujahidin in Bosnia, but their numbers were in the hundreds, not thousands. The war in Chechnya had also attracted European foreign fighters, but in miniscule numbers. As discussed earlier, although the Iraq war has been a main motive for terrorists in Europe, a limited number of Europeans traveled to Iraq as foreign fighters for various reasons. European security services have indicated that dozens departed from major countries considered hubs for jihadism, such as the UK and France, whereas handfuls departed from smaller countries.

Although larger numbers of European Muslims have taken part in national conflicts in countries such as Pakistan, Algeria and Somalia, these hardly supersede Syria. Most Europeans fighting in Syria were extremists on departure and part of the new generation, mobilized through semi-political rallies and social media. At first they tended to join al-Qaida-affiliated groups such as Jabhat al-Nusra and Ahrar al-Sham, and a Chechen group known as Jaysh al-Muhajireen wa'l-Ansar. However, from 2014, most Europeans would join ISIS. ISIS was a spin-off from al-Qaida in Iraq, which re-invented itself after suffering major defeats against American forces and nearly being decimated in 2007–8.

After 2008 the group resurrected itself, and recruited from among ex-Baathist military and Sunni clans marginalized by the Shia-dominated government in Baghdad. Under the leadership of a religious student radicalized by the US invasion and his own imprisonment at the hands of the Americans, Abu Bakr al-Baghdadi, the group further boosted its power through multiple jailbreaks during 2012, freeing prisoners who joined its ranks.[9] The group gradually evolved into a formidable fighting force and initiated terrorist campaigns in Iraq while simultaneously infiltrating and trying to take control of the jihad in Syria. Upon entering Syria the group announced its leadership over al-Qaida's affiliate Jabhat al-Nusra (JAN), something the latter rejected. This sparked a major conflict which resulted in armed confrontation between JAN and ISIS in Syria, and competition between al-Qaida and ISIS for overall leadership of transnational jihadism. The conflict peaked when al-Baghdadi boldly declared himself caliph of the "Islamic State" (IS) on 29 June 2014, expecting all Muslims and mujahidin to follow his commands.

In this situation al-Zawahiri and al-Qaida received support from allies and old school ideologues (such as Qatada). The ideologues said al-Baghdadi lacked religious legitimacy and should submit to the Taliban leader Mullah Omar, who enjoyed the position of commander of the faithful.[10] However, major successes on the battlefield against security forces in Iraq and competing groups in Syria bolstered IS's image as an invincible group and it continued to attract recruits. There were multiple reports that fighters defected from other groups in Syria, including Jabhat al-Nusra, to join IS. There were also defections from other al-Qaida affiliates to IS, for example from AQIM, although the scope was unknown.[11] Moreover, IS had a special appeal to recruits from the West because of its massive and skillful exploitation of social media, and because it had the support of the main entrepreneurs of the new generation in Europe, Bakri and Choudary. Moreover, the myth of the Islamic State was exacerbated by the group's terrifying, high-definition videos of mass executions of Iraqi soldiers during the blitzkrieg capture of Mosul and threat to Baghdad, and the beheadings of Western hostages while calmly warning President Obama.

By the late fall of 2014 IS was a worthy competitor to al-Qaida in being the world's most dangerous terrorist organization. Over a short period of time the group made Raqqa in Syria the Islamic State's capital and took control of cities alongside Iraq's river belts and oilfields generating massive revenues. IS further gained access to weapons when demoralized Iraqi Army forces fled their positions. The group established state-like structures, including a bureaucracy and health system, and a veritable army of some 20,000 to 30,000 fighters.

While advancing on the local battlefield IS also threatened to launch attacks in Western countries if the West intervened. However, although there have been several terrorist plots in Europe that were linked to ISIS/IS in some way or another since late 2013, the exact nature of such links remained poorly understood at the time of writing. Preliminary analyses indicated that most IS-linked plots in Europe since 2013 were initiated by independent sympathizers and affiliates, rather than the group's central leadership.[12] While there were signs that IS was starting to affect the terrorist threat to Europe, at the very least by way of inspiration, the period 2011–15 was dominated by a number of incidents that could be linked to al-Qaida's networks.

Al-Qaida still in the game

Most plots linked to al-Qaida and its affiliates were group-based and pursuing mass casualty attacks. However, some of them also involved single-actors planning smaller, discriminate attacks. The exact level and nature of al-Qaida's involvement tended to be opaque. Most plots were linked to Af-Pak and Yemen, but there were also a couple of incidents which had vague links to al-Shabaab and AQIM.[13]

In April 2011 German authorities disrupted an al-Qaida-linked cell in Düsseldorf. It was composed of the German-Moroccans Abdeladim El-Kebir and Jamil Seddiki, and the German-Iranian Amid Chaabi. The entrepreneur, El-Kebir, an engineering student, had attended training in Waziristan in 2010 where he had been tasked by the al-Qaida handler Younis al-Mauritani (alleged to have supervised the Europlot in 2010) to carry out mass casualty bomb attacks in Germany (most likely against a bus or a bus station).[14] Like the doctors' cell in Britain in 2007, the terrorists were planning a second explosion targeting fleeing victims and first responders. El-Kebir was said to have recruited and indoctrinated the other cell members, and they started assembling bomb-making materials and scouting targets before being arrested. In a chilling email to contacts in Waziristan, the plotters declared "Oh, our Sheikh, we are upholding our promise. We will begin the slaughter of the dogs."[15]

In May, one individual referred to as Halil S., who escaped the first crackdowns, was pursuing a hand weapons-based attack (Mumbai-style) on his own, seeking advice and receiving instructions from al-Awlaki in Yemen. He was captured in December. Also in May, German authorities dismantled yet another cell composed of former German Taliban Mujahideen, who had joined al-Qaida, and were sent on a mission to Germany. This cell was disrupted at an early stage, but investigations turned up a highly interesting USB stick, which contained encrypted al-Qaida strategy documents and a report outlining al-Qaida's role in 7/7 and the airliner plot, written by Rashid Rauf. The documents revealed details about how al-Qaida's section for external operations was recruiting Europeans and preparing them for attacks in Europe.

In addition to the German cases, several plots uncovered in the UK underscored the continued significance of the Pakistan axis. One cell uncovered in Birmingham in September 2011 was plotting suicide attacks in Britain carrying IEDs in rucksacks.[16] The terrorists had been experimenting with IEDs and discussing attack scenarios. They estimated that they would be able to kill more people than 7/7. The entrepreneur of the plot was the British-Pakistani Irfan Naseer and the cell also included the foot soldiers Irfan Khalid and Ashik Ali who similarly hailed from Pakistan. Naseer had attended HuM training facilities and connected with al-Qaida handlers in Waziristan during the spring of 2011. Sources suggested that the plotters had planned to use fertilizer for the bombs and to detonate them via the use of timers.

In April 2012, UK anti-terrorism police dismantled a cell composed of British-Pakistanis and British-Bengalis in Luton believed to be plotting an attack in Britain on behalf of al-Qaida in Af-Pak, or its branch in Yemen. In this case, no information surfaced about meetings between the plotters and al-Qaida handlers, but the prosecution argued that leader of the cell had received instructions from al-Qaida in Pakistan, and that his second-in-command was in charge of sending recruits to Pakistan for training.

Those arrested had been involved in a wide range of support activities for militants in Pakistan, before surveillance indicated that a concrete plot to attack a military facility was in the making. The plot involved a novel modus operandi as the terrorists planned to use a model car to carry an IED through the gate of the army center they were targeting. While there was a link to Pakistan, the terrorists also possessed a famous text by al-Awlaki detailing forty-four ways to support jihad, and planned to build the bomb devices based on recipes from AQAP's *Inspire* magazine.[17] Regardless of whether the plot could be traced to Pakistan or Yemen, it illustrated how al-Qaida-linked jihadis in Europe were increasingly going after military targets.

Another bombing plan uncovered in the UK in July 2012 pointed in the same direction. Anti-terrorism police arrested a jihadi convert and former security guard, Richard Dart (twenty-nine), and two British-Pakistanis, Imran Mahmood and Jahangor Alom, on suspicion of plotting to kill British intelligence officers, including heads of MI5 and MI6.[18] All three were acolytes of Choudary who went to Pakistan to obtain terrorist training. Mahmood and Alom stayed in Pakistan for longer periods and worked to recruit other Britons for training in the country. Only one of them, Mahmood, was proven to have undergone training, however. Investigators retrieved samples of nitroglycerin, RDX (a military high explosive) and PETN from the rucksack he was carrying on journeys to Pakistan.

The plotters discussed carrying out attacks in Wootton Bassett, the town where British soldiers were being commemorated. The convert Dart had been part of one of the al-Muhajiroun spin-offs supported by Choudary called "Muslims against Crusades" which was banned in 2011. This group rallied for emirates to be established in Britain, against British military involvement in Muslim countries and also clashed with the EDL on several occasions. Asked to comment on his sway over the plotters, Choudary said he had influenced them, but that he had told them to fight jihad outside the UK and not at home. However, he added that other preachers, such as al-Awlaki, encouraged Western Muslims to attack at home.[19]

A plot uncovered in Spain also had a strong link to Pakistan.[20] This was again an atypical case because of the national origins of the militants as well as their modus operandi. In August 2012, Spanish and French authorities made coordinated arrests of suspected terrorists hailing from Chechnya, Turkey and Dagestan. They were believed to be preparing an attack in Gibraltar, possibly using para-gliders to bomb a shopping center. The suspects were in possession of explosives and suspicious videos. The purported entrepreneur of the cell, a Dagestani former Russian Special Forces soldier, was said to have connected with al-Qaida and the Uzbek Islamic Jihad Union (IJU) in Waziristan in 2010 and to have taken part in terrorism-related activities internationally before he was captured.

Of the Af-Pak-linked incidents, the one best exemplifying the heterogeneity of the threat to Europe from 2011 may have been the attacks on French soldiers and a Jewish children's school by the French-Algerian Mohammed Merah in Montauban and Toulouse, Southern France, in March 2012.[21] Merah worked alone, but had international ties and was trained in Waziristan. He was part of the new generation of European jihadis, yet he also mixed with veterans who had a long history with jihadism in Europe. He was motivated by personal grievances, grievances over French campaigns in Muslim countries and Israeli incursions in Palestine. Although he was active online, he also interacted face-to-face with Islamists in France and internationally during his travels.

Merah first killed three French soldiers in two separate assaults with an automatic pistol, approaching and escaping the attack scene on a motorbike. In the first attack he lured a soldier to meet him by answering an advert pretending he was selling his motorbike, and in the second soldier attack, four days later, he shot uniformed paratroopers who had returned from Afghanistan, by an ATM-machine. In the last attack, he drove his motorbike up to a Jewish children's school and massacred three children and a rabbi.

He escaped the scene of the attack and was later rounded up in his apartment where he barricaded himself in with an arsenal of weapons (including pistols, a submachine gun and a shotgun) determined to fight until death. After a thirty-two-hour siege, during which he contacted the media and talked to police negotiators, special police forces penetrated the apartment, forcing Merah to jump off his balcony while continuing to fire his gun mid-air. He was shot dead by police snipers before hitting the ground. Merah staged the first lethal jihadi attacks in France since the 1990s.

However, there had been multiple planned atrocities in France throughout the 2000s, which had been thwarted by a security apparatus with much experience in combating jihadism and which had adopted tough measures to deal with the threat. After the GIA campaign in 1990s, the Frankfurt cell (2000), the Beghal network (2001) and the Chechen network (2002), there was less jihadi activity for a few of years before the amount of plots rose again in the wake of the invasion of Iraq, and this also applied to France. In 2004, members of the Chechen network who avoided the arrests of 2002 were plotting attacks with poison. In 2005, the GIA recruiter Safe Bourada assembled a cell planning to attack French security services and Orly airport when he was released from prison. In 2008 a cell headed by Rany Arnoud, who tried but failed to join the Iraqi jihad, also plotted an attack against the security apparatus, and in 2009 the aforementioned Adlène Hicheur was arrested for discussing attacks in France with AQIM. In 2010, French security services then thwarted a plot to assassinate the leading Muslim cleric Dalil Boubakeur by a group of militants who had spent time in Af-Pak.

Merah was part of an intensifying threat in France and this situation would grow worse. The threat erupted from local French extremist networks which were Algerian-based and grew out of historical support networks for the GIA and FIS in the country. Throughout the 2000s these networks had linked up to the global jihad and supported jihad in Afghanistan and Iraq.

Mohammed Merah was a typical French jihadi and a misfit. He had an abusive father and drifted into crime at an early age. His parents separated and he was put in protective care for a while due to neglect by his mother. Facing troubles at school he soon dropped out and pursued a life of petty crime. He was arrested when he was seventeen and mixed with Islamists in jail where he became radicalized. He was easy prey as his family sympathized with the Algerian GIA and FIS, and he had grown up hearing extremist rhetoric over Algeria and had been exposed to anti-Semitism and radical Salafism from an early age. His sister and brother were also extremists who supported jihadism and the sister defended his attacks in the media. Another brother was moderate and rejected the views of his siblings.

Via his brother and sister, Merah connected with recruitment networks in France and Belgium sending Europeans to Iraq and Af-Pak, via Syria and Egypt. He mingled with a recruitment network in Toulouse led by a Syrian, and the Islam4UK equivalent Forsane Alizza, something that put him on the radar of the security services. After his radicalization had accelerated inside jail under the influence of imprisoned jihad entrepreneurs, Merah started traveling throughout the Middle East and entered Afghanistan for the first time in 2010. He then spent time in Waziristan in 2011.

Merah was also very active online and would surf jihadi websites, using social media for extremist purposes. He consumed jihadi propaganda and violent videos. In one incident he was reported to police by the mother of a young boy to whom he had shown beheading videos. As revenge he went to the boy's house and stood outside waving a sword while shouting al-Qaida slogans.

The security services may have been fooled by Merah's extrovert extremism, as the most dangerous terrorists are usually secretive. As seen in previous chapters (e.g. the case of Fritz Gelowicz), this was not always the case with European jihadis. It is believed that Merah became more introvert and security conscious after reading Abu Musab al-Suri's book on decentralized jihad. However, the French security services were fully aware of Merah's trips to Af-Pak because he was online, and because he kept in touch with a case officer who wanted to interview him about the trips. Merah said he was looking for a wife.

When besieged in the apartment in Montauban, Merah told negotiators he had trained with al-Qaida in Waziristan and had been given money for the attack. He also said his individual al-Qaida instructor had told him to go after American or Canadian targets and use a bomb as a weapon, whereas Merah preferred to strike French targets using handguns instead, telling the handler that bomb ingredients were under surveillance in France. He further said that he had not planned to attack the Jewish school, but took the opportunity when he was driving around on his motorbike looking for another soldier to kill. Merah filmed his attacks with a sports camera wrapped to his chest. Somewhat curiously, given the fact he was so social media-savvy, he emailed the videos, edited as jihad propaganda to Al Jazeera, which decided not to air any of it.

An al-Qaida-affiliated group named Jund al-Khilafa claimed responsibility for Merah's attacks online and said they had trained him in Waziristan. This group was led by the Swiss-Tunisian Moez Garsallaoui, the husband of Malika El-Aroud. Garsallaoui and El-Aroud (the wife of one of the Tunisian suicide bombers who killed Ahmad Shah Massoud for al-Qaida before the 9/11 attacks) had been operating as propagandists and jihad recruiters out of Belgium until the former left for Waziristan in 2008 and the latter was arrested. There were speculations Garsallaoui could have been Merah's handler on behalf of al-Qaida, although there exists no evidence to confirm this. It is further believed that the Swiss-Tunisian was killed in an American drone strike in Pakistan in late 2008.[22]

Merah had extensive network ties and support and could be described as a bottom-up solo-terrorist. However, Merah also inspired copycat attacks by individuals and groups who had limited connections to organized networks. One such plot was uncovered in February 2013, for example, when the Moroccan Mohammed Echaabi was arrested in Valencia, Spain. Drawing inspiration from Merah, he was plotting attacks on public figures or other targets in Spain or another European country, and he had attempted to obtain explosives and firearms for this purpose. Echaabi originally intended to travel to Gaza aiming to launch an attack on Israeli interests. Unlike Merah, he did not have known connections to terrorist networks and educated himself online.[23]

In another incident, in March 2013, three suspected terrorists were detained in Marignane, near Marseilles, and accused of plotting a bomb attack. Police uncovered a makeshift bomb laboratory in the house of one of those arrested. The plotters had made tributes to Merah on Facebook, and investigators confiscated small amounts of the explosive TATP and firearms among their belongings.[24]

Soldier killers

Although Merah managed to stage the first lethal attacks in France since the 1990s and inspired copycats, it was another single actor that introduced targeted attacks against soldiers in uniform as a modus operandi among jihadis in Europe; the Sauerland cell also targeted American soldiers, but more discriminately—targetting civilians as well.

In January 2011 the young Kosovar Arid Uka shot and killed two American soldiers and wounded several others at Frankfurt international airport. Together with Roshonara Choudhry, Arid Uka is considered the clearest example of lone wolf jihadism in Europe. Uka entered a parked shuttle bus and started firing at the American servicemen sitting in seats while shouting the jihadi slogan "Allahu Akbar." Fortunately, his gun jammed and Uka escaped, but he was hunted down and captured by two of the victimized soldiers. Uka was believed to have been triggered spontaneously by a feature movie, which displayed American soldiers who were gang-raping a young Iraqi girl. However, as pointed out by Guido Steinberg, this was not just any feature movie. Uka was watching a propaganda movie by IMU (Islamic Movement of Uzbekistan), using material from an American movie.[25]

He also maintained contacts with well-known Salafis in Frankfurt and other parts of Germany via social media, but was not part of any organized group. He came from a religious family and did relatively well in school, but like many lone terrorists he suffered from some psychological problems. He had withdrawn from friends and family in the months leading up to the attacks, spending much of his time surfing jihadi websites. Interestingly, he asked a soldier at the airport whether the servicemen were heading for Afghanistan before he attacked, and said he would have averted the plot if they were heading home.

Crude attacks on soldiers increased after Malik Nidal Hassan's deadly operation at Fort Hood in 2009, which was strongly promoted by al-Qaida's main outlet for operational advice in recent times, AQAP's *Inspire* magazine. *Inspire* magazine also praised Uka's attacks in Frankfurt, and called for follow-up attacks. Like the attacks on the Muhammad cartoonists, attacks on soldiers while off duty had a high symbolic value at low cost.

From al-Qaida's perspective, soldier attacks were far better suited than mass casualty attacks to generate needed support, as the latter had come under harsh critique because of Muslims being killed alongside unbelievers. AQAP in Yemen was at the forefront of calling for soldier attacks, but IS would also pick up the tread. Al-Awlaki talked about the permissibility of attacking Western soldiers in their home countries and *Inspire* magazine no. 9 (2012) also specified military personnel as targets as did other issues. The spokesman for IS, Abu Mohammad al-Adnani, called for attacks on military personnel in a statement issued in September 2014.[26]

On 22 May 2013, a crude attack taken directly out of *Inspire* magazine occurred on the streets of London. Two Britons of Nigerian decent, Michael Adebolajo (twenty-eight) and Michael Adebowale (twenty-two), killed a soldier in the British Army, Fusilier Lee Rigby, near the Royal Artillery Barracks in Woolwich, southeast London. The assailants ran Rigby down with a car before hacking him to death with knives and a meat cleaver, attempting to decapitate the victim while shouting "Allahu Akbar."[27] When police arrived on the scene the jihadis charged against them armed with an old revolver which misfired, injuring the shooter alone. The killers remained at the murder scene and talked to bystanders while allowing them to film. They said the attack was aimed at the British soldier as revenge for Muslims he had killed in Iraq and Afghanistan.

Investigations revealed that Adebolajo and Adebowale had been a part of the UK Islamist scene surrounding al-Muhajiroun spin-offs and Anjem Choudhry for a long time, and had featured in several terrorist investigations, although in the periphery of networks plotting attacks. Adebolajo had also tried but failed to join al-Shabaab in Somalia, and both of them had been in touch via phone or online with AQAP in Yemen. In one online exchange with a contact in Yemen, Adebowale had declared his intention to kill a British soldier, but this message was not accessed by the security services until after the attack.[28] In the UK they had been involved in support activism and protests against Muhammad cartoons, and consumed extremism online, including AQAP's *Inspire* magazine. Adebolajo had been arrested in Kenya in 2010 on his way to join al-Shabaab in Somalia. He was also believed to have interacted with other British extremists and al-Shabaab associates residing in the country.

Adebolajo seems to have been the entrepreneur. The Nigerian hailed from a Christian family. He was known to have ethnic Britons as friends and to be intelligent, but struggled with his relationship to authority figures. He converted and started to radicalize in connection with the death of a nephew and increasingly over the invasion of Iraq. He started to mingle with Islamists and also pursued criminal activities, including selling drugs.

While Adebolajo was troubled, his radicalization involved political thought processes. He was known to debate politics from an early age, and studied for a politics degree at university before he dropped out. Adebowale was a misfit and a gang member from an early age. He dealt drugs and spent time in a youth prison, and he also witnessed a brutal murder when a drug deal went wrong. As a result of this experience he began suffering from post-traumatic stress disorder.

As troubled converts from Woolwich, Adebolajo and Adebowale drifted towards al-Muhajiroun in Greenwich and London, and the two would come to act as part of Britain's extremist networks. They participated in missionary recruitment (dawa-stalls) and protests, pursued online jihadism and communicated with militants abroad. According to the official intelligence report, in the run-up to the attacks both plotters had contacts with individuals linked to AQAP Yemen, including Adebowale's aforementioned message via Facebook that he wanted to murder a British soldier.

Only five days after the killing of Lee Rigby, on 27 May 2013, a convert named Alexandre Dhaussy attacked a French soldier patrolling a train and subway traffic hub in the La Défense financial area of Paris.[29] The attacker jumped the guard and stabbed him in the neck with a box-cutter. Dhaussy was likely a Woolwich copycat. However, he was known to the police as a Salafi who had been increasingly radicalized over the preceding years, but did not seem to have been part of an organized jihadi network, or to have traveled to jihad zones.

While Mohammed Merah, Arid Uka, the Woolwich plotters and other soldier killers seemed driven primarily by Western invasions of Muslim countries, they also had other grievances such as the plight of Palestinians and insults against Islam. However, several other incidents provided clearer examples of the radicalizing power of anti-Islam. Largely because of the Danish cartoons, they also illustrated the continued increase of terrorist plotting in Scandinavia.

Targeting anti-Islam

In September 2011 four people were arrested over a plan to assassinate the Swedish artist Lars Vilks at an exhibition at the Røda Sten cultural center in Aarhus, Denmark.[30] The plotters were of Somali and Iraqi origins, and one of the men did online research into Vilks's self-announced visit to the exhibition, and bought a pocket knife which was believed to be the weapon. The evidence was not sufficient to have the alleged plotters convicted on terrorism or murder charges and they were only fined for carrying a knife in a public place.

In the same month the Danish cartoonist Kurt Westergaard had to cancel his participation in a book launch at Litteraturhuset cultural center in central Oslo because of an alleged assassination plot.[31] Coinciding with the news about Westergaard's return to Denmark, heavily armed operators from the police's emergency response unit (Delta) arrested a suspected terrorist for a minor traffic offence. Police believed that the suspect had access to automatic weapons and explosives suitable for assassination plans. Although he was never identified, media sources strongly indicated that this was Arfan B., the aforementioned Norwegian-Pakistani who was central in building an Islamist extremist network in Norway from 2009 onwards.[32]

An incident in Britain in June 2012 exemplified how reciprocal radicalization between Islamists and anti-Islam could trigger plots and affect target selection. A gang composed of British-Pakistani and British-Bengali extremists from Birmingham prepared a terrorist attack on a rally organized by the EDL in Dewsbury, UK. The cell was discovered by coincidence during routine traffic control, driving from Dewsbury to Birmingham after learning that the EDL rally had ended early.[33] One of their cars contained a number of knives, machetes, swords and a sawn-off shot gun, in addition to a pipe bomb made out of fireworks and nails and ball bearings meant to function as shrapnel. The terrorists admitted intending to attack EDL on the grounds that the organization had insulted the Prophet Muhammad and they all received lengthy prison sentences.

Similarly, in February 2013, a plot in Denmark illustrated that attacks in that country were not confined to *Jyllands-Posten* and the cartoonists, but also targeted all of those who had expressed anti-Islamic views. An individual dressed as a mailman approached the home of a former journalist and a fiercely outspoken Islam-critic Lars Hedegaard in Copenhagen, and attempted to murder him with a handgun. The attacker fired one shot but it missed Hedegaard's head, after which the gun malfunctioned in an attempt to fire another. The attacker then fled the scene. Investigations revealed that the attack was pre-planned, and a car he had rented was placed outside Hedegaard's house two weeks before the attack, likely for reconnaissance. Hedegaard has been a highly controversial figure in Danish public debate and even went on trial on racism charges based on his harsh critique of Islam. However, he was found not guilty by the Danish High Court.

It later transpired that the attacker in all likelihood was a twenty-six-year-old Danish-Lebanese man who was part of the extremist scene in Denmark and had links to people who had been involved in the Glostrup case. He had spent time in Lebanon before the attack, and after fleeing the scene of the attack he traveled to Syria where he allegedly mixed with jihadis. It is not clear which group he was affiliated with. He was arrested in Turkey on his way to Denmark again on 14 April 2014.[34] It was later rumored that he had been released from jail in exchange for Turks who were held hostage by IS.

The targeting of anti-Islamic figures also included politicians. In March 2013, German authorities arrested four extreme Salafis suspected of plotting to assassinate the right-wing politician and leader of the Pro NRW Party, Markus Beisicht. Police raids were launched against three radical Islamist associations dubbed Dawa FFM, Islamische Audios and An-Nussrah, all of which had an online presence and engaged in fundraising, recruitment and propaganda activities on behalf of jihadi movements. Two of the suspects were apprehended while they were driving a car near the politician's residence, and police confiscated one firearm and explosives among their belongings. It was later revealed that one member of the group had already attempted to bomb

Bonn Central Station in December 2012 with a device made out of an ammonium nitrate (fertilizer) mixture, which failed to explode.[35]

While the jihadi terrorism threat in Europe is clearly becoming more discriminate, it remains to be seen how the sizeable contingent of European foreign fighters in Syria will affect the threat in the time ahead.

Blowback

The war in Syria and the rise of IS will more than likely create a blowback effect on patterns of Islamist terrorism in Europe. By welcoming Europeans in its ranks IS has built a capacity which could be exploited for international terrorism, either as a means to deter Western interference in the conflict, or as a means to outflank al-Qaida in the realm of international terrorism. In 2014 IS stood out as the most potent insurgent/terrorist group the world has ever seen. At the same time, it made many enemies and lost support of old school jihadis loyal to al-Qaida.

The first plots in Europe with links to Syria after the outbreak of the insurgency sprang out of support networks for al-Qaida's Syrian branch, Jabhat al-Nusra, which was most popular among European foreign fighters before the rise of the Islamic State. In September 2012, two terrorists threw a hand grenade into a Jewish bakery in a Paris suburb. One of them, a former delinquent turned religious, was rounded up and shot dead in an exchange of fire with the police in early October. Jeremie Sidney (thirty-three) had, according to the typical pattern among French jihadis, become radicalized in jail and joined a militant network dubbed the "Cannes-Torcy network" by French security officials, which was involved in recruitment for al-Qaida's wing in the Syrian jihad, Jabhat al-Nusra (JAN), and dissemination of jihadi propaganda.

In Sidney's apartment, investigators discovered a make-shift bomb factory, a target list of Jewish associations, jihadi training manuals and anti-Semitic propaganda. The network had declared war on France and praised Mohammed Merah, dubbing his attacks "the Battle of Toulouse."[36] After this incident, which seemed homegrown, by a network supporting JAN, there have been no other plots in Europe that could be traced to JAN. This makes sense as JAN was dominated by Syrians and focused on the battle against the regime before clashing with ISIS/IS. It should be noted that members of the Cannes-Torcy network who traveled to Syria were believed to have joined the ranks of ISIS/IS when that group emerged as the most popular among the Western foreign fighters in 2013–14.[37]

It did not take long after ISIS/IS had become the preferred choice among European foreign fighters until plots began occurring in Europe which had links to the group. In October 2013, MI5 intercepted four individuals believed to be plotting a Mumbai-style terrorist attack in London. The plotters were young Britons hailing from Turkey, Algeria, Azerbaijan and Pakistan. Apparently, they had actively been trying to obtain weapons suitable for a guerilla-style attack. Two of the suspects were released, but one Turkish-Briton and an Algerian-Briton were charged with terrorist offences. The trial was shrouded in secrecy, but the charged were said to have had spent time with ISIS in Syria.

After returning to the UK they had kept a low profile for several months, but there had reportedly been contacts between them and one alleged handler in Syria referred to as "Ahmed".[38] What is known from the trial against the purported entrepreneur of the plot, Erol I., is that the prosecution believed they were preparing indiscriminate mass casualty attacks on civilians with bombs and Kalashnikovs, and that they also had considered assassinating Tony Blair.[39] Erol I. was in the end sentenced for possessing a bomb manual, but found not guilty of planning an attack, in March 2015. The case highlighted the difficulty of assessing foiled terrorist plots. The security services regarded the plot as very real and dangerous, and surely they still do, whereas in the legal sense there was no attack plan.[40]

In a case uncovered in February 2014, French police arrested twenty-three-year-old Ibrahim Boudina, in the Cote d'Azur region in Nice, South France.[41] The suspected terrorist possessed 900 grams of the explosive TATP and a handgun, and was suspected of plotting to bomb the Nice Carnival. According to the media he had assembled a rudimentary IED, which included bolts and nails meant as shrapnel. It is thought that the plot was modeled on the Boston Marathon bombings, which had in turn been based on the modus operandi and bomb recipes discussed in AQAP's *Inspire* magazine.

The suspect joined the insurgency in Syria alongside jihadi outfits in September 2012 and returned in early 2014. He was known to have ties to the Cannes-Torcy network, which had been involved in recruitment for JAN, and whose members carried out an attack with a hand grenade on a Jewish bakery in the Paris. He acted together with a French-Tunisian extremist who had been his friend since childhood. The two of them had posted threats on social media that France should be punished. However, they were also known to have undergone radicalization during Arabic-language studies in Cairo, and to have wanted to die as martyrs in Syria.

Boudina was known as an entrepreneur among a small extremist group in Cannes. He had been using videos of atrocities carried out by the Assad regime to recruit people for the Syrian jihad. He had also told friends that if he was unable to become a mujahid in Syria, he would launch jihad in France instead. Investigations further revealed that Boudina had voiced support for the actions of Mohammed Merah in southern France in 2012. He had escaped the police crackdowns against the Cannes-Torcy network and slipped into Syria via Turkey. Investigators believed that after fighting first with JAN, Boudina was among those who defected to ISIS and that he was affiliated with that group at the time of his arrest. He returned to France via Greece carrying bomb recipes on a USB-stick and hid in a rented luxury apartment in Nice when agents intervened and had him arrested. It was not established whether Boudina acted on behalf of ISIS, or initiated the plot on his own.

However, ISIS was stepping up threats against the West in social media at the time and several subsequent incidents involved ISIS/IS affiliates. The first deadly incident linked to ISIS was the attack on 24 May 2014 by the twenty-nine-year-old French-Algerian Mehdi Nemmouche, who entered the Jewish Museum in Brussels and opened fire at visitors and staff with a Kalashnikov.[42] The attack left four people dead, three at the scene and one in hospital. The attacker had disguised himself and managed to escape the scene. Like Mohammed Merah, he wore a sports camera strapped to his chest to film the atrocity, but the device failed to record. The terrorist was arrested six days later at a railway station in Marseilles. He was carrying the assault weapon with him wrapped in ISIS's infamous black flag. It turned out he had spent one year in Syria with ISIS after becoming radicalized by interacting with Islamists over the five years he had spent in French jails. The pattern was all too familiar.

Nemmouche's profile was almost identical to Mohammed Merah's and he eulogized the Toulouse killer. Nemmouche hailed from Roubaix, the city that gave its name to the notorious gangster-terrorists headed by Christophe Caze operating in France in the 1990s. He has been described as a misfit and drifter who dabbled in crime and was sent to jail for armed robberies. While Nemmouche claimed he was innocent and did not talk to interrogators, witness accounts of his activities in Syria provided a window into his motives. In Syria he had become part of a crew of ISIS hostage-takers said to be behind the abduction, heinous torture and beheadings of Syrian and foreign hostages, including the journalists James Foley and Steven Sotloff who were beheaded by the group's British executioner "Jihadi John" in propaganda videos threatening the West. Two French journalists who were released described Nemmouche as one of the most brutal hostage-takers and a torturer. They described how he portrayed Merah as a hero and indicated that he wanted to commit an attack five times as big as Merah's, for example during the Bastille Day Parade in Paris.[43]

Intriguingly, Nemmouche also expressed admiration for Khaled Kelkal who attacked France for the GIA, and according to *Libération*, like many other French jihadis he saw the al-Qaida-linked Djamel Beghal as his guru.[44] Nemmouche, Merah and Beghal all served time in the Fleury-Mérogis Prison south of Paris, but details of their interaction were not known at the time of writing.[45] While ISIS's involvement in the museum-shootings could not be established through claims by the group or otherwise, the attacks were premeditated and well organized. Nemmouche made sure to fly via several destinations in Asia back to France, and had recorded a voice-recording, in which he said he would attack Jews and set Belgium on fire.

However, although by 2014 ISIS or IS was becoming the strongest group in jihadism, its ties to plots in Europe were often hard to unpack. While most European foreign fighters were joining IS, some were also fighting with competing groups, such as Jabhat al-Nusra and Ahrar al-Sham. Moreover, before traveling to Syria, many of the European foreign fighters had been part of support networks in Europe that had catered to al-Qaida, the Taliban and other groups in Af-Pak, as well as al-Qaida's Iraqi branch—which was now going solo. They harbored conflicting loyalties, to "brothers" whom they cooperated with in Europe, old school al-Qaida and the new version of al-Qaida in Iraq, Islamic State.

To complicate matters further, intelligence leaks brought attention to another network operating out of Syria since 2012, called the "Khorasan Group." This group or network was said to take orders from central al-Qaida and bring together resources from al-Qaida's affiliates in Af-Pak, Yemen and other places in a specialized project aimed at launching ambitious terrorist attacks in the West.[46] The network, which has been supervised by al-Qaida veterans such as Muhsin al-Fadli (who previously oversaw al-Qaida's networks in Iran), is believed to organize training activities in different locations in Syria, recruiting Westerners for attacks. Western intelligence services assess that the group remains a potent threat, perhaps an even greater one than IS when it comes to international attacks.

Although details were murky, at least one incident in recent times raised questions that a Khorasan "sleeper" could have been involved.[47] In June 2014, a British extremist returning from Syria was suspected of plotting an attack on the scale of 7/7. The plot was believed to involve both handguns and bombs, and the suspect received instructions from a shadowy al-Qaida figure in Syria. The contact in Syria was known to design plots directed against Western countries and was making contacts with would-be terrorists in the UK and other European countries for this purpose. The UK suspect was said to have brought with him substantial amounts of cash which he used to buy weapons and bomb-making materials. He kept in touch with the Syria contact after returning home, and he also teamed up with another accomplice before the security services intervened.

While an increasing number of plots have involved people who have spent time in Syria and Iraq, there have also been a rising number of terrorist plans by independent sympathizers. A worrying incident in Austria in October 2014 illustrated how very young people might be manipulated to commit terrorism by interacting with IS online.[48] A fourteen-year-old Turkish boy, Mertkan G., was arrested in Austria on suspicion of plotting to bomb a train at Vienna's Westbahnhof and other crowded areas in the city, before fleeing Syria to join IS. He had been living in Austria for eight years and had conducted research online on how to build improvised cluster-bombs like the ones used in the Boston Marathon attack. He had also voiced support for IS and interacted with IS members on social media. According to media reports, the Turkish boy had been offered the equivalent of 25,000 USD and a special position within IS if he executed the attacks. The offer was made online and the reports said two other boys who remained at large had received similar offers. The fourteen-year-old had not yet built bomb devices, but he had carried out reconnaissance at the time of the arrest. Other media reports referred to the boy as a lone wolf, without any contacts. The lone wolf from Vienna illustrated how the full specter of cell configurations was at play in Europe at the end of 2014.

In January 2015, while I was finalizing this book, an attack occurred in Paris which horrifyingly demonstrated how the trends discussed throughout the study were converging. The following account of the attacks against the offices of *Charlie Hebdo* and a kosher supermarket in Paris concludes this history of jihadi terrorism in Europe.

Full Circle: The Attacks on Charlie Hebdo

I had originally intended to conclude this book by summing up the main patterns in the emergence of terrorist plots in Europe and discussing what could happen next. Then, the jihadis summed it up themselves in a shock attack on the offices of the satirical magazine *Charlie Hebdo*, which had published cartoons of the Prophet. On 7 January two black-clad masked gunmen wearing body armor threatened a worker at the magazine for the door code, stormed inside and killed a guard, the magazine's editor and several staff members. They acted calmly and addressed the editor by his nickname "Charb" before killing him. Like Theo van Gogh, *Charlie Hebdo* did not satirize Islam specifically, but ridiculed fundamentalists of all faiths, including politicians and other public figures.

The terrorists killed as many as they could, only sparing one female worker, reassuring her they did not kill women. Another female staff member was shot and killed but it was not clear if this was intentional. On their way out the gunmen shouted that they had avenged the Prophet and that they had "killed Charlie Hebdo", before shooting a Muslim policeman arriving at the scene.[49] Heavily armed with Kalashnikovs, they managed to escape by car after firing rounds at a police vehicle that was attempting to block their way. After crashing their escape car, they hijacked a taxi and told the driver they were members of al-Qaida in Yemen (AQAP). A massive manhunt was launched, but the attackers went underground.

On the day of the attack on the offices of *Charlie Hebdo*, there was also a shooting against a jogger, which initially seemed to be unrelated. The next day a police woman was shot dead by another terrorist who turned out to be behind the shooting against the jogger (who survived) as well. The other terrorist shooter had prior connections to the gunmen attacking the offices of *Charlie Hebdo*, but it was not entirely clear if, or to what extent, they were coordinated.

The gunmen from the first attacks, the French-Algerian brothers Chérif Kouachi and Saïd Kouachi, were observed by several witnesses during the manhunt, including an incident when they robbed a gas station. They were heavily armed with automatic rifles, bombs and even a rocket launcher. They were rounded up two days later after taking a hostage into a storage facility in an industrial area near a village north of Paris.

Simultaneously, the man behind the attack on the police woman and the jogger, French-Malian Amedy Coulibaly, took hostages in a Jewish supermarket in Paris, threatening to kill them unless those who had attacked the offices of *Charlie Hebdo* were given free passage. Confusingly, this attacker told the press that he was connected to the Kouachi brothers and IS, not AQAP, and that the attacks were coordinated. All of the terrorists were killed by Special

Forces in the counter-terrorism operation and four hostages died. In total, seventeen people were killed in the deadliest jihadi attacks thus far in France.

Operationally, the attacks combined historical trends seen among jihadi terrorists in Europe. They were mass casualty (more than ten deaths), and at the same time discriminate (aimed at cartoonists, Jews and police). The terrorists spared one person they referred to as "civilian" and the mentioned woman, but they also had bombs suitable for indiscriminate attacks.[50]

The attacks on the magazine's offices and the separate shootings were hit-and-runs, but the terrorists were all obviously prepared to become martyrs as they charged against the police shooting (like Mohammed Bouyeri and the Woolwich killers) in the end. Coulibaly had recorded a martyrdom video, whereas videos by the Kouachi brothers had not yet surfaced at the time of writing. They did, however, tell the police negotiators that they intended to become martyrs during the siege.

Another intriguing operational aspect was the dissimilarities between the two attacks. Chérif and Saïd Kouachi who attacked the magazine's offices clearly worked together, whereas Coulibaly acted as a solo-terrorist, although he may have received help from his French-Algerian wife Hayat Boumeddiene in the run-up to the attacks (she fled the country before the attacks started). Coulibaly claimed that he coordinated with the brothers, but this was never confirmed by them it seems. The French-Malian also said he was operating on behalf of IS, whereas the brothers stated to witnesses and the press that they were members of AQAP.

As was the case with Mohammed Merah and Mehdi Nemmouche's attacks in 2012 and 2014, the Kouachi brothers had bought sports cameras to video their attacks, but did not use them. The different modus operandi at play in the attacks in Paris in January 2015 involved a mix of previous patterns seen in Europe. The terrorists' backgrounds and radicalization were even more intriguing from a historical perspective.[51]

This last case perfectly demonstrates the historical continuity of European jihad networks emanating from the Afghan-Arab movement, the role of jihad entrepreneurs in terrorist cell formation and the constant interplay between extremist networks in Europe and mujahidin in conflict zones. It also highlights how personal frustrations and crises become politicized when interacting with jihadi networks, creating a highly complex motivational landscape.

All of the motives seen in the history of jihadism in Europe were expressed by the Kouachi brothers and Coulibaly. In addition to personal failures, they were angered by the invasions of Iraq and Afghanistan, the plight of

Palestinians, arrests of Islamists in Europe (including their own) and acts they considered anti-Islamic (cartoons).

This last case also demonstrates how travel to conflict zones and interaction with groups abroad provided plotters with encouragement, justification, skills and mental capacity to go through with attack plans in Europe. However, were it not for homegrown radicalization at the hands of entrepreneurs, they would likely not have connected with foreign terrorists groups in the first place. Like most jihadi terrorists in Europe in the 2000s they had been part of the recruitment network for Iraq and one of them was arrested for his role in it.

The Kouachi brothers were part of a network in the nineteenth arrondissement Paris, gathering around a self-taught preacher named Farid Benyettou who was a central figure in the French recruitment network for the Iraqi jihad in the years following the invasion.[52] Focusing much on the transgressions at Abu Ghraib, Benyettou was said to have recruited a dozen fighters for which he received a six-year prison sentence. It should be noted that Benyettou never called for an attack in France. On the contrary, he seems to have preached that French Muslims were restricted by a covenant of security. He was released from prison due to his cooperation with law enforcement and he condemned the attacks on the offices of *Charlie Hebdo*. However, in the mid-2000s he was clearly an entrepreneur drawing young men into jihadism.

Among them were Kouachi brothers, who were misfits by all accounts. They hailed from a broken home and were eventually orphaned. They lived frustrating lives drifting between odd jobs, doing soft drugs and listening to rap music in their spare time. In Ramadan 2004, the older brother, Cherif, decided he would try to go to Iraq, but was intercepted by the security services and arrested. He was prosecuted and sentenced, and spent some time in the Fleury-Mérogis Prison after 2008.

At this point, the story took a highly interesting turn seen in light of the cases analyzed in this book. In prison Cherif Kouachi came under the spell of Djamel Beghal, the entrepreneur of the network plotting attacks for al-Qaida in Europe in 2001, discussed in Chapter Four. Beghal had become a go-to-guy among Islamists in French jails. This was also the case with several other ex-GIA members who were part of the networks operating in the 1990s, including Safe Bourada and Smaïn Aït Ali Belkacem.

A similar pattern was seen in the UK and other European countries, where imprisoned terrorists gained status among inmates and became the center of attention. Similar to Beghal, the former GIA leader Rachid Ramda gained a martyr status in British jails, as did radical preachers such as Hamza and Qatada, and terrorist cell entrepreneurs such as Omar Khyam of the Crawley group.

Beghal seems to have had a profound influence on Cherif Kouachi, and when Beghal was released in 2010 (under a strict security regime) he received visits from all of those involved in the attack on the offices of *Charlie Hebdo* and the Jewish supermarket at his home in Murat, Cantal, including Coulibaly's wife Hayat Boumeddienne. Shortly after, Beghal was rearrested in connection with a plot to free Smaïn Aït Ali Belkacem, the "mujahid" sent by GIA-leader Djamel Zitouni to construct bombs for the Paris attacks in 1995 (Chapter Three). The jailbreak plot was meant to involve both the Kouachi brothers and Coulibaly. However, while Coulibaly and Beghal went to prison for the plans, the evidence against the Kouachi brothers did not hold up in court.

At this juncture, the generations of jihad in Europe crossed paths in an omen of what was to come. In line with the familiar pattern of jihadism in Europe, there was also a link to the UK, as Beghal had been a key figure in the British jihadi scene in the circles of Qatada and Hamza in the late 1990s and early 2000s.[53] After the Belkacem affair, the Kouachi brothers continued as activists of the new generation among French extremist circles, both online and through engaging with jihadis internationally.

According to a Yemeni journalist, Said Kouachi spent time in Yemen in 2009–10 and in 2011.[54] It has been alleged that he shared an apartment with the underwear-bomber Umar Farouk Abdulmutallab in 2009, and that he may have met al-Awlaki before he was killed in 2011. According to some sources, the brothers traveled together to Yemen in 2011 and received training from AQAP. In a statement to a French television station during the French counter-terrorism operation in 2015, Cherif Kouachi said they had received financing for the attack from AQAP and al-Awlaki.

As for the self-declared IS member Coulibaly, his radicalization paralleled the Kouachi brothers in terms of network contacts and motives. Coulibaly's hatred of French law enforcement and desire for revenge seems to have been the main driving force, however.[55] The police had shot dead a close friend of his when the pair were committing a robbery, which was most likely one reason why he first went after police when he joined the attacks. In prison he met and befriended Beghal, and as with many other terrorists discussed in this book, he was impressed by his charisma.

Seeing Beghal as his religious guide he kept in touch with him after being released from jail. He also introduced his wife, Boumeddienne, to him and the couple visited the entrepreneur when he was released. Because of his criminal background and familiarity with guns, Beghal considered Coulibaly an asset in his plan to free Belkacem. Coulibaly gathered weapons and ammunition for the plot and received a five-year prison sentence for his involvement.

When Coulibaly's father died from cancer during his incarceration and he was not allowed to visit him, it added to his rage. After his release in March 2014 he reunited with his wife, went on hajj and visited his father's grave in Mali. Although Coulibaly claimed he was a member of IS, there were no sources at the time of writing confirming he fought with the group in Syria–Iraq.

There is no doubt that Coulibaly clearly identified with IS, that he considered himself a soldier of the Caliphate and that his attack was retaliation for Western attacks against the group. He also made several phone calls threatening to attack the police. However, Coulibaly's endgame was to target Jews. As shown throughout this book, Palestine was a central theme in the radicalization of European jihadis, and Jews were a default target for all cells, networks and groups over time. Even if terrorists prioritized national struggles or international jihad in Af-Pak, Iraq or other places, Palestine was still a partial motive, and a trigger in a number of instances.

Like most plots examined in this book, the attacks in France in January 2015 involved an intricate interplay between personal factors and group dynamics, between extremists in Europe and groups overseas, between social grievances and religious–political ideology. Ever since 1994, terrorist cells in the region have combined bottom-up and top-down elements. Some terrorists have worked in groups and others alone. In line with other research, the subjects presented in this book did not stand out compared to non-terrorists in terms of social profile. What distinguished them was that they became part of networks growing out of the Afghan jihad under the influence of entrepreneurs. The entrepreneurs fed them with conspiracy theories, and could do so more effectively in the age of social media.

The book has also shown how Europe played an essential role in the evolution of transnational jihadism. In the 2000s European countries were both support bases and targets for al-Qaida. Throughout the 2000s al-Qaida and likeminded groups became bent on deterring and punishing Europeans for their efforts in the War on Terror. For this purpose they relied on recruits from Europe. The threat was further accentuated by a consensus that Europeans had broken security pacts with Muslims. Furthermore, Europeans were unable to halt the radicalization of a new generation of extremists, fueled by the Arab Spring and the rise of IS.

I have shown how jihadi terrorism in Europe has been multi-layered, entrepreneur-driven and shaped to a large extent by foreign armed groups and foreign fighters. With an estimated 3,000 to 5,000 European Islamists fighting in Syria, patterns of jihadism in Europe are bound to be affected. Although research has shown that a minority of foreign fighters become international terrorists, those that do tend to become entrepreneurs in networks and cells.

This book has focused on actors, but its analysis also has policy implications. The European jihadi phenomenon is driven forward by tight-knit networks of individuals motivated mostly by wars in the Muslim world. The networks emerge and behave similarly in different countries, indicating that the networks to a large extent explain themselves and that societal explanations have less impact. At the foreign policy level, European states need to work to resolve the conflicts that motivate the terrorists, and think carefully about how to intervene in Muslim countries.

In the domestic arena, European states must mitigate acute threats and prevent networks from growing further. Intelligence capacities need to be strengthened to monitor growing numbers of foreign fighters. The security services must find out as much as possible about what they are up to when in conflict zones, so as to foresee and intercept plots. Special Forces need to adapt their training in order to cope with the terrorists' diversifying modus operandi.

My typology of terrorists and the conclusion that cells rarely emerge in the absence of entrepreneurs has implications for threat assessments and counter-radicalization. Extremists need to be monitored very closely to spot suspicious constellations of entrepreneurs, protégés, misfits and drifters that could be a cell in the making.

Furthermore, it must be made as difficult as possible for the former to manipulate the latter to commit violence, whether it happens in radical mosques, prisons or online. As entrepreneurs and protégés are generally intelligent activists, it may in some instances be possible to reason with them and steer them towards non-violent activism instead. If not, they need to be constrained as much as possible, or rendered harmless.

As for the misfits and drifters who constitute the majority, but became part of extremism more coincidentally, they are generally less committed than entrepreneurs. They should therefore in principle be easier to guide out of extremism. A project in Aarhus, Denmark, with the intention of reintegrating Danish foreign fighters into society exemplifies how de-radicalization of such types may involve mundane matters, such as assistance in finding a job or somewhere to live; someone non-extremist to talk to; or psychological counselling.[56] Misfits and drifters also include very young people, or even children.

As shown by the plot involving the fourteen-year-old Turkish immigrant to Austria, youngsters are easy prey for terrorists. Moreover, it should be highlighted that many militants hail from the same family, such as the Kouachi brothers. This calls for paying special attention to younger siblings of terrorists and foreign fighters who look up to them as role models. Targeted de-radicalization tailored to the needs of different types of terrorists seems to be the best way forward to reduce recruitment to jihadism in Europe.

Finally, there has been a tendency to tie the threat from jihadism in the West to broader societal developments and failed integration in particular. There are several examples in this book that terrorists were poorly integrated and had been exposed to racism or anti-Islamic ideas. This was usually the case with misfits and drifters, whereas entrepreneurs seemed integrated by most accounts. Policies to improve integration would hardly affect entrepreneurs.

It might be argued that integration policies could reduce the pool of potential recruits for extremists as they tend to target disaffected youths. This effect is impossible to measure and there will always be an abundance of disenfranchised immigrants in Europe compared to small numbers of extremists, relatively speaking. Also, if immigration policies were a main driving force, countries pursuing different policies would experience different threat levels. This is hardly the case.

The UK is known for a multi-cultural approach to immigration, whereas France has pursued assimilation and has generally experienced higher tensions related to immigration. Yet the two countries experience very similar threats from Islamist terrorism, partly due to their foreign policies in the Muslim world and partly because jihadis managed to established support networks in French and British cities. Integration should be pursued for its own value of creating better societies and not linked to terrorism. Counter-measures against jihadism should primarily be tailored to the individual in order to disintegrate concrete networks and cells.

EPILOGUE

ISLAMIC STATE'S EFFECT ON EUROPEAN JIHADISM[1]

On 17 August 2017, a group of Islamic State (IS) jihadis executed a terrorist attack in Barcelona. A van ploughed into crowds of pedestrians at Las Ramblas, the most famous street in the city. Shortly thereafter, another vehicle attack shook the nearby coastal city of Cambrils. Sixteen people were slain and more than 130 others were wounded. The terrorists had initially planned to car-bomb the Sagrada Familia church, but had to alter their plans when the apartment they used as a bomb factory exploded by accident.

Before the dust had settled from the attacks in Spain, another occurred, this time in Northern Europe, in the Finnish city of Turku (Åbo). An IS jihadi, a Moroccan asylum seeker, attacked pedestrians with a knife at the market square. Two women were killed and eight other people were wounded. The attacks in Spain and Finland were, each in their own way, typical of the current jihadi threat in Europe, which has escalated since IS emerged in June 2014.[2] There has clearly been an "IS-effect" on European jihadism, and IS has become a more severe threat in the region than al-Qaida ever was.

What is the "IS-effect" on the terrorist threat in Europe? Why are we seeing such an effect? How did IS become a bigger threat in Europe than al-Qaida? How dangerous is the IS threat compared to other terrorist threats in the region? Who are the IS terrorists in Europe? What motivates them? How do they join terrorist networks? And lastly, what can be done to prevent and counter the elevated threat Europe has faced since the rise of IS? Based on what I have learnt through fifteen years of studying European jihadism, this epilogue offers my take on how and why the jihadi threat to Europe has transformed since the rise of IS in 2014.

As shown in this book, Western Europe has faced threats from al-Qaida-linked networks since the mid-1990s (when the GIA attacked France)—threats that steadily became more frequent throughout the 2000s. Lethal attacks struck commuter trains in Madrid in 2004, and the London Tube as well as a London bus in 2005. There have also been numerous smaller attacks and plots, such as the attempts to kill the Danish cartoonists who drew the Prophet Muhammad in 2005. Since 2014, nearly all plots in Europe have been linked to IS, whereas very few have been linked to al-Qaida. The "IS-effect" on European jihadism can be characterized by the following:

- Never before have there been so many terrorist plots per year in Europe. 2017 saw nearly one plot occur every week (if we count both well-documented plots and the vague ones described in the appendix). Al-Qaida never came close to such numbers.
- Never before have so many plots gone under the radar of security services and resulted in attacks.
- Never before have so many people been killed by jihadi terrorism in Europe. In fact, more people have been killed since the rise of IS (339) than in the previous twenty years (267).

What creates the IS-effect?

There are three main and interlinked explanations. First, the number of potential jihadi terrorists to monitor in Europe has rapidly increased. This is a direct consequence of the high number of Europeans (4–7000) who traveled to the

Graph A: Well-documented plots (1994–2017). Source: FFI data updated December 2017

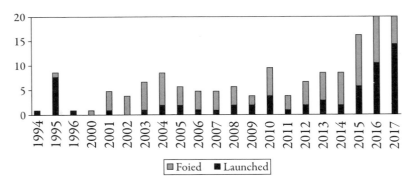

Middle East as foreign fighters. Second, the jihadis operate in new ways and with more stealth, making it harder to intercept attacks. Third, security services lack the personnel and legal tools necessary to surveil, arrest, and prosecute all of the potential attackers.

Why the rise in potential attackers?

This mainly has to do with the "Arab Spring" and the outbreak of the war in Syria in 2011. These developments breathed new life into European jihadi networks that were weakened around the time of Osama bin Laden's death in 2011. European jihadis—especially Anjem Choudary's Islam4/Sharia4-network—who at that time supported al-Qaida, recruited thousands of young Europeans to fight the Syrian regime. His network channeled the volunteers to Syria via Turkey to join al-Qaida-affiliated militias.

Soon al-Qaida's Iraqi arm penetrated Syria and gained territorial control. The group challenged al-Qaida's central leadership and declared itself an independent organization. The group proclaimed that it had reestablished the caliphate and that all Muslims must swear fealty to this new entity known as the "Islamic State". By being the most brutal, strongest and richest fighting force, and more importantly, a "state", IS became more popular than al-Qaida with European recruits. This is the most important reason behind IS dominating the threat in Europe today.

We do not know enough about how IS became the organization of choice for the European foreign fighters, or how European jihadis managed to mobilize so many new recruits IS's use of propaganda and media productions targeting a young western audience clearly played a central role. So too did the existence of a transnational European network of Islam4/Sharia4 branches, and radical preachers who pledged allegiance to IS—notably Anjem Choudary—influencing the new generation of European jihadis.

Foreign fighters constitute the core capacity for IS to build attack networks in Europe. Similar to al-Qaida, IS uses people who have lived in Europe, and who are familiar with the societies they operate in, to launch attacks in European countries. Attackers are typically recruited from the foreign fighters, or their networks at home. The most immediate reason for the steep increase in plots and lethal attacks is therefore that Europe's jihadi networks have rapidly grown in size. Moreover, these large networks have a powerful organization backing them (IS), which has used the foreign fighters to establish bridgeheads in Europe.

The importance of foreign fighters

Foreign fighters have played a crucial role in creating the IS-effect in Europe. However, not all of them constitute a threat. Research has shown that only a small minority of Muslims who seek out conflict zones end up becoming international terrorists.

One reason for this, discussed extensively in this book, is that while there is general agreement among jihadis about the legality of fighting Arab dictators, launching attacks in countries offering protection to Muslims remains ideologically controversial. According to some stipulations in Islamic theology, it is forbidden for Muslims to attack countries offering them political asylum and sanctuary. As shown in chapter one, al-Qaida was harshly criticized by other jihadis after 9/11 because the attackers had obtained visas to the U.S. and thereby entered the country as guests. This may seem odd to someone not familiar with how jihadis discuss theology. Yet, there is considerable disagreement among jihadis about whether or not it is permissible for a Muslim who has entered a "covenant of security" with a non-Muslim country (by being a citizen or having obtained political asylum or other permits such as a visa) to attack the country in question.

Among an extreme minority this is not an issue. In their eyes, covenants of security stopped applying the moment Western countries invaded Muslim countries, prevented Muslims from freely practicing their religion (e.g. by banning veils), or allowed insults against the Prophet Muhammed to take place.

However, though they are a minority, they make the threat to Europe far more severe. History has shown that people with experience as foreign fighters play crucial roles in jihadi networks. They become "entrepreneurs": resourceful, ideological activists who recruit misfits and drifters into terrorist networks and cells, and connect them with militant groups in conflict zones. However, stronger networks and entrepreneurs are not the only explanation for the IS-effect. Another reason for this effect is that IS operates in ways that make it hard for security services to intercept attacks.

Tactical moves

Solo-terrorism is one of several tactical moves. Attackers who have little contact with an organized network, or who only communicating with these networks via encrypted apps, are difficult to stop. It was al-Qaida that initiated solo-attacks in Europe, but IS has taken this tactic further. Presently, about half of the plots in Europe involve single actors (most of them instructed by IS's networks).

Graph B: Data presented in Petter Nesser, Anne Stenersen, and Emilie Oftedal, "Jihadi Terrorism in Europe: The IS Effect," Perspectives on Terrorism, 10, no. 6 (20 December 2016)

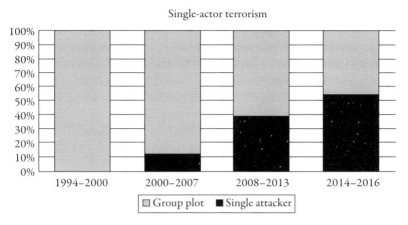

Single-actor terrorism

Another tactical move is the weaponization of everyday tools such as knives, or means of transportation from rental cars to large trucks. Bombs have historically been al-Qaida's weapon of choice in Europe. This also seems to apply to IS. However, attackers are not always able to procure the necessary ingredients and successfully assemble their devices. For instance, the IS cell in Barcelona initially planned to carry out car-bomb attacks, but was forced to resort to simpler means when their bomb factory exploded. As we have seen, many al-Qaida cells in Europe were intercepted when procuring ingredients, and many operations failed for technical reasons. Knife or vehicle attacks are usually less lethal, but nearly impossible to stop. Furthermore, as became evident in Nice (2016), Berlin (2016), Stockholm (2017) and Barcelona (2017), vehicle attacks can be highly lethal when carried out against crowds. This is why IS has increasingly used and promoted this tactic to its followers.

A third tactical move is gaining access to a country by smuggling terrorists in among refugees. This was done by the IS network behind the attacks on the Bataclan (2015) and the Brussels Airport (2016); several of the attackers entered Europe posing as refugees. Similarly, the Tunisian IS member, Anis Amri, who drove a van into the Christmas market in Berlin in December 2016, was a solo-terrorist with refugee status. Typically, the terrorists transported as refugees are foreign fighters who have previously have lived in Europe. Al-Qaida too employed people with local knowledge for its attacks in the West.

A fourth tactical move behind the IS-effect is the use of encrypted apps such as WhatsApp and Telegram to communicate with entrepreneurs (who have typically been European foreign fighters working for IS's international operations division) in Syria or other conflict zones. The attacker who rammed a vehicle into the Berlin Christmas market in 2016 received instructions from IS via encrypted apps, as did the terrorist of Libyan descent who bombed the Ariana Grande-concert in Manchester in May 2017. He was reportedly in contact with an IS member in Syria via the encrypted communication app Zello. He asked his contact, whom he referred to as "Sheikh" (religious supervisor), if the attacks were legitimate. The sheikh gave him permission to go through with the attacks and stressed that he should "show no mercy to civilians".[3]

The challenges security services face

Up against mushrooming networks and altered tactics, European security services face formidable capacity challenges. Thousands of Europeans have fought alongside IS and potentially belong to transnational terrorist networks, making it impossible for security services to closely monitor everyone.

The large influx of refugees to Europe has made identifying potential threats even more difficult. as has the rapid development in communication technologies, which makes it possible for terrorists to communicate via encrypted platforms that are cheap or free.

The biggest challenge is deciding who poses a threat. Some returning foreign fighters have been prosecuted for war crimes or terrorist planning. Some are disillusioned and have left extremism behind. Others remain extreme but have put armed struggle on hold. Among those who have not returned, many are reported dead, but there are multiple examples of foreign fighters who have "risen from the dead" and operate as terrorists under a fake identity.

Moreover, persons who were prevented from going to Syria (often friends and relatives of people who reached the conflict zone at an earlier stage) have plotted attacks. One example is the all-female cell that attempted to carry out a car-bomb attack outside Notre Dame in 2016. The women never made it to Syria, but were connected to French jihadis, and received instruction from entrepreneurs in Syria.

The terrorist threat can be measured as the difference between the terrorists' capacity to carry out attacks, and the security services' capacity to thwart attacks. For the moment, the terrorists seem to be one step ahead in Western Europe.

Do we exaggerate the threat?

Europe has a long history with terrorism. Left-wing terrorists have fought for a communist world order, right-wing terrorists have fought for fascism—wanting to revive an imagined glorious past—, and separatist terrorists have demanded independence for minorities. Some believe that the jihadi threat is less severe than other terrorist threats in Europe,[4] pointing to data showing that separatist groups top the terrorism statistics in Europe. The comparison is not valid for several reasons.

The data in question are pulled from sources such as the World Terrorism Database (WTD) or Europol's T-Sat report. Anyone who has worked with these data is aware of their limitations. Europol's definition of terrorism varies with each member state, and WTD's definition of terrorism is broad, encompassing sabotage and vandalism. Because of this, firecrackers in a garbage bin in Corsica can end up being equated to the jihadi attacks in Madrid in 2004 which killed 192 and wounded some 2000 others. Thousands of attacks have been attributed to Corsican separatists since the movement emerged in 1975, up until its dissolution in 2014. During this period they have been responsible for the deaths of 40 people. Despite the high number of attacks, we hardly think of Corsican terrorism as a European problem. The same cannot be said for jihadism.

According to data collected by the Norwegian Defence Research Establishment (FFI), jihadis have initiated at least 200 terrorist plots in Western Europe since 1994 (consult the book's appendix for a chronology of planned and executed attacks). More than 65 attacks have been executed, over 600 people have been killed, and thousands have been injured. Moreover, the number of deaths would most probably have been much higher had European security services not paid special attention to jihadism after 9/11. Multiple mass-casualty plots have been foiled, such as the plot to blow up a number of trans-Atlantic jets departing from the UK in 2006.

It is true that European separatist groups such as the Irish Republican Army (IRA) and the Basque separatist group Euskadi Ta Askatasuna (ETA) have killed more people than European-based jihadis, but the former groups have been active for much longer. During the 2000s, al-Qaida posed a much greater threat. Due to hard work, and sometimes pure luck, European security services have prevented a large number of attacks that could have potentially been very lethal.

Separatist groups mostly operate within specific countries, whereas jihadism is a transnational phenomenon affecting all of Europe. Unlike the jihadis, separatists have primarily pointed their arms at representatives and symbols of governments, rather than pursuing mass-casualty attacks against random citizens. Separatists are sometimes also open to taking a seat at the negotiating table, as they usually have demands they need met. Jihadis, on the other hand, pursue ideologically-speaking "maximalist goals". Their ambitions extend beyond existing state boundaries, and they take part in conflicts across multiple countries, making negotiations less feasible.

A comparison with left- or right-wing terrorism is more suitable. Like jihadism, these are ideological and transnational movements. However, important distinctions must be made. European left-wing extremists have, unlike jihadis, rarely targeted random citizens, and have killed relatively few compared to the other European terrorist movements. Left-wing extremism was severely weakened by the end of the Cold War, when the symbolically important ideal of the Soviet Union disappeared, and with it the financial support that left-wing groups had received from the Eastern Bloc. This has hampered mobilization on the far left, although things could change in the future.

As for right-wing extremism, it generally thrives in times of mass migration. Right-wing extremists are a source of substantial levels of violent hate-crime in Europe. With increasing polarization over immigration, right-wing extremism might cause significant societal and political problems in the region in the time to come. At the same time, research has shown that the levels of organized terrorism by right-wing extremists in Europe have actually been decreasing over time.[5] Right-wing extremists have indeed executed lethal terrorist attacks in the region, but they have seldom been as lethal as the mass-killings in Norway in 2011, when a right-wing, anti-Islam extremist bombed a government building in Oslo and went on a shooting spree at a political youth camp on an island outside the capital, killing a total of 78 people. A plausible explanation for this decline in right-wing terrorism is that political representation obtained by anti-immigration parties across Europe has functioned as some sort of safety valve, putting violence on hold. Another, more important explanation, could be that right-wing extremists are not involved in armed conflict in the same way as jihadis. The main source of terrorism is and has always been armed conflict, and terrorists with combat experience are more dangerous than those without.

There should thus be little doubt that jihadism currently constitutes the main terrorist threat to Europe, and there is an acute need to reduce it. The frequent lethal jihadi attacks are currently seriously harming Europe, and contribute to the steadily increasing polarization over immigration issues and the role of Islam in society. In the worst-case scenario, this could develop into political instability and violent conflicts in the region. Jihadism is likely the biggest, most dangerous and durable terrorist threat Europe has ever faced. How can we prevent and counter jihadism and the IS-effect in Europe? The first step towards this is to establish a sound understanding about how and why people join IS's European terrorist campaign.

How do plots occur?

Many look upon IS's terrorism in Europe as new and very different from al-Qaida's. It has been alleged (mostly erroneously) that IS pursues different objectives, attracts different people, and recruits differently. A typical argument is that, while al-Qaida had strategic aims of pressuring European states to abandon their alliance with the U.S., IS only seeks to randomly kill as many people as possible, with a view to polarizing European societies and creating chaos.

There is also a widespread misperception that European IS terrorists are merely criminals and losers, and far less religious than those who worked for al-Qaida. Even an esteemed scholar, Olivier Roy, largely reduces Europe's jihadism phenomenon to a youth revolt in religious disguise, despite ample evidence in this book and elsewhere that religious ideas and political motives shaped the actions of jihadi terrorist cells in the region.[6] Another common misperception is that most of the IS terrorists targeting Europe are "lone wolves", terrorists who act on their own without any interaction with organized networks.

It is problematic to make sweeping generalizations based on incomplete data. If one looks at the evolution of European jihadism over time, and compares IS's terrorist campaign in Europe since 2014 with the historical threat outlined in this book, one will see that not much has changed apart from the growing scope of the threat. The differences between IS and al-Qaida are nearly negligible in Europe. As described earlier, the IS-effect means that networks have grown and the number of attacks has increased, but the core dynamics of recruitment and cell formation remain the same.

Many of the terrorists operating for IS in Europe were until very recently part of al-Qaida-networks. IS by and large want to achieve the same goals as al-Qaida with their attacks in Europe, and there are no fundamental differences in who, and how the groups recruit. The terrorists are recruited via transnational networks and true "lone wolves" are very rare.

In order to explain the escalating threat, many point to failed integration and social discontent. Others argue that the increased threat is a direct consequence of increased immigration. In reality, such factors have limited impact on the emergence of jihadi terrorist cells in Europe, threat levels, or which countries are targeted.

The jihadi terrorist threat in Europe is a transnational phenomenon, and in order to obtain a nuanced and realistic understanding of how terrorist cells emerge, we need to pay attention to the interplay between jihadi networks inside Europe and jihadi groups in conflict zones. The most important element in this interplay is the group of terrorists addressed here as "entrepreneurs"—those who recruit others, build terrorist cells and direct them.

Who are the terrorists?

It is impossible to come up with easy answers as to who the terrorists are and what drives them. There are commonalities among those being recruited, but at the same time there is substantial variation when it comes to their backgrounds and how they are radicalized. This applied to al-Qaida's European networks and is true for IS's networks in the region now.

Research on foreign fighters and terrorists is complicated because of incomplete data and privacy laws that make it difficult to establish databases suitable for sound quantitative research. The scattered and imperfect data indicate that the typical European jihadi is a young Muslim man who is less educated and has a lower-than-average income. There also seems to be an overrepresentation of people with criminal records.[7] Yet, there is substantial variation, both between countries and within countries. For example, criminals and disadvantaged people dominate the French jihadist scene, whereas in the UK, one also finds many students of middle class background among jihadi recruits. Within both al-Qaida and IS networks, whether we are looking at foreign fighters or members of terrorist cells, one will come across young teenagers, men approaching their fifties, women, ethnic European converts, persons from privileged backgrounds, and talented students. And, regardless of whether we are talking about al-Qaida or IS, the most resourceful people (who in theory could have chosen a different path than jihadism) are the ones pulling the strings.

What characterizes the majority of European IS recruits tells us something about who might be susceptible to recruitment. At the same time, there are many exceptions to the typical profile, and the average IS-recruit does not differ from millions of European Muslims who do not resort to terrorism. The mantra of this book has been that terrorist cells in Europe emerge through an intricate interplay between driving forces on different levels, in the Muslim world and in Europe, between group dynamics and personal issues. One driving force we cannot ignore is the effect of Western military interventions.

Interventions matter

When jihadis justify attacks in Europe they usually emphasize two factors: military interventions in Muslim countries and "insults" against Islam and the Prophet Muhammad.[8] The military interventions seem to matter the most. Some also point to the ban on veils, arrests of Muslims (jihadis), and European support for Israel. Moreover, the colonial history of European countries is a recurring topic. As discussed thoroughly in chapter two of this book, the statistics on jihadi plots in Europe since the 1990s show that there are spikes in activity in connection with military interventions in Muslim countries.

The first spike came in 1995, when France was accused of continuing its colonial rule in Algeria by supporting the military regime against the Islamists during the civil war. The al-Qaida-connected Algerian terrorist group GIA, declared war on France and executed a string of attacks in French cities (chapter three). The next spike came after the US-led invasion and occupation of Iraq in 2003. Al-Qaida-affiliated cells bombed commuter trains in Madrid (2004) and the London Tube and a London bus (2005), and multiple (potentially highly lethal) attack plots were thwarted. The third spike in attack activity came with the establishment of IS in 2014.

There were a few terrorist plots linked to ISIS before the announcement of IS in June 2014,[9] but their number increased drastically when the anti-IS coalition was established and began to bomb the group in the fall of 2014. From then on, European countries were part of the anti-IS coalition while thousands of European Muslims joined IS. This was bound to have consequences. IS's leaders have consistently sworn to exact revenge against countries attacking the group, and IS terrorists have shouted "this is for Syria" when they strike in Europe.

The geographical distribution of terrorist plots in Europe over time shows that countries with the heaviest military footprint in the Muslim world, France and Britain, are the most targeted. Conversely, countries with less military involvement in Muslim countries such as Italy and Sweden are less targeted. This is despite the fact that all four of these countries experience high levels of Muslim immigration and that all of them face major challenges with regards to integration. It should also be noted that the last wave of terrorist plots in France actually began before the rise of IS, in the wake of the country's intervention in Mali, which was launched in December 2012.

Another indication that military interventions motivate terrorists is that many plots target military personnel or installations. There have been several attacks on uniformed soldiers in Europe, both by al-Qaida and IS terrorists. Nonetheless, military interventions cannot be the main explanation for the terrorist threat. A large number of Muslims in Europe condemn Western interventions in Muslim countries, but only a very small number resort to terrorism.

Networks matter more

This book has demonstrated that both al-Qaida and IS cells can be traced back to the networks that were established in the region from the early 1990s onwards. As discussed in Chapter One, these networks were set up by veterans of the Afghan Arab foreign fighter movement in the 1980s' Afghan jihad. Their aim was to support jihadis fighting regimes in the Arab-Muslim world with money, weapons, and fighters.

As shown in Chapter One, the UK became the nerve center for these networks, because the most important leaders and ideologues settled there. The networks branched out all over Europe. They grew larger and stronger through the recruitment of young European Muslims and cooperation with jihadis in Algeria, Bosnia, Afghanistan, Pakistan, Somalia, Iraq, Syria and Libya. When al-Qaida declared "global jihad"[10] in 1998, the European jihadi networks became an important weapon against the US's European allies. European jihadis, who travelled as foreign fighters to conflict zones, were recruited and trained by al-Qaida to execute attacks in their home countries. For this reason, the countries in Europe with most foreign fighters have been the most exposed to terrorist plotting. The threat to the UK severely increased in the mid-2000s when al-Qaida in Af-Pak recruited British-Pakistani foreign fighters as terrorists. Sweden experienced its first jihadi suicide bombing in 2010, after militants with longtime residence in Sweden rose to leadership positions in IS's forerunner, al-Qaida in Iraq. The pattern has repeated itself with IS. The primary reason why France has experienced so many attacks since 2014 is that French foreign fighters obtained leadership functions in IS's division for international operations.

The IS-linked terrorist plots in Europe involve the new generation of European jihadis discussed in Chapter Nine. This new generation emanated from within al-Qaida's networks in the region and the al-Muhajiroun movement, and formed new entities under names such as Islam4UK, Sharia4Belgium, Sharia4Holland, Sharia4Spain, Fursan Alizza (France), The Prophet's Umma (Norway), and Kaldet til Islam (Denmark). When IS emerged as the strongest jihadi actor in Syria, members of these networks sided with this group rather than al-Qaida. As noted, the exact reasons why the Europeans preferred IS remain unclear, but it is significant that Anjem Choudary and his Islam4/Sharia4-movement sided with the "Caliphate" when it clashed with al-Qaida in Syria.

There are, however, very close and concrete links between Europe's old al-Qaida networks and new-generation ones. Multiple investigations have shown that experienced veterans of the old networks, most of whom have spent time in conflict zones, function as entrepreneurs—creators of the new terrorist cells made up of young recruits. This pattern of older generations becoming recruiters was also common within al-Qaida's European networks, and is a common feature of the IS-effect on European jihadism.

Entrepreneurs matter most

This book has introduced a typology for analyzing jihadi terrorist cells in Europe, the point being to arrive at a more nuanced and differentiated understanding of how people join terrorist networks. It is also a tool for assessing the relative weight of different drivers. The typology was originally designed for analyses of terrorist cells, but in the simplified form I present here, it also has relevance for the study of extremism more broadly.

The entrepreneurs are the ones who build and direct terrorist cells and recruit their members. They tend to be more resourceful, political and ideological than other terrorists, and function as the link between a cell and groups in conflict zones. They usually go through a lengthier radicalization process than the other cell members, and have typically spent time in conflict zones as foreign fighters. The entrepreneurs are the minority within terrorist networks, but they are the ones in control. They also act as agents for jihadi insurgent groups in conflict zones. Because of them, the terrorist threat inside Europe is more influenced by factors outside the region than most realize.

The misfits are characterized by personal grievances and problems. Here we find youths who have drifted into crime, substance abuse and have become outsiders in society for different reasons. They are lured in by the terrorist cell entrepreneur and his closest associates, who offer them a fresh start, community, spirituality, and a political cause to fight for.

The drifters are the random recruits who do not differ from the vast majority of European Muslims who do not take part in terrorist activities. In this category we find underprivileged people, but also resourceful ones. It is mainly friendship, kinship, or loyalty to someone on the inside that draw them into a cell.

This categorization implies that there are three main pathways to terrorism: the ideological (the entrepreneur), the grievance-based (the misfit) and the social (the drifter). However, given the role of the entrepreneur vis-a-vis the other types, there is a logical hierarchy between the different factors deciding when and where jihadi cells emerge in Europe: 1) there have to be entrepreneurs and networks in place for there to be an attack; 2) the entrepreneur (and the group he represents) must be able to convince recruits (politically and ideologically) of the legality of an attack; and 3) the entrepreneur might also exploit misfits' grievances or drifters' social ties in the construction of a cell.

This pattern has repeated itself throughout the history of European jihadism, from the first attacks in the mid-1990s until the latest attack wave attributed to IS, and it applies to those portrayed as "lone wolves" by the media as well. Because jihadism is rooted in an extreme form of Islam, the terrorists must obtain approval from someone they look upon as a religious authority (an entrepreneur or ideologue) before launching an attack. This requires interaction with other extremists within the networks. Perhaps the most important difference between the al-Qaida threat in the 2000s and the IS threat to Europe since 2014, is that new, encrypted communication apps have made it possible for IS to recruit, convince and train terrorists online, to an extent that al-Qaida never was able to.

IS's solo-terrorists in Europe are therefore rarely the "lone wolves" they tend to be portrayed as. Investigations reveal that they have both physically and virtually interacted with networks. A case in point is that of the solo-terrorist who bombed the Ariana Grande-concert in Manchester. Prior to the attack the perpetrator consulted an IS entrepreneur whom he addressed as "Sheikh", and received the latter's approval. He also frequently travelled to Libya, and allegedly fraternized, and possibly trained, with jihadis there.

Based on what is known so far about the IS attack in Barcelona, the entrepreneur appears to have been the Moroccan Abdelbaki Es Satty. He was considered to be a religious authority by IS supporters, and he recruited Moroccan drifters in Catalonia. The Barcelona cell demonstrates the historical links between today's threat and the networks of the past. Es Satty was reportedly radicalized while spending time in jail, where he was influenced by a member of the terrorist cell that bombed the Madrid commuter trains in 2004. The case resembles that of the cell behind the attacks on Charlie Hebdo and the Jewish supermarket in Paris in January 2015. As discussed in the book's conclusion, the attackers had been influenced by the veteran Algerian jihadi Djamel Beghal, who was part of the GIA's networks in the 1990s, and who supervised a terrorist cell for al-Qaida in 2001, for which he was convicted and jailed. Both in prison, and when he was out on parole in 2010 (before he was rearrested), he continued to inspire young French jihadis, several of whom have plotted attacks for al-Qaida and IS in Europe.

Another possible example of this dynamic occurred in the summer of 2017, when two terrorists were arrested in Wattignies near Lille in France for preparing a terrorist attack. One of them was also suspected of having recruited for IS. The purported terrorists had been in regular contact with the imprisoned jihadi Lionel Dumont, the leader of the GIA spin-off known as the Roubaix Gang, which operated as a terrorist group in France in the mid-1990s (see chapter three). One of the Wattignies plotters had previously occupied the cell next to Dumont's during a stint in prison. During a search of Dumont's prison cell in connection with the Wattignies plot, French security agents confiscated handwritten notes containing references to IS. Dumont said he had received them from the alleged plotters, and denied any involvement whatsoever.[11]

All of the above highlights that, in order to be able to formulate appropriate counter-measures to today's terrorist threat, it is essential to understand how terrorists operate within historically rooted networks, and that people join the networks for different reasons.

How can the threat be reduced?

We currently lack sufficient knowledge about what works and what does not work when it comes to preventing European jihadism. The debates about the rising threat in Europe have mainly revolved around Muslim immigration, failed integration and social exclusion.

Europe no doubt faces major challenges with regards to the integration of Muslims, and as we have seen, social misfits are preyed upon and exploited by terrorist entrepreneurs. Yet, these are not the most important explanations for why terrorist plots occur. Active terrorist cells emerge in countries with high

Muslim immigration (Germany) and low (Finland), in countries with diverging integration policies (UK vs France), and in segregated suburbs (Molenbeek) as well as affluent areas (North Kensington).[12] The cells emerge where entrepreneurs and their networks gain footholds.

Consequently, the most important steps that need to be taken to reduce the threat are to intercept the entrepreneurs, and restrain network connections (online and off-line) between extremists in Europe and groups in conflict zones. As entrepreneurs are relatively resourceful, they hardly become jihadis for lack of different options. They are people with strong religious-political convictions. In an ideal world, the most effective counter-measure would have been to de-radicalize entrepreneurs and channel them into non-violent, democratic forms of activism. Unfortunately, this is unrealistic in many, if not most instances. Their cemented views make it necessary to increase surveillance and police measures targeting them. Concrete measures could include a total ban on all forms of foreign fighter activity, and longer prison sentences for advocating terrorism and terrorist recruitment. European security services need more resources to monitor networks that have grown dramatically after the Arab Spring. It is more important than ever that security services be able to identify the constellations of entrepreneurs, misfits and drifters that could be cells in the making. At the same time, it is also harder than ever to do so. If security services are to monitor and disturb recruitment processes that increasingly happen online via encrypted apps, they will need the necessary authorization and tools to be able to monitor this traffic.

Military action against groups threatening Europe can of course be necessary. However, because interventions in Muslim countries affect the threat level in Europe, they need to occur as little as possible, and harming civilians must be avoided at all costs (which of course must be a goal in itself regardless of how it affects the international terrorist threat). Only then will it become difficult for entrepreneurs to convince recruits that there is a "war on Islam".

Better integration, increased social welfare benefits, and a reduction of socio-economic inequalities will not stop terrorist attacks in Europe. Yet, societies with successful integration and equality can make it harder for terrorists to take advantage of misfits. Such societies will also be better equipped to deal with the effects of attacks when they do take place.

Because misfits are targets of terrorist recruitment, socio-economic measures targeting people subject to recruitment might make the recruiters' job harder. Measures could be anything from helping them to obtain jobs, housing, or medical care. Those working on prevention will need to know who the entrepreneurs are, as well as who they are looking to target. This requires cooperation and information sharing between preventers, the local community, and the families of those in the danger zone.

Drifters are difficult to influence beyond the wider policies of improving integration and social justice. These are, nevertheless, problems that will need to be dealt with to maintain a stable and functioning democracy, and such policies will hardly have a measurable effect on the threat levels. Very few people are needed to cause a great deal of harm, and entrepreneurs will always be able to get their hands on enough people to carry out attacks, if they are allowed to operate as freely as they did in Europe in the 1990s and 2000s.

The threat from transnational jihadism in Europe is unprecedented, and show few signs of abating. With each attack, public frustration and polarization appears to grow considerably. We will probably see more countermeasures with negative side-effects being put in place. Increased surveillance challenges privacy laws. More armed police or military patrols in European cities are measures we would prefer not to see in open and liberal European societies. Yet this is something we probably will have to accept more of in the time to come if we are to reduce the threat level and secure stability in the region.

NOTES

INTRODUCTION

1. See e.g. Alison Pargeter, *The New Frontiers of Jihad: Radical Islam in Europe*, Philadelphia: University of Pennsylvania Press, 2008; Peter R. Neumann, *Joining Al-Qaeda: Jihadist Recruitment in Europe*, Abingdon: Routledge, 2009; Rik Coolsaet, *Jihadi Terrorism and the Radicalisation Challenge: European and American Experiences*, Farnham: Ashgate, 2011; Magnus Ranstorp, *Understanding Violent Radicalisation: Terrorist and Jihadist Movements in Europe*, London: Routledge, 2010; Robert S. Leiken, *Europe's Angry Muslims: The Revolt of the Second Generation*, Oxford: Oxford University Press, 2012; Angel Rabasa and Cheryl Benard, *Eurojihad: Patterns of Islamist Radicalization and Terrorism in Europe*, New York: Cambridge University Press, 2014.

2. See e.g. Michael Taarnby Jensen, "Recruitment of Islamist Terrorists in Europe," Aarhus: Danish Ministry of Justice, 2005; Peter Neumann, "Europe's Jihadist Dilemma," *Survival*, 48, 2 (1 June 2006), pp. 71–84; Anja Dalgaard-Nielsen, "Violent Radicalization in Europe: What We Know and What We Do Not Know," *Studies in Conflict & Terrorism*, 33, 9 (16 Aug. 2010), pp. 797–814; Javier Jordan, "Analysis of Jihadi Terrorism Incidents in Western Europe, 2001–2010," *Studies in Conflict & Terrorism*, 35, 5 (2012), pp. 382–404; Petter Nesser, "Ideologies of Jihad in Europe," *Terrorism and Political Violence*, 23, 2 (2011), pp. 173–200; Jeffrey M. Bale, "Jihadist Cells and 'IED' Capabilities in Europe: Assessing the Present and Future Threat to the West," Strategic Studies Institute, May 2009; Petter Nesser and Anne Stenersen, "The Modus Operandi of Jihadi Terrorists in Europe," *Perspectives on Terrorism*, 8, 6 (2014); Javier Jordan, "The Evolution of the Structure of Jihadist Terrorism in Western Europe: The Case of Spain," *Studies in Conflict & Terrorism*, 37, 8 (3 Aug. 2014), pp. 654–73.

3. See e.g. Albert Benschop, "Chronicle of a Political Murder Foretold: Jihad in the Netherlands," University of Amsterdam, 2005; Fernando Reinares, "The Madrid Bombings and Global Jihadism," *Survival*, 52, 2 (2010), pp. 83–104; Fernando

Reinares, *¡Matadlos!*, Barcelona: Galaxia Gutenberg, 2014; Guido Steinberg, *German Jihad: On the Internationalization of Islamist Terrorism*, New York: Columbia University Press, 2013; Raffaello Pantucci, *"We Love Death as You Love Life": Britain's Suburban Mujahedeen*, London: Hurst, 2015.

4. See Bruce Hoffman, "The Myth of Grass-Roots Terrorism," *Foreign Affairs*, June 2008; Bruce Hoffman and Fernando Reinares, "Al-Qaeda's Continued Core Strategy and Disquieting Leader-Led Trajectory," Madrid: Elcano, 2013.

5. Marc Sageman, *Leaderless Jihad: Terror Networks in the Twenty-First Century*, Philadelphia: University of Pennsylvania Press, 2008.

6. See e.g. Bruce Hoffman, *Inside Terrorism*, New York: Columbia University Press, 2006; Alex Schmid (ed.), *The Routledge Handbook of Terrorism Research*, reprint edn, New York: Routledge, 2013.

7. See e.g. Camille Tawil, *Al-qaida wa akhawatiha, qisat al-jihadiin al-Arab*, Beirut: Dar al-Saqi, 2008; Seth G. Jones, *In the Graveyard of Empires: America's War in Afghanistan*, reprint edn, New York: W.W. Norton, 2010.

8. See e.g. Roel Meijer (ed.), *Global Salafism: Islam's New Religious Movement*, New York: Oxford University Press, 2014, and Stéphane Lacroix, *Awakening Islam: The Politics of Religious Dissent in Contemporary Saudi Arabia*, trans. George Holoch, Cambridge, MA: Harvard University Press, 2011.

9. Brynjar Lia and Thomas Hegghammer, "Jihadi Strategic Studies: The Alleged Al Qaida Policy Study Preceding the Madrid Bombings," *Studies in Conflict & Terrorism*, 27, 5 (1 Sep. 2004), pp. 355–75.

10. For a hierarchical understanding of al-Qaida consult the well-informed blog Long War Journal http://www.longwarjournal.org/. I see the phenomenon as somewhat less hierarchical, more in line with J. M. Berger, "War on Error," *Foreign Policy*, 5 Feb. 2014.

11. Clark McCauley and Sophia Moskalenko, *Friction: How Radicalization Happens to Them and Us*, Oxford: Oxford University Press, 2011. For a critical discussion of terrorists' normalcy, see John Horgan, *The Psychology of Terrorism*, 2nd edn, Abingdon, Oxon: Routledge, 2014.

12. For a historical account of the foreign fighter phenomenon more broadly, see David Malet, *Foreign Fighters: Transnational Identity in Civil Conflicts*, Oxford: Oxford University Press, 2013.

13. Thomas Hegghammer, "Should I Stay or Should I Go? Explaining Variation in Western Jihadists' Choice between Domestic and Foreign Fighting," *American Political Science Review*, 107, 1 (2013), pp. 1–15.

14. Neumann, *Joining Al-Qaeda*.

15. See e.g. Anne Stenersen, "The Internet: A Virtual Training Camp?" *Terrorism and Political Violence*, 20, 2 (9 Apr. 2008), pp. 215–33; Petter Nesser, "How Did Europe's Global Jihadis Obtain Training for their Militant Causes?" *Terrorism and Political Violence*, 20, 2 (2008), pp. 234–56; Rüdiger Lohlker, *New Approaches*

to the Analysis of Jihadism: Online and Offline, Göttingen: Vandenhoeck & Ruprecht, 2011; Andrew Zammit, "Explaining a Turning Point in Australian Jihadism," *Studies in Conflict & Terrorism*, 36, 9 (1 Sep. 2013), pp. 739–55.

16. See Edwin Bakker, "Jihadi Terrorists in Europe," Haag: Clingendael, 2006; Marc Sageman, *Understanding Terror Networks*, Philadelphia: University of Pennsylvania Press, 2004; Sageman, *Leaderless Jihad*.

17. For an excellent theorization of radicalization, see Quintan Wiktorowicz, *Radical Islam Rising: Muslim Extremism in the West*, Lanham, MD: Rowman & Littlefield, 2005. For reviews of the literature, see Anja Dalgaard-Nielsen, "Violent Radicalization in Europe: What We Know and What We Do Not Know," *Studies in Conflict & Terrorism*, 33, 9 (2010), pp. 797–814; McCauley and Moskalenko, *Friction*; Peter R. Neumann, "The Trouble with Radicalization," *International Affairs*, 89, 4 (1 July 2013), pp. 873–93.

18. See Emmanuel Karagiannis, "European Converts to Islam: Mechanisms of Radicalization," *Politics, Religion & Ideology*, 13, 1 (2012), pp. 99–113.

19. Sageman, *Understanding Terror Networks*.

20. For a similar classification see "Våldsbejakande Islamistisk Extremism i Sverige," Säpo, 2010. The report categorized 200 Swedish extremists into four types: (1) the person who is "acting out" in opposition to the social surroundings (resembling my misfit); (2) the contemplator (resembling my entrepreneur); (3) the person who joins through family connections; and (4) the contact-seeker (the latter two paralleling my misfits and drifters). The difference between the model is that the latter is more detailed and inter-relational, and designed to capture cell dynamics and links to international networks.

21. See e.g. Alexander L. George and Andrew Bennett, *Case Studies and Theory Development in the Social Sciences*, Cambridge, MA: MIT Press, 2005.

1. FROM AFGHANISTAN TO EUROPE

1. See e.g. Olivier Roy, *Islam and Resistance in Afghanistan*, Cambridge: Cambridge University Press, 1990; Barnett R. Rubin, *The Fragmentation of Afghanistan: State Formation and Collapse in the International System*, New Haven, CT: Yale University Press, 2002; Seth G. Jones, *In the Graveyard of Empires: America's War in Afghanistan*, New York: W.W. Norton, 2010.

2. Gilles Kepel, *Muslim Extremism in Egypt: The Prophet and Pharaoh*, Berkeley: University of California Press, 2003.

3. Thomas Hegghammer and Stéphane Lacroix, *The Meccan Rebellion: The Story of Juhayman Al-'Utaybi Revisited*, Bristol: Amal Press, 2011.

4. Camille al-Tawil, *Al-jama'a al-musallaha fi al-jazair*, Beirut: Dar al-Nahar, 1998.

5. Brynjar Lia, *Architect of Global Jihad: The Life of Al-Qaeda Strategist Abu Mus'ab Al-Suri*, New York: Oxford University Press, 2009.

6. See e.g. Robert D. Kaplan, *Soldiers of God: With Islamic Warriors in Afghanistan and Pakistan*, New York: Vintage, 2001.

7. For an overview of young Saudis' motives for going, see Thomas Hegghammer, *Jihad in Saudi Arabia: Violence and Pan-Islamism since 1979*, Cambridge: Cambridge University Press, 2010.

8. Tawil, *Al-qaida wa akhawatiha*, pp. 13 ff. and Omar Saghi, Thomas Hegghammer and Stéphane Lacroix, *Al Qaeda in Its Own Words*, ed. Gilles Kepel and Jean-Pierre Milelli, trans. Pascale Ghazaleh, Cambridge, MA: Belknap Press, 2010.

9. Tawil, *Al-qaida wa akhawatiha*, pp. 30 ff.

10. For example, one Algerian recruited by Azzam, Qari Said, first fought with Afghan warlords, then joined MAK and subsequently al-Qaida before he was sent back to Algeria with money to set up a jihad group and became co-founder of the GIA, see Tawil, *Al-qaida wa akhawatiha*, pp. 105 ff. and Chapter Three of this book. Many Algerian and Egyptian "Afghans" became involved in terrorist plots in Europe.

11. The camp started out with twelve trainees, increased to twenty-five in 1985 and had around 200 fighters in 1986, see ibid., p. 17.

12. For an account of the battle, see Bergen, *The Osama Bin Laden I Know*, pp. 53 ff. and Tawil, *Al-qaida wa akhawatiha*, pp. 18–19.

13. Bergen, *The Osama Bin Laden I Know*, pp. 74 ff. and Tawil, *Al-qaida wa akhawatiha*, pp. 30 ff.

14. For an informed analysis of al-Qaida's ideology and praxis see e.g. Jarret M. Brachman, *Global Jihadism: Theory and Practice*, London: Routledge, 2008.

15. National Commission on Terrorist Attacks, *The 9/11 Commission Report*, New York: W.W. Norton, 2004, p. 56.

16. Based on Anne Stenersen, "Overview of Al-Qaida Leaders and Facilitators of External Operations," 2012 (on file with author); Rohan Gunaratna and Anders Nielsen, "Al Qaeda in the Tribal Areas of Pakistan and Beyond," *Studies in Conflict and Terrorism*, 31, 9 (1 Sep. 2008), pp. 775–807; Leah Farrall, "Al-Qaeda: The Evolution of Command and Control," Jane's Strategic Advisory Services, Nov. 2009; Duncan Gardham, "Al-Qaeda's 'International Operations Wing,'" *Telegraph*, 7 Jan. 2011 and interview with European security official, Jan. 2015.

17. Seth G. Jones, "Al Qaeda in Iran," *Foreign Affairs*, 29 Jan. 2012.

18. Bruce Hoffman and Fernando Reinares (eds), *The Evolution of the Global Terrorist Threat: From 9/11 to Osama Bin Laden's Death*, New York: Columbia University Press, 2014, pp. 29 ff.

19. See e.g. Jason Burke, *Al-Qaeda: The True Story of Radical Islam*, London: Penguin, 2007.

20. Tawil, *Al-qaida wa akhawatiha*, pp. 46 ff.

21. Anne Stenersen, *Al-Qaida's Quest for Weapons of Mass Destruction: The History behind the Hype*, Saarbrücken: VDM Verlag Dr Müller, 2008.

22. *The 9/11 Commission Report*, p. 500, n. 5 (Chapter 6).

23. Gunaratna and Nielsen, "Al Qaeda in the Tribal Areas of Pakistan and Beyond."

24. Saif al-Adel, "Al-sira al-jihadiyya li al-qaid al-dabah abi musab al-zarqawi," GIMF, 2007.

25. Omar bin Laden, Najwa bin Laden and Jean Sasson, *Growing up Bin Laden: Osama's Wife and Son Take us Inside their Secret World*, New York: St. Martin's Press, 2009, p. 128.

26. *The 9/11 Commission Report*, p. 58, and lecture by CTC's Vahid Brown at conference in Oslo 19–21 Mar. 2009.

27. Emerson Vermaat, "Bin Laden's Terror Networks in Europe," Mackenzie Institute, 2002.

28. See Alex Strick van Linschoten and Felix Kuehn, *An Enemy We Created: The Myth of the Taliban–Al Qaeda Merger in Afghanistan*, New York: Oxford University Press, 2014; Anne Stenersen, *Brothers in Jihad: The Alliance between Al-Qaida and the Taliban*, New York: Cambridge University Press, forthcoming, 2016.

29. Gunaratna and Nielsen, "Al Qaeda in the Tribal Areas of Pakistan and Beyond." For a study of the Haqqani network see Vahid Brown and Don Rassler, *Fountainhead of Jihad: The Haqqani Nexus, 1973–2012*, Oxford: Oxford University Press, 2013.

30. Al-Adel, "Al-sira al-jihadiyya li al-qaid al-dabah abi musab al-zarqawi."

31. For a good overview of al-Qaida's alliancing with Arab groups after 2001 consult Camille Tawil, "Al-wajh al-akhar li al-qaida," *Al-Hayat*, 25 Sep. 2010.

32. See e.g. Mohammed Hafez, *Suicide Bombers in Iraq: The Strategy and Ideology of Martyrdom*, Washington, DC: United States Institute of Peace, 2007, pp. 189 ff.

33. Brachman, *Global Jihadism*, and Meijer, *Global Salafism*, pp. 22 ff.

34. "Minbar al-tawhid wa al-jihad," 22 Jan. 2015, http://www.tawhed.ws/.

35. Houriya Ahmed and Hannah Stuart, "Hizb ut-Tahrir: Ideology and Strategy," The Centre for Social Cohesion, 2009, p. 27.

36. Manuel Torres Soriano, "Spain as an Object of Jihadist Propaganda," *Studies in Conflict & Terrorism*, 32, 11 (30 Oct. 2009), pp. 933–52.

37. Manuel Torres Soriano, "The Road to Media Jihad: The Propaganda Actions of Al Qaeda in the Islamic Maghreb," *Terrorism and Political Violence*, 23, 1 (7 Dec. 2010), pp. 72–88.

38. Nesser, "Ideologies of Jihad in Europe."

39. Ibid. See also "Anwar al Awlaki: 44 Ways of Supporting Jihad," KavkazCenter, 2009, http://www.kavkazcenter.com/eng/content/2009/02/16/10561.shtml (accessed 15 Jan. 2015).

40. Nesser, "Ideologies of Jihad in Europe."

41. See Andrew Geddes, *The Politics of Migration and Immigration in Europe*, 1st edn, London: Sage, 2003; Rabasa and Benard, *Eurojihad*, pp. 8 ff.

42. Ed Husain, *The Islamist: Why I Became an Islamic Fundamentalist, What I Saw*

Inside, and Why I Left, New York: Penguin, 2009, pp. 19 ff.; James Brandon, "British Universities Continue to Breed Extremists," *CTC Sentinel*, 4, 1 (2011).

43. Gilles Kepel, *Allah in the West: Islamic Movements in America and Europe*, Stanford: Stanford University Press, 1997.

44. Quintan Wiktorowicz, "Anatomy of the Salafi Movement," *Studies in Conflict & Terrorism*, 29, 3 (1 May 2006), pp. 207–39.

45. See description of moral policing by the Beghal network in Martin Bright et al., "The Secret War," *Guardian*, 30 Sep. 30, 2001 and Chapter Four. Many members of the cells analyzed in this book practiced *hisba* against family, friends, their communities or others they saw as violating the moral codes of Islam.

46. Lia, *Architect of Global Jihad*.

47. Umar Abd al-Hakim, "Mukhtasar shahadati ala al-jihad fi al-jazair," Silsila al-Zahirin ala al-Haqq, 2004, p. 27 (on file with author).

48. Ibid.

49. Ibid., p. 21.

50. Ibid.

51. *The 9/11 Commission Report*; Brynjar Lia and Åshild Kjøk, "Islamist Insurgencies, Diasporic Support Networks, and their Host States: The Case of the Algerian GIA in Europe *1993–2000*," Kjeller: FFI, 2001; Sean O'Neill and Daniel McGrory, *The Suicide Factory: Abu Hamza and the Finsbury Park Mosque*, London: Harper Perennial, 2010.

52. Omar Nasiri, *Inside the Jihad: My Life with Al Qaeda*, New York: Basic Books, 2008, p. 283.

53. Dominique Thomas, *Le Londonistan: La Voix du djihad*, Paris: Michalon, 2003.

54. "'I Will Be a Martyr'—This is How the Islamists in Handcuffs Speak," *Il Nuovo*, via FBIS, 5 Dec. 2003.

55. Lorenzo Vidino and Steven Emerson, *Al Qaeda in Europe: The New Battleground of International Jihad*, New York: Prometheus Books, 2005.

56. Al-Hakim, "Shahadati ala al-jihad fi al-jazair," p. 23.

57. Evan Kohlmann, *Al-Qaida's Jihad in Europe—Afghan–Bosnian Network*, New York: Berg, 2004. See also Bjorkman in Ranstorp, *Understanding Violent Radicalisation*, pp. 231 ff.

58. Reinares, *¡Matadlos!*.

59. Nick Fielding and Yosri Fouda, *Masterminds of Terror*, Edinburgh: Mainstream, 2011. See also Peter Finn, "Hamburg's Cauldron of Terror," *Washington Post*, 11 Sep. 2002.

60. Rik Coolsaet and Tanguy Struye de Swielande, "Belgium and Counterterrorism Policy in the Jihadi Era (1986–2007)," Policy Paper, Egmont, 2007.

61. Benschop, "Chronicle of a Political Murder Foretold".

62. Morten Skjoldager, *Truslen Indefra—De Danske Terrorister*, Copenhagen: Lindhardt og Ringhof, 2009.

63. "Våldsbejakande Islamistisk Extremism i Sverige"; Lars Akerhaug, *Norsk Jihad* (Kagge Forlag, 2013); Brynjar Lia and Petter Nesser, *Militant Islamism in Norway: From Expat Politics to Violent Activism* (forthcoming book, 2016).

64. The biography of Qatada is taken from Petter Nesser, "Abū Qatāda and Palestine," *Die Welt Des Islams*, 53, 3–4 (1 Jan. 2013), pp. 416–48. For a broader analysis of his ideology see Mohammed Abu Rumman and Hassan Abu Hanieh, *The Jihadi Salafist Movement in Jordan after Zarqawi: Identity, Leadership Crisis and Obscured Vision*, Amman: Friedrich-Ebert-Stiftung, 2009. I have also gleaned insights from Abu Musab al-Suri's account of his interaction with Qatada in London, see al-Hakim, "Shahadati ala al-jihad fi al-jazair."

65. Interview with Dominique Thomas, author of *Le Londonistan*, Mar. 2008.

66. Al-Hakim, "Shahadati ala al-jihad fi al-jazair"; Lia, *Architect of Global Jihad*, p. 158.

67. The biography is based upon O'Neill and McGrory, *The Suicide Factory*.

68. "Abu Hamza and the Islamic Army; Day by Day; A Chronology of Events Surrounding the 'Bomb Plot' and Kidnapping," *Al-Baab*, 1999.

69. Benjamin Weiser, "Life Sentence for British Cleric Who Helped Plan 1998 Kidnappings in Yemen," *The New York Times*, 9 Jan. 2015.

70. The biography is based on Wiktorowicz, *Radical Islam Rising*; Mahan Abedin, "Al-Muhajiroun in the UK: An Interview with Sheikh Omar Bakri Mohammed," *Spotlight on Terror*, 2, 5 (25 May 2005); Nick Lowles and Joe Mulhall, "The Gateway to Terror: Anjem Choudary and the Al-Muhajiroun Network," London: Hope not Hate, 2014 and Omar Bakri Mohammed, *The World Is Divided into Two Camps ... Daar Ul-Kufr and Daar Ul-Islaam*, London: Ad-Da'wah Publications, 2004.

71. Mohammed, *The World Is Divided into Two Camps*, p. 7.

72. The sources do not carify whether or not Bakri had his PhD from Saudi Arabia formally approved.

73. Nasiri, *Inside the Jihad*, p. 273.

74. Lowles and Mulhall, "The Gateway to Terror."

75. Ibid.

76. Nasiri, *Inside the Jihad*, pp. 266, 280 ff.

77. See e.g. "Radd al-shaykh abi qatada ala al-qardawi," YouTube, 22 Apr. 2008, https://www.youtube.com/watch?v=CCnwgYAU-W4 (accessed 20 Jan. 2015).

78. See e.g. Abu Hamza, "How to Live Islamically in the Land of the Kuffar," Hesba, 1999 (on file with author).

79. Interview with Sean O'Neill, co-author of *The Suicide Factory*, Apr. 2008.

80. O'Neill and McGrory, *The Suicide Factory*, 85.

81. "Supporters of Shariah Online," 2003, http://www.geocities.com/suporters_of_sharia/; Supporters of Shariah newsletters, June 1998 through March 2000 (on file with author).

82. See, for example, the cleric's humorous lecture on toilet etiquette, Omar Bakri,

"Adab of Visiting the Toilet 00 by Shaikh Omar Bakri Muhammad" (Salafimedia. com via YouTube, 9 Dec. 2010), http://www.youtube.com/watch?v=4oauvRFywpc (accessed Jan. 2011).

83. Wiktorowicz, *Radical Islam Rising*, pp. 85 ff.

84. See discussion on whether Omar Bakri Mohammed is a spy or not at Expergefactionist, "Azzam Publication's Statement about O. Bakri," Islamic Awakening Forum, 16 May 2005, http://forums.islamicawakening.com/f20/ azzam-publications-statement-about-o-bakri-467/ (accessed 8 Feb. 2015).

85. Nasiri, *Inside the Jihad*, 106.

86. For a study of subcultural features of jihadism, see Thomas Hegghammer (ed.), *Jihad Culture*, Cambridge: Cambridge University Press, forthcoming. See also discussion of Salafi-jihadis' construction of an imagined community and political imageries online in Frazer Egerton, *Jihad in the West: The Rise of Militant Salafism*, Cambridge: Cambridge University Press, 2011.

87. E.g. "MMS Sheikh Abu Hamza" (Internet Archive), https://archive.org/details/ mms-shaykh-abu-hamza?start=179.5 (accessed 26 Jan. 2015).

88. Dar al-Islam is also referred to as Dar al-Salam (the abode of peace), whereas Dar al-Kufr is referred to as Dar al-Aman (the abode of safety) when covenants are in place, and Dar al-Harb (the abode of war) or Dar al-Jihad (the abode of jihad) when covenants are broken. For an exposition of the principles by a jihadi living in the West, see Omar Bakri Mohammed, *The World Is Divided into Two Camps ... Daar Ul-Kufr and Daar Ul-Islaam*, London: Ad-Da'wah Publications, 2004. See also Omar Bakri Mohammed, "Covenant of Security" (Salafimedia.com via YouTube, 10 Dec. 2010), https://web.archive.org/web/20110226072355/http:// www.youtube.com/watch?v=lpln7DhStto (accessed 15 Jan. 2015).

89. Mohammed, "Covenant of Security."

90. Osama bin Laden, "O People of Islam," Al-Sahab, 2006 (on file with author).

91. James Brandon, "Virtual Caliphate: Islamic Extremists & Their Websites," London: Center for Social Cohesion, 2008, p. 93.

92. Mohammed, *The World Is Divided into Two Camps*, p. 67.

93. Sean O'Neill and Yaakov Lappin, "Britain's Online Imam Declares War as he Calls Young to Jihad," *Times*, 17 Jan. 2005. The statement read "I believe the whole of Britain has become Dar ul-Harb ... the kuffar has no sanctity for their own life or property ..." and he urged his followers to join jihad "wherever you are." He added that "Al Qaeda and all its branches and organisations of the world, that is the victorious group and they have the emir and you are obliged to join. There is no need ... to mess about."

94. Newsnight, BBC, 1 Aug. 2005.

95. Abu Qatada, "Iman Series," 2008, http://freepdfs.net/iman-series-kalamullahco m/9943b703a50cdbf23b8fc8068200834b/ (accessed 8 Feb. 2015).

96. Jamil El-Banna et al. vs George W. Bush President of the United States et al., United States District Court of Colombia, 2004.

97. Hamza, "How to Live Islamically in the Land of the Kuffar."
98. "Islamic Ruling on the Covenant of Security with Kuffar by Shaikh Abdullah Faisal" (al-Ghurabaa via YouTube, 31 May 2013), https://www.youtube.com/watch?v=srF8r_LB4gg (accessed 12 January 2015).
99. Dr Fadl, "Tarshid al-jihad fi misr wa al-alam," *Al-Jarida*, 8 Mar. 2007.
100. Ayman al-Zawahiri, *The Exoneration—Chapter 7: The Visa and the Safe-Conduct (Aman)*, At-Tibyan, 2008.
101. Ibid.
102. Ayman al-Zawahiri, "The Open Meeting with Shaykh Ayman Al-Zawahiri Part One," Al-Sahab Media Production, 2008.
103. See e.g. Anthony F. Lemieux et al., "*Inspire* Magazine: A Critical Analysis of its Significance and Potential Impact through the Lens of the Information, Motivation, and Behavioral Skills Model," *Terrorism and Political Violence*, 26, 2 (1 Apr. 2014). The story of al-Awlaki is told in Jeremy Scahill, *Dirty Wars: The World is a Battlefield*, New York: Nation Books, 2013.

2. SCOPE AND MODUS OPERANDI

1. The chapter is primarily based upon and uses text from an article I co-authored with Anne Stenersen, see Nesser and Stenersen, "The Modus Operandi of Jihadi Terrorists in Europe" (with permission from Stenersen). For other studies of the modus operandi of jihadi terrorists in Europe, see e.g. Jeffrey M. Bale, "Jihadist Cells and 'IED' Capabilities in Europe: Assessing the Present and Future Threat to the West," Strategic Studies Institute, May 2009; Teun van Dongen, "The Lengths Terrorists Go To: Perpetrator Characteristics and the Complexity of Jihadist Terrorist Attacks in Europe, 2004–2011," *Behavioral Sciences of Terrorism and Political Aggression*, 6, 1 (2014), pp. 58–80.
2. Emilie Oftedal, "The Financing of Jihadi Terrorist Cells in Europe," Kjeller: FFI, 2015.
3. The table includes both well-documented (C1 and C2) plots and vague incidents (C3).
4. Thomas Hegghammer, "Global Jihadism After the Iraq War," *The Middle East Journal*, 60, 1 (1 Jan. 2006), pp. 11–32.
5. "Youtube.com Og Facebook.com—De Nye Radikaliseringsværktøjer," Copenhagen: CTA, 2010.
6. "Al-Qaeda Threatens France with Revenge over Burka Stance," *Telegraph*, 1 July 2009.
7. Nesser and Stenersen, "The Modus Operandi of Jihadi Terrorists in Europe," p. 3.
8. Such an approach resembles, to some extent, what Neumann and Smith refer to as "strategic terrorism," which implies that terrorist groups will eventually shift away from indiscriminate violence and move towards activities designed to boost the group's legitimacy, consult Peter R. Neumann and M.L.R. Smith, "Strategic

Terrorism: The Framework and its Fallacies," *Journal of Strategic Studies*, 28, 4 (Aug. 2005), pp. 571–95.

9. Nesser and Stenersen, "The Modus Operandi of Jihadi Terrorists in Europe," p. 11.

10. Anne Stenersen, *Al-Qaida's Quest for Weapons of Mass Destruction: The History behind the Hype*, Saarbrücken: VDM Verlag Dr Müller, 2008.

11. "Exclusif—Transcription Des Conversations Entre Mohamed Merah et Les Négociateurs," *Libération*, 17 July 2012.

12. Terrorism research has shown how terrorists tend to emulate each other, a phenomenon accelerating in the age of social media, see e.g. Midlarsky et al., "Why Violence Spreads," *International Studies Quarterly*, 24, 2 (June 1980), pp. 262–98; Alex P. Schmid and Janny de Graaf, *Violence and Communication: Insurgent Terrorism and the Western News Media*, London: Sage, 1982; Brigitte L. Nacos, "Revisiting the Contagion Hypothesis: Terrorism, News Coverage, and Copycat Attacks," *Perspectives on Terrorism*, 3, 3 (2009).

13. Brynjar Lia, *Globalisation and the Future of Terrorism: Patterns and Predictions*, London: Routledge, 2007, p. 13. For studies of terrorists' target selection, see also C.J.M. Drake, *Terrorists' Target Selection*, New York: St. Martin's Press, 1998; Adam Dolnik, *Understanding Terrorist Innovation: Technology, Tactics and Global Trends*, London: Routledge, 2009.

14. "Qualities of an Urban Assassin," *Inspire*, 9 (Winter 2012), p. 37.

15. Helen Davidson, "ISIS Instructs Followers to Kill Australians and Other 'Disbelievers,'" *Guardian*, 23 Sep. 2014.

16. Nesser and Stenersen, "The Modus Operandi of Jihadi Terrorists in Europe," p. 10.

17. "Qualities of an Urban Assassin," *Inspire*, 2 (2010), pp. 53–7.

18. Oftedal, "The Financing of Jihadi Terrorist Cells in Europe".

19. Anne Stenersen and Petter Nesser, "Jihadism in Western Europe Dataset," Kjeller: FFI, 2015.

3. THE ALGERIA FACTOR (1994–2000)

1. See e.g. John Phillips and Martin Evans, *Algeria: Anger of the Dispossessed*, London: Yale University Press, 2008; Shapiro in Martha Crenshaw (ed.), *The Consequences of Counterterrorism*, New York: Russell Sage Foundation, 2010, pp. 255 ff.

2. See e.g. Luis Martinez and John Entelis, *The Algerian Civil War*, New York: Columbia University Press, 2000; Hugh Roberts, *The Battlefield: Algeria 1988–2002, Studies in a Broken Polity*, London and New York: Verso, 2003. Roberts also highlights the role of Algerian guerilla traditions, see "Logics of Jihadist Violence in North Africa," in *Jihadi Terrorism and the Radicalization Challenge in Europe*.

3. See e.g. Charles-Robert Ageron and Michael Brett, *Modern Algeria: A History from 1830 to the Present*, Trenton, NJ: Africa World Press, 1992.

4. Ray Takeyh, "Islamism in Algeria: A Struggle between Hope and Agony," *Middle East Policy*, 10, 2 (2003), pp. 62–75.

5. Tawil, *Al-jamaa al-musallaha fi al-jazair*, pp. 54 ff.

6. Ibid., pp. 18 ff.

7. Lia and Kjøk, "Islamist Insurgencies, Diasporic Support Networks, and their Host States," 20.

8. Kepel, *Allah in the West*, 192.

9. Tawil, *Al-qaida wa akhawatiha*, p. 112.

10. Lawrence Wright, *The Looming Tower: Al-Qaeda and the Road to 9/11*, New York: Vintage, 2007, p. 189.

11. Tawil, *Al-qaida wa akhawatiha*, p. 99.

12. Tawil, *Al-jamaa al-musallaha fi al-jazair*, pp. 66–7.

13. Tawil, *Al-qaida wa akhawatiha*, p. 112.

14. Verdict against Benahmed et al. (Tribunal de Grande Instance Paris, 2006). The verdict describes activities at a guesthouse for Algerians in Peshawar and the Khalden camp administered by GIA-members and al-Qaida affiliates Montaz, Abu Jaffar, Abu Doha and Rachid Ramda who was one of the entrepreneurs of the attacks in France.

15. Noureddine Jebnoun, "Is the Maghreb the "Next Afghanistan"? Mapping the Radicalization of the Algerian Salafi Jihadist Movement," Washington, DC: Georgetown University, 2007.

16. For discussions of networks in Maghreb consult Tawil, *Al-jamaa al-musallaha fi al-jazair*. For networks in Europe see Coolsaet and Struye de Swielande, "Belgium and Counterterrorism Policy in the Jihadi Era (1986–2007)" and Lia and Kjøk, "Islamist Insurgencies, Diasporic Support Networks, and their Host States" (e.g. the depiction of the "Chalabi-network," p. 32). For a fascinating (alleged) insider account, see Nasiri, *Inside the Jihad*, pp. 3 ff. See also Richard J. Chasdi, *Tapestry of Terror: A Portrait of Middle East Terrorism, 1994–1999*, Boston: Lexington Books, 2002.

17. See interview with GIA recruiter in Peter Taylor, "The Third World War: Al-Qaida, the Breeding Ground," BBC, 2004.

18. E.g. a website called ISLAMREPORT run by GIA supporters in the United States (American Islamic Group).

19. Tawil, *Al-jamaa al-musallaha fi al-jazair*, p. 76.

20. Ibid., p. 123.

21. Camille Tawil, "Lakhdaria Emir Reveals Secrets and Internal Liquidations of the Mountain, GIA Emir was Accused of Becoming Shiite after Some Elements Received Training in Lebanon—Part III," *Al-Hayat*, 13 June 2007.

22. Ibid., and Tawil, *Al-qaida wa akhawatiha*, p. 201.

23. GIA ideology can be read from its magazines *al-Shahada* and *al-Ansar*, and a booklet by Djamel Zitouni entitled *Hidaiyyat rabb al-alamin*. For an outline of the main ideas of this book consult Tawil, *Al-jamaa al-musallaha fi al-jazair*, p. 216.

24. Al-Hakim, "Shahadati ala al-jihad fi al-jazair," p. 22.

25. Abu Abdulrahman Amin, "Open Letter to all Muslims" (ISLAMREPORT, American Islamic Group, 1995).

26. Tawil, *Al-qaida wa akhawatiha*, p. 201.

27. See e.g. Thomas Sancton, "Anatomy of a Hijack," *Time*, 24 June 2001. The hijackers handed out money to the passengers, something which was interpreted as a sign they were on a martyrdom mission; author's interview with European security official, Mar. 2009.

28. Lia and Kjøk, "Islamist Insurgencies, Diasporic Support Networks, and Their Host States".

29. Nick Fraser, "How to Kill an Arab," *Critical Quarterly*, 40, 3 (1998), p. 16.

30. "Off the Rails: The 1995 Attempted Derailing of the French TGV (High-Speed Train) and a Quantitative Analysis of 181 Rail Sabotage Attempts," Washington: Mineta Transportation Institute (MTI), 2010.

31. Robert Pape, *Dying to Win: The Strategic Logic of Suicide Terrorism*, New York: Random House, 2005. Algerian jihadis (GIA/GSPC/AQIM) rarely employed suicide attacks as a tactic before GSPC joined al-Qaida in 2007, see Hanna Rogan, "Violent Trends in Algeria Since 9/11," *CTC Sentinel*, 1, 12 (2008).

32. "The Armed Islamic Group Communiqué on the Algiers Martyrdom Operation" (ISLAMREPORT (American Islamic Group), 25 Feb. 1995).

33. For an account of the overall social profile of the network consult "Off the Rails", pp. 7 ff.

34. Hassane Zerrouky, "Attentats de 1995: Comment Le GIA a Tissé Sa Toile," *l'Humanité*, 1 June 2009.

35. Nasiri, *Inside the Jihad*, p. 39.

36. Patricia Tourancheau, "'La Révolution Était Une Obligation Religieuse,'" *Libération*, 1 Oct. 2007.

37. Consult Tawil, *Al-qaida wa akhawatiha*, pp. 69, 123 and al-Hakim, "Shahadati ala al-jihad fi al-jazair," p. 30.

38. Jason Bennetto, "Paris Bombs 'Planned in London,'" *The Independent*, 4 Nov. 1995.

39. Zerrouky, "Attentats de 1995: Comment Le GIA a Tissé Sa Toile."

40. "Safé Bourada, L'un Des Chefs Des Attentats de 1995," *Libération*, 27 Sep. 2005.

41. Fraser, "How to Kill an Arab," p. 6.

42. The network consisted of three cells: (1) the Chasse-sur-Rhône logistics cell composed of Safe Bourada, David V., Joseph J., Said D., Said Y., Slimane R. and Touami M.; (2) the Vaulx-en-Velin operative terrorist cell composed of Khaled Kelkal, Karim Koussa, Farid Mellouk, Abdelkader B. and Nasredinne S.; and (3) the Lille logistics cell composed of Smaïn Aït Ali Belkacem, Mohamed Drici, Ali ben Fattoum, Adelkader M. and Neji N.

43. Zerrouky, "Attentats de 1995: Comment Le GIA a Tissé Sa Toile."

44. Ibid.

45. Fraser, "How to Kill an Arab."

46. Bruce Crumley, "Terror Takes The Stand," *Time*, 6 Oct. 2002.

47. Al-Tawil, *Al-jama'a al-musallaha fi al-jazair*, p. 162.

48. Abu Abdulrahman Amin, "Open Letter to All Muslims" (ISLAMREPORT (American Islamic Group), 16 Jan. 1995). Interestingly, the terrorists who attacked and took hostages at a British-Norwegian gas facility in in Amenas, Algeria, in 2013 also called themselves "Those Who Sign in Blood." The group was led by Mokhtar Belmokhtar an ex-GIA, AQIM-leader who formed his own group, see Myra MacDonald, "Insight: In Amenas Attack Brings Global Jihad Home to Algeria," *Reuters*, 24 Jan. 2013.

49. Al-Tawil, *Al-jama'a al-musallaha fi al-jazair*, p. 196.

50. Alan Riding, "The Militant Group Behind the Hijacking," *The New York Times*, 27 Dec. 1994.

51. Al-Tawil, *Al-jama'a al-musallaha fi al-jazair*, p. 195.

52. Abu Abdulrahman Amin, "Min amir al-jama'a al-musallaha abi abd al-rahman amin ila rais faransa Jacques Chirac," *Al-Ansar*, 118 (12 Oct. 1995), pp. 7–8.

53. "Algerian Rebels Claim Planting Bombs in France," *Los Angeles Times*, 8 Oct. 1995.

54. Amin, "Open Letter to All Muslims," 16 Jan. 1995.

55. James Phillips, "The Rising Threat of Revolutionary Islam in Algeria," The Heritage Foundation, 9 Nov. 1995.

56. Omar Ashour, "Islamist De-Radicalization in Algeria: Successes and Failures," *The Middle East Policy Brief*, 21 (Nov. 2008).

57. Tawil, "Emir Reveals Secrets."

58. "Faransa, ila ayna al-mufarr," *Al-Ansar*, 118 (12 Oct. 1995), p. 9.

59. As quoted in Lia, *Architect of Global Jihad*, p. 156.

60. Abu Hamza, *Khawaarij & Jihad*, Birmingham: Makhtabah Al-Ansar, 2000, p. 153.

61. Ibid., p. 152.

62. Fraser, "How to Kill an Arab," p. 7.

63. Ibid.

64. Hal Bernton, "The Terrorist Within; the Story Behind One Man's Holy War against America," *Seattle Times*, 23 July 2002.

65. Norimitsu Onishi, "Japan Arrests 5 Who Knew Man Possibly Tied to Qaeda," *The New York Times*, 27 May 2004.

66. A list of passionate tributes to Ramda from a fellow prisoner published by the website Cageprisoners included a "who's who" of UK-based jihadis convicted of terrorist offences in Europe and internationally, consult "Statements on Rachid Ramda from Prison" (Cageprisoners, 2006), http://old.cageprisoners.com/articles.php?id=7500 (accessed 15 Jan. 2015).

67. Sebastian Rotella, "The Enemies in Their Midst," *Times*, 5 Sep. 2006.

68. Coolsaet and Struye de Swielande, "Belgium and Counterterrorism Policy in the Jihadi Era," p. 2.

69. Tawil, *Al-qaida wa akhawatiha*, p. 244.

70. "Islamism, Violence and Reform in Algeria: Turning the Page (Islamism in North Africa III)," International Crisis Group, 30 July 2004.

71. Interview with European security official, March, 2009.

72. Jean-Pierre Filiu, "The Local and Global Jihad of Al-Qa'ida in the Islamic Maghrib," *The Middle East Journal*, 63, 2 (2009), pp. 213–26.

4. TOWARDS GLOBAL JIHAD IN EUROPE (2000–3)

1. Simon Reeve, *The New Jackals: Ramzi Yousef, Osama Bin Laden, and the Future of Terrorism*, Boston: Northeastern, 1999.

2. "Nass bayan al-jabha al-islamiyyaa al-alamiyya li al-jihad ala yahud wa al-salibiyin," *Al-Quds Al-Arabi*, 23 Feb. 1998.

3. Reeve, *The New Jackals*.

4. Pervez Musharraf, *In the Line of Fire: A Memoir*, New York: Free Press, 2008, p. 239.

5. *The 9/11 Commission Report*, p. 191.

6. Musharraf, *In the Line of Fire*, p. 149.

7. *The 9/11 Commission Report*, p. 169.

8. Musharraf, *In the Line of Fire*, p. 239.

9. Tawil, "Al-wajh al-akhar li al-qaida."

10. *The 9/11 Commission Report*, p. 165.

11. "Shoe-Bomber Supergrass Testifies in US," BBC, 23 Apr. 2012.

12. The plot is described in e.g. Musharraf, *In the Line of Fire*, p. 241, and disputed in e.g. Ian Cobain and Richard Norton-Taylor, "CIA Used False Heathrow Terror Plot Confession to Justify Waterboarding," *Guardian*, 9 Dec. 2014.

13. Verdict against Benahmed et al., pp. 27 ff.

14. Ibid., pp. 184–5.

15. See USA vs Abu Doha (United States District Court Southern District of New York, 2001); United States of America vs Mokhtar Haouari (United States District Court Southern District of New York, 2001) and Bernton, "The Terrorist Within; the Story Behind One Man's Holy War against America."

16. See e.g. Abu Rumman and Hanieh, *The Jihadi Salafist Movement in Jordan*, and Joas Wagemakers, *A Quietist Jihadi: The Ideology and Influence of Abu Muhammad Al-Maqdisi*, Cambridge: Cambridge University Press, 2012.

17. Mary Anne Weaver, "The Short, Violent Life of Abu Musab Al-Zarqawi," *The Atlantic*, Aug. 2006.

18. Steven Brooke, "The Preacher and the Jihadi," *Current Trends in Islamist Ideology*, Vol 5, (2005), 52–66.

19. Therefore, he first named the group Army of the Levant (jund al-sham), verdict against Shadi Abdalla [Abdullah] (Oberlandsgericht Düsseldorf 2003), p. 14.

20. Al-Adel, "Al-sira al-jihadiyya li al-qaid al-dabah abi musab al-zarqawi."

21. Indictment of Shadi Abdullah (2003), 15.
22. Assaf Moghadam and Brian Fishman, *Fault Lines in Global Jihad: Organizational, Strategic, and Ideological Fissures*, New York: Routledge, 2011, pp. 194 ff.
23. Josh Rogin Lake Eli, "Will Iran Sell Out Al Qaeda for Nukes?" *The Daily Beast*, 25 Sep. 2014.
24. See e.g. USA vs Abu Doha (United States District Court Southern District of New York, 2001), p. 7.
25. See Steinberg and Holtmann in Hoffman and Reinares, *Global Terrorist Threat*.
26. Hafez, *Suicide Bombers in Iraq*, pp. 189 ff.
27. Verdict against Benali [Beandali] (Oberlandsgericht Frankfurt am Main, 2003), p. 49.
28. "Five in Italy Convicted of Al-Qaida Ties," *AP* via FBIS, 2 Feb. 2004.
29. Verdict against Benali [Beandali] (Oberlandsgericht Frankfurt am Main, 2003), p. 17.
30. Ibid., pp. 21 ff.
31. Ibid., pp. 9 ff.
32. Verdict against Benahmed et al., 89.
33. Bernton, "The Terrorist Within; the Story Behind One Man's Holy War against America."
34. *Expertise Collective Des Terrorismes En Europe: Échanges Entre Chercheurs et Services Chargés À La Lutte Anti-Terroriste, Actes et Synthèses*, Institut National des hautes études de Sécurité (INHES), 2006, p. 33.
35. Taylor, "The Third World War."
36. Ibid.
37. Verdict against Benali [Beandali] al., pp. 11 ff.
38. "Repentant Algerian Tells of Bomb Plot: Muslim Militant, 'Horrified' by Sept. 11, Says His Target Was French Synagogue," *Washington Post*, 24 Apr. 2002.
39. Verdict against Benali [Beandali] al., p. 14.
40. Ibid., p. 11.
41. Ibid., p. 49.
42. Ibid., pp. 28–9.
43. Ibid., p. 30.
44. Taylor, "The Third World War."
45. "Repentant Algerian Tells of Bomb Plot."
46. Ibid.
47. Ibid.
48. Verdict against Benali [Beandali] al., p. 36.
49. Pierre-Antoine Souchard, "Man Says He Was Recruited by Bin Laden for Suicide Attack on U.S. Embassy in Paris," *AP*, 2 Oct. 2001.
50. "Dutch Terror Plot Trial Begins," *CNN*, 2 Dec. 2002.
51. Bright et al., "The Secret War."

52. Ibid.

53. Musharraf, *In the Line of Fire*, p. 237.

54. For a discussion of the matter see e.g. Peter Finn and Joby Warrick, "Detainee's Harsh Treatment Foiled No Plots," *Washington Post*, 29 Mar. 2009. See also reporting on Zubaydah's diaries in "Zubaydah Diaries Shed New Light on Twin Towers and Links to Bin Laden," *Al Jazeera*, 12 Nov. 2013.

55. See e.g. Nasiri, *Inside the Jihad*, pp. xi, 2, 241–2, 273. See also Henry Schuster, "Inside the Jihad," *CNN*, 20 Nov. 2006.

56. Robert Mendick, "Leicester Terrorist Cell That Laid Seeds of Paris Atrocity," *Telegraph*, 17 Jan. 2015.

57. Verdict against Beghal et al. (Tribunal de Grande Instance de Paris, 2005), p. 146.

58. See e.g. Jeffrey B. Cozzens, "Al-Takfir wa'l Hijra: Unpacking an Enigma," *Studies in Conflict & Terrorism*, 32, 6 (June 2009), pp. 489–510.

59. Mark Eeckhaut, "Trabelsi Wanted To Kill Americans," *De Standaard* via FBIS, 28 May 2003.

60. "French Police Gain Insight into Network Suspected of Planning Attack on US Embassy," *Le Monde* via FBIS, 20 Oct. 2001.

61. C.J.M Drake, *Terrorists' Target Selection*, New York: St. Martin's Press, 1998.

62. See e.g. Steven Erlanger and Chris Hedges, "Terror Cells Slip through Europe's Grasp," *The New York Times*, 28 Dec. 2001.

63. "Djamel Beghal" (As-Sabirun, 5 June 2013), https://web.archive.org/web/20130605025620/http://www.assabirun.com/the-stories-of-as-sabirun/djamel-beghal/ (accessed via webarchive, Jan. 2015).

64. Erlanger and Hedges, "Terror Cells Slip through Europe's Grasp."

65. Verdict against Beghal et al., p. 21.

66. Nesser in in Ranstorp, *Understanding Violent Radicalisation*, pp. 87 ff.

67. Indicative of Beghal's wish and ability to influence and control the fate of others, he once was involved in the abduction of the children of a Libyan friend from their British mother in Norwich, UK, in 2000, in order to transport them to Libya: "Father Accused of Plot to Abduct Children to Libya," *Times*, 20 Apr. 2005.

68. Bright et al., "The Secret War."

69. Erlanger and Hedges, "Terror Cells Slip through Europe's Grasp."

70. Elaine Sciolino, "Portrait of the Arab as a Young Radical," *The New York Times*, 22 Sep. 2002.

71. Bruce Crumley, "The Boy Next Door," *Time*, 12 Nov. 2001.

72. Verdict against Beghal et al., pp. 28–9.

73. Sebastian Rotella and David Zucchino, "In Paris, a Frightening Look at Terror's Inconspicuous Face," *Los Angeles Times*, 21 Oct. 2001.

74. Verdict against Beghal et al., p. 36.

75. Ibid., p. 39.

76. Bergen, *The Osama Bin Laden I Know*, pp. 269–72.

77. "French Trial Links Madrid and Casablanca Bombs," *Reuters*, 7 Apr. 2004.

78. Andrew Osborn in Brussels, "Al-Qaida Trial Opens in Belgium," *Guardian*, 23 May 2003.

79. "Terror Suspect Says Osama is 'Like a Father,'" *AP*, 15 Nov. 2002.

80. Ibid.

81. "Trabelsi Wanted To Kill Americans."

82. Ibid.

83. Warren Hoge with Desmond Butler, "Threats and Responses: Europe on Alert; Blair Warns of New Qaeda Threats, but Says Britain Won't Succumb to Panic," *The New York Times*, 12 Nov. 2002.

84. "Bin Laden's Invisible Network," *Newsweek*, 119, 45 (2001).

85. "Portrait of the Arab as a Young Radical."

86. Ibid.

87. Ibid.

88. Ibid.

89. Ibid.

90. "French Police Gain Insight into Network Suspected of Planning Attack on US Embassy."

91. "Portrait of the Arab as a Young Radical."

92. Ibid.

93. "Bin Laden's Invisible Network."

94. Alexandria Sage and Chine Labbé, "French Attacks Inquiry Centers on Prison 'Sorcerer' Beghal," *Reuters*, 15 Jan. 2015.

95. See e.g. Steinberg, *German Jihad*, pp. 44 ff.

96. Djamel Moustafa stood out because he was Algerian and seemingly not a cell member. He became involved through Abdullah who asked him to supply a gun with silencer, ammunition and hand grenades. Indictment of Mohamed Abu Dhess et al. (Der Generalbundesanwalt beim Bundesgerichthof, 2003), pp. 29 ff.

97. Jason Burke, "Terror Cell's UK Poison Plot," *Guardian*, 25 May 2003.

98. Indictment of Mohamed Abu Dhess et al., p. 62.

99. Interrogation of Shadi Abdullah dated 15 May 2002 (courtesy Peter Bergen).

100. Indictment of Mohamed Abu Dhess et al., p. 70.

101. Ibid., p. 9.

102. Ibid., pp. 21 ff.

103. Verdict against Shadi Abdalla [Abdullah], pp. 4 ff.

104. Bergen, *The Osama Bin Laden I Know*, p. 262.

105. Ibid., pp. 262 ff.

106. Geir Moulson, "Jordanian Admits He's Aide of Al-Qaida," *AP*, 24 June 2003.

107. Dominik Cziesche et al., "As If You Were at War," *Spiegel* via FBIS, 22 Mar. 2004.

108. Dominik Cziesche and Georg Mascolo, "A Lost Boy," *Spiegel* via FBIS, 27 Dec. 2004.

109. Steinberg, *German Jihad*, p. 47.
110. "German Court Finds Terror Suspects Guilty," *Deutche Welle*, 26 Oct. 2005.
111. Interrogation of Shadi Abdullah, 15 May 2002.
112. Verdict against Benahmed et al. (Tribunal de Grande Instance Paris, 2006), p. 89.
113. Ibid., pp. 253–4.
114. Ibid., p. 89.
115. Ibid., p. 91.
116. Ibid., p. 171.
117. Ibid.
118. Ibid., pp. 70, 103.
119. Ibid., p. 88.
120. Murad Batal Shishani, "Abu Hafs and the Future of Arab Fighters in Chechnya," *Terrorism Monitor*, 3, 7 (2005).
121. Verdict against Benahmed et al., p. 94.
122. Ibid., p. 80.
123. Ibid., p. 125.
124. Ibid., p. 250.
125. Ibid., p. 142.
126. Ibid., p. 100.
127. Ibid., p. 80.
128. Ibid., p. 100.
129. Ibid., pp. 91–2.
130. Ibid., p. 125.
131. Ibid., p. 130.
132. Ibid., p. 75.
133. Ibid., p. 253.
134. Ibid., p. 139.
135. Ibid., p. 135.
136. Craig S. Smith, "French Court Sentences 25 Islamic Extremists," *The New York Times*, 15 June 2006.
137. Jon Henley, "Al-Qaida Terror Plot Foiled, Say French Police," *Guardian*, 12 Jan. 2004.
138. Johanna Mcgeary and Paul Quinn-Judge, "Theater of War," *Time*, 28 Oct. 2002.
139. Paul Tumelty, "The Rise and Fall of Foreign Fighters in Chechnya," *Terrorism Monitor*, 4, 6 (26 Jan. 2006).
140. Verdict against Benahmed et al., p. 90.
141. Ibid., p. 146.
142. "Terrorist Cell Dismantled in France Reportedly Planned Russian Embassy Attack," *Le Monde* via FBIS, 29 Dec. 2002.
143. Verdict against Benahmed et al., p. 145.
144. Ibid., p. 146.

145. Ibid., pp. 172–3.
146. Ibid., p. 121.

5. THE IRAQ EFFECT (2003–5)

1. Murdiyah, "The Martyred & Imprisoned Scholars," Islamic Awakening Forum, Jan. 2008, http://forums.islamicawakening.com/f47/martyred-imprisoned-schol-ars-24452/. Umm Musab al-Gharib, "Babar Ahmed and Imprisoned Muslims," Islamic Awakening, Jan. 2006, http://forums.islamicawakening.com/f20/babar-ahmed-imprisoned-muslims-722 (accessed 15 Jan. 2015).
2. James Brandon, "Unlocking Al-Qaeda: Islamist Extremism in British Prisons," Quilliam Foundation, 2009; James A. Beckford, Danièle Joly and Farhad Khosrokhavar (eds), *Muslims in Prison: Challenge and Change in Britain and France*, New York: Palgrave Macmillan, 2006.
3. Brandon, "Virtual Caliphate", p. 60.
4. James Brandon, "Unlocking Al-Qaeda", p. 45.
5. Peter Bergen and Paul Cruickshank, "Al Qaeda in Iraq: Self-Fulfilling Prophecy," *Mother Jones*, 31 Oct. 2007.
6. "Zawahiri's Letter to Zarqawi (English Translation)," New York: CTC, 2006.
7. Thomas Hegghammer, "Global Jihadism after the Iraq War," *Middle East Journal*, 60 (2006), p. 1.
8. "Bin Laden's Iraq Plans," *Newsweek*, 15 Dec. 2003.
9. Moghadam and Fishman, *Fault Lines in Global Jihad*, pp. 39 ff.
10. Guido Steinberg, "The Iraqi Insurgency; Actors, Strategies and Structures," Berlin: SWP, 13 Dec. 2006.
11. Based on review of Thomas Hegghammer, "Dokumentasjon om Al-Qaida: Intervjuer, Kommunikéer og andre Primærkilder," Kjeller: FFI, 2003; "Al-Qaida Statements 2003–2004: A Compilation of Translated Texts by Usama Bin Ladin and Ayman Al-Zawahiri," Kjeller: FFI, 2005; "Al-arshif al-jami'a li-kallimat wa khutabat imam al-mujahidin usama bin muhammad bin ladin," Shabakat al-Buraq al-Islamiyya, 2007; "Compilation of Usama Bin Ladin's Statements 1994–January 2004," FBIS, 2004, http://www.fas.org/irp/world/para/ubl-fbis.pdf (accessed 20 Jan. 2015).
12. Warren Hoge with Desmond Butler, "Threats and Responses: Europe on Alert; Blair Warns of New Qaeda Threats, but Says Britain Won't Succumb to Panic," *The New York Times*, 12 Nov. 2002.
13. "Bin Laden Tape Hails Bali, Issues New Threats," *Sydney Morning Herald*, 13 Nov. 2002.
14. "'Al-Qaeda' Statement: Full Text," BBC, 21 May 2003. Likely he mistook Norway for Denmark. Norway did not send troops to Iraq because the invasion lacked a UN mandate.
15. "Compilation of Usama Bin Ladin's Statements 1994—January 2004," p. 265.

16. "Al-risala al-ula li-shu'ub uruba," (dated 14 Apr. 2014) in "Al-arshif al-jami'a li-kallimat wa khutabat imam al-mujahidin usama bin muhammad bin ladin," p. 203.

17. "Headscarf Ban May Cause Attack on France," *Daily Times*, 26 Feb. 2004.

18. Indictment of the Madrid bombers, 1357–1358 (Juzgado Central De Instruccion N 6 Audiencia Nacional Madrid, 2006).

19. Ibid., p. 1265.

20. Frank Cifullo, Jeffrey Cozzens and Magnus Ranstorp, "Foreign Fighters—Trends, Trajectories & Conflict Zones," (HSPI, 2010).

21. Brian Fishman, "Al-Qa'ida's Foreign Fighters in Iraq: A First Look at the Sinjar Records," New York: CTC, 2008.

22. Hafez, *Suicide Bombers in Iraq.*

23. Exceptions include a possible plan by Ansar al-Islam members in Germany to bomb a military hospital in 2003, a plot to assassinate the Iraqi prime minister on a visit to Germany in 2004 by people from the same group, a plot to attack the French security services and Orly airport in 2005, a plot to bomb trains in Germany by Lebanese students in 2006, a failed plot to bomb a nightclub in London and Glasgow international airport in 2007 and the failed suicide bombing in Stockholm, Sweden, in 2010.

24. Interview with European security official, 2008.

25. Verdict against Lokman Amin Hama Karim (Oberlandsgerich Munchen 2006), p. 106.

26. Ibid., pp. 39 ff.; Sebastian Rotella, "A Road to Ansar Began in Italy," *Los Angeles Times*, 28 Apr. 2003; Prosecutors statement in case against members of Ansar al-Islam cells in Italy (translated excerpts) (Tribunale di Milano, 2003).

27. "Bayan al-jama'a al-mujahida bi al-maghreb," document dated 16 June 1997 (on file with author).

28. Ibid.

29. Rogelio Alonso and Marcos García Rey, "The Evolution of Jihadist Terrorism in Morocco," *Terrorism and Political Violence*, 19, 4 (8 Oct. 2007), pp. 571–92.

30. Craig Whitlock, "How a Town Became a Terror Hub," *Washington Post*, 24 Nov. 2005.

31. Mia Bloom, "Bombshells: Women and Terror," *Gender Issues*, 28, 1–2 (6 May 2011), pp. 1–21.

32. Interview with European security official, 2008.

33. Craig Whitlock, "In Europe, New Force for Recruiting Radicals: Ansar Al-Islam Emerges as Primary Extremist Group Funneling Fighters Into Iraq," *Washington Post*, 18 Feb. 2005.

34. "Germany: Videos Show Islamists Built Infrastructure in West Long Before 9/11," *Focus*, 31 Dec. 2004.

35. Verdict against Lokman Amin Hama Karim (Oberlandsgerich Munchen, 2006).

36. "Al-Hayat Cites Detainees on Moroccan Al-Qa'ida Group That Enlists Volunteers For Iraq," *Al-Hayat* via FBIS, 29 Nov. 2005.

37. "Detained Moroccans' Confessions Said to Detail Al-Zarqawi's Targets, Plans," *Al-Hayat* via FBIS, 5 Dec. 2005.

38. Hafez, *Suicide Bombers in Iraq*, pp. 196–7 and indictment of the Madrid bombers, 1306–1307.

39. Timothy Holman, "Background on the 19th Network, Paris, France, 2000–2013," Across the Green Mountain (blog), 8 Jan. 2015.

40. The authoritative account of M-11 is Reinares, *¡Matadlos!*. My case study is based largely on the indictment of the Madrid bombers (Juzgado Central De Instruccion N 6 Audiencia Nacional Madrid, 2006) and Reinares in Hoffman and Reinares, *Global Terrorist Threat*.

41. "11-M Massacre En Madrid," *El Mundo*, 2004, http://www.elmundo.es/documentos/2004/03/espana/atentados11m/.

42. Interview with European security official, Sep. 2004.

43. Indictment of the Madrid bombers, p. 1133.

44. Ibid., p. 465.

45. Interview with European security official, Sep. 2004.

46. Reinares, "The Madrid Bombings and Global Jihadism," p. 88.

47. Reinares, in Hoffman and Reinares, *Global Terrorist Threat*, pp. 42 ff.

48. Ibid.

49. Indictment of the Madrid bombers, pp. 201–2.

50. Lia, *Architect of Global Jihad*, pp. 199–208.

51. Indictment of the Madrid bombers, p. 1212.

52. Ibid., p. 1346.

53. Ibid., p. 1364.

54. Ibid., p. 1244.

55. Hoffman and Reinares, *Global Terrorist Threat*, p. 42.

56. Indictment of the Madrid bombers, p. 793.

57. James Graff, "Terror's Tracks," *Time*, 11 Apr. 2004.

58. Elaine Sciolino, "From Tapes, a Chilling Voice of Islamic Radicalism in Europe," *The New York Times*, 18 Nov. 2005.

59. Interview with European security official, Sep. 2004.

60. Indictment of the Madrid bombers, p. 1146.

61. Ibid., p. 1358.

62. Ibid., p. 528.

63. Ibid.

64. Ibid., p. 474.

65. Ibid., p. 1217.

66. Graff, "Terror's Tracks."

67. Indictment of the Madrid bombers, p. 1365.

68. Ibid., p. 1226.

69. Hegghammer, *Jihad Culture*.

70. Indictment of the Madrid bombers, p. 1227.

71. Ibid., p. 286.

72. Ibid., p. 1137.

73. Andrea Elliott, "Where Boys Grow Up to Be Jihadis," *The New York Times*, 25 Nov. 2007.

74. Indictment of the Madrid bombers, pp. 269, 271, 1224.

75. Elliott, "Where Boys Grow Up to Be Jihadis."

76. Indictment of the Madrid bombers, pp. 230–2.

77. Elliott, "Where Boys Grow Up to Be Jihadis."

78. Indictment of the Madrid bombers, pp. 1351, 1360.

79. "Morocco to Madrid, A Bomb Suspect Grew Radicalized," *Wall Street Journal*, 19 Mar. 2004.

80. Indictment of the Madrid bombers, p. 1226.

81. Ibid., p. 1372.

82. Ibid., pp. 793, 1372.

83. "Transcript of Purported Al Qaeda Videotape," *The New York Times*, 14 Mar. 2004.

84. Ibid.

85. Ibid.

86. Lia and Hegghammer, "Jihadi Strategic Studies."

87. Elliott, "Where Boys Grow Up to Be Jihadis."

88. "Al-risala al-ula li-shu'ub uruba" (dated 14 Apr. 2014).

89. Ibid.

90. Reinares, *¡Matadlos!*.

91. Toby Sterling, "Changes Sway Holland Slaying Suspect," *AP*, 8 Nov. 2004.

92. See Benschop, "Chronicle of a Political Murder Foretold: Jihad in the Netherlands," and Petter Nesser, "The Slaying of the Dutch Filmmaker: Religiously Motivated Violence or Islamist Terrorism in the Name of Global Jihad," Kjeller: FFI, 2005.

93. Lorenzo Vidino, "The Hofstad Group: The New Face of Terrorist Networks in Europe," *Studies in Conflict & Terrorism*, 30, 7 (2007), pp. 579–92.

94. For similar views, see Bart Schuurman, Quirine Eijkman and Edwin Bakker, "The Hofstadgroup Revisited: Questioning its Status as a 'Quintessential' Homegrown Jihadist Network," *Terrorism and Political Violence*, (published online June 2014), 1–20, and Beatrice de Graaf in Hoffman and Reinares, *Global Terrorist Threat*, pp. 101 ff.

95. Interview with European security official, 2005.

96. Benschop, "Chronicle of a Political Murder Foretold".

97. "Theo van Gogh" *The Independent*, 4 Nov. 2004.

98. Nesser, "The Slaying of the Dutch Filmmaker", p. 10.

99. Benschop, "Chronicle of a Political Murder Foretold".

100. Ibid.

101. Thomas Hegghammer, "The Iraqi Hostage Crisis: Abductions in Iraq April–August 2004," Kjeller: FFI, 2004.
102. Nesser, "The Slaying of the Dutch Filmmaker," p. 22.
103. "Ayaan Hirsi Ali: My Life under a Fatwa," *The Independent*, 27 Nov. 2007.
104. Ian Traynor, "I Don't Hate Muslims. I Hate Islam,' Says Holland's Rising Political Star," *Guardian*, 17 Feb. 2008.
105. Theo Van Gogh and Ayaan Hirsi Ali, *Submission*, 2004.
106. Judit Neurink, "'Mujahideen of the Lowlands' on Trial in the Netherlands," *Terrorism Monitor*, 3, 24 (21 Dec. 2005).
107. Interview with European security official, 2005.
108. "Dutch Intelligence Service Employee Jailed for Leaking Secrets," *Radio Netherlands*, 15 Dec. 2005.
109. Marc Sageman et al., *Women Warriors for Allah: An Islamist Network in the Netherlands*, Philadelphia: University of Pennsylvania Press, 2010.
110. Sebastian Rotella, "European Women Join Ranks of Jihadis," *Los Angeles Times*, 10 Jan. 2006.
111. Benschop, "Chronicle of a Political Murder Foretold".
112. Beatrice de Graaf in Hoffman and Reinares, *Global Terrorist Threat*, p. 113.
113. Benschop, "Chronicle of a Political Murder Foretold".
114. Interview with European security official, Nov. 2006.
115. "Syrian Mystery Man Sought in Van Gogh Case," *Radio Netherlands*, 3 Dec. 2004.
116. Benschop, "Chronicle of a Political Murder Foretold".
117. Ibid.
118. Nesser, "The Slaying of the Dutch Filmmaker".
119. Benschop, "Chronicle of a Political Murder Foretold".
120. Nesser, "The Slaying of the Dutch Filmmaker," p. 11.
121. Rudolph Peters in Coolsaet, *Jihadi Terrorism and the Radicalisation Challenge*, pp. 145 ff.
122. Emerson Vermaat, "Hofstad Trial Continues: Nouredine El Fatmi—A Terrorist and Seducer of Teenage Girls by Emerson Vermaat," Militant Islam Monitor (blog), 15 Jan. 2006.
123. Interview with European security official, 2005.
124. Benschop, "Chronicle of a Political Murder Foretold".
125. Ibid.
126. Interview with European security official, 2005.
127. Toby Sterling, "Muslims Arrested in Van Gogh Murder Belong to Militant Group," *AP*, 13 Nov. 2004.
128. Juan Avilés, "The Madrid Massacre: The Iraq Connection," Madrid:Elcano, 2004.
129. Benschop, "Chronicle of a Political Murder Foretold"; Nesser, "The Slaying of the Dutch Filmmaker," p. 24.

130. "Open Letter to Hirshi Ali," 2004, http://www.faithfreedom.org/forum/viewtopic.php?t=5270 (accessed Jan. 2005).
131. Ibid.
132. Ibid.
133. Ibid.
134. Interview with European security official, 2005.
135. Benschop, "Chronicle of a Political Murder Foretold".
136. Ibid.

6. THE PAKISTAN AXIS (2004–6)

1. Irfan Husain, "The Battle for Hearts and Minds," *Dawn*, 6 Oct. 2001.
2. Abu Esa al-Hindi, *The Army of Madinah in Kashmir*, Birmingham: Maktabah Al Ansaar, 1999.
3. Sarah Lyall, "What Drove 2 Britons to Bomb a Club in Tel Aviv?" *The New York Times*, 12 May 2003.
4. John Tagliabue, "French Police Detain 6 Suspected of Ties to Shoe Bomber," *The New York Times*, 26 Nov. 2002; "UK Officer 'May Have Been Target,'" *CNN*, 2 Feb. 2003.
5. Clutterbuck in Hoffman and Reinares, *Global Terrorist Threat*, pp. 81 ff.
6. "Terror Suspects Had Video of Spain's Twin Towers," *Expatica*, 20 Sep. 2004.
7. Reinares in Hoffman and Reinares, *Global Terrorist Threat*, pp. 334 ff.
8. "David Coleman Headley Sentenced to 35 Years in Prison for Role in India and Denmark Terror Plots," US Department of Justice, 24 Jan. 2013.
9. Steinberg, *German Jihad*, pp. 139 ff.
10. Ahmed Rashid, *Descent into Chaos: The U.S. and the Disaster in Pakistan, Afghanistan, and Central Asia*, revised edn, New York: Penguin Books, 2009. See also Steve Coll, *Ghost Wars: The Secret History of the CIA, Afghanistan, and Bin Laden, from the Soviet Invasion to September 10, 2001*, New York: Penguin Books, 2004; and Imtiaz Gul, *The Most Dangerous Place: Pakistan's Lawless Frontier*, New York: Penguin Books, 2011.
11. Audun Kolstad Wiig, "Islamist Opposition in the Islamic Republic: Jundullah and the Spread of Extremist Deobandism in Iran," Kjeller: FFI, 2009.
12. Mariam Abou Zahab and Olivier Roy, *Islamist Networks: The Afghan–Pakistan Connection*, New York: Columbia University Press, 2006.
13. Christine Fair, "Militant Recruitment in Pakistan: Implications for Al Qaeda and Other Organizations," *Studies in Conflict & Terrorism*, 27, 6 (1 Nov. 2004), pp. 489–504.
14. Ibid.
15. "Pakistan: Madrasas, Extremism and the Military," International Crisis Group, 2002.

16. Sabrina Tavernise, "Pakistan's Islamic Schools Fill Void, but Fuel Militancy," *The New York Times*, 3 May, 2009.

17. Stephen Philip Cohen, "The Jihadist Threat to Pakistan," *The Washington Quarterly*, 26, 3 (1 June 2003), pp. 5–25.

18. Musharraf, *In the Line of Fire.*

19. Qandeel Siddique, "The Red Mosque Operation and its Impact on the Growth of the Pakistani Taliban," Kjeller: FFI, 2008.

20. Gul, *The Most Dangerous Place.*

21. Linschoten and Kuehn, *An Enemy We Created*; Anne Stenersen, *Brothers in Jihad: The Alliance Between Al-Qaida and the Taliban*, New York: Cambridge University Press, forthcoming, 2016.

22. Fielding and Fouda, *Masterminds of Terror*, pp. 53–73.

23. Musharraf, *In the Line of Fire.*

24. Fielding and Fouda, *Masterminds of Terror*, pp. 53 ff.; Musharraf, *In the Line of Fire*, pp. 225 ff.

25. Adrian Levy and Cathy Scott-Clark, *The Meadow: Where the Terror Began*, New York: HarperCollins, 2012.

26. Stephen Tankel, "Lashkar-E-Taiba in Perspective," New America Foundation, 2010.

27. Gunaratna and Nielsen, "Al Qaeda in the Tribal Areas of Pakistan and Beyond."

28. Ibid., p. 784.

29. Noor Khan had fought with al-Qaida in Afghanistan, and was working with IT and media for the organization from Lahore, while liaising with extremists in the UK. Allegedly, Noor Khan was recruited by KSM in 2002 and he had been involved in preparing British-Pakistanis for missions (which included the plot to ram airliners into Heathrow) from camps in the Shakai Valley; see ibid., p. 782.

30. "Could 7/7 Have Been Prevented? Review of the Intelligence on the London Terrorist Attacks on 7 July 2005," London: Intelligence and Security Committee of Parliament, May 2009, p. 10.

31. Peter Bergen and Paul Cruickshank, "Al Qaeda-on-Thames: UK Plotters Connected," *Washington Post*, 30 Apr. 2007.

32. Opening statement Regina vs. Omar Khyam et al., no. 310 (The British Crown, 2006).

33. Ibid., no. 126.

34. Ibid., no. 112.

35. Ibid., no. 67.

36. Ibid., no. 129.

37. Ibid., no. 143.

38. Ibid., no. 142.

39. Ibid., no. 173.

40. Gunaratna and Nielsen, "Al Qaeda in the Tribal Areas of Pakistan and Beyond," p. 786.

41. Ibid.
42. Sami Yousafzai, Ron Moreau and Mark Hosenball, "The Regathering Storm," *Newsweek*, 26 Dec. 2006.
43. "Harb al-mustada'fin", al-Sahab, 2005 (on file with author).
44. Opening statement Regina vs Omar Khyam et al., no. 69 (The British Crown, 2006).
45. Ibid., no. 116.
46. Ibid., nos. 54 and 55.
47. Ibid., no. 241.
48. Rosie Cowan, Richard Norton-Taylor and Audrey Gillan, "Police Search Emails for Trail to Pakistan," *Guardian*, 1 Apr. 2004.
49. Ibid.
50. "Could 7/7 Have Been Prevented?, Review of the Intelligence on the London Terrorist Attacks on 7 July 2005" (London: Intelligence and Security Committee of Parliament, May 2009), pp 7 ff.
51. Olga Craig and Adam Lusher, "The Making of a Terrorist," *Telegraph*, 6 May 2007.
52. "Plot Suspect 'Happy' after 9/11," BBC, 14 Sep. 2006.
53. Interview with European security official, Apr. 2006.
54. Opening statement Regina vs Omar Khyam et al., no. 142.
55. Chris Greenwood et al., "Are Syria Charities a Front for Jihadists? Fears Convoys in the Country Are Being Used to Help Militants after Thousands in Cash is Seized," *Mail*, 13 Feb. 2014.
56. Peter Taylor, "Real Spooks: Transcript," BBC, 30 Apr. 2007.
57. "Profile: Jawad Akbar," BBC, 30 Apr. 2007.
58. "Profile: Anthony Garcia," BBC, 30 Apr. 2007.
59. Anthony Garcia's bothers Lamine and Ibrahim Adam escaped prosecution in the Crevice case and disappeared. Ibrahim later turned up as a suspect in plans to launch terrorist attacks in the United States, the UK and Norway in 2010, Frode Hansen and Harald Klungtveit, "Terror-Ettersøkte Ibrahim (23) Skulle hjelpes inn i Norge med falsk pass," *Dagbladet*, 16 July 2010.
60. "Mohammad Momin Khawaja," *CBC*, 24 Oct. 2006.
61. "Momin Khawaja Constitutes the Canadian End of the Conspiracy," *Ottawa Citizen*, 23 Mar. 2006.
62. "Supergrass Tells of Terror Fight," BBC, 24 Mar. 2006.
63. Opening statement Regina vs Omar Khyam et al., no. 67.
64. "Profile: Omar Khyam," BBC, 30 Apr. 2007.
65. "Plot Suspect 'Happy' after 9/11."
66. Ibid.
67. Opening statement Regina vs Omar Khyam et al., no. 132.
68. Ian Cobain and Richard Norton-Taylor, "'Because British Soldiers Are Killing Muslims,'" *Guardian*, 30 Apr. 2007.

69. Simon Israel, "Babar Admits Assassination Plot," *Channel 4 News*, 30 Mar. 2006.
70. Main sources for the case study are "Report of the Official Account of the Bombings in London on 7th July 2005," London: UK Government, 11 May 2006, and "Could 7/7 Have Been Prevented?, Review of the Intelligence on the London Terrorist Attacks on 7 July 2005" (London: Intelligence and Security Committee of Parliament, May 2009).
71. "Wasiya fursan ghaswat London," al-Sahab, 2006, (on file with author).
72. Rachel Briggs et al., "Anatomy of a Terrorist Attack, What the Coroner's Inquests Revealed about the London Bombings," London: RUSI, 2011.
73. "Wasiya fursan ghaswat London."
74. Abu 'Ubayda al-Maqdisi, "Shuhada fi zaman al-ghuraba," Al-Fajr, 2006 (courtesy Anne Stenersen).
75. Ibid.
76. "Osama Bin Laden: 7/7 Bombers Met with Al-Qaeda Leader's Courier before London Attacks," *Mirror*, 15 May 2011.
77. "Profile: Shehzad Tanweer," BBC, 6 July 2006.
78. For a detailed timeline of the attacks, see Briggs et al., "Anatomy of a Terrorist Attack," pp. 3 ff.
79. Paul Cruickshank et al., "Documents Give New Details on Al Qaeda's London Bombings," *CNN*, 30 Apr. 2012.
80. Paul Tumelty, "An In-Depth Look at the London Bombers," *Terrorism Monitor*, 3, 15 (28 July 2005).
81. "British Muslims Monthly Survey," September 1997, volume V, no 9.
82. Shiv Mali, "My Brother the Bomber," *Prospect*, 135 (30 June 2007).
83. "Edgware Road: Mohammad Sidique Khan," *Times*, 14 July 2005.
84. Sean O'Neill and Daniel McGrory, "Abu Hamza and the 7/7 Bombers," *Times*, 8 Feb. 2006.
85. Raghava Sudarsan, "Friends Describe Bomber's Political, Religious Evolution, 22-Year-Old Grew up Loving Western Ways and Wanting for Little," *Washington Post*, 29 July 2005.
86. Ibid.
87. Ibid.
88. Peter Foster and Nasir Malick, "Bomber Idolised Bin Laden, Says Pakistan Family," *Telegraph*, 21 July 2005.
89. Ian Cobain, "The Boy Who Didn't Stand Out," *Guardian*, 14 July 2005.
90. Tumelty, "An In-Depth Look at the London Bombers."
91. Jeremy Armstrong, "My Hasib Must Have Been Brainwashed," *Mirror*, 2 Aug. 2005.
92. Tumelty, "An In-Depth Look at the London Bombers."
93. Simon Tomlinson, "White Widow 'Is Alive and Living with Al-Qaeda Husband in Somalia,'" *Mail*, 14 Nov. 2014.

94. "Profile: Sheikh Abdullah Al-Faisal," BBC, 25 May 2007.

95. "London Bomber: Text in Full," BBC, 2 Sep. 2005.

96. "Wasiya fursan ghaswat London."

97. Ibid.

98. "Jamal Lindsay-Warrior of Allah," al-Firdaws, 2006 (on file with author).

99. O'Neill and Lappin, "Britain's Online Imam Declares War as He Calls Young to Jihad."

100. Kevin Sullivan and Joshua Partlow, "Young Muslim Rage Takes Root in Britain, Unemployment, Foreign Policy Fuel Extremism," *Washington Post*, 13 Aug. 2006.

101. Marina Jimenez and Hamida Ghafour, "Infant Reported to Be Tool of Terror Scheme," *Globe and Mail*, 14 Aug. 2006.

102. "Terror Charges: Police Statement," BBC, 21 Aug. 2006.

103. For a very detailed account of operational aspects and international links, see Cruickshank in Hoffman and Reinares, *Global Terrorist Threat*, pp. 224 ff.

104. Vikram Dodd, "Airline Bomb Plotters' Links to Al-Qaida and Other Convicted Terrorists," *Guardian*, 7 Sep. 2009.

105. Don Van Natta Jr, Elaine Sciolino and Stephen Grey, "Details Emerge in British Terror Case," *The New York Times*, 28 Aug. 2006.

106. Dodd, "Airline Bomb Plotters' Links to Al-Qaida and Other Convicted Terrorists."

107. Ibid.

108. Paul Cruickshank and Tim Lister, "Documents Give New Details on Al Qaeda's London Bombings," *CNN*, 30 Apr. 2012.

109. Gunaratna and Nielsen, "Al Qaeda in the Tribal Areas of Pakistan and Beyond," p. 791.

110. Ibid.

111. Hamida Ghafour and Doug Sanders, "Suspects Were from Moderate Muslim Families," *Globe and Mail*, 11 Aug. 2006.

112. Gordon Corera, "Bomb Plot—the Al-Qaeda Connection," BBC, 9 Sep. 2008.

113. Cruickshank in Hoffman and Reinares, *Global Terrorist Threat*, p. 233.

114. "Airline Urges Liquids Review after Trial," BBC, 8 Sep. 2008.

115. Oliver Evans, "Terror Profile: Assad Sarwar," *Bucks Free Press*, 8 Sep. 2008.

116. "Profiles: Airline Plot Accused," BBC, 7 Sep. 2009.

117. Julie Hyland, "Contradictions, Anomalies, Questions Mount in UK Terror Scare," *The Muslim News*, 17 Aug. 2006.

118. Haroon Siddique, "Airliner Bomb Plot: Profiles of the Defendants," *Guardian*, 7 Sep. 2009.

119. "My Friend: The Football Fan Who Dreamed of Being a Doctor," *Guardian*, 15 Aug. 2006.

120. "Inside This Building, a Terror Suspect Ran a London University's Islamic Group: Was it Also a Recruiting Ground for 'Holy War'?" *Telegraph*, 13 Aug. 2006.

121. Duncan Campbell et al., "Pakistan: Terror 'Ringleader' Admits Al-Qaeda Link," *Guardian*, 14 Aug. 2006.
122. Raffaello Pantucci, "A Biography of Rashid Rauf: Al-Qa'ida's British Operative," *CTC Sentinel*, 5, 7 (2012).
123. "Suicide Videos: What They Said," BBC, 4 Apr. 2008.
124. Ibid.
125. Ibid.
126. Ibid.
127. Ibid.
128. Ibid.
129. Ibid.
130. Ibid.
131. Ibid.
132. Ibid.
133. Ibid.
134. Ibid.
135. Ibid.

7. THE NORTHERN FRONT (2005–8)

1. "Tegningesagen i Al-Qaidas Ideologiske Perspektiv," Copenhagen: CTA, 16 June 2009.
2. Bin Laden, "O People of Islam."
3. Ibid.
4. "Tegningesagens fortsatte betydning for Terrortruslen mod Danmark," Copenhagen: CTA, 2013.
5. The best source of information about the case is the book by the Danish journalist and author Skjoldager, *Truslen Indefra—De Danske Terrorister*. I also interviewed Skjoldager on 6 May 2009 and reviewed judicial documents.
6. Indictment of Mirsad Bektasevic and Abdulkadir Cesur (Court of Bosnia and Herzegovina Sarajevo, 2006).
7. Skjoldager, *Truslen Indefra*, p. 194.
8. Anne Speckhard, Mubin Shaikh and Jessica Stern, *Undercover Jihadi: Inside the Toronto 18—Al Qaeda Inspired, Homegrown Terrorism in the West*, McLean, VA: Advances Press, 2014.
9. Sebastian Rotella, "A World Wide Web of Terrorist Plotting," *Los Angeles Times*, 16 Apr. 2007.
10. Skjoldager, *Truslen Indefra*, p. 175.
11. "Baggrund: De Tre Danske Terrorsager," *Berlingske Tidende*, 4 Sep. 2007.
12. Skjoldager, *Truslen Indefra*, p. 224.
13. Indictment of Mirsad Bektasevic and Abdulkadir Cesur (Court of Bosnia and Herzegovina Sarajevo, 2006), p. 11.

14. Rade Maroevic and Daniel Williams, "Terrorist Cells Find Foothold in Balkans," *Washington Post*, 1 Dec. 2005.

15. Previously they had belonged to the Waqf mosque supervised by the late Abu Laban who was one of the main organizers of the delegation traveling to the Middle East to instigate protests against the Muhammad cartoons.

16. Skjoldager, *Truslen Indefra*, p. 127.

17. Ibid., pp. 120 ff.

18. Ibid., pp. 112–14.

19. Ibid., p. 139.

20. Michael Taarnby Jensen, "Jihad in Denmark: An Overview and Analysis of Jihadist Activity in Denmark 1990–2006," Copenhagen: DIIS, 2006, p. 22.

21. Skjoldager, *Truslen Indefra*, pp. 93 ff.

22. Morten Skjoldager and Nilas Heinskou, "Ung terrormistænkt hjalp Said Mansour," *Politiken*, 20 Dec. 2006.

23. "Jag Längtar till Sverige," *Expressen*, 9 Aug. 2007.

24. Rita Katz and Michael Kern, "Terrorist 007, Exposed," *Washington Post*, 26 Mar. 2006.

25. "Våldsbejakande Islamistisk Extremism i Sverige".

26. "Det Svider i Hjartat, En film om de Svenske Martyrerna," Laika Film & Television, 2006.

27. Skjoldager, *Truslen Indefra—De Danske Terrorister*, p. 164.

28. William Kole, "Are Terrorists Recruiting 'White Muslims'?" *Seattle Times*, 18 Apr. 2006.

29. Skjoldager, *Truslen Indefra*, p. 183.

30. "Tiltalte: Jeg er ikke ekstremist," *Dagbladet Information*, 11 Jan. 2008.

31. Skjoldager, *Truslen Indefra*, pp. 134 ff.

32. Søren Astrup, "Terrorsigtede Forvirrede Om Gruppens Leder," *Politiken*, 15 Feb. 2007.

33. Indictment of Mirsad Bektasevic and Abdulkadir Cesur (Court of Bosnia and Herzegovina Sarajevo, 2006), p. 3.

34. Skjoldager, *Truslen Indefra*, pp. 172 ff.

35. Ibid., p. 175.

36. Ibid.

37. Ibid., p. 239.

38. See e.g. Martin Burcharth, "Denmark's Problem with Muslims," *The New York Times*, 12 Feb. 2006.

39. Ann-Sophie Hemmingsen, "The Attractions of Jihadism," Copenhagen: DIIS, 2007, p. 94.

40. Tine Johansen and Lisbeth K. Larsen, "Terrortiltalt Indrømmer Sprængninger," *Ekstra Bladet*, 15 Aug. 2008.

41. Hemmingsen, "The Attractions of Jihadism," p. 221.

42. Siddique, "The Red Mosque Operation and its Impact on the Growth of the Pakistani Taliban".
43. Skjoldager, *Truslen Indefra*, p. 261.
44. Interview with journalist and author of *Truslen Indefra*, Morten Skjoldager, 6 May 2009.
45. Skjoldager, *Truslen Indefra*, p. 275.
46. Paul Cruickshank, "The Militant Pipeline between the Afghanistan–Pakistan Border Region and the West," New America Foundation, 2010, p. 18.
47. Skjoldager, *Truslen Indefra*, p. 276.
48. Interview with journalist and author Morten Skjoldager, 6 May 2009.
49. "Terrortiltalt kan ikke lide nøgne damer," *Ekstra Bladet*, 14 Aug. 2008.
50. Skjoldager, *Truslen Indefra*, p. 277.
51. Hemmingsen, "The Attractions of Jihadism," p. 86.
52. Skjoldager, *Truslen Indefra*, pp. 239 ff.
53. A collection of German press clippings by Hintergrund provided most of the information for the analysis, see "Recherche 'Koffer-Bomben,'" Hintergrund, 20 July 2009; http://www.hintergrund.de/2007070821/globales/terrorismus/recherche-koffer-bomben.html (accessed 3 Feb. 2011). It has been corroborated with the original sources.
54. Craig Whitlock, "Student Gets Life in German Train-Bombing Plot," *Washington Post*, 10 Dec. 2008.
55. Tine Gade, "Fatah Al-Islam in Lebanon: Between Global and Local Jihad," Kjeller: FFI, 2007, p. 50.
56. "'Koffer-Bomben.'"
57. "German Security Services Reveal Bomb Threat to Justice Ministry," *Deutche Welle*, 12 Jan. 2008.
58. "Germany Opens Inquiry into Terror Attack Claim," *Spiegel*, 12 Jan. 2008.
59. "Terror Suspect Extradited to Germany; Police Seek Third Bomber," *Deutche Welle*, 6 Apr. 2007.
60. Andreas Ulrich, "Failed Bomb Plot Seen as Al-Qaida Initiation Test," *Spiegel*, 9 Apr. 2007.
61. Hubert Gude and Josef Hufelschulte, "Kind of Napalm—Terrorism Suspect Al-Haydib Chief Planner Behind Suitcase Bombings, Accomplice Claims," *Focus* via FBIS, 13 Sep. 2006.
62. Philipp Holtmann, "Virtual Leadership in Radical Islamist Movements," IDC working paper, 2011, p. 10.
63. "Train Plotter Jailed in Germany," BBC, 9 Dec. 2008.
64. "Mutmaßliche Kofferbomber Sollen Netzwerk Angehört Haben," *Focus*, 6 Jan. 2007.
65. "Newspaper Editor Was Bomb Target," *Copenhagen Post*, 4 Oct. 2007.
66. Gunther Latsch et al., "Every Investigator's Nightmare," *Spiegel*, 28 Aug. 2006.

67. "'Koffer-Bomben.'"

68. Fatima Rida, "The Role of the European West in Producing Mujahideen and Sending Them to Lebanon," *Al-Hayat*, 17 Dec. 2008.

69. "Failed Bomb Plot Seen as Al-Qaida Initiation Test."

70. "Lebanese Man Convicted in 2006 Plot to Bomb German Trains," *AP*, 19 Dec. 2007.

71. Ayman al-Zawahiri, "Message to the Muslim Turkish People" (via Flashpoint Partners, 15 Aug. 2010), https://azelin.files.wordpress.com/2010/08/dr-ayman-al-zawahiri-e2809cmessage-to-the-muslim-turkish-peoplee2809d.pdf (accessed 15 Jan. 2015).

72. "A Chat with the Commander of Islamic Jihad Union Ebu Yahya Muhammed Fatih ..." Sehadet Vakti, 31 May 2007.

73. Simone Kaiser, Marcel Rosenbach and Holger Stark, "Operation Alberich: How the CIA Helped Germany Foil Terror Plot," *Spiegel*, 10 Sep. 2007.

74. Yassin Musharbash, "Sauerland Cell Testifies: Jihadists Describe Hatred of US as Reason for Terror Plot," *Spiegel*, 8 Dec. 2009.

75. Guido Steinberg, "The Islamic Jihad Union," Berlin: SWP, 2008.

76. Marcel Rosenbach and Holger Stark, "Aladin's Stories," *Spiegel*, 8 Oct. 2007.

77. Martin Knobbe, "Terrorverdächtiger Fritz Gelowicz; Interview Mit Einem 'Gefährder,'" *Stern*, 13 Sep. 2007.

78. "Operation Alberich: How the CIA Helped Germany Foil Terror Plot."

79. "Sauerland Cell Testifies."

80. Cerwyn Moore, "Uzbek Terror Networks: Germany, Jamoat and the IJU," *Terrorism Monitor*, 8 Nov. 2007.

81. "Islamic Jihad Union Threatens Attacks Outside Germany," *Spiegel*, 12 Sep. 2007.

82. Thomas Sanderson, Daniel Kimmage and David Gordon, "*From the Ferghana Valley to South Waziristan*," Washington: CSIS, 2010.

83. Marcel Rosenbach and Holger Stark, "The Bomb Plot; Terror from the German Heartland," *Spiegel*, 9 Apr. 2009.

84. Steinberg, *German Jihad*, p. 60.

85. Nicholas Kulish and Souad Mekhennet, "In Plot Suspect, Germany Sees Familiar Face," *The New York Times*, 7 Sep. 2007; "Dark Side; Southern German Towns Become Hub of Jihadism," *Neue-Ulmer Zeitung*, 17 Sep. 2007.

86. "Sauerland Cell Testifies."

87. "No Justice for El-Masri, Germany Drops Pursuit of CIA Kidnappers," *Spiegel*, 24 Sep. 2007.

88. "Sauerland Cell Testifies."

89. Ibid.

90. Ibid.

91. "The Bomb Plot; Terror from the German Heartland."

92. "Operation Alberich: How the CIA Helped Germany Foil Terror Plot."

93. "Sauerland Cell Testifies."
94. Steinberg, "The Islamic Jihad Union".
95. "Osamas Deutscher General," *Stern*, 2 Aug. 2005.
96. Yassin Musharbash, "German Jihadists: Al-Qaida Fighter from Bonn Believed Dead," *Spiegel*, 19 Jan. 2009.
97. Mark Daly, "Inside Scotland's Terror Cell," BBC *Scotland*, 16 Dec. 2008.
98. The prosecutor pushed A.'s role as "an important member" although he was not involved in operational activities. He was in frequent contact with the attackers. Investigators retrieved "extreme religious and ideological material" from his computer "consistent with his extreme political beliefs," Regina vs Bilal Talal Abdul Samad Abdulla and Mohammed Jamil Abdelqadader Asha, opening note (Woolwich Crown Court, 2008), pp. 9 ff.
99. Ibid., p. 2.
100. Chris Greenwood, "London Glasgow Terrorist Attacks: The Men in the Dock," *The Independent*, 16 Dec. 2008.
101. Regina vs Bilal Talal Abdul Samad Abdulla and Mohammed Jamil Abdelqadader Asha, opening note (Woolwich Crown Court, 2008), p. 14.
102. Ibid., p. 17.
103. Ibid., pp. 9 ff.
104. Greenwood, "London Glasgow Terrorist Attacks: The Men in the Dock."
105. Shiraz Maher, "Glasgow Bombs: The Doctor I Knew," *New Statesman*, 5 July 2007.
106. Evan Thomas and Mark Hosenball, "Doctor of Death," *Newsweek*, 16 July 2007.
107. Ibid.
108. Sean O'Neill, Steve Bird and Michael Evans, "Glasgow Bomber Bilal Abdulla Was in Iraq Terrorist Cell," *Times*, 17 Dec. 2008.
109. "Doctor of Death."
110. Regina vs Bilal Talal Abdul Samad Abdulla and Mohammed Jamil Abdelqadader Asha, p. 64.
111. "Glasgow Bomber Bilal Abdulla Was in Iraq Terrorist Cell."
112. Ibid. and "Glasgow Airport bomber's email to brother," *Telegraph*, 11 Apr. 2008.
113. Regina vs Bilal Talal Abdul Samad Abdulla and Mohammed Jamil Abdelqadader Asha, p. 81.
114. Ibid., pp. 76, 76, 79.
115. "Al Muhajir Says Al Qaeda in Iraq Behind London and Glasgow Car Bombings," *CBS*, 14 Oct. 2008.

8. DECENTRALIZATION (2008–10)

1. Steinberg, *German Jihad*, pp. 30–1.
2. Hegghammer, *Jihad in Saudi Arabia*.
3. Lia, *Architect of Global Jihad*.

4. See e.g. Ramon Spaaij, *Understanding Lone Wolf Terrorism: Global Patterns, Motivations and Prevention*, New York: Springer, 2011; Jeffrey D. Simon, *Lone Wolf Terrorism: Understanding the Growing Threat*, New York: Prometheus Books, 2013.

5. See e.g. Anthony F. Lemieux et al., "Inspire Magazine: A Critical Analysis of its Significance and Potential Impact through the Lens of the Information, Motivation, and Behavioral Skills Model," *Terrorism and Political Violence*, 26, 2 (1 Apr. 2014), pp. 354–71.

6. "Youtube.com Og Facebook.com—De Nye Radikaliseringsværktøjer," Copenhagen: CTA, 2010.

7. Fernando Reinares, "A Case Study of the January 2008 Suicide Bomb Plot in Barcelona," *CTC Sentinel*, 2, 1 (2009). I also reviewed the WikiLeaks cable "Spain: Al-Qaida Ties Emerge in Trial for Plot against Barcelona Subway," 22 Dec. 2009.

8. Open Judgment, Special Immigration Appeals Commission (SIAC), 18 May 2010.

9. See e.g. Paul Cruickshank, "The Militant Pipeline," p. 38.

10. Open Judgment, Special Immigration Appeals Commission (SIAC), 18 May 2010.

11. Bill Roggio, "Pakistani Army Kills Senior Al Qaeda Commander Tasked with Attacking the West," Long War Journal (blog), 6 Dec. 2014.

12. Statement of Najibullah Zazi, 9 July 2010 (on file with author).

13. Verdict against Mikael Davud et al., 30 Jan. 2012, p. 52.

14. Verdict against Mikael Davud et al., 30 Jan. 2012, p. 42.

15. "TV 2 Vil Anmelde Bhatti for Trusler," *NRK*, 18 Nov. 2011.

16. US-based militants had been involved in cases, such as Babar in the Crawley group, but this time the main plotters were citizens of the United States.

17. "David Coleman Headley Sentenced to 35 Years in Prison for Role in India and Denmark Terror Plots," US Department of Justice, 24 Jan. 2013.

18. Oh Onook, Manish Agrawal and H. Raghav Rao, "Information Control and Terrorism: Tracking the Mumbai Terrorist Attack through Twitter," *Information Systems Frontiers*, 13, 1 (25 Sep. 2010), pp. 33–43.

19. Steinberg, *German Jihad*, p. 35.

20. Verdict against Munir Awad et al. (Retten i Glostrup, 2012); Magnus Ranstorp, "Terrorist Awakening in Sweden?" *CTC Sentinel*, 4, 1 (2011). See also Per Gudmundson, "Gudmundson: Svenska Hjärnan Bakom Attentaten Mot Jyllands-Posten Intervjuad," Gudmundson (blog), 28 Apr. 2012.

21. See Ramón Spaaij and Mark S. Hamm, "Key Issues and Research Agendas in Lone Wolf Terrorism," *Studies in Conflict & Terrorism* (forthcoming) and "The Threat from Solo Terrorism and Lone Wolf Terrorism," Copenhagen: *CTA*, 5 Apr. 2011.

22. Petter Nesser, "Research Note: Single Actor Terrorism: Scope, Characteristics and Explanations," *Perspectives on Terrorism*, 6, 6 (12 Dec. 2012).

23. See Paul Gill, John Horgan and Paige Deckert, "Bombing Alone: Tracing the Motivations and Antecedent Behaviors of Lone-Actor Terrorists," *Journal of*

Forensic Sciences, 59, 2 (1 Mar. 2014), pp. 425–35 and Ramon Spaaij, *Understanding Lone Wolf Terrorism.*

24. Michael Daly, "When Your Son Is a Suicide Bomber," *The Daily Beast*, 3 Apr. 2014.
25. See e.g. Raffaello Pantucci, "A Typology of Lone Wolves: Preliminary Analysis of Lone Islamist Terrorists," London: ICSR, 2011.
26. "Exeter Giraffe Restaurant Bomber Regrets Attempted Terrorist Attack, Says Mother," *Exeter Express and Echo*, 9 May 2014.
27. "How One Extremist Rejected Violence," BBC, 2 July 2013.
28. "Milan Bomber Had Accomplices, More Explosives—Police," *Reuters*, 13 Oct. 2009.
29. Federico Bordonaro, "The October 2009 Terrorist Attack in Italy and its Wider Implications," *CTC Sentinel*, 2, 10 (2009).
30. Verdict against Doukaev (Københavns Byret, 2011).
31. Scott Sayare, "CERN Scientist Sentenced to 5 Years in Terrorism Case," *The New York Times*, 4 May 2012.
32. Scott Stewart, "The Curious Case of Adlene Hicheur," Stratfor, 21 Oct. 2009.
33. Paul Cruickshank, "Revelations from the Underwear Bomber Trial," *CNN*, 14 Oct. 2011.
34. "Rajib Karim: The Terrorist Inside BA," BBC, 24 Feb. 2011; Raffaello Pantucci, "Al-Awlaki Recruits Bangladeshi Militants for Strike on the United States," *Terrorism Monitor*, 9, 7 (17 Feb. 2011).
35. Verdict against Geele (Vestre Landsret, 22 June 2011).
36. Magnus Ranstorp, "Terrorist Awakening in Sweden?" *CTC Sentinel*, 4, 1 (2011).
37. Ibid.
38. Ibid.
39. "Stockholm Bomber Got Training in Iraq: Official," *Al-Arabiya*, 7 Feb. 2015.
40. Per Gudmundson, "Gudmundson: Nasserdine Menni Skyldig—Var Taimour Abdulwahabs Finansiär," Gudmundson (blog), 20 July 2012, http://gudmundson.blogspot.no/2012/07/nasserdine-menni-skyldig-var-taimour.html (accessed 13 Jan. 2015).
41. See e.g. Joseph Carter, "Case Study: Roshonara Choudhry" Theriskyshift (blog), 23 Jan. 2013, http://theriskyshift.com/2013/01/case-study-roshonara-choudhry/ (accessed 10 Jan. 2014).

9. A HETEROGENEOUS THREAT (2011–2015)

1. Stig Jarle Hansen, *Al Shabaab in Somalia: The History and Ideology of a Militant Islamist Group, 2005–12*, Oxford: Oxford University Press, 2013.
2. For a well-informed account of Choudary's significant involvement in setting up Sharia4Belgium, consult Ben Taub, "Journey to Jihad," *New Yorker*, 1 June, 2015.
3. Consult Lars Akerhaug, *Norsk Jihad* (Kagge Forlag, 2013) and Brynjar Lia and

Petter Nesser, *Militant Islamism in Norway: From Expat Politics to Violent Activism* (fortcoming, 2016).

4. Brynjar Lia and Petter Nesser, "Norske Muslimske Fremmedkrigere," *Nytt Norsk Tidsskrift*, 31, 4 (2014), pp. 399–416.

5. Asle Bentzen, "Syria-bakmann:—65 fra Norge til Syria for å Kjempe med Islamister," *TV2*, 28 Sept. 2013.

6. Anders Behring Breivik, "2083: A European Declaration of Independence," 2011.

7. "Zawahiri Gives General Guidelines for Jihad Regarding Military, Propaganda," SITE, 13 Sep. 2013.

8. Michael Holden, "Up to 5,000 European Fighters in Syria Pose Risk—Europol," *Mail*, 13 Jan. 2015.

9. Charles Lister, "Profiling the Islamic State," Doha: Brookings, 2014; Richard Barrett, "The Islamic State," Soufan Group, Nov. 2014.

10. Kevin Jackson, "The Forgotten Caliphate," Jihadica (blog), 31 Dec. 2014, http://www.jihadica.com/ (accessed 7 Jan. 2015).

11. "Algeria's Al-Qaeda Defectors Join IS Group," *Al Jazeera*, 14 Sep. 2014.

12. Thomas Hegghammer and Petter Nesser, "Assessing Islamic State's Commitment to Attacking the West," *Perspectives on Terrorism* 9, no. 4 (2015).

13. These incidents included two Danish-Somalis linked to al-Shabaab who were arrested for discussing weapons, attack methods and targets, an alleged plot by British al-Shabaab associates to stage attacks in connection with the London Olympics in 2012 (a plot believed to have been ordered by bin Laden and overseen by al-Shabaab leaders and the "white widow" of 7/7 bomber Jermaine Lindsay) and some incidents in France, where suspected terrorists had been in touch with AQIM. However, these cases were poorly or dubiously documented in open sources and will not be commented on further. Descriptions of the plots may be accessed in the electronic appendix (www.hurstpublishers.com/book/islamist-terrorism-in-europe)

14. Steinberg, *German Jihad*, p. 236.

15. "Court Jails Al Qaeda-Linked Düsseldorf Cell Members," *Deutche Welle*, 13 Nov. 2014.

16. Chris Greenwood, "Jailed, Terror Gang behind Plot to Rival 7/7 and Transform Birmingham into a 'Little War Zone'... but One May Be Free in Eight Years," *Mail*, 26 Apr. 2013.

17. Duncan Gardham, "Men Appear in Court Charged with Plotting to Attack Territorial Army with Model Car," *Telegraph*, 30 Apr. 2012.

18. "Muslim Convert from BBC Documentary Pleads Guilty to Terrorism Charges," *Guardian*, 15 Mar. 2013.

19. Vikram Dodd, "Three Jailed for Discussing Possible Terror Attack," *Guardian*, 25 Apr. 2013.

20. Paul Cruickshank, "3 Suspected Islamist Terrorists Arrested in France," *CNN*, 1 Mar. 2013.

21. The case study of Merah's attacks is based on Virginie Andre and Shandon Harris-Hogan, "Mohamed Merah: From Petty Criminal to Neojihadist," *Politics, Religion & Ideology*, 14, 2 (2013), pp. 307–19; "Exclusif—Transcription Des Conversations Entre Mohamed Merah et Les Négociateurs," *Libération*, 17 July 2012, the chronology of incidents presented in the appendix, and interview with European security official, Nov. 2014.

22. Paul Cruickshank, "Taking Tea with a Terrorist," *CNN*, 17 Oct. 2012.

23. "'Lone wolf' terrorist alleged to have planned attacks held in custody," *El Pais*, 12 Feb., 2014.

24. Ian Sparks, "Plot to blow up Eiffel Tower and Louvre foiled," *Scotsman*, 5 July, 2015.

25. Steinberg, *German Jihad*, p. 4.

26. Helen Davidson, "ISIS Instructs Followers to Kill Australians and Other 'Disbelievers,'" *Guardian*, 23 Sep. 2014.

27. Case study based on "Report on the Intelligence Relating to the Murder of Fusilier Lee Rigby," London: Intelligence and Security Committee of Parliament, 2014; Dominique Casciani, "A Journey towards Violence," *BBC*, 19 Dec. 2013.

28. "Report on the Intelligence Relating to the Murder of Fusilier Lee Rigby," p. 15.

29. "Islamic convert charged with attempting to kill French soldier," *Telegraph*, 31 May, 2013.

30. "Terrormisstänkta greps vid Röda sten," Säkerhetspolisen (Säpo), http://www.sakerhetspolisen.se/publikationer/fallstudier-och-artiklar-fran-arsbocker/terrorism/terrormisstankta-greps-vid-roda-sten.html (not dated, accessed Jan., 2015).

31. Gunnar Hultgreen, "Skulle Drepes med Sprengstoff," *Dagbladet*, 17 Sep. 2011.

32. Ibid.

33. Vikram Dodd, "Jihadist Gang Jailed for Plot to Bomb EDL Rally," *Guardian*, 10 June 2013.

34. "Fakta: Det Ved vi Om Lars Hedegaards Formodede Attentatmand," *Danmarks Radio*, 12 Oct. 2014.

35. "Attentats-Versuche: Prozess Gegen Terror-Verdächtige," *Kölner Stadt-Anzeiger*, 21 Aug. 2014.

36. "France's Interior Minister: Hundreds of Potential Terrorists," *The Jewish Chronicle*, 11 Oct. 2012.

37. Paul Cruickshank, "Raid on ISIS suspect in the French Riviera," *CNN*, 28 August, 2014.

38. Tom Whitehead, "Erol Incedal jailed for three-and-a-half years over bomb-making manual," *Telegraph*, 1 April, 2015.

39. Ian Cobain, "Terrorism Trial Hears of Possible Plot to Assassinate Tony Blair," *Guardian*, 14 Oct. 2014.

40. Lucy Crossley and Duncan Gardham, "British Law Student Cleared of Plotting 'Mumbai-style' Terror Attack and Targeting Tony and Cherie Blair after Secret Trial," *Mail*, 26 March, 2015.

41. "Un Attentat Islamiste Probablement Déjoué Sur La Côte d'Azur," *LaDépêche.fr*, 26 Mar. 2013.

42. "France—Brussels Shooter 'Planned Bastille Day Atrocity' in Paris," *France 24*, 8 Sep. 2014; "Mehdi Nemmouche, de Roubaix Aux Basses Œuvres Jihadistes)," *Libération*, 26 July 2014.

43. "France—Brussels Shooter 'Planned Bastille Day Atrocity' in Paris."

44. "Mehdi Nemmouche, de Roubaix Aux Basses Œuvres Jihadistes," *Libération*, 26 July 2014.

45. "After the Atrocities," *Economist*, 17 Jan. 2015.

46. See e.g. Bill Roggio and Thomas Joscelyn, "Analysis: CENTCOM Draws Misleading Line between Al Nusrah Front and Khorasan Group," Long War Journal (blog), 7 Nov. 2014.

47. Duncan Gardham, "Revealed: Briton Who Was Jihadi in Syria and Came Home to Bomb UK," *Mail*, 6 July 2014.

48. Justin Huggler, "Isil Jihadists 'Offered Teenager $25,000 to Carry out Bombings in Vienna,'" *Telegraph*, 30 Oct. 2014.

49. Adam Sage, "We have avenged Muhammad. We have killed Charlie Hebdo," *Times*, 8 Jan. 2015.

50. "Frenchman Says He Came Face to Face with Charlie Hebdo Attacker: 'I Shook His Hand,'" *Telegraph*, 9 Jan. 2015.

51. See e.g. Rukmini Callimachi and Jim Yardley, "Chérif and Saïd Kouachi's Path to Paris Attack at Charlie Hebdo," *The New York Times*, 17 Jan. 2015.

52. Timothy Holman, "Background on the 19th Network, Paris, France, 2000–2013," Across the Green Mountain (blog), 8 Jan. 2015, https://acrossthegreenmountain. wordpress.com/2015/01/08/background-on-the-19th-network-paris-france-2000–2013/ (accessed 9 Jan. 2015).

53. Robert Mendick, "Leicester Terrorist Cell That Laid Seeds of Paris Atrocity," *Telegraph*, 17 Jan. 2015.

54. "Untangling a Deadly Web: The Paris Attacks, the Suspects, the Links," *CNN*, 14 Jan. 2015.

55. See e.g. Stacy Meichtry, Noémie Bisserbe and Benoît Faucon, "Paris Attacker Amedy Coulibaly's Path to Terror," *Wall Street Journal*, 14 Jan. 2015.

56. Jon Henley, "How Do You Deradicalise Returning Isis Fighters?" *Guardian*, 12 Nov. 2014.

EPILOGUE: ISLAMIC STATE'S EFFECT ON EUROPEAN JIHADISM

1. This epilogue is based on analyses presented in the first edition of the book and an article I authored with Anne Stenersen and Emilie Oftedal, "Jihadi Terrorism in Europe: The IS-Effect," *Perspectives on Terrorism*, 10, no. 6 (20 Dec. 2016), http://www.terrorismanalysts.com/pt/index.php/pot/article/view/553. Text has been

translated from two essays I wrote, in Norwegian, for the Norwegian Institute for Foreign Affairs (NUPI), "Terror i Europa: IS-effekten," (27 Sept. 2017), and "IS-terror i Europa: hvordan dannes terrorceller?" (1 Nov. 2017). I thank Brynjar Lia and Henrik Gråtrud for comments and advice.

2. The group was previously known as Islamic State of Iraq and Syria (ISIS).

3. "The Manchester Bomber 'Received Permission' from ISIS in Syria and a Recruiter in Dallas", *Newsweek*, 14 Aug. 2017, http://www.newsweek.com/manchester-attack-bomber-received-permission-isis-syria-recruiter-dallas-650300.

4. See e.g. Dean Obeidallah, "Are All Terrorists Muslims? It's Not Even Close," *The Daily Beast*, 14 Jan. 2015, https://www.thedailybeast.com/articles/2015/01/14/are-all-terrorists-muslims-it-s-not-even-close.

5. See Jacob Aasland Ravndal, "Right-Wing Terrorism and Violence in Western Europe: Introducing the RTV Dataset", *Perspectives on Terrorism*, 10, no. 3 (14 June 2016), http://www.terrorismanalysts.com/pt/index.php/pot/article/view/508. There has been an uptick in rightwing terrorist plots over the last couple of years, but the scope of attack-related activities is not comparable to that of jihadi terrorist plotting.

6. See Olivier Roy, *Jihad and Death: The Global Appeal of Islamic State*, London: Hurst, 2017. Consult also this article on the critique of Roy's perspective based on a recent book on French jihadis by David Thompson: Jonathan Derbyshire, "The Voices of France's Jihadist Foot Soldiers", *Financial Times*, 6 Feb. 2017, https://www.ft.com/content/ce70df74-cdde-11e6-864f-20dcb35cede2.

7. "Crime as Jihad: Developments in the Crime-Terror Nexus in Europe," *CTC Sentinel*, 18 Oct. 2017, https://ctc.usma.edu/posts/crime-as-jihad-developments-in-the-crime-terror-nexus-in-europe.

8. What the militants themselves say about why they do what they do has too often been ignored when analyzing motivations and drivers.

9. This is usually presented as an argument that IS was targeting Europe all along. However, one must remember that the ISIS-linked plots before the announcement of the anti-IS coalition, for example the French Riviera bomb plot in January 2014 or the Brussels Jewish Museum shooting in March 2014, involved people who had been part of al-Qaida-affiliated networks that targeted Europe. For example, the ISIS-linked French Riviera bomb plotter, Ibrahim Boudina had been a member of a French support network for al-Qaida's Syrian arm Jabhat al-Nusra, dubbed the "Cannes-Torcy Network". This network recruited fighters for Jabhat al-Nusra and members also executed a terrorist attack with a hand grenade against a Jewish Bakery in a Paris suburb in 2012. See "Raid on ISIS Suspect in the French Riviera—CNN.Com", CNN, accessed 15 Jan. 2015, http://www.cnn.com/2014/08/28/world/europe/france-suspected-isis-link/index.html.

10. The declaration called for attacks against Americans and Jews, civilians as well as military personnel all over the world.

11. "Enquête—Lionel Dumont, Membre Du Gang de Roubaix, Serait Lié Au Terroriste Présumé de Wattignies," *La Voix Du Nord*, 11 July 2017, http://www.lavoixdunord.fr/190428/article/2017-07-11/lionel-dumont-membre-du-gang-de-roubaix-serait-lie-au-terroriste-presume-de.

12. An IS-linked terrorist cell in the UK was for example intercepted in 2014 in the affluent North Kensington west of London see Richard Spillett, "Drive-by Gang Came from Same London Terror Area as Jihadi John", *Mail Online*, 23 Mar. 2016, http://www.dailymail.co.uk/news/article-3506567/London-s-neighbourhood-terror-Drive-gang-came-area-Jihadi-John-ISIS-poster-boy-July-21-bombers.html.

INDEX

INDEX